THE TEMPLE OF MITHRAS LONDON

Excavations by W F Grimes and A Williams at the Walbrook

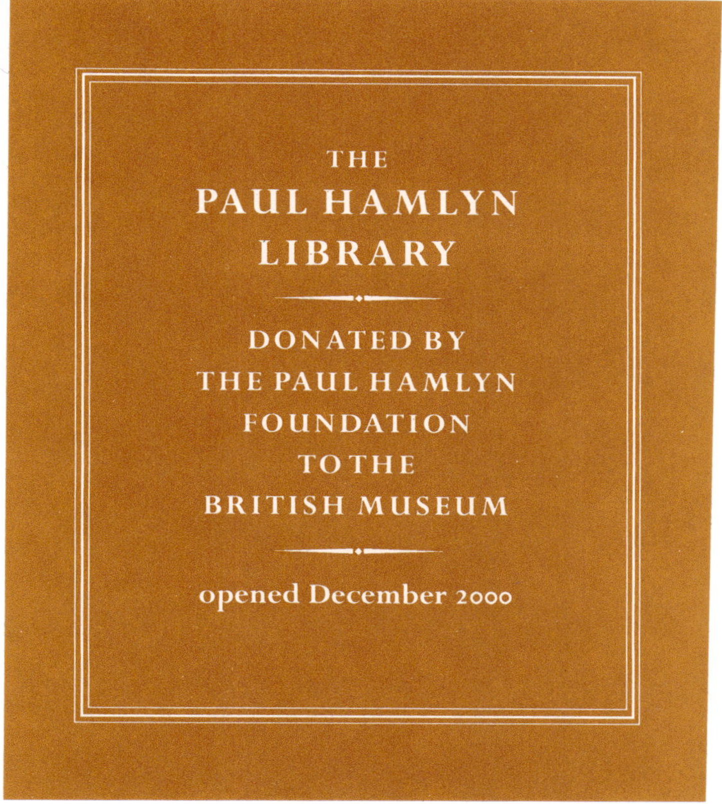

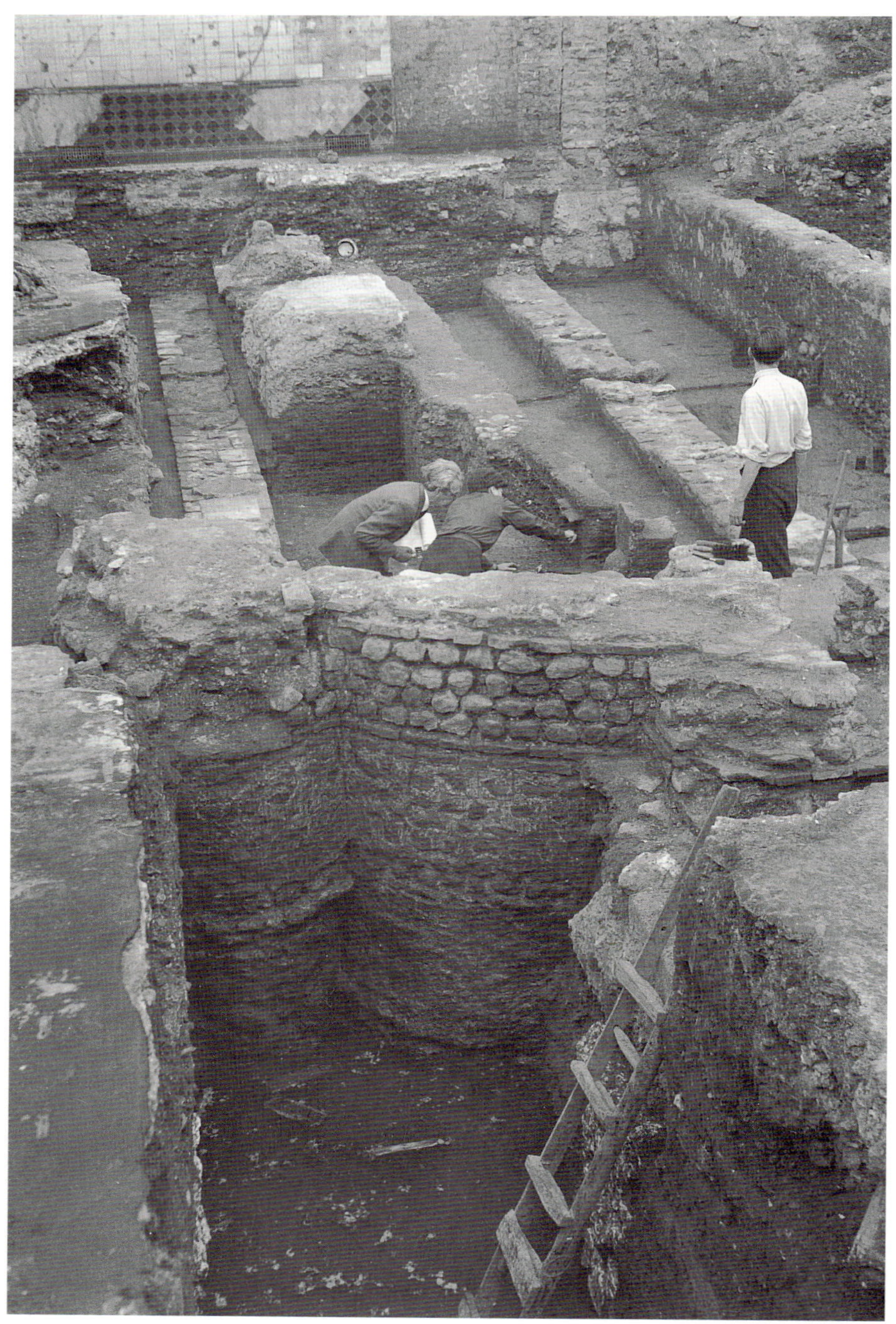

W F Grimes and Audrey Williams recording details of the floor sequence at the west end of the Mithraeum

THE TEMPLE OF MITHRAS, LONDON

Excavations by W F Grimes and A Williams at the Walbrook

John D Shepherd

with contributions from
I Betts, J Bird, S Bowman, T Brigham, I Cornwall,
B Dickinson, J Groves,
J Hall, K Hartley, M Hassall, M Henig, E Knox,
A Lawson, S Macready, K Matthews,
R Merrifield, D Peacock, V Rigby, J Sidell, J Toynbee,
I Tyers, S Walker and A Wardle

and illustrations by S Banks, N Griffiths, W F Grimes,
P Levine, G Marsh, C Thomas and T Wellman

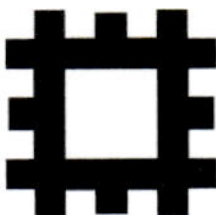

ENGLISH HERITAGE

1998

ARCHAEOLOGICAL REPORT 12

First published by English Heritage, 23 Savile Row, London W1X 1AB

Printed by Snoeck-Ducaju & Zoon

ISBN 1 85074 628 1
Product code XC10851

Editor: Guy de la Bédoyère
Design: Jeannette van der Post

Contents

Illustrations

Note: Numbers on sections refer to layers. Black represents timber in sections and tile in elevations.
Where timber and tile appear in the same elevation, the timber has been labelled.

Unless otherwise stated, photographs © Museum of London.

List of tables

Preface

This report upon the Walbrook Mithraeum is one in a series of projects and publications prepared by the Museum of London with support from English Heritage from documents and finds contained within the archive of the late Professor W F Grimes (the Grimes London Archive, part of the London Archaeological Archive, Museum of London). This extensive archive contains the documentation and finds for 63 sites excavated and examined by Grimes in the City of London and its immediate hinterland between 1946 and 1967, the majority of which were summarised in *The excavation of Roman and mediaeval London* in 1968 (Grimes 1968). Two of these excavations, at Gutter Lane and Gresham Street, were carried out under the auspices of the Society of Antiquaries in 1946, but the remainder were the work of the Roman and Mediaeval London Excavation Council (RMLEC) with Grimes as Honorary Director of excavations.

The Roman and Mediaeval London Excavation Council

The Roman and Mediaeval London Excavation Council (RMLEC) evolved over a 30-month period. In May 1944 Kathleen Kenyon, as Secretary of the Council for British Archaeology (CBA), drew attention in the London and national press to the need for controlled archaeological examination of the many bomb-damaged sites in London prior to their redevelopment. Raymond Smith, Librarian and Curator at the Guildhall and a member of CBA, also realised the need for such work to be carried out, even though, he added, Kenyon's expectation of immediately carrying out an excavation in 'the region of Ludgate Hill' (*Evening Standard,* 8 May 1944) was premature. Indeed the area in question, part of the Fleet valley, was only recently redeveloped for the first time since the Second World War after archaeological excavations had been carried out by the Museum of London's Department of Urban Archaeology.

In May 1945 James Mann, Director of the Society of Antiquaries of London, and Ian Richmond, then Vice-President of the Society, informed the Lord Mayor that the Antiquaries wished to form a joint committee, under the presidency of the Lord Mayor, to carry out archaeological research in the City of London. These preliminary overtures for the formation of a committee were not met with enthusiasm by the Corporation of London and its senior officials. After a short while, but with difficulties, the Improvements and Town Planning Committee of the Corporation of London was persuaded to allow a deputation consisting of James Mann, Ian Richmond and William Grimes, the Assistant Archaeology Officer to the Ordnance Survey, to attend a meeting on 13 July 1945. Their intention was to put forward the case for the setting up of a 'joint committee re: the excavation of Roman London' (WFG-PC 1945). The result of this meeting was that Raymond Smith was permitted to serve on this committee, which was called the 'Roman London Committee'.

In the same year (1945), Grimes became Keeper and Secretary of the London Museum. On behalf of the Roman London Committee of the Society of Antiquaries of London he began trial work on the two sites in the City referred to above, Gutter Lane (archive site code WFG25) and Billiter Square (WFG51). A new approach was made to the new Lord Mayor, the Rt Hon Sir Bracewell Smith, to act as President of the committee (renamed Roman London Excavation Committee), so that Grimes could work in the City with authority and as a means of attracting additional sponsorship. This second appeal was successful and the Lord Mayor's willingness to act as President of the Committee led to its formal inaugural meeting in the Mansion House on 26 September 1946. Before this meeting Grimes, as 'Director of Excavations' proposed changing the title from the 'The Roman London Excavation Committee' to 'The Roman and Mediaeval London Excavation Council' (RMLEC) so that:

a) with the title of 'Council' it might be seen to be a 'parent body rather than an *ad hoc* appendage to a pre-existing organisation' and
b) the inclusion of 'mediaeval' [sic] would 'avow clearly our concern also with the later periods.'
(WFG-PC 18 September 1946)

This title was duly adopted, with the archaic spelling of the later period in the title (not Grimes's preferred choice) insisted upon by a certain member of the Council (Grimes 1968, 221). Efforts were immediately begun to raise support and funds for the examination and excavation of sites in the City of London. The greatest support always came from the Government through grants for excavation and post-excavation work from the Ministry of Works and its successors the Ministry of Public Buildings and Works, the Department of the Environment, the Historic Buildings and Monuments Commission and English Heritage.

With the assistance of the executive of the Council and a number of skilled and trusted employees, especially Audrey Williams, A J Haydon, Fred Beasley, George Rybot and Gordon Atkinson, Grimes examined a further 61 sites in and around the City of London. These sites were excavated while he was still the Director of the London Museum and subsequently, from 1955, Director of the Institute of Archaeology, University of London. In 1962 the decision was made to wind up the excavation policy of the previous 15 years, although St Mary's Aldermanbury was to be excavated by RMLEC in 1967, and to concentrate upon the processing and publication of the large volume of data which he and his assistants had accumulated.

His intention was to precede the full and detailed publication of sites or groups of sites with a general survey of the activities of RMLEC. His 1968 book, *The excavation of Roman and mediaeval London,* was the result.

Since the late 1960s this large quantity of data has been steadily processed by a succession of research assistants, including Ahmed Youssef, Joanna Bird, Chris Thomas, Percival Turnbull, Sarah Macready and John Shepherd. But throughout the 70s and the early 1980s, as the costs of archaeological excavation and research rose alarmingly, the honest intention so often expressed in his 1968 volume of producing a definitive account of his work became more and more idealistic. Paradoxically, his ambitions were not helped by a new generation of archaeologists who, for the most part, laudably accelerated the rate of research and excavation, thus putting additional pressure on the few public funds which were available for post-excavation and research. As *'anno domini* crept up on him', as he would say, the task of getting the material into a format which could be published became ever greater. But the RMLEC archive was never neglected. The comment above concerning the continuing support of the Government departments in the 1970s and early 80s must be repeated here. The importance of his work was always acknowledged and some funds made available, so that even if the work was not completed during this period, the RMLEC archive was at least maintained and processed.

The Museum of London and the Grimes London Archive

In January 1988, Professor Grimes, the late Dr Hugh Chapman (then the Deputy Director of the Museum of London) and Peter Marsden (then Section Head of Field Section I in the Museum's Department of Urban Archaeology) signed an agreement that would transfer to the Museum of London the full responsibility for ensuring the maintenance and the publication of the RMLEC material. In June 1988 this archive, to be called the Grimes London Archive, was placed in the care of the Prehistoric and Roman Department of the Museum of London, now the Department of Early London History and Collections, with the Roman Curator Jenny Hall as Manager and the present author, John Shepherd, then of Field Section I in the DUA and the last of Grimes's full-time research assistants, as Curator of the archive. Grimes left a number of specific verbal intructions on what should be published and how certain elements of the archive should be presented, but he allowed the Museum of London the freedom to determine the proper publication strategy. Sadly, Professor Grimes died, aged 83, on Christmas Day 1988. Since 1990 the Museum of London has been working in coordination with Gill Andrews and Roger Thomas of English Heritage to ensure the correct archiving and processing of this material. Full assessments had been completed in 1992 and publication proposals submitted in keeping with English Heritage's *Management of archaeological projects* (1991; known as MAP2). The Walbrook Mithraeum was the first. Other proposals included the excavations of St Bride's Church, Fleet Street (Milne 1997), the Roman fort in the Cripplegate area (Shepherd, forthcoming) and the medieval and post-medieval occupation in the Cripplegate area (Milne, forthcoming). These publications in the English Heritage archaeological monograph series will cover less than a half of the entire archive. To ensure the full circulation of all of the data contained within the archive a gazetteer of the Grimes London Archive, giving summarised accounts of the excavations on all of Grimes's sites with full bibliographical references for published and archival material, is to be published by the Museum of London to complement Grimes's own account of his excavations so lucidly presented in the 1968 volume (Shepherd, forthcoming).

The Temple of Mithras report

The Roman Temple of Mithras, Walbrook, is undoubtedly the best known of Grimes's discoveries in the City of London. Much to his bemusement he received a CBE for this find, an award that he would have preferred to have had bestowed upon him for the discovery of the Cripplegate fort. Even as an archaeological discovery, the fame of the Temple has only recently been matched by that of the Rose Theatre in Southwark. Both sites attracted a great, perhaps too great, amount of publicity. Of course, publicity can and often does have a positive effect for archaeology, especially urban archaeology. But for the Mithraeum in 1954 and the Rose Theatre in 1989 the publicity and the debate, at times woefully misinformed, led to the many and various parties being drawn into confrontation.

This report includes an assessment of this press and public interest into the Mithraeum affair of 1954. However, the main priority has been to put into print for the first time as full an account as possible of the excavations themselves. It is, of course, unfortunate that Professor Grimes was not able to complete this work himself, but an analysis of why or how this came about is unnecessary and hardly constructive. What is especially regrettable is that we have lost the ideas and interpretations of not only Professor Grimes but those others who worked so closely with him, especially Audrey Williams. It is for this reason that the main part of this report is concerned primarily with reproducing as objectively as possible the data recovered by Grimes and Williams. This has been ordered according to their own main interpretations of the archaeological sequence which can be found within published interims (especially Grimes 1968), lecture notes, site documentation and other research notes contained within the archive.

The only revision of any real significance has been to the archive pottery report. This was originally prepared by Joanna Bird and completed in the early 1970s. Professor Grimes, Joanna Bird and Sarah Macready, research assistant to Professor Grimes during the late 1970s and the present author's predecessor, made use of this pottery report to establish the main stratigraphic framework (the stratigraphic 'Groups'). In the light of increased research into Romano-British ceramics, especially of the late Roman period so relevant here, Bird's original work on the coarse pottery was updated with her authorisation by Jo Groves of the Museum of London Archaeology Service. Bird has updated the report on the samian from the site herself for inclusion here. As a result some fine alterations have had to be made to the 1970s framework. A more detailed account of the method used to prepare this report is described below *(Chapter 1, The preparation of this report)*

Professor Grimes's own belief that 'Whatever its other claims to fame the Mithraic temple will go down in history as a discovery on which more nonsense has been written and spoken than almost on any other' (letter to the Editor of *The Times,* 15 June 1957) has always been at the front of my mind. Unfortunately, many past studies of the Walbrook Mithraeum, and indeed Roman Mithraism in general, are riddled with what Dr Martin Millett reminds us are called 'factoids...pieces of information which have been so commonly repeated that they are indistinguishable from facts' (Millett 1990, xvi). Now that the evidence for the London temple is presented here the 'informed' debate can, at last, begin.

Museum of London
October 1995

Acknowledgements

This report has been in the making for more than 40 years and, as one would expect, has included the involvement of a great many individuals and institutions. I have been able to identify a number of these who contributed to the work, both excavation and post-excavation, conducted by Professor Grimes and his senior site supervisor Audrey Williams, and I am only too pleased to be able to mention them below. To all of those people and institutions, wherever or whatever they may be, who find that they have been left out I would like to pass on my sincere thanks for their contributions, which ultimately made my work easier.

Grimes and Williams received much assistance during the excavations from 1952–4. First of all the generous cooperation of the site owners, Messrs Legenland (especially Major Brigland and Mr Edwards) and the contractors, Messrs Humphreys, must once again be emphasised, as too should the invaluable contribution of Mr Owen Campbell Jones, the architect of Bucklersbury House. It was he who initially contacted Grimes while the redevelopment was still on the drawing board.

None of this work could have been achieved without the continual support of the executive committee of the RMLEC, in particular R Asheton MP, Sir H Bell, Sir A Bossom, D A J Buxton, N Cook, P Corder, N Davey, G C Dunning, Miss K Kenyon, C Harrison, Sir J Mann, G Nicholson MP, A H Oswald, Sir I A Richmond, R Syme and Miss M V Taylor. Four other executive council members, R Smith, the Librarian and Curator of Guildhall, F J Forty, the City Engineer, B H St John O'Neil, the Chief Inspector of Ancient Monuments (who tragically died a few weeks after the temple had ceased to be front page news), and his successor P K Baillie Reynolds, gave Grimes and RMLEC invaluable assistance, support and advice not just on this site but on many others throughout the City. A special debt is due to the Council's Secretary, J A Giuseppe, and Treasurer, J F Head, who, with Grimes, successfully achieved so much in the City for which our generation of archaeologists is only too grateful. Finally, on the administrative side, in the London Museum and at the Institute of Archaeology, Professor Grimes was ably supported by his secretaries, Jean McDonald and Margery Hunt.

The sculptures have already been published in a separate volume but the inclusion of summaries of their descriptions here justifies restating our thanks to those who contributed to that volume. Professor J M C Toynbee made by far the greatest contribution; her report on the sculptures was published posthumously in 1986. S E Ellis of the Department of Mineralogy, British Museum (Natural History), provided visual identifications from samples removed with care and caution by Professor J Skeaping, Department of Sculpture, Royal College of Art. Casts were made by A G Prescott and electrotypes of the canister made by Dr H J Plenderleith, M J Hughes and J R S Lang.They all contributed much specialist advice.

Environmental advice and technical information came from E Knox (peat), G Hart (Scientific Officer at the Timber Development Association Ltd), I Cornwall (soil) and F Zeuner (general advice), the last two colleagues of Professor Grimes at the Institute of Archaeology. Arthur Trotman, Conservation Officer at the Guildhall Museum and later the Museum of London, worked on the less stable finds, not only from the Mithraeum but from many of the RMLEC's sites in the City.

More recently much of the work on the pottery and finds, on which so much of the finds component of this report is based, was carried out by Joanna Bird and Sarah Macready. Their contributions were gratefully acknowledged by Professor Grimes and the current author wishes to point out his indebtedness to so much of their work. Chris Thomas, Patricia Levine and students of the Institute of Archaeology, under the supervision of H Stewart, prepared the pottery and samian drawings. Gilly Marsh did a number of small finds drawings, but the majority were done by Professor Grimes himself. Finds processing in the early 1970s was carried out by Ahmed Youssef.

Above all, however, thanks must go to the team of excavators who achieved so much with so few resources. It is never easy working under the full glare of the press and public but their ability to do so successfully has meant that 40 years later this report could be compiled. Of those many who took part, and unfortunately the archive does not contain a staff list for this period, a special tribute must go to Audrey Williams. Her hand appears in much of the recording and the interpretation of the site sequence. It is only fitting that she should appear in the title alongside Professor Grimes.

I must thank the former Director of the Museum of London, Max Hebditch CBE, and all my colleagues in the Department of Early London History and Collections, particularly Jenny Hall who has managed the Grimes programme, for all their help and support. I would like to thank Dr Peter Marsden and (if only it could have been personally) the late Dr Hugh Chapman for initiating this and the other Grimes projects in 1988. All of us involved with the Grimes archive are most grateful to English Heritage for funding these projects, in particular to Val Horsler, Dr Ellen McAdam, Roger Thomas and Dr Geoff Wainwright, but especially to Gill Andrews, who has given so much valuable guidance, advice and support.

I would also like to thank Gustav Milne, of the Museum of London and University College, London, my collaborator on the Grimes projects, Dr Ralph Merrifield who contributed so much to the study of the Walbrook and the temple since the 1950s but who sadly died before this report was completed, Dr Simon James, and Professor Mike Fulford for giving so many useful comments towards the completion of this volume.

My thanks also go to Page Bird, Mark Geraghty and Sandra Green of the Historic Maps Department for locating Ministry of Works elevation drawings and survey notebooks.

A number of people at the Museum of London's Archaeology Service (MoLAS) have assisted in this project. Angela Wardle and Jo Groves both revised and updated earlier catalogues of finds and pottery. Jane Sidell updated and edited the animal bone report and Ian Tyers supplied wood identifications. Another invaluable contribution has come from Tracy Wellman, MoLAS Drawing Office, who has successfully been able to edit Professor Grimes's original site drawings in accordance with the instructions he gave me at my last meeting with him in the summer of 1988. Nick Griffiths has made an equally valuable contribution with regard to the small finds drawings. All involved with the project would like to thank them for their presentation of our work.

I have received much secretarial advice and help from Roz Sherris, Museum of London, and would also like to record my thanks to Julia Buckley and David Hawkins, work experience students, who gave me a great deal of practical help during the final stages of the preparation of the volume.

My final thoughts and respect go out to Professor Grimes, for whom I worked as assistant in the early 1980s, and to Audrey Williams, his unsung assistant in 1954, without whom he simply would not have been able to achieve as much as he did.

Professor Grimes believed strongly in interpreting sites from the position of maximum information — a philosophy which would explain his frustration with the many members of the press (and a few academic colleagues) who produced such startling ideas about the temple while it was still being excavated. Unfortunately, and paradoxically, the absence of a definitive publication such as this on the Walbrook temple has prevented others from examining the evidence in detail for themselves and sharing the maximum amount of information available for the site. When I collected his archive from his home in 1988, Professor Grimes told me that he was sincerely and doubly disappointed about this. First, because he was not able to complete the report sooner and so facilitate the work of so many others, especially those involved in the reawakening of Mithraic studies in the late 1960s and 1970s, and secondly, a feeling no doubt shared by the vast majority of archaeologists, because he was not going to be able to complete the report himself. I have followed as best as possible the instructions he gave me, and where I have had no guidance from Professor Grimes, I am confident that I have presented the data in the form which he would have intended. I can only hope, however, that the volume as a whole, including the collection of discursive essays, would have met with his approval. I am certain that he would not be displeased that a more informed debate about the temple can at last begin.

Summary

In 1952 the Roman and Mediaeval London Excavation Council (RMLEC) began work on a series of trenches that crossed the valley of the Walbrook stream on the Bucklersbury House redevelopment site. The new building was being constructed on a blitz site and was the largest project of its kind in the reconstruction of the City of London following the Second World War. The aim of this excavation was to obtain information about the true nature of the Walbrook valley and its stream. The RMLEC, under the directorship of W F Grimes, had been carrying out similar carefully planned excavations on sites throughout the City since 1946, but the discovery of a well preserved Roman building beneath the basement slab in the easternmost of these trenches was to bring the activities of the RMLEC and its director to a far wider audience. The discovery of a marble head of Mithras on the very last day of scheduled excavation, 18 September 1954, was to set in train a string of events that still figure strongly in the post-war folklore of London.

Although the Temple and the rich hoard of sculptures found in it are well known from a number of interim accounts published by Professor Grimes and Professor Jocelyn Toynbee, a definitive account of the archaeology of the building was not produced at the time. Likewise, a full presentation of the data regarding the Walbrook valley, the original incentive for the excavation, was not completed in Grimes's lifetime. This volume seeks to rectify this situation.

The Bucklersbury House redevelopment site is described and the excavations placed in context. The original aims of the excavation and the methods of Grimes and his RMLEC team on the site between 1952 and 1954 are also examined. Subsequent post-excavation work and the methods employed to bring this site to publication are also described.

The report chronicles the extraordinary events which came about as a result of the discovery of the sculpture depicting the head of Mithras. It is arguable that the temple is best remembered not just for this and the other sculptures, which compare so favourably with anything found in the north-west provinces, but for the incredible public interest shown in its discovery. This included tens of thousands of visitors to the site, the interest of all of the broadsheet and popular newspapers, television newsreel, the archaeological establishment and the Government, in the form of the Minister and staff of the Ministry of Works, the Treasury, the Cabinet office, and no less a person than the Prime Minister, Sir Winston Churchill. Chapter 2 describes the events which occurred in those few weeks from the end of September to the beginning of October in 1954, making use of those Ministry, Treasury and Cabinet documents now available for study in the Public Records Office.

The evidence from the excavations is presented in Chapters 3 and 4. As Professor Grimes himself intended, the existence of a temple on this site, and a mithraeum at that, has not been allowed to divert our attention away from the original aims of the excavation, namely the examination of the Walbrook valley as an important topographic feature of Roman London. A full account of the pre-temple deposits is therefore included as well as the evidence for the building itself, constructed around the middle of the third century, and the nature of the Walbrook valley contemporary with it.

The sculptures from this site are among the best known finds from Roman London, but they make up only a very small part of the total finds assemblage. Grimes was aware that the valley might have changed its appearance in the course of the Roman period and therefore ensured a thorough finds recovery programme to enable these changes to be dated. Although this material had been sorted in the 1950s, it still presents a valuable resource for our understanding of the valley as well as the temple. The finds are presented in Chapter 5, in an abbreviated form, with the scant environmental material which still survives from the site in Chapter 6.

Chapter 7 places the site as a whole in context in Roman London. The temple, however, has a far wider importance and significance, the full study of which is far beyond the scope of the current publication programme. It is hoped, therefore, that the brief comments, in conjunction with the details of the excavation itself, will form the foundation for others better qualified in the study of Roman Mithraism to place the temple and its contents in their proper, international context. It must also be noted that the possibility, presented here by Dr Martin Henig (Appendix 1), that the temple was dedicated to Bacchus during the first quarter of the fourth century following the burial of the Mithraic sculptures, adds a new dimension to this important building.

Résumé

En 1952, le groupe archéologique, appelé à cette époque *Roman and Mediaeval London Excavation Council* (RMLEC), entreprit des travaux de prospection avec une série de tranchées placées en travers de la vallée du ruisseau Walbrook sur le chantier de reconstruction de Bucklersbury House. Le nouveau bâtiment allait être construit sur un site bombardé lors du Blitz, et représentait le plus grand projet parmi les chantiers de reconstruction de la City (City of London) au lendemain de la Deuxième Guerre Mondiale. L'objectif de cette fouille était d'obtenir des connaissances sur la véritable nature du ruisseau Walbrook et de sa vallée. Depuis 1946, le RMLEC sous la direction de WF Grimes avait déjà entrepris des fouilles soigneusement organisées sur des sites dans la City. Mais ce fut la découverte d'un bâtiment romain bien préservé sous les fondations, dans la tranchée la plus à l'est, qui allait bientôt signaler les activités du RMLEC et celles de son directeur à la connaissance d'une plus vaste audience. En effet lors du tout dernier jour officiel de fouille, le 18 septembre 1954, la découverte d'une tête en marbre du dieu Mithra déclencha toute une série d'évènements qui existent encore vivement dans la "petite Histoire" londonienne de l'après-guerre.

Bien que le Mithraeum et son riche assemblage de sculptures soient bien connus grâce à un certain nombre de comptes rendus provisoires, édités par les Professeurs Grimes et Jocelyn Toynbee, un rapport archéologique complet du Mithraeum n'a jamais été écrit à l'époque de la fouille. Pareillement un compte rendu des informations concernant la vallée du Walbrook, qui avait été l'objectif premier derrière les fouilles, ne fut jamais terminé durant la vie de Grimes. Ce volume va tenter de rectifier cette situation.

Dans le chapitre 1, le site du chantier à Bucklersbury House est décrit et les fouilles sont mises en contexte. Les objectifs initiaux de fouille et les méthodes de travail de Grimes et de son équipe sur le site entre 1952 et 1954 sont aussi examinés. Les travaux post-fouilles ultérieurs et les méthodes actuelles employées pour permettre la publication de ce site y sont aussi décrits.

Le chapitre 2 décrit les évènements extraordinaires qui se produisirent à la suite de la découverte sur le site de la tête de Mithra. On peut soutenir que le Mithraeum se grava dans la mémoire des gens non pas pour cette fameuse tête de Mithra et les autres sculptures, qui, il faut souligner, peuvent être placées parmi les plus beaux exemples trouvés dans la province du nord-ouest, mais pour l'immense intérêt montré par la population pour leur découverte. Cet intérêt se traduisit par des dizaines de millier de visiteurs sur le site, par le journal télévisé et la couverture par toute la presse écrite, par l'intérêt vif du milieu archéologique et celui du gouvernement, notamment du Ministre et du bureau des Travaux publiques, du ministère des Finances, du Cabinet et non moins du Premier Ministre Sir Winston Chirchill. Ce chapitre décrit les évènements qui eurent lieu durant ces quelques semaines de la fin septembre au début octobre 1954, utilisant les papiers ministériels, ceux de la Trésorerie et du Cabinet, aujourd'hui disponibles aux Archives Nationales.

Les chapitres 3 et 4 présentent les excavations en elles-même. Comme l'avait désiré le Professeur Grimes, la présence d'un Mithraeum sur le site n'a pas fait dévier notre attention de l'objectif initial de la fouille, à savoir l'examination de la vallée du Walbrook. De plus, un rapport complet des couches antérieures au temple, les éléments prouvant l'existence du Mithraeum lui-même et la nature de la vallée du Walbrook lors de l'utilisation du Mithraeum sont inclus. Les sculptures provenant de ce site font partie des trouvailles d'époque romaine les plus connues à Londres, mais elles ne représentent qu'une très petite partie du total des objets trouvés. Grimes savait que la vallée du Walbrook avait peut-être changé à travers l'époque romaine, ainsi il s'assura que la récupération des objets fut minutieuse de telle manière à pouvoir dater ces changements. Bien que ces matériaux ont été classés dans les années 50, ils présentent encore aujourd'hui une ressource précieuse d'information pour notre compréhension de la vallée et du temple. Les objets sont présentés d'une façon abréviée dans le chapitre 5, puis dans le chapitre 6 sont décrits les matériaux, bien que peu abondants, mais que nous possedons encore depuis les fouilles en 54.

Pour finir le volume, le chapitre 7 situe le site dans son juste contexte, celui de Londres à l'époque romaine, et pour le Mithraeum à sa-véritable place parmi les cultes mystiques de l'Empire Romain. Il est aussi suggéré dans un papier annexé par Docteur Martin Henig, que le temple avait été probablement dédié à une nouvelle divinité, celle de Bacchus, après l'ensevellissement des sculptures durant le premier quart du quatrième siècle. Nous espérons que ces contributions non seulement compléteront les recherches encore plus récentes faites sur la nature de la vallée du Walbrook à l'époque romaine, mais aussi initiera un débat plus informé sur le temple de Mithra du Walbrook.

Zusammenfassung

1952 begann das Komitee der römischen und mittelalterlichen Ausgrabungen in London (The Roman and Mediaeval London Excavation Council, ie RMLEC) mit den Arbeiten an einer Reihe von Gräbern, die das Tal des Walbrook-Baches auf dem Bucklersbury Haus-Sanierungsgelände durchqueren. Das neue Gebäude wurde auf einem bombengeschädigten Gelände gebaut und war beim Wiederaufbau der Innenstadt von London nach dem 2. Weltkrieg das größte Projekt seinesgleichen. Das Ziel dieser Ausgrabung war, Informationen über die wahre Beschaffenheit des Walbrook Tales und dessen Bach zu ermitteln. Seit 1946, unter der Leitung von W F Grimes, hatte die RMLEC ähnlich sorgfältig geplante Ausgrabungen auf Geländen überall in der Innenstadt durchgeführt, aber die Entdeckung eines gut erhaltenen römischen Gebäudes unter der Platte des Untergeschosses in den östlichst gelegenen Gräbern hatte den Effekt, die Aktivitäten des RMLEC und dessen Direktor der weiten Öffentlichkeit zuzubringen. Die Entdeckung des Mithras-Marmorkopfes am allerletzten Tag der geplanten Ausgrabungen, dem 18. September 1954, hatte die Folge eine Reihe von Begebenheiten in Gang zu bringen, welche heute noch einen wichtigen Platz in der Folklore der Londoner Nachkriegszeit einnehmen.

Obwohl das Mithras-Heiligtum und ein Schatz gefundener Skulpturen durch eine Anzahl von Pr. Grimes und Pr. Jocelyn Toynbee veröffentlichten Zwischenberichten gut bekannt waren, hatte man damals keinen eindeutigen Bericht über die Archäologie dieses Gebäudes herausgegeben. Gleichermaßen verhält es sich mit der Darlegung des Berichtes über die ursprüngliche Absicht der Ausgrabungen des Walbrook-Tales, die zu Lebenzeit Pr. Grimes nicht vollendet worden waren. Dieser Band versucht diesem Verfehlen nachzukommen.

Das 1. Kapitel beschreibt das Bucklersbury-Haus Sanierungsgelände und die in diesem Rahmen stattgefundenen Ausgrabungen. Darüberhinaus wird die ursprüngliche Absicht der Ausgrabungen und Vorgangsweisen Pr. Grimes und seines RMLEC-Teams am Gelände zwischen 1952 und 1954 untersucht. Auch werden subsequente Ausgrabungsarbeiten und Methoden beschrieben, mit denen versucht worden ist, dieses Gelände publik zu machen.

Das 2. Kapitel beschreibt die außergewöhnlichen Ereignisse, die sich anläßlich der Entdeckung des Mithras-Kopfes an diesem Gelände abgespielt haben. Der Standpunkt läßt sich vertreten, daß man das Mithras-Heiligtum nicht nur wegen des Fundes des Kopfes und anderer Skulpturen in guter Erinnerung behält, da sie sich, mit allen anderen, in den nordwestlichen Provinzen gefundenen Artifakten, verglichen, positiv verhalten, sondern auch wegen des bei der Entdeckung regenerierten, unglaublichen, öffentlichen Interesses. Das betrifft Zehntausende von Besuchern auf diesem Gelände, das Interesse aller seriösen Zeitungen und der Boulevardpresse, die Fernsehnachrichten, das archäologische Etablissement und Mitglieder der Regierung, wie den Minister selbst und das Personal des Ministeriums für 'Works' (unter anderem verantwortlich für die Erhaltung von historischen Gebäuden, heute ein Teil der Abteilung des englischen Nationalgutes), das Finanzministerium, das Kabinettbüro und sogar den Premierminister, Sir Winston Churchill. Dieses Kapitel beschreibt die Ereignisse dieser Wochen ab Ende Septembers bis zum Anfang des Oktobers 1954, mit Hilfe von Unterlagen der Ministerien, des Finanzministeriums und Kabinetts, die heute im Nationalarchiv (in Deutschland Bundeszentralarchiv) zum Studium zur Verfügung gestellt sind.Das 3. Kapitel befaßt sich mit dem Beweismaterial der Ausgrabungen selbst. Den Wünschen Pr. Grimes gemäß, ließ man nicht zu, daß die Aufmerksamkeit von dem ursprünglichen Ziel der Ausgrabungen - nämlich die Ermittlung des Walbrook-Tales als Einheit - auf die Existenz des Mithras-Heiligtums an diesem Gelände abgelenkt wurde. Es beinhaltet einen vollständigen Bericht über Ablagerungen vor der Zeit des Tempels, sowie auch das Beweismaterial für die Existenz des Mithras-Heiligtums selbst und die Beschaffenheit des zeitgenössischen Walbrook-Tales

Die Skulpturen des Geländes zählen zu den bekanntesten Funden aus dem römischen London, trotzdem sind sie nur ein kleiner Bruchteil der Sammlung. Grimes war sich bewußt, daß das Aussehen des Tales sich warscheinlich im Laufe der Römerzeit verändert hatte, deshalb tat er alles um ein gründliches Bergungsprojekt der Funde zu garantieren, damit diese Änderungen datiert werden konnten. Obwohl das Material in den 50er Jahren dieses Jahrhunderts aussortiert wurden, bildet es heute noch ein wertvolles Quellenmaterial für unser Verständnis des Tales sowie auch das des Tempels. Das 5. Kapitel befaßt sich in gekürzter Form mit den Funden und das 6. Kapitel mit dem noch erhaltenen, geringen Umweltsmaterial.

Um den Band zu vervollständigen, endet das 7. Kapitel mit der Lage des Geländes als Ganzes in Kontext mit dem römischen London gesehen und, im Falle des Mithras-Heiligtums, mit seinem rechtmäßigen Platz unter den mystischen Kulten des Römischen Reiches. In einem von Dr. Martin Henig angehefteten Essay, vermutet dieser, daß der Tempel nach dem Vergraben der Skulpturen während des ersten Viertels des vierten Jahrhunderts warscheinlich einer neuen Gottheit, dem Bacchus, gewidmet wurde. Man möchte hoffen, daß diese Beiträge, zusammen mit den Ergebnissen der Ausgrabungen, das Fundament für andere, im Bereich des römischen Mithraismus besser qualifizierte, Studien liegt und den Tempel zusammen mit den Funden in einem angemessenen international Kontext sieht.

A SONG TO MITHRAS

Mithras, God of the Morning, our trumpets waken the Wall!
'Rome is above the Nations, but Thou art over all!'
Now as the names are answered, and the guards are marched away,
Mithras, also a soldier, give us strength for the day!

Mithras, God of the Noontide, the heather swims in the heat,
Our helmets scorch our foreheads, our sandals burn our feet.
Now in the ungirt hour, now ere we blink and drowse,
Mithras, also a soldier, keep us true to our vows!

Mithras, God of the Sunset, low on the Western Main,
Thou descending immortal, immortal to rise again!
Now when the watch is ended, now when the wine is drawn,
Mithras, also a soldier, keep us pure till the dawn!

Mithras, God of the Midnight, here where the great bull dies,
Look on Thy children in darkness. Oh, take our sacrifice!
Many roads Thou hast fashioned: all of them lead to the Light!
Mithras, also a soldier, teach us to die aright!

1 The RMLEC Bucklersbury House excavations 1952–4

The redevelopment site

The Bucklersbury House development was planned as one of the largest office constructions of its era in the City of London. It consisted of a £4 million office scheme with ground floor shops, bars and restaurants and, in parts, double basements to accommodate parking space and building services. The building had been commissioned by the site owners, Messrs Legenland, and designed by Owen Campbell Jones. The work was carried out by the contractors Messrs Humphreys. It was located at the very centre of the City (Figs 1 and 2) in an area which had been highlighted by the Improvements and Town Planning Committee of the Corporation as one which was bound to attract special attention from prospective developers (Holden and Holden 1951, 216, 256). The entire project was completed in the spring of 1962.

This redevelopment site was situated immediately south-west of Mansion House and the Bank of England and to the north of Cannon Street Station (NGR TQ 32590 80995). The street called Walbrook, on the east side of the site, was and still remains a vital pedestrian link between the station and the financial heart of the City (Fig 3). Cannon Street and Budge Row marked the southern limits of the site, with Sise Lane on the west, Queen Victoria Street on the north-west side and Bucklersbury on the north. The site was therefore an irregular five-sided plot of land covering an area of *c* 1.5 acres. The alignments of all of these roads remain the same except for two: Budge Row, which was converted during redevelopment into an access and exit road for car parks under another office block called Temple Court, and Sise Lane, whose status has been reduced to that of a narrow pedestrian thoroughfare.

Budge Row, Sise Lane and Walbrook followed the lines of medieval streets of those names. Cannon Street, also of medieval date, was widened during the nineteenth century and remains the same today. Queen Victoria Street, as the name indicates, was built in 1869. It was during the construction of this road that the Bucklersbury mosaic was discovered (*Illustrated London News*, 29 May 1869), and it now forms the centrepiece of the Roman Gallery of the Museum of London. This discovery attracted very large crowds of sightseers, an event which was to be repeated in 1954 with the discovery of the Mithraeum (see Figs 16 and 17).

On the eve of the Second World War this area was typical of much of the City of London and the streets immediately surrounding it. The nineteenth-century

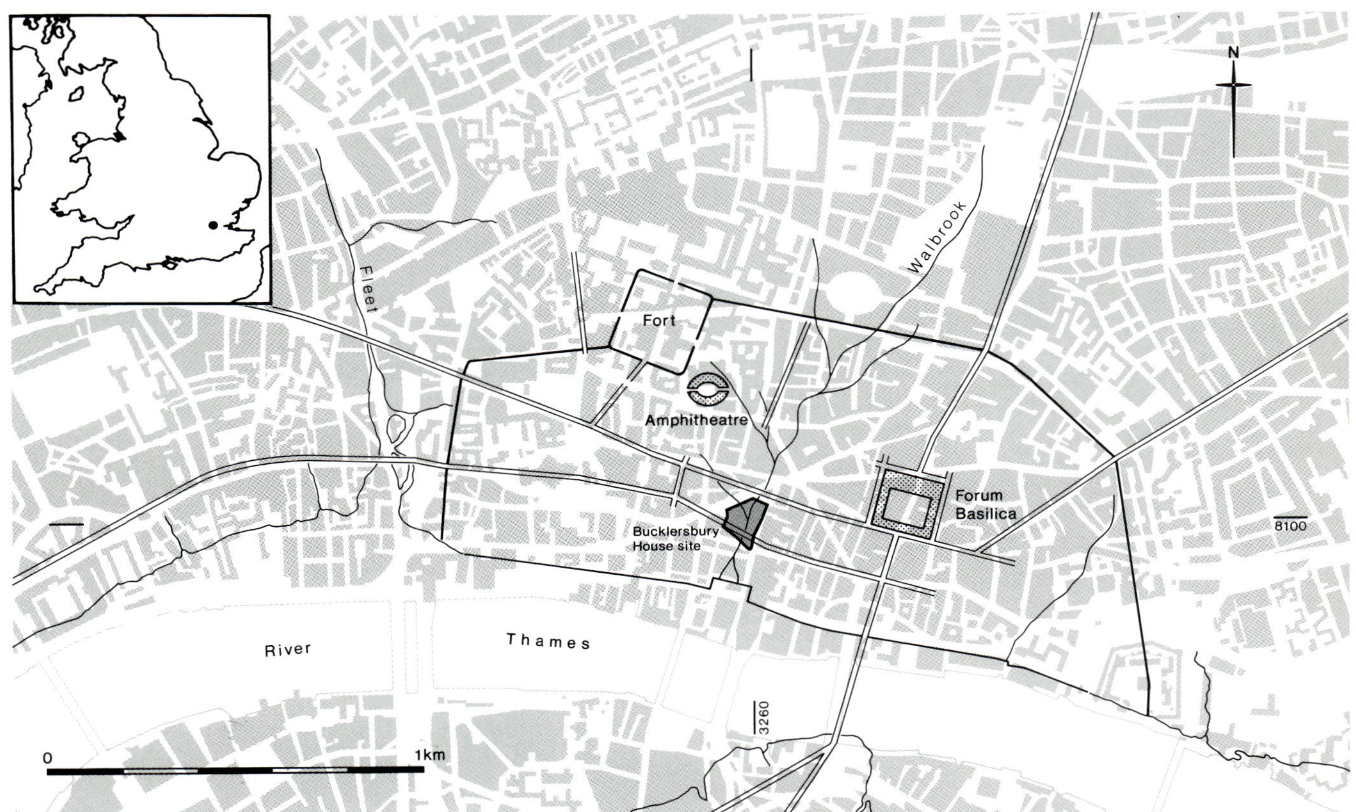

Fig 1 General location plan showing study area

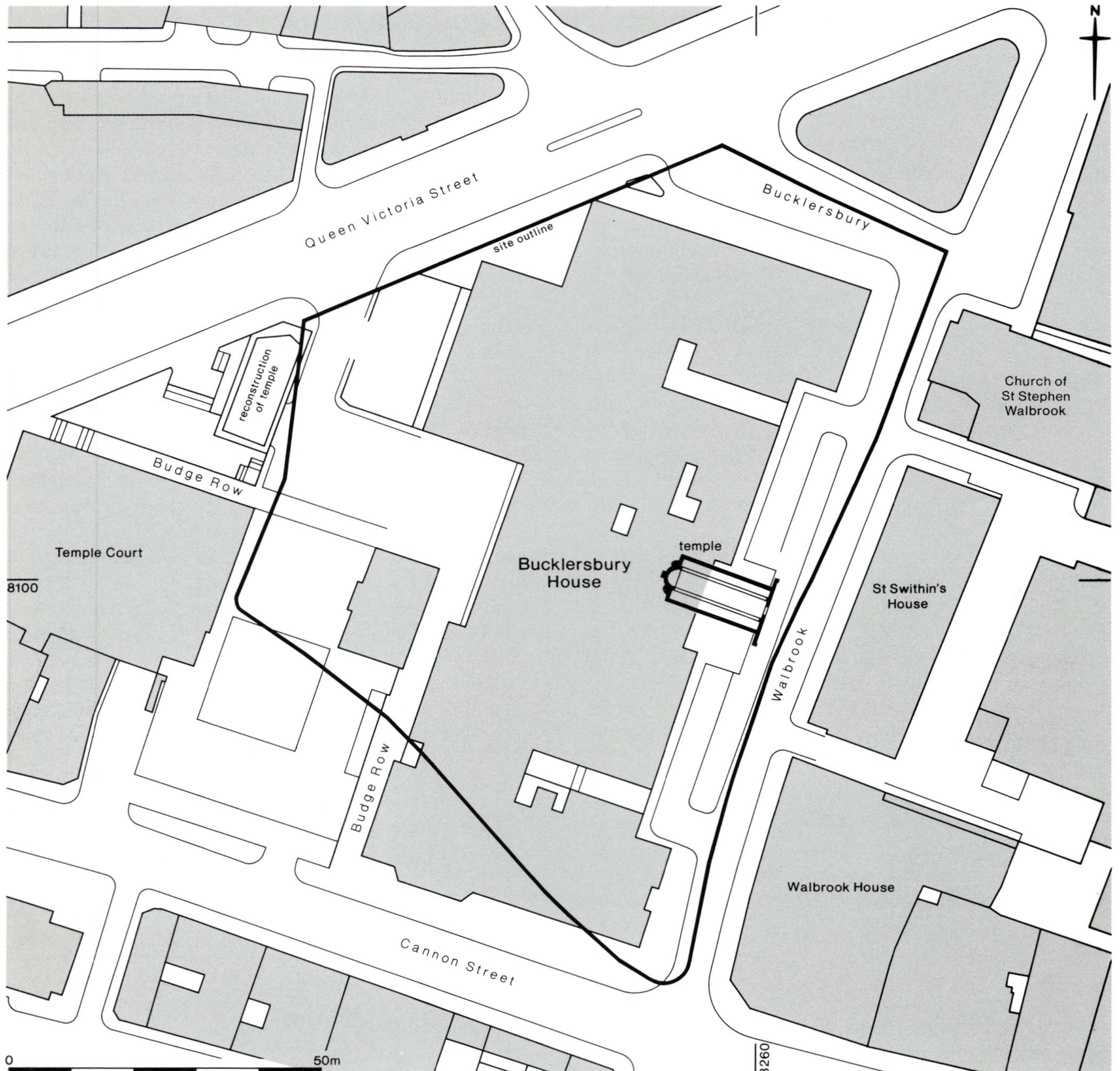

Fig 2 Modern OS map showing 1954 site outline and the site of the temple. The position of the Mithraeum reconstruction is shown to the north-west of the site

construction of Queen Victoria Street had led to much rebuilding on either side, but apart from this new diagonal alignment the majority of the properties followed the alignments and property lines of previous centuries. These fronted onto the narrow medieval streets such as Walbrook. With the migration from the City of London of the greater part of the residential population during the nineteenth century, such areas became used as office blocks for all manner of services and industries, which the City attracted as a financial and commercial centre. In the area of the future redevelopment site these properties were densely packed.

In 1941, the west side of Walbrook alone housed 51 business concerns (Post Office Directory 1941). These included 11 firms of accountants, 6 firms of solicitors, 6 insurance brokers, 3 merchants and 2 property developers. The remaining businesses included a bank, a dentist, a chiropodist, a bookseller, three cafés (including two Lyons cafés), a hosier, a tailor, one public house (The Deacon Tavern, later to be relocated in the Bucklersbury House redevelopment) and a typing pool. To the west of these, the area was filled with a large office conglomeration called Mansion House Chambers, connected by a warren of narrow alleys, which housed over 300 other businesses.

Fig 3 Details of the pre-Second World War properties taken from the 1896 OS map (darker tone indicates 1889 building overlying Temple)

These buildings were built of brick, many with stone facades or cladding, with mainly timber interior fittings — floors, stairways, wall-panelling, shelving and furniture. Such buildings were notorious as fire-traps and many fires were recorded throughout the City. One devastating blaze occurred on 19 November 1897. One hundred warehouses and blocks of offices in what is now the Barbican and Museum of London region of the City were destroyed in just a few hours, causing the greatest loss of property in the City since the Great Fire of 1666.

It is not surprising therefore that the bombing of the City, in 1940 and 1941 in particular, caused great devastation in areas filled with such small, compact and easily combustible buildings (Fig 4). On the night of 29 December 1940, high-explosive bombing accompanied by incendiaries caused the almost total destruction of a great swathe of property stretching from the Cripplegate area to the north, including the area rebuilt after 1897, southwards to the wharves on the Thames waterfront and east to west from Cheapside and Cannon Street to Fleet Street. Set in the midst of this destruction, St Paul's Cathedral, although struck by incendiaries and bombs, was not severely damaged.

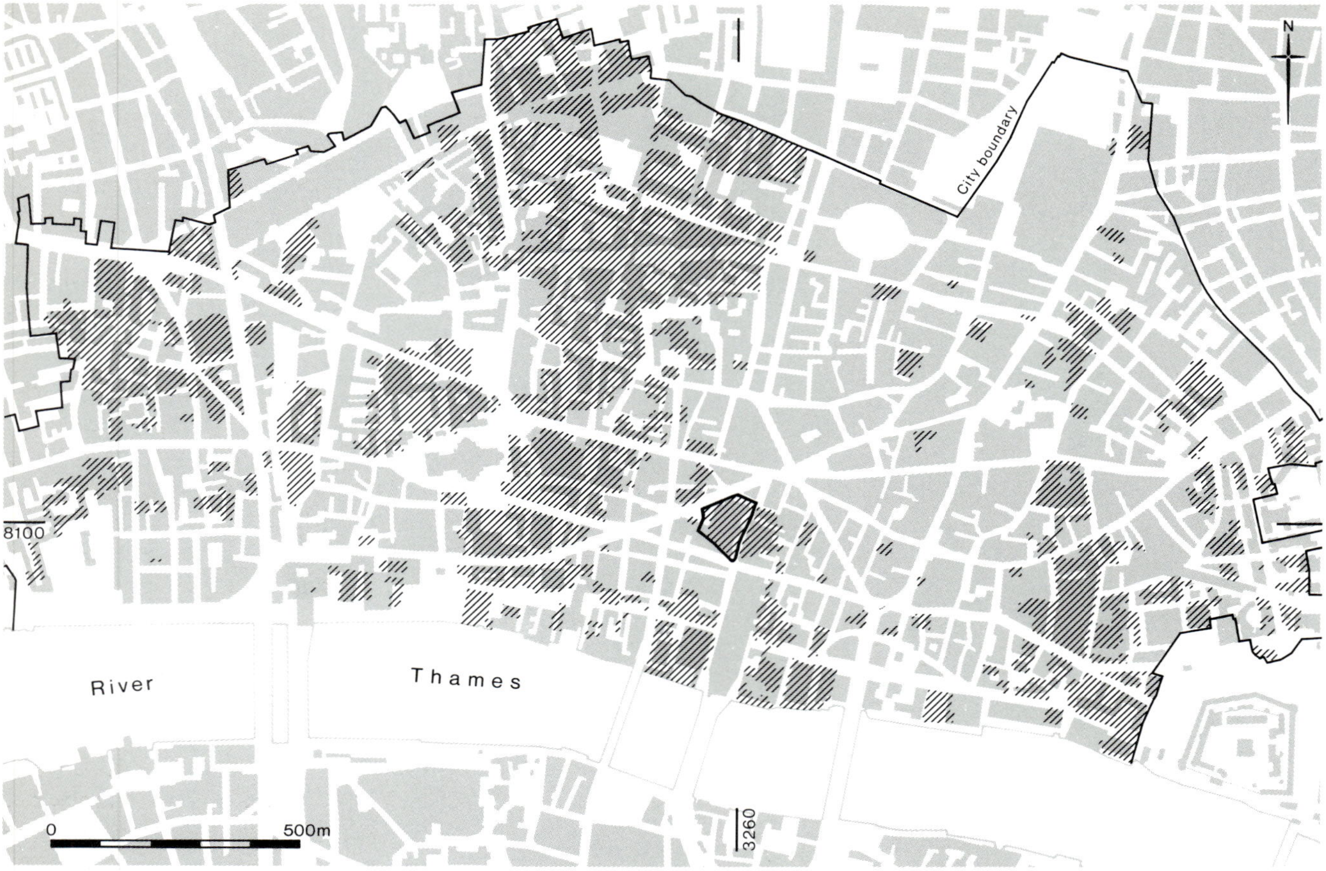

Fig 4 Extent of bomb damage throughout the City

Fig 5 Looking south down Walbrook on the morning of 11 May 1941. St Stephen's, Walbrook, is on the left (Cross and Tibbs Collection: reproduced with the permission of the Chief Commissioner of the Metropolitan Police)

The site in question was also damaged on that and subsequent occasions, but the most serious and ultimate damage came on the night of 10 May 1941. On that night, the severe attack on the entire area of London was recorded in the London County Council records as follows (John Reynolds pers comm):

1436 killed
1800 seriously injured
8000 streets impassable
2154 fires attended
210 medium fires recorded
20 major fires recorded
37 serious fires recorded
9 conflagrations recorded

Two of the conflagrations comprised the area of this site and an area on the north side of Queen Victoria Street extending to Cheapside (Fig 5). Across the site only the gutted shells of buildings remained standing and only 21 Bucklersbury, 21 Walbrook, and 19 and 27–32 Budge Row remained intact and usable for business purposes. The basements of 26 Budge Row were also utilised as offices. On the Queen Victoria Street frontage a large Air Raid Protection (ARP) static water tank was constructed for future fire-fighting purposes. The remaining shells of buildings were dismantled for safety and the basements filled with their rubble. The site remained in this condition from 1941 until 1952 (Fig 6).

The site as a whole was 'one on which archaeologists had long turned covetous eyes' (Grimes 1968). St John O'Neil, the Chief Inspector of Ancient Monuments, summarised the importance of this site well in a memorandum to his superiors in the Ministry of Works in May 1952. This was in connection with seeking a licence to remove rubble so that Grimes could extend the scale of his operations:

> This area is of the greatest potential importance archaeologically because of the depth of ancient deposits in the filled-in bed of the Walbrook and because this seems to have been the hub of earliest London. This is known from scattered finds of the past few decades and from trial cuttings, already dug, which have revealed part of a substantial Roman building. (PRO Works 142592 memo from O'Neil, 9 May 1952)

As will be seen, it was the presence of the Walbrook stream which was the immediate attraction to the archaeologists.

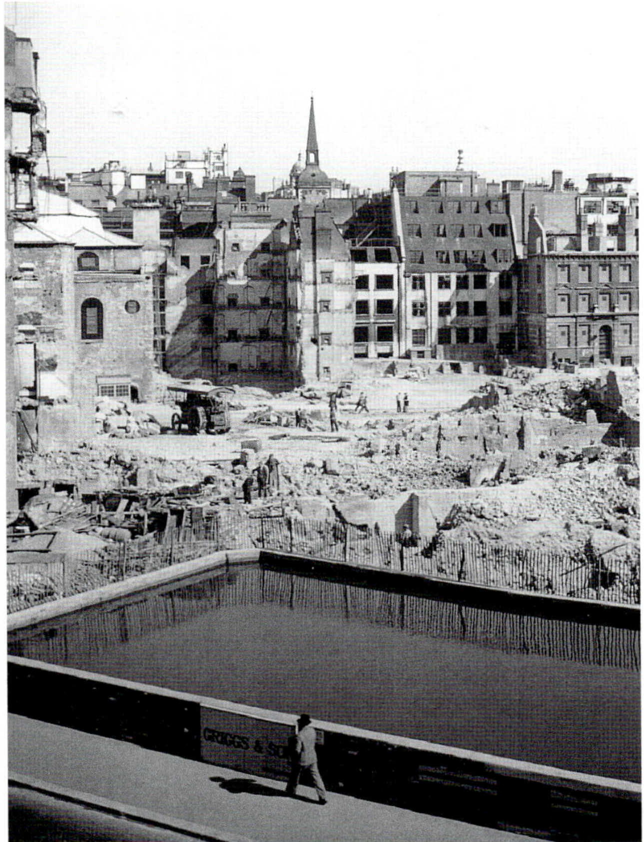

Fig 6 Looking south-east across the bomb-damaged site c 1944 showing the extent of the destruction. The ARP temporary water tank is in the foreground (Cross and Tibbs Collection)

The aims of the excavation

In August 1951, Mr Owen Campbell Jones, the architect of Bucklersbury House and senior partner in a firm of architects, contacted Grimes to bring to his attention the imminent redevelopment of the site. His wish was to make an agreement for the provision of a controlled archaeological excavation on the site in advance of any large-scale groundworks.

On other sites in the City of London, especially in the Cripplegate area, such a request would have led to the immediate presence of a RMLEC team. These were made up of a group of skilled labourers, selected by Grimes and the officers of the executive committee, who were paid competitive professional rates. They were supervised by trusted members selected from their own ranks or, as was the case for more important sites, by Grimes's assistant Audrey Williams. Mrs Williams joined RMLEC after a productive and active field and research career with St Albans Museum and the team in Canterbury, which had conducted similar work to that being carried out in the City of London under the directorship of Sheppard Frere. Her role in the Mithraeum excavation was an important factor in its success.

It was not until the early months of 1952, however, that Grimes was able to mobilise a team for the Bucklersbury House site. This was due to a number of factors. First of all, RMLEC was already stretched financially, and therefore physically, by its presence on other important sites. St Bride's Church was being excavated in its totality by the Council and Grimes was still maintaining a large presence in the Cripplegate area to determine the full extent and scale of the Roman fort, which he had identified only two years earlier. Secondly, the post-war shortage of building materials required applications for licences from the relevant Government offices for equipment such as timber for shoring. Progress on this site was hampered in particular by the need for a Government licence to clear the bomb-rubble from the basements of the area. This was in addition to the need for licences to cover timber for preparatory groundworks on the site and the steel for the structure of Bucklersbury House itself. Applications were submitted by the developers for both early in 1951. No decision was made on either until the latter part of 1952.

For these reasons the first work carried out on the site early in 1952 was regarded as exploratory only. Because no permission had yet been granted to the developers to remove the large quantities of bomb-rubble which still filled the many basements on the site, Grimes located his first cuttings in those areas which were clear of rubble.

The primary aim of the entire exercise on this site was to record an east–west profile through the Walbrook valley. Work conducted by the Guildhall Museum on the St Swithun's House site on the east side of the Walbrook, under the supervision first of Adrian Oswald but primarily of Ivor Nöel Hume,

Fig 7 Aerial view of the site looking south-west in October 1954 (Grimes)

had shown that the western side of that site contained deposits which resembled the waterlogged fills of the Walbrook stream seen in previous observations. Those excavators believed that the stream at this point along its course was probably *c* 80m wide and that the waterlogged deposits they had discovered in 1949–50 represented the eastern edge of that watercourse (Wilmott 1991, 12).

The cutting locations

Whether Grimes accepted in 1952 the generally held belief that the Walbrook flowed in a broad watercourse in a north–south direction across the Bucklersbury House site is not certain. If he was not aware of the real form of the stream, a narrow water channel *c* 4m wide in a wide, shallow valley *c* 90m across, then his original cutting locations would appear to have been placed with the intention of achieving a section through the stream itself (Cuttings A, C and F; see Fig 10) and a north–south lateral section down the course of the stream close to its centre (Cutting B). As will be seen, these cuttings actually examined a section across the Roman occupation in the stream valley from the west to the east bank (Cuttings A and C). They located the narrow stream bed in the centre (Cutting F), and the north-south cutting revealed further the nature of occupation on the west bank (Cutting B).

When work first commenced on the Bucklersbury House site in early 1952, therefore, three cuttings (A, B and F) were opened and the site name of 'Bucklersbury' (WFG44) was given to them. These were originally cuttings WFG44 I, II and III respectively. Cutting C was opened in the spring of 1952 and the site given the address of 'Walbrook' (WFG45), named after the street. Cutting C was evidently placed

Fig 8 The basements of nos 7—8 Walbrook (foreground) with Cutting C and no 38 Mansion House Chambers (rear) with Cutting F in 1953 (G F Walsh)

Fig 9 Detail of the apse beneath the basement slab of nos 7–8 Walbrook in 1953 (G F Walsh)

to complement cuttings A and F, but it was after the discovery of the apsidal building immediately under the basement slab in Cutting C that the two sites, WFG44 = 'Bucklersbury' and WFG45 = 'Walbrook', were amalgamated to form WFG44/45, variously known as 'The Walbrook site', 'The temple site', 'The Mithraeum site', 'The Walbrook/Mithraeum site','The temple of Mithras site' or 'The Bucklersbury House site'. For the purposes of this report, the site will be known as the 'Bucklersbury House site', the name of the entire redevelopment and the site name used by the Guildhall Museum to accession finds from their own examinations of the site and the excavations and observations of Grimes's RMLEC team between 1952 and 1955. Documents and finds in the Grimes London Archive can be found under the site code WFG44/45, still named Walbrook/Mithraeum.

As mentioned above, the positioning of all of the cuttings was dictated, in part, by the ease of access to the basements (Fig 7). Bomb-rubble still filled many of the basement areas. Indeed, some had been backfilled and turned into car parks. Fortunately, a relatively open passage existed running east to west across the site at its widest part, and after Grimes had received the relevant permission from the Ministry of Works this line was cleared further. Early photographs of the excavations show rubble banked up into the corners of basement areas, freeing just the central area for excavation (Figs 8 and 9). This phase of clearance preceded the full clearance of the basements by the contractors in 1953 and 1954.

Once this line had been selected, the precise positions of the cuttings were then determined by the existing basement walls and foundations. These were based upon long-established property, ward and parish boundaries which, in turn, had been influenced by the approximate north to south flow of the Walbrook stream (Wilmott 1991, 11, fig 2) and subsequently by the route of the street called Walbrook. The detailed locations of the cuttings, with subsequent expansions in 1954, were as follows (see Fig 10):

Cutting A (comprising AA and AB)

This cutting was located in the basements of 18, 25 and 46 Mansion House Chambers on what was later identified as the west bank of the Walbrook. This approximately east–west–oriented cutting was perpendicular to the supposed central axis of the Walbrook stream. At first this cutting was 65ft (19.80m) long and 5ft (1.52m) wide but was subdivided into two (Cuttings AA and AB) upon the discovery of broad and deep post-medieval foundations at the western end. Cutting AA was on the west of these foundations and was restricted to the basements of 18 Mansion House Chambers. Its new length was 3.45m. Cutting AB, on the east of these foundations, stretched across the basements of 25 and 46 Mansion House Chambers and was 14.55m in length.

Cutting AB was later subdivided again by an unexcavated baulk beneath a slight north–south post-medieval foundation but no subdivision by cutting notation was made.

Cutting B (comprising BA and BB)

This long cutting was located in the basements of 46–8, and 58–63 Mansion House Chambers. It was perpendicular to the extreme east end of Cutting AB and was positioned parallel to the supposed central axis of the Walbrook stream. It was later shown to be located on the west bank of the Walbrook.

Cutting B was also later subdivided into two on account of deep and large post-medieval foundations. Cutting BA, to the north of the foundations, was approximately 25ft (7.62m) long and 5ft (1.52m) wide. Cutting BB, to the south, was 48ft (14.63m) long, and also 5ft (1.52m) wide. Cutting BB was also later subdivided by unexcavated baulks under shallow post-medieval foundations and a late Roman masonry platform (Figs 30–1). As with Cutting AB, no additional cutting numbering was deemed necessary.

The Cutting C complex (comprising CA, CB, CC, CD and CE)

The initial Cutting C was located in the rear basement of 8 Walbrook in an east–west line, continuing the line of Cuttings AA, AB and F to the west (Fig 10). It was therefore perpendicular to the supposed central axis of the Walbrook stream and was later found to be located on the east bank of the Walbrook.

Fig 10 The location of the preliminary cuttings in 1952

At a very early stage in the excavation in 1952, however, the walls of a well preserved Roman apsidal building (only later, in 1954, identified as a Mithraeum) were discovered (Figs 8 and 9). This led to Cutting C being enlarged into five areas (CA–CE inclusive) which extended the area of excavation to cover 7–9 Walbrook (Fig 11). These cuttings were as follows:

Cutting CA was located at the west end and on the north side of the central axis of the Mithraeum. It included the north sleeper-wall in this area and part

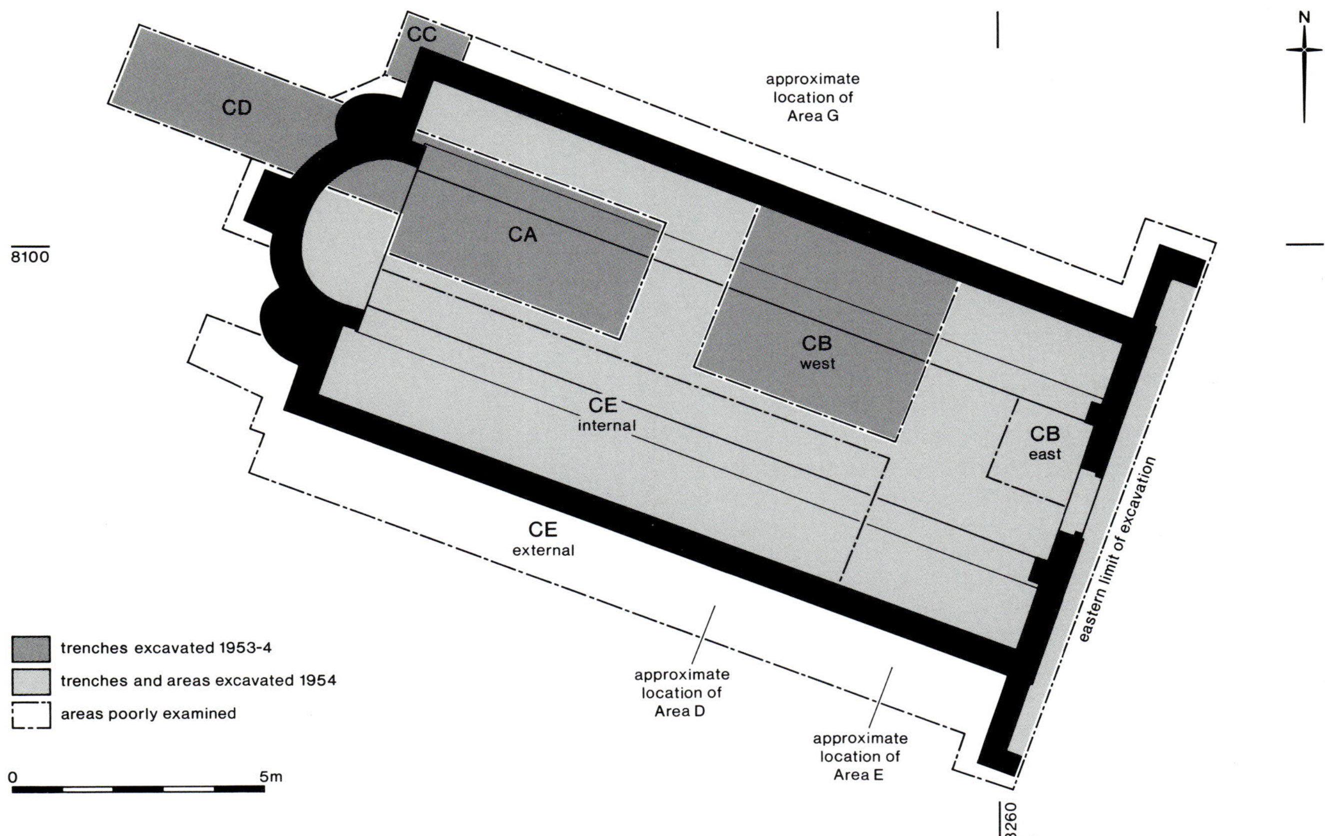

Fig 11 The location of the cuttings (C complex) over the Mithraeum in 1954

of the north aisle. The apse foundation separated it from Cutting CD to the west and a late Victorian foundation dictated its eastern limit.

Cutting CB continued the line of Cutting CA, extending eastwards towards the eastern limit of excavation. In 1954 this cutting was extended on the east side of a Victorian foundation. The western part was 4.34m in length, the eastern part 5.15m (Fig 10; see also Fig 91 for the full length of the recorded sections in Cutting CB).

Cutting CC was a small excavation outside the north-west corner of the Mithraeum. No details survive for this cutting but it would appear to have been a small sondage alongside a late Victorian foundation, which had damaged the corner of the Roman building, dug in order to examine the external features of the temple. It was later consumed by the open area excavation of the temple.

Cutting CD was located on the west side of the Mithraeum apse wall, continuing the line of Cutting CA to the east. The external face of the apse and the north buttress were the eastern limits of this cutting. The eastern limit was dictated by a massive basement foundation. On the other side of this was Cutting F.

Cutting CE was an open area which, in effect, covered the greater part of the interior of the Mithraeum from the southern faces of Cuttings CA and CB to the south, west and east walls of the Mithraeum on the south side of the central axis of the temple. Unlike Cuttings CA, CB and CD, which were excavated totally down to the top of natural levels, the base of Cutting CE was restricted to those layers which Grimes had identified as being those which immediately predated the construction of the Mithraeum. Cutting CE also includes those deposits examined outside the south-west corner and outside the south wall of the temple. This included a medieval well which cut into the south wall of the temple.

Cutting D

See below.

Cutting F (no subdivisions)

This cutting was located in the basements of 38–40 Mansion House Chambers (Fig 10). It was oriented east to west on the western side of the foundation which dictated the west limit of Cutting CD (Fig 8). It was anticipated that its position would cross the central axis of the Walbrook stream, but as it proved it located the actual course of the narrow Walbrook itself, including details of its revetting, and the west bank of the stream.

Cuttings D, E and G

Three other small cuttings were located around the exterior walls of the Mithraeum (Fig 11). Cuttings D and E, in 9 Walbrook, were positioned up against the south wall to the east of the medieval well. Cutting G, in 7 Walbrook, was positioned to the north of the west end of the Mithraeum. All three areas were consumed during the general opening-up of the area in 1954 and were not retained during the main part of the excavation. The Cautopates sculpture and an altar *(Chapter 5, The finds catalogue, Period 2 finds, VIII/IX/X.4 and 6)*, however, were found in Cutting D.

The excavation and recording techniques

It is evident from the locations of the cuttings and the subsequent division of these cuttings into smaller units that the modern foundations and intrusions caused considerable problems on this site. Grimes's team were not well equipped for heavy breaking-out work. The limited funds for this excavation did not extend to the hiring of compressors or drills, so the breaking of the concrete basement slabs had to be carried out with 14lb hammers and cold chisel points!

However, it will be seen below that the modern foundations covering and, in places, cutting into the Mithraeum walls and floors have an important bearing upon the site, especially in connection with three of the sculptures *(Chapter 5, The finds catalogue, Period 2 finds, IX.44, 45 and 46)*. These, it was said, were found 'in the Walbrook' in 1889. It is therefore of significance that the foundations which overlay the temple were laid in that year during the rebuilding of 5–8 Walbrook. This was the only building work which took place in Walbrook (the street) during 1889.

Modern foundations were not the only problems which had to be overcome. Every cutting on the site was bedevilled at a very early stage by groundwater problems. Manual pumps were used to clear the water but eventually the working conditions became intolerable and work had to cease late in 1952. It was not until 1953 that the Corporation of London supplied Grimes's team with a mechanical pump and gave him permission to pump groundwater into one of the few unblocked live drains running across the site.

The excavation of the cuttings was carried out by Grimes's team of hired, skilled labourers with occasional assistance from a few trusted volunteers. Because of supervision problems and the dangers inherent on busy building sites in the City, Grimes was wary of encouraging too much volunteer help (see Grimes 1968, 222–4 for a full explanation of his recruitment policy). The team was supervised by a trained archaeologist, in this case Audrey Williams. She supervised the day-to-day work on the site and reported to Grimes on his frequent visits to the City during 1952 and 1954 from his other duties as Director of the London Museum.

The cuttings were excavated as far as possible as single contexts in their proper stratigraphic sequence. However, not every 'context' was recorded in detail and finds retrieval and retention were selective and erratic. The RMLEC recording method is briefly described here.

Firstly, as has been noted above, each cutting was allocated its separate and unique label. At Bucklersbury House an alphabetic code was used (A to G), but numerical cutting codes were used on sites elsewhere in the City. The cuttings were excavated by pick, shovel and trowel but detailed recording and finds retrieval occurred only when a judgement had been made concerning the significance of a particular deposit or level.

In the course of excavation notebooks were filled with context and feature details including sketches. Before the discovery of the head of Mithras Grimes would visit the site only intermittently, because in addition to his duties at the London Museum his presence was required on the other RMLEC excavations in the City. After the identification of the building as a Mithraeum, although he spent much of each day on the site, his time was taken up with official and media duties. Most of the recording in these notebooks was therefore by Audrey Williams, with numerous annotations, observations and comments by Grimes.

Finds were placed in paper bags, with the context information written onto them at the cutting-side. At the end of each working day the bags were collected and the context information entered into a finds log book. At this stage each group of finds was given a unique number which became known as its 'Bag number'. Thus F715 would be 'Bag' 715 from Cutting F. This method meant that associated bags of finds might become separated but each group within each bag would remain a closed unit. However, this system accounts for the, at times, confusing scatter of bag numbers, with high numbers appearing stratigraphically higher than some bags with low numbers.

There are two significant disadvantages to this system for any modern researcher dealing with Grimes's records. First, unless the information placed in the finds log book was precise and specific, giving relationships to known features or other bags, the period of time since their retrieval in 1952–4 and the present has resulted in a number of inconsistencies. Regrettably, any bag group which has the slightest ambiguity associated with it must be regarded as unstratified. We are fortunate here that the Mithraeum and Walbrook site attracted so much attention and revealed such dramatic results. Extra attention was paid to the precise recording of finds groups. Nevertheless, a few bags can still not be located either on plan or in section and so must remain in the unstratified category.

The second disadvantage, which for comparative purposes is more frustrating, is that only those layers from which finds were kept are certain to have a detailed context description. Sometimes the section drawings are annotated with context information for layers without finds, but this is for a small percentage only of the total number of identifiable contexts within a cutting. However, this criticism is perhaps a little unfair, since, in truth, Grimes's pioneering work on such a scale in the City of London laid the foundation for so much which has been carried out since — in terms not only of archaeological knowledge but also of methods and techniques. It is a tribute to him that he was able to develop a system with such limited resources which so competently recorded the archaeological sequences on 63 sites.

Whenever necessary Grimes would personally carry out the photography of the site. Much emphasis was placed by him on a full photographic record and the completion of this report has been made easier by having available a large stock of negatives and slides. Many of these photographs have been reproduced in this volume. Unfortunately the intervening 40 years have seen a marked deterioration in the quality of many negatives. The reader is therefore asked to be additionally tolerant about the quality of their reproduction here.

All site surveying and measurement of cutting locations were carried out by Grimes. In the case of the Mithraeum itself, his task was made easier by the need of the Ministry of Works to make a scale model of the temple before it was eventually 'saved'. The ground plan of the temple and the elevations of the interior and exterior, redrawn here, were prepared by architects of the Ministry of Works. The ground plan was used and annotated by Grimes for his 1968 volume. Edited versions of the plan and elevations are reproduced here. The elevations can be found on Figures 62–70 and the phase plans on Figures 61, 97, 100, 103 and 126.

The sections were drawn by Grimes at a scale of 1:48. He was gifted with the ability to draw in miniature and the amount of information he was able to convey on a section drawing at such a scale has proved remarkable. It has been mentioned above that Grimes left the Museum of London a number of instructions about the publication of this archive. One specific point, of a personal nature, was that we should make as much use as possible of his original artwork, and we are happy to report that we have been able to do so. The section drawings and finds drawings have been enhanced by our illustrators, but they remain essentially Grimes's own work (Fig 12).

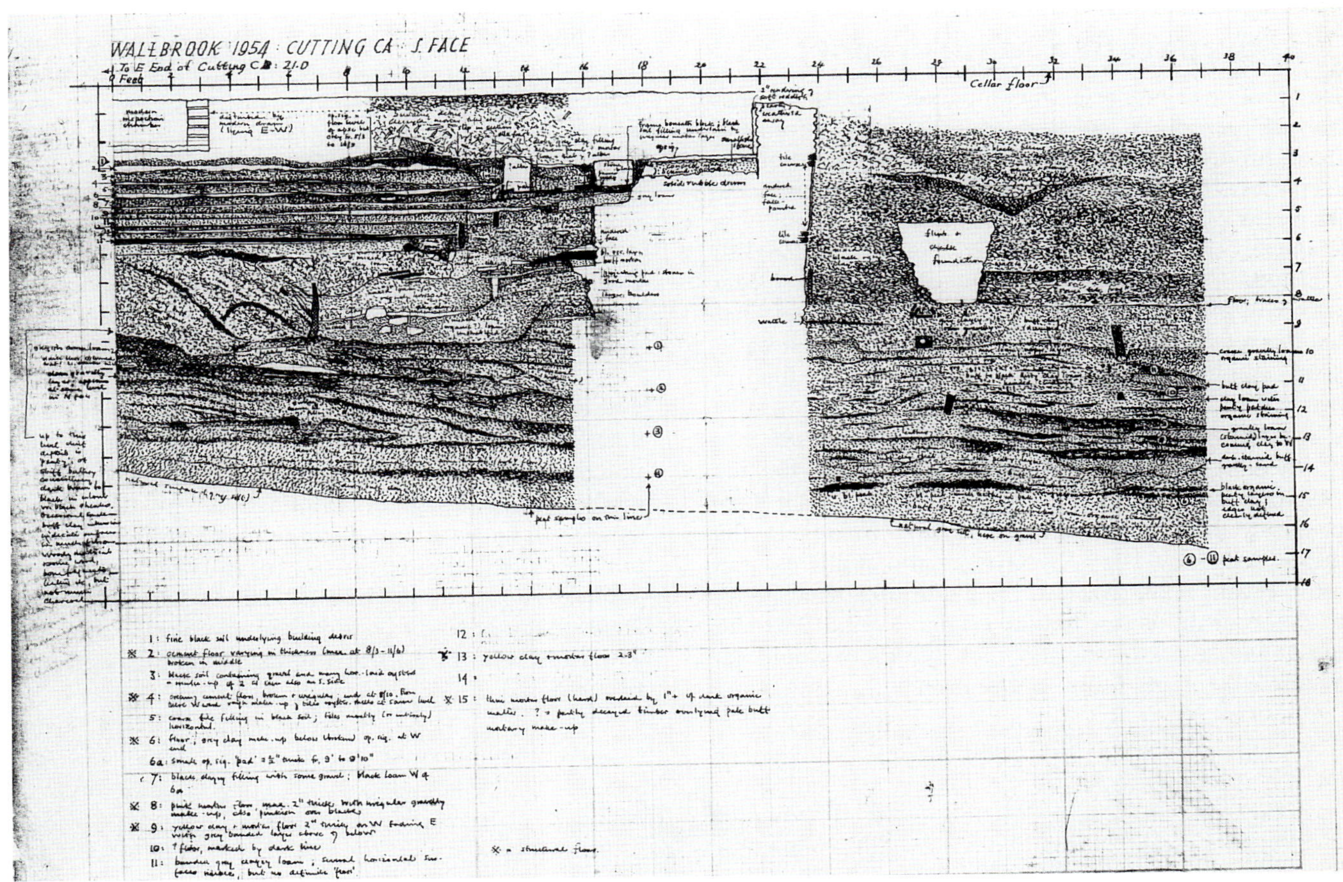

Fig 12 The section drawing of Cuttings CA and CD as drawn by Grimes. The frontispiece shows him consulting with Audrey Williams over this drawing. The longitudinal sections of the temple have been reversed in this report to place west on the left. Compare with Figure 41 (MoL)

Once a section had been drawn the numbers of the individual finds bags were projected onto the section, thus showing their relative positions. The section drawings are therefore an important component of this archive. This is in keeping with Grimes's original excavation aim of recording as complete a section as possible through the fills of the Walbrook stream and valley.

Post-excavation work on the large body of finds and documents from this excavation began almost immediately once the excavation was completed. Finds were washed by RMLEC and Guildhall Museum staff. The owners of the site, Legenland, generously donated the finds from these excavations to the Guildhall Museum. Research on these and other finds, including the bulk finds such as pottery and animal bone, was carried out intermittently from the mid-1950s to the late 1970s. The most important achievements during that long period were Professor Jocelyn Toynbee's sculpture report, Joanna Bird's coarse pottery, samian and small finds reports, and Sarah Macready's animal bone report and editing of the coarse pottery report. It has been mentioned above that much of this has had to be updated, but the contribution made to this final report on the Walbrook valley and the temple of Mithras by these pieces of work has undoubtedly been immense.

The preparation of this report

The project of preparing the documents in the Grimes archive pertaining to this site for publication has been funded by English Heritage and based in the Department of Early London History and Collections, Museum of London. The procedural document The management of archaeological projects (English Heritage 1991), although designed with more recent and complete archaeological archives in mind, has been implemented as fully as possible, although naturally some concessions and compromises have had to be made.

At an early stage in the assessment of the archive as a whole it was noted that the documents for the Mithraeum contained a number of items which were evidently drafts of the structural text written in the 1950s and early 1960s by Grimes and Williams, and more recent texts (late 1970s) by Grimes which refer to the work of his research assistants, Joanna Bird and Sarah Macready. It was apparent that these would act as the basis of any future publication.

These outline preparatory texts concentrated upon the temple itself and the deposits immediately below the temple. Unfortunately no drafts existed for the other cuttings on the site. These drafts have therefore been included here with context information and other cross-references supplied by the present author from a variety of documents in the archive. The section drawings and site notebooks have been the most important in this respect.

Grimes had divided the stratigraphy across the entire site into 11 main stratigraphic groups. The re-analysis of the pottery showed that the grouping together of a number of layers, especially in the latest of Grimes's groups, Groups VII to XI inclusive, could no longer be justified. For instance, on the basis of research work conducted in the early 1970s, Group VIII contained deposits from Cuttings AB, BB, CA, CB, CE and F. The re-analysis of this material in the early 1990s, taking into account the advances made in pottery studies in the ensuing 20 years, especially in late Roman ceramics, showed that the material in this group on the west bank of the stream (Cuttings AB, BB and F) was later than that in the Mithraeum on the east bank (Cuttings CA, CB and CE). To rectify this and other inconsistencies, some of these original groups have therefore been divided. There is now a total of 15 stratigraphic groups.

Roman numerals, as used by Grimes, have been used throughout this report to identify these groups. These have been divided into two main periods separated by the approximate construction date of the temple, ie AD 240–50:

Period 1 The Walbrook valley up to *c* AD 240–50, which includes Groups I–VII inclusive and Group XII

Period 2 The temple and the Walbrook valley from *c* AD 240–50, which includes Groups VIII–XI inclusive and Groups XIII–XV inclusive.

The site documents and finds for this site, with more detailed information on certain aspects such as the pottery assemblages and the pre-Mithraeum sequence, are held by the Museum of London. These can be consulted, along with the documents and finds for the other RMLEC sites in the City of London, on written application to the Archaeological Archive Manager, Department of Early London History and Collections, The Museum of London, 150 London Wall, London, EC2Y 5HN.

2 *'There's a fascination frantic in a ruin that's romantic'*: the Mithras Affair, September and October 1954

Prologue

With the words of the Lord High Executioner from Gilbert and Sullivan's operetta, *The Mikado*, Sir David Eccles, the Minister of Works, opened his final assessment of the chances for the preservation of a Temple of Mithras in the City of London to a meeting of the Cabinet of Her Majesty's Government, chaired by the Prime Minister, Sir Winston Churchill. Just how this came to be necessary is a story which is well worth the telling. It shows the fragile relationship between Government departments, contractors and developers, and archaeologists during the post-war period of reconstruction in the City. It shows also the intense interest shown by the public in this find which, although fuelled by a news-hungry and sensation-seeking press, served as the catalyst for subsequent events. It is tempting to draw comparisons between the events of 1954 and those of more recent 'headline' archaeological finds in London. This is not the place, however, to discuss the politics of London archaeology in the capital over the last 50 years, but as a contribution to this at times volatile topic and to make this study of the Walbrook valley and the excavation of the temple of Mithras complete, the events which took place off-site during those few weeks at the end of September and the beginning of October 1954 are presented below.

The following commentary makes use of press reports, contemporary accounts of the affair, and Ministry of Works, Treasury and Cabinet documents, now available for scrutiny in the Public Records Office. This chapter is not intended to be critical of any individual or organisation. Nor does it attempt to pass any sort of judgement on any aspect of the proceedings and their ultimate outcome. Grimes, at the centre of events, made his opinion more than clear (1968, 230–7). But in retrospect it will become apparent that throughout the entire affair there was never a coordinated attempt by all the parties involved to address the problem of the temple itself. Each group worked individually. No national policy existed to cope with such an occurrence and none was subsequently prepared to make ready any contingencies for future occasions of this kind — even though all of the parties represented among the documents here (the views of the developers have never been properly recorded) readily admitted that archaeological excavation in the City had to be carried out and that it was most likely that other spectacular discoveries of this kind were waiting to be made. As will be seen, some tentative suggestions were made, by the Ministry itself, to organise further excavation in the City around a programme of rescue and research. This revolutionary idea floundered as the affair progressed and eventually faded from the agenda once the media interest in the temple had waned. Not once was the Government or the nation asked what they felt about their heritage and how they should regard it. Perhaps this might be expecting too much, but such lost opportunities are a recurring feature of those months in the autumn of 1954.

The beginning

The discovery of the temple of Mithras was, according to Grimes, 'in the nature of a fluke...I had no choice where to dig: there was no heaven-sent inspiration to guide the siting of the trench that revealed the temple' (1968, 237). Such fortuitous discoveries abound in the history of archaeology. But whatever the circumstances of the discovery, there is little doubt that the London Mithraeum must rank high among the archaeological discoveries made in this country, if only because of the type of building, its state of preservation, and the rich sculptures found in association with it. Together all of these factors make it a monument which compares favourably with others in the Roman Empire.

Although the archaeologist may refer to the architectural details of the building, archetypal of urban Mithraism, and the high quality of the cult images which it contained, it is of interest that the Walbrook Temple remains very strong in the memory and folklore of the population of the City of London, perhaps even of the country as a whole. A great many people outside the discipline of archaeology still recall those last two weeks in September 1954 when the building was first identified as a Mithraeum. Many still take pride in having queued, some for many hours and having travelled great distances, to see the temple first-hand, and many can still recall Grimes's name. And a generation after the occasion, until its discovery was recently eclipsed by that of the Rose Theatre in Southwark, there were still some in the building industry who would shudder at the very mention of the temple. As Merrifield aptly put it, 'If you wish to see building contractors cower and property developers turn pale, you need only whisper the words "Temple of Mithras", (1965, 18).

The 'Temple of Mithras Affair' and the public clamour to see it preserved caused a sensation which was reported in great detail in newspapers around the country (Fig 13). The great national broadsheets led the outcry with a high moral tone but small provincial and local newspapers described the building and, through their editorials and letters pages, added their opinions to the national debate. In an unprecedented case, the temple appeared on a Movietone newsreel

Queue for Mithras

MINISTER SEES TEMPLE RELICS

DEMOLITION HALTED FOR ARCHÆOLOGISTS

ROMAN TEMPLE IN LONDON

LESSONS OF PRESENT DISCOVERY

SEPTEMBER 22 1954

BIG CROWDS AT ROMAN RUIN

POLICE MARSHAL QUEUES

MANY UNABLE TO ENTER

MORE FINDS AT ROMAN SITE

THE TEMPLE'S FATE

BUILDING OVER ROMAN RUIN

DUE TO START TO-DAY

'MOST BEAUTIFUL' HEAD IS FOUND

Woman shows it to queuers

BIG NEW FIND AT TEMPLE

Crowds see 1,800-year-old Roman god dug up

Daily Mail

NO. 18,199 THREE HALFPENCE FOR QUEEN AND COMMONWEALTH SATURDAY, SEPTEMBER 25, 1954

ROMAN TEMPLE MAY BE SAVED

Work again postponed as experts race report

CAN THEY, CAN'T THEY SAVE THE TEMPLE?

Still Hope of Reprieve for Roman Temple

COST OF PRESERVING ROMAN TEMPLE

STUDY BY MINISTRY

COST WOULD BE £500,000

Churchill awaits findings

Friday, October 15, 1954

New discoveries on Roman Temple site

DIGGING NEARLY COMPLETE

MITHRAS AND MUSSOLINI

DECISION NEAR ON TEMPLE

CHANCE OF MORE DISCOVERIES

LATEST FIND IN TEMPLE OF MITHRAS

INSCRIBED MARBLE TABLE

TEMPLE OF MITHRAS IS SAVED FOR LONDON

Fig 13 A small collection of the headlines from September and October 1954

which was no doubt seen by hundreds of thousands, and many tens of thousands of people made the effort to queue, some for many hours, to visit the site. On one such occasion a small crowd tried to storm a police barricade to gain access to the site!

At a more academic level, eminent archaeologists, architects and building engineers of the day engaged in a tangled public debate. Should such monuments be preserved *in situ*? Would it be the same if it was moved? Should the archaeological records be regarded as a suitable replacement for the real thing? Who should pay if it was preserved? Would anyone be interested in it once it had been preserved? And what would be the implications for London and other towns in the country if a precedent was established over the Walbrook Temple? Questions about the temple were asked in the House of Commons. The Minister of Works and his men visited the site and at Prime Minister Sir Winston Churchill's request the temple was twice discussed in Cabinet.

Finally, as far as the events of 1954 are concerned, the decision to move the building led to triumphant banner headlines proclaiming 'Temple Saved' and the immediate public concern faded away. The temple was dismantled and stowed away in no real order in the corner of a redundant churchyard. It would appear that in 1954 all parties were satisfied with this final compromise, but subsequently Professor Grimes and senior officials in the Ministry of Works did not approve of the way the architects intended to incorporate the Mithraeum into the new Bucklersbury House. As Baillie Reynolds, Chief Inspector of Ancient Monuments, said in 1959 when refusing a request to supply Ministry workers to rebuild the monument, it would be '...on the wrong site, at the wrong level and on the wrong orientation' (MoW memorandum, 13 July 1959). Their protestations, however, were in vain and in 1962 a structure vaguely resembling the Mithraeum was reproduced on the south side of Queen Victoria Street, using the original building materials.

But how did all of the parties concerned arrive at this final decision? How was it that such a well preserved ancient monument as the Walbrook Temple of Mithras could not be preserved *in situ*? Who campaigned for its survival and who wished it to be destroyed? And what was discussed in those Cabinet meetings?

The building had been reported in the press througout the summer of 1954. An article in *The Sphere* magazine, in an interview with Grimes, described the building as part of a well built house or public building. The preliminary excavations (Cuttings CA and CD) exposed the north sleeper-wall and part of the apse. It ends with the comment that 'It is probable that the current excavations are the most important made in the City of London for a very long time'.

By the middle of September more of the interior had been excavated and the presence of the channelled altar-stone *(Chapter 5, The finds catalogue, Period 2 finds, IX.49,* Figs 105 and 205*)* confirmed the growing belief that the building was a temple. *The Sphere* showed an interest once again and reported that the end of the excavation was approaching and the temple would have to be ripped down to make way for a 14-storey block of offices. But there was no public response.

It was at the very end of the excavation that public interest in the site was finally engaged. On Saturday 18 September, the final day of the excavation, The *Daily Telegraph* published a very short article noting the fact that London was to lose 'the remains of the only Roman Temple found within its precincts'. In an interview, Grimes noted that the building was the first in London to be completely excavated and was remarkably well preserved. The cult was, as yet, unknown but 'relics of a number of eastern cults' were reported (eg the roundel, *Chapter 5, The finds catalogue, Period 2 finds, IX/X.1,* Fig 213, found in July 1954).

During the morning of this Saturday, as final recording work was being done, the head of Mithras *(Chapter 5, The finds catalogue, Period 2 finds, IX.38,* Fig 180) was discovered and was photographed 'by one of those press-photographers who always seem to be about' (Grimes 1968, 231). Almost nonchalantly, the excavation closed at lunch-time and the team dispersed. Grimes 'departed for the country' (1968, 231).

The next day, Sunday 19 September, *The Sunday Times* published the photograph of the head of Mithras, the building was finally identified as a mithraeum and the public were warned once again of the imminent destruction of the building beneath a block of modern offices.

It is fascinating and bewildering to think that while the identity of the cult of the temple remained unknown or at least uncertain the public interest in this monument failed to materialise. But once Mithras had arrived on the scene the public imagination was ignited — the City of London, financial centre of the country, home to Mammon, was harbouring yet another cult just as mysterious, that of Mithras.

Spurred on by the *Telegraph* and *The Times* reports a number of people, including reporters and photographers, visited the site, which to all intents had now been abandoned by the archaeologists. Photographs in the newspapers the next day showed people climbing over the building and showing, as Grimes said in retrospect, 'an unhealthy interest in some of its more fragile features' (1968, 231) (Fig 14). Since the situation at that time was that the archaeologists had left the site and the machines were to move in the very next day to destroy the temple, these visitors ought to be forgiven for showing such enthusiastic interest. For good or ill, it could even be said that many of them initiated the subsequent affair. Some of them were sufficiently moved by this Temple of Mithras and so shocked by the thought of its loss that they went down to Printing House Square and lodged their complaints at *The Times* office.

On Monday 20 September events began to accelerate and the number of interested parties increased alarmingly. *The Times* ran a story, accompanied by the photograph of the Sunday crowd enthusiastically inspecting the site, which described the building in some detail — with some errors of fact and interpretation of the kind which frequently bedevil archaeological journalism (it was described as lying on the west bank, not the east bank, of the Walbrook and it was supposed to have had a triple-apsed east end). In this article the first reference is made by Grimes to the sculptures found in 1889 (not 1896 as recorded by *The Times's* archaeological correspondent), in particular the relief of Mithras Tauroctonos with an inscription by Ulpius Silvanus, veteran of the Second Augustan Legion, which probably marked the dedication of the Mithraeum *(Chapter 5, The finds catalogue, Period 2 finds, IX.46,* Fig 196).

These details aside, the most important and influential part of *The Times's* coverage of the story concerned the ultimate fate of the temple. The article mentioned the 'several callers at *The Times* offices [who] protested against the likelihood of this remarkable discovery being destroyed by immediate constructional work for a new office building'. *The Times* feared that it was too late to interfere with contractors who were due to start demolition that very morning.

In its conclusion, the article made four important points:

1 The design of the new building would not accommodate the temple.
2 The terms of agreement under which the site was excavated provided for its return to the owners upon completion of the archaeological work (an agreement which, by ending his work at Saturday lunchtime, Grimes was evidently intent on keeping).
3 The bodily removal of the structure to another place would not be welcomed by archaeologists since it would lose its significance away from the site.
4 Though the individual finds, including the head of Mithras, would find their way to an appropriate place for safekeeping the public might expect more than just the contents of the temple to be preserved.

All of these points would be raised again during the debate over the next couple of weeks. Immediately, however, it was *The Times's* editorial which accompanied

Fig 14 Visitors to the site on Sunday 19 September as recorded by a Times photographer (©Times Newspapers Limited, 1954)

the article published on the Monday which prompted immediate Government action. The effect of this editorial was such that it is repeated here in full:

> A Temple for Destruction
>
> Archaeological work ended on Saturday on the remarkable remains of a Roman Temple of MITHRAS excavated by the Roman and Mediaeval London Excavation Council on a site between Cannon Street and Queen Victoria Street, adjoining Walbrook, and within a few yards of Cannon Street station. Some sixty feet in length of this building have been uncovered showing the layout of a triple apse west end, and a double line of pillars dividing, as it were, a nave from two aisles. Even on the last day a remarkable carved head of MITHRAS was unearthed. The excavation is still far from complete, and it seems that it never will be completed. Within a matter of hours from the writing of these words the whole structure, with anything else that may be hidden under adjoining parts of the site, is apparently due to be bulldozed out of existence to make way for the foundations of a new (and, no doubt, much-needed) building.
>
> There is something grievously wrong with our planning if an important antiquity of this sort can be destroyed almost before it has been seen. What other civilised nations may think of the matter is a point upon which one can only speculate apprehensively. It is no wonder that many of those who visited the site yesterday (some of whom came to *The Times* office to lodge their protests) were asking why no arrangements could be made either to arch over the remains in a sort of crypt, or to remove them stone by stone for re-erection elsewhere.

Phrases such as 'bulldozed out of existence' and 'destroyed almost before it had been seen' conjure up an impression of what the leader-writer of *The Times* regarded as an act of wanton vandalism that was about to be enacted in the centre of the City of London on something that was the property of the nation as a whole. No doubt this pending destruction outraged many. But it may be that the most telling statement here, which sent tremors through the British establishment all the way to 10 Downing Street, was the thought that other 'civilised nations' would be aghast at this act of British barbarism.

The Government intervenes

That very day, at the suggestion of the Prime Minister, Sir Winston Churchill (CAB 128/27; C.C(54), no. 49), Sir David Eccles, the Minister of Works, and others from his Ministry visited the site in the company of Grimes (Fig 15). We do not know his exact brief from the Prime Minister, but the notes following his visit included the following (paraphrased from WORKS14/2592 — The Minister's Brief):

> **Item 1** That the Ministry had made grants to RMLEC totalling £12,300 since 1948 and that very little had been given by anyone else.
> **Item 3** That the building, Bucklersbury House, to be built on the site was estimated to cost £4,000,000 and that a licence of £2,750,000 had already been issued. The building had been planned in detail and any change would be costly. The building contractor had cooperated fully with RMLEC.
> **Item 4** That there were powers to protect the temple under the Ancient Monuments Acts. Firstly, the temple could be listed under the Acts as a monument of national importance. This would hold up demolition and would require three months' notice to be given of any intention to destroy or damage it. Once the Ministry had been notified of a threat of destruction a preservation order could be made and the monument taken into compulsory guardianship. This would require payment of compensation to the owners of the site.

The Ancient Monuments Acts did not specify the basis on which compensation should be paid but the presence of an ancient monument would reduce considerably the value of the Bucklersbury House site, on which £1,000,000 had already been spent. Compensation on any basis would be a very large sum and in preserving the monument the rebuilding of an important area of the City would be delayed.

> **Item 6** None of the archaeologists who had been engaged on the site had suggested to the Minister that the ruins should be preserved permanently. A full record had been made of the area excavated, finds had been removed for safekeeping and, in general, the arrangements made for completing the examination of the remains had been accepted as satisfactory.
> **Item 7** That there were likely to be other finds of archaeological importance in the City was accepted. The archaeologists were on the alert to recognise finds of importance at the earliest possible moment so that steps could, if possible, be taken to preserve them. To this end RMLEC would continue to receive support within the limits of the Ancient Monuments vote.

These notes make a number of points very clear and it is apparent that from the outset the financial implications of preserving the temple were the most influential, above any others.

The point that the Ministry had been making by far the largest contribution for a long time to the archaeological work in the City (Item 1) was certainly true. There was never any hesitation on the part of the Ministry of Works from the very first request from RMLEC for government funding. This would continue, in one form or another and with a few short breaks, for many years. Indeed, this support has continued until this very day, thus permitting this report to be written. During the same period up to 1954, the Corporation of London had contributed only 250 guineas (£262.50).

Later, however, when the arguments for preservation were becoming louder, the Ministry's financial contribution to RMLEC would be used to make a disingenuous statement releasing the Ministry of any obligation to pay for the preservation of the temple, to the effect that without the substantial funding by the Ministry of Works the site might never have been excavated in the

Fig 15 W F Grimes and Sir David Eccles examine the temple on Monday 20 September

first place and might well have been destroyed without anyone ever knowing of its very existence.

Item 3, concerning the cost of the building scheme itself, is the most important here. At £4,000,000 the Bucklersbury House scheme was the most expensive of its kind in the City of London during the early 1950s. By September 1954 £1,000,000 had already been spent on the site (see Item 4 above). The protection of the temple under the Ancient Monuments Acts would have had serious repercussions not only for this site in the City but also for others throughout the country for which the scale and content of the archaeological deposits were unknown. For instance:

a) If monuments were ultimately taken into guardianship considerable, and expensive, delays to rebuilding would result.
b) The presence of a monument on a site would cause a reduction in the value of a site due to the restraints that its presence would have on future redevelopment schemes. Also, any redesign might result in a dramatic reduction of space which could be let, as would have been the case with Bucklersbury House. This would have caused the loss of rents.
c) A large sum of money would have to be paid out to the developers to compensate for these losses.
d) Additional restraints might be placed on building design (see below).

It is obvious that the burden placed upon the Government by item c) was just too great to bear. Furthermore, the prospect of slowing down redevelopment and alienating developers in a period of post-war reconstruction could never be considered.

Back on the site, as a result of the meeting that day (Monday) with the Minister and representatives of the site owners (Legenlands), Grimes and his team were given time to continue their excavations in order to rescue as much data as possible about the temple. 'Preservation by record' was their brief. The morning newspaper reports had again attracted public interest but this time, on a working day, the crowds were far larger than those which had visited the site over the weekend. The concern of the police for public safety (and order) resulted in Grimes being obliged to announce that official visiting times for members of the public would come into effect the following day. This was to be from 4.30pm to 6pm every evening for a week.

The following day, Tuesday 21 September, the Minister was to present the results of the previous day's site visit to his colleagues in Cabinet. At this meeting chaired by Sir Winston Churchill the 'Roman Temple in the City of London' was on an agenda which included:

1 France's rejection of the European Defence Community Treaty (a move which threatened European unity)
2 Friction with China over Formosa (the US government's dilemma: not to commit forces would damage morale in Formosa and encourage com-munists; to commit forces may result in war with China)
3 The signing of the Pacific Charter (which the Cabinet felt had to be signed after the Cyprus issue had come before the UN because of the embarrassment that would be caused by the principle of self-determination)
4 Military airfields
5 The retirement of Vice Admiral J Hughes Hallett
6 Roman Temple in the City of London
7 Commonwealth Prime Ministers' meeting
8 Industrial disputes, docks and railways

Nestled among such great matters of state and foreign affairs a debate about the fate of a small mid-third-century Roman temple looks oddly out of place. But on reflection it is probably appropriate that the case of the temple of Mithras did reach such prominence in Government debate. Though not exactly a crisis in itself, the matter was certainly cause for concern. As outlined above, the preservation of the temple would almost certainly lead to large Government expenditure to compensate not only for any delays in rebuilding but also for the loss of revenue caused by these delays and any revised building designs. On a political level, the rebuilding of the City could not be seen to be restrained by such matters. To do so would almost certainly incur the dissatisfaction of property owners, developers and contractors with Government policy. And there were the public interest and votes to consider.

With all of these considerations in mind, therefore, the brief memorandum presented by Sir David Eccles to the Cabinet was as follows (CAB 129/70, C.(54)294, Tuesday 21 September 1954, Copy no. 59):

> CABINET
> ROMAN TEMPLE IN THE CITY OF LONDON
> Memorandum by the Minister of Works
>
> 1 The Ministry of Works has made grants of £12,300 over the last six years to the Roman and Mediaeval London Excavation Council to help them dig for Roman remains on bombed sites.
> 2 The Council has discovered the foundations of a Temple of Mithras dating from 150 AD *(sic)* on the Bucklersbury House site, Walbrook. The building owner and contractors have cooperated with the archaeologists, but the time has come when further delay in preparing the site will cause them considerable financial loss. The ruin is nothing much to see and none of the archaeologists I met on the site suggested we should stop the new building altogether in order to preserve the foundations permanently. It is however important to carry the work to the point where the ground plan of the temple can be fully plotted and recorded. This will take a week or two more digging and I

arranged with the owners and contractors to agree to this in spite of the loss and delay involved. Everyone seemed satisfied with the proposal.
3 I do not recommend any action to preserve the remains of the temple. There are likely to be other finds as the rebuilding of the City proceeds, and I shall continue to give the Excavation Council all the support which is possible within the limits of the Ancient Monuments Vote.

D. Eccles
Ministry of Works
Monday 20th September 1954

The following was the conclusion of the meeting (CAB 128/27, C.C.(54), No. 49, Tuesday 21 September 1954, 11.30am).

Conclusions of a Meeting of the Cabinet
ROMAN TEMPLE IN THE CITY OF LONDON

6 The Cabinet had before them a memorandum by the Minister of Works (C.(54)294) about the discovery of the foundations of a Temple of Mithras, dating from 150 AD, on the Bucklersbury house site, Walbrook, on which building construction was about to begin.

The Minister of Works said that the discovery had been made by the Roman and Mediaeval London Excavation Council with the assistance of grants made by this Department. At the Prime Minister's suggestion, he had visited the site and had arranged that building construction should be postponed for a further week or two in order to enable the archaeologists, if possible, to unearth and record fully the ground plan of the temple. The owners of the site and the building contractors had cooperated with the archaeologists and agreed to this further delay, in spite of the financial loss it would entail. It would not, however, be reasonable or justifiable on archaeological grounds, to postpone the new building construction indefinitely. Indeed, if further investigation showed that the ground plan of the temple was considerably more extensive, it would not be possible to unearth it completely without undermining Walbrook thoroughfare.

The Cabinet took note with approval of this statement.

Mithras fever sweeps the nation

In the City, work continued on the excavation of the temple. Grimes's work at the London Museum had to be suspended and he found himself continually at the beck and call of journalists. This Tuesday saw the discovery of the neck of Mithras which fitted exactly with the head discovered on Saturday.

Fig 16 The crowds visit the Bucklersbury mosaic, found during the building of Queen Victoria Street in 1869

Fig 17 ... and in 1954 only the monument and the costumes have changed

The evening, however, saw the first of the now famous queues of visitors to the site. Whereas it is, perhaps, possible to say that the unsupervised visitors on Sunday and the majority of those office workers who sought out the site on Monday had a genuine interest in the temple and its future, the same cannot be said of the crowds who subsequently flocked to the site. The announcement that the site would be officially open to the public in the evenings for the rest of the week attracted many who visited out of mere curiosity. A great many of these, whose expectations had been raised by the excitement in the press, were to be disappointed by what they saw.

The article on the temple of Mithras in *The Times* on Wednesday 22 September, for by now the temple attracted daily coverage ('concerned more with disseminating news than with imparting information', Grimes 1968, 232), led with the spectacle of the crowds seeking to visit the site on the previous evening. The scene must have been reminiscent of the discovery of the mosaic at Bucklersbury in 1869, a similarly spectacular find which captured the imagination of the public (Figs 16 and 17). The mosaic fared better than the Mithraeum. It was lifted and survives now as a principal exhibit in the Roman Gallery of the Museum of London.

Fig 18 Part of the queue stretching down Walbrook

In 1954, 'marshalled' by police, the visitors to the site queued along Budge Row and all the way along Walbrook as far as the Bank underground station by Mansion House and the Bank of England (Fig 18). Many at the head of this queue had been there for up to 90 minutes before the official 4.30pm opening, and as more City offices closed the queue grew longer and longer. At one stage it was said that the tail of the queue was in Poultry and the east end of Cheapside — almost 300m from the site entrance. By 6.00pm, *The Times* claimed, a great many remained and clamoured to be let in, and an extension of 30 minutes was arranged. But this was still insufficient time to let everyone in the queue gain access to the site. Some left outside at 6.30pm objected to not being told earlier that their wait would be futile, others slipped past the police attempting to block the wide entrance to the gates and, at one time, a surge of city office-workers bore down on the entrance to the site, causing the police to link arms in a successful attempt to bar their trespass onto the site. By dusk, when it was not only too dark to see anything of the temple but extremely dangerous for anyone to be on an unlit building site, there was still a short queue of people outside the site.

The papers also ran the results of the Minister's deliberations of Monday and Tuesday. The main points were emphasised:

a) the remains could not be preserved because they could not be included in the proposed building
b) to redesign that building would be a costly business and would probably involve the Government in the payment of large sums by way of compensation
c) on the advice given to him, the Minister did not believe that it was worthwhile moving the remains to a new site
d) work on the temple would proceed for two weeks

The temple, then, was to be destroyed. Only the records of the archaeologists and the artists invited to paint the site for posterity would remain. The crowds who came to see the site from this day onwards now included in their numbers those who wanted to see the temple before it disappeared forever. And now that the Ministry had made its decision the debate was to include the opinions of academics and members of the public printed in the letters pages of the national newspapers.

Meanwhile, in Whitehall...

For the staff of the Ministry of Works, to their credit, the episode was not regarded as over. They were concerned about the growing public pressure to see the monument preserved. Although they were not willing to be persuaded by public emotions, they rightly believed that more justification for the Minister's decision not to save the temple had to be given.

On the Thursday (23 September) a Ministry of Works departmental note minutes a discussion between Sir David Eccles and Mr Root, the Ministry Secretary. The Press 'agitation' was the subject of the meeting and more publicity for the case against preservation had to be obtained. A number of points were agreed:

a) The opening by the Minister of *The Times* exhibition of photographs of ancient monuments would afford an opportunity for the Minister to speak publicly about the case against preserving the temple. He would stress the limitations of the Ancient Monuments Vote, the good work being done with this money, for instance in connection with historic houses, and emphasise that had it not been for the Ministry's contribution of £12,300 towards the work of RMLEC the temple probably would not have been found at all. The City's paltry contribution of 250 guineas was mentioned here to stress this point.
b) The Minister wanted the full costs of preservation to be prepared and given to the press. Root agreed about preparing the estimate but said that this infor mation should be given to the Press only as a last resort — ie, if other arguments had failed to convince.
c) On another matter, Root had suggested to Grimes that RMLEC should turn the interest aroused by the

discovery of the temple to the raising of money for further excavation. He also said that the Ministry might increase its contribution if a plan for extended excavation in the City could be submitted to it.

d) Finally, the Ministry had received a number of letters from the public urging for the temple's preservation. A letter on the following lines was agreed, to be sent to these and future correspondents:

> The Minister has asked me to say how grateful he is for the interest you have shown in this matter. He would himself very much have liked to preserve the remains of the temple. The fact is however that the funds at the disposal of the Ministry for the excavation and preservation of Ancient Monuments are severely limited, and the cost of preserving this temple and compensating the owners of the site for their loss might well amount to several times the annual total of work of this nature throughout the whole Kingdom. It is of course true that the present government has through the Historic Buildings Act added to these funds, but the calls on all monies at the Ministry's disposal for these purposes are heavy, and the kind of sum needed to preserve the temple of Mithras could not be found.

It is worthwhile taking note here of the Ministry's dilemma and, at the same time, highlighting its officials' genuine concern regarding this affair. They were well aware that the cost of preserving this one monument *in situ* was, in financial and political terms, too high to bear. The Minister's notes and the comments made to Cabinet on the Tuesday show that these were the most important determining factors from the start. However, the Ministry was responsive to the public pressure to preserve the temple. Whether this response was merely appeasement or a genuine concern is debatable. Considering the drain that the preservation of the temple would almost certainly have made upon the limited resources available and the financial and political implications that would almost certainly have resulted if the temple, as preserved, became a precedent this response could justifiably be explained as a 'damage limitation exercise'. It is difficult now to judge. But what is of interest is the Ministry's continuing concern, even at this stage when they were receiving criticism of their responsibilities concerning this matter, to support and apparently to increase formally, by means of a detailed excavation/research programme in the City, the funds they made available to RMLEC. As we have already indicated, the Ministry was never unwilling to debate the need for archaeological work in the City. If anything, its officials were willing to promote such work. They had readily acknowledged in the years immediately after the end of the Second World War, long before the temple of Mithras affair had caught the attention of the public, that such work was essential. But their renewed interest in continuing this funding might appear overcharitable were it not for the fact that other parties had entered the debate through the letters pages in *The Times* that morning.

Letters to the Editor — and the Prime Minister

The most influential of these, it would seem, was the communication from Sir Mortimer Wheeler, signed as President of the Society of Antiquaries, London. Wheeler's letter, emphatic and authoritatively presented with his customary military metaphors, touched upon two points. The first concerned the 'general question of the policy underlying the exploration of the devastated areas of the City'. The site, he noted correctly, had been available for excavation for two years and the building itself had been exposed for many months. The pace of archaeological exploration was proceeding at too leisurely a pace. Though the quality of work was unimpeachable, its scale was 'pathetically inadequate':

> A large part of a hundred acres which, after deep rebuilding, will never again be available for archaeological exploration still awaits excavation if we are to reconstruct any considerable part of London's Roman and Mediaeval past. To attempt this, as at present, with four or five pairs of hands is like attacking a battleship with a peashooter. The first requisite is adequate provision for exploration on a scale commensurate with the problem. Anything less is both unworthy and, in a phase of renewed building activity, uneconomic.

The following day, Friday 24 September, in a meeting with the Ministry's Press officer, Mr Howarth and the site owners, Legenland, it was agreed that a further extension of one week would be given to the archaeologists and that the Press would be told that the Ministry and the site-owners were calculating the costs for preservation. Mr Howarth, in classic civil service language, said that he would let *The Times* know this but, 'he will not give them the impression that it is probable that the decision not to attempt to preserve the temple will be reversed.'

In layspeak this would appear to mean that the result of calculating the costs for preservation would confirm the Minister's original decision.

On the same day, unknown to the Ministry, Grimes entered the political fray as a supporter for preservation of the temple. He wrote the following letter directly to the Prime Minister:

> Dear Prime Minister
>
> I hesitate to trouble you in the matter of the Roman Temple in Walbrook, but my excuse for doing so must be the interest which I understand you have expressed in the site.

The temple is of course a unique monument for London and has certain features which are not at present paralleled in this country. Public interest in this site is intense. The spectacle of the many thousands of people who have queued to see it and have filed past it reverently is at once impressive and moving.

There is clearly a widespread feeling that the building should be preserved for posterity.

I have every reason to believe that the site-owners (who throughout have been most sympathetic to the research activities of the Excavation Council) are still prepared to go to considerable trouble to find a means of preserving the monument. But the problem is one of finance and there seems to be no doubt that they cannot afford to face the considerable loss which would be involved in the permanent sterilisation of this part of a costly building on an expensive site.

A sum of £200–£300,000 has been mentioned, unofficially, as the amount which would be involved in making the necessary new dispositions in the building. It is obvious that such a figure could not be raised within the necessary time-limit by any public subscription, and I venture respectfully to suggest that this is a case which might well justify government intervention.

Without such intervention, the temple is doomed to destruction in about ten days' time — a fate which I believe the owners themselves would deplore and which would be the subject of much criticism from the general public.

The contents of this letter were telephoned to the Prime Minister at Chartwell on Saturday, 25 September. A copy of the letter with a note from the Prime Minister's Private Secretary reached the Ministry of Works on Monday, 27 September. The note said 'The PM has now seen Mr. Grimes' letter of

Fig 20 'Rebuilding London — if they have to preserve these Roman discoveries' (Moon, Daily Sketch, 26 September 1954)

Sept. 23 about the Roman Temple in Walbrook and would like Sir David Eccles to report on the matter again at the next meeting of Cabinet'.

The matter continued to be front page news in the press and the site continued to be visited by large crowds. As should only be expected in such circumstances, the debate about the preservation of the temple drew some humorous responses from the satirists who saw such things in a more cynical light (Figs 19–21). It even encouraged others to put their poetic talents to work. *The Statesman and Nation* invited contributions and published the following on 16 November 1954, over a month after the affair had subsided.

Fig 19 'Start about here and the first man to find a Roman temple gets docked a quid' (David Langdon, Punch, 6 October 1954)

On Turning up a Roman Temple with a Mechanical Navvy

Here, where the legionary slept at church parade,
Dreaming of Heaven and Lalage, all roses,
Big Business buries all that Mithras made,
and the bull dozes.
Robert Murray

Where pious Romans were filled up
With tales of Mithras and his glories,
Mammon now gets a nice build up
In several much taller storeys.
P.M.

Cover the Roman Temple in,
Mithras-worshipping was sin;
Christian lifts will shortly slam on
Fourteen storeys preaching Mammon
Ethel Talbot Scheffauer

Fig 21 'St Paul's is in danger and needs your help' — Lord Simonds (Punch, 27 October 1954)

Betwixt the cloaks and the canteen
Is where the temple would have been.
Sir Gorgius Midas could not spare
The time and space to leave it there.
R J P Hewison

Invictus
The Sun God lay so long with speechless lips
They thought him dead, and broke his tomb divine,
But he, awakening from his long eclipse,
Transformed their mundane building to a shrine.
E Leach

On, bulldozers, to your task,
While the antiquarians fuss;
Cloud-gloomed Britain well may ask
What's the sun-god done for us?
Stanley J Sharples

Big Business claims this ancient temple's site
Where Romans worshipped Mithras, God of Light:
Our Age puts out the faintly glowing spark,
For money-making's easier in the dark.
(NB — See Heartbreak House, *Act 1. SHOTOVER: Give me deeper darkness. Money is not made in the light.)*
Allan M Laing

The Church Triumphant rests on battles won
Over Mithraic cults of blood and stone;
While Christendom reveals its pagan id,
Touched to the tune of half a million quid.
Lakon

Erstwhile he slaughtered bulls that dozed on site:
But move his sanctum — and the God of Light,
The fearsome lord of nuclear conflagration,
Might blow to bits the statesman and the nation!
R Pavry

Christ drove the money-changers out;
But their successors, stung, no doubt,
By his opprobrious decision,
Reserve a basement for Religion.
W.P.B

Reduced to Rubble Mithras' shrine departs,
"Sic transit gloria" — on builders' carts:
A thousand ages ere 'tis necessary
To cry, "The glory that was Bucklersbury!"
J E Terry

Charivaria also had a contribution to make in *Punch,* October 1954:

Setback in the City
When a chartered surveyor
With erudite air
Has approved your foundations and drains
It seems a bit thick
That some clot with a pick
Should identify Roman remains.

The final decision

On Tuesday 28 September, Eccles and his officers and representatives of the site owners met to discuss the cost of preserving the temple *in situ.* Three points concerned the latter:

a) costs arising from the delays due to alterations of plans
b) necessary restrictions of the building due to foundation problems
c) difficulties arising from proposed tenants's occupancy of office space which was urgently needed and which had already been agreed would be available by a certain date

On item a), it was pointed out that at least eight months' delay would result from the alteration to the existing plans. This would include the resubmission of altered plans for the approval of various authorities after a delay of at least two months during which architects and engineers would prepare the amended plans. On top of this eight months' delay, as minimum, would be the costs for these architects and engineers as well as interest on money already invested. Eight months' loss of income from the building, estimated to be in the vicinity of £550,000 per annum gross, would also have to be included. Interest had been calculated as running at £1000 per week.

The problem of the foundations, b), principally concerned the type of soil on the site. According to two firms of consultant engineers, the foundations could only be constructed by piling a few feet apart. If the necessity of bridging over the temple was agreed then at least five stories of the proposed section of the building above the temple would have to be deleted, as well as a sub-basement and basement. The entrance to the new building would also have to be relocated in any new design because it was over the site of the temple.

Finally, regarding item c), many lettings had already been accomplished and proposed tenants were unlikely to agree to further delays. Various approvals of plans and the receipt of building licences (see above) had already taken five years.

The total costs of these delays, as presented to the Cabinet, were given as £680,000 (see below). However, the main outcome of this meeting was that it emerged that the owners were willing, at their own expense, to re-erect the remains of the temple on one of the open spaces of the site, thus allowing the public access to the remains of the temple. This generous offer was a most welcome piece of news for the Ministry.

At the Cabinet meeting the next day the temple was discussed was again following Grimes's letter to the Prime Minister. The record of the discussion is as follows (CAB 129/71, C.(54)301, Wednesday 29 September 1954, Copy no. 56):

CABINET
ROMAN TEMPLE IN THE CITY OF LONDON
Memorandum by the Minister of Works

There's a fascination frantic
In a ruin that's romantic
W. S. Gilbert

1. Since the Cabinet discussed the temple of Mithras on 21 September (C.C.(54) 61st Conclusions, Minute 6) the public desire for its preservation has, if anything, increased.
2. Archaeologists generally, and my Chief Inspector of Ancient Monuments, continue to tell me that the temple is not as important as several other discoveries of remains now being made. If more money were available for preserving ancient monuments they would prefer to spend it elsewhere.
3. On the other hand the public imagination has been deeply stirred by the drama of Mithras versus Mammon. I cannot tell whether, if the temple were off the danger list, it would prove an exception to our unvaried experience that Roman remains attract very few visitors. The new factor in this case is television newsreel which has been the Chief agent in creating interest. But I doubt if this interest would last.
4. The following is the owner's estimate of the cost of preserving the temple on its present site:
a) Structural costs
(Retaining walls around temple-bridge etc) £110,000
b) Cost arising from delay: 6 months' net revenue £155,000
6 months' interest on capital £35,000
c) Loss on rentable accommodation £380,000
Grand total £680,000
5. My consulting engineers advise me that the subsoil is so spongy and unstable that the 60ft span of the arch over the temple could not carry more than two storeys against the seven planned.
6. This sum has to be compared with my Vote for preserving historic monuments and buildings:

	1951/2	1953/4	1954/5
	£	£	£
Preserving			
Monuments	275,000	405,000	450,000
Excavation	15,000	15,000	20,000
Historic Houses	0	10,000	250,000
Total	290,000	430,000	720,000

This year we are spending more than twice [as much as] any Government has spent on this service.
7. There is work of the value of more than £4 million waiting to be done to bring the 600 monuments already in my charge to a satisfactory state of repair.
8. Sir Alan Lascelles and Lord Dundee, Chairman of the English and Scottish Historic Buildings Councils, report that the £250,000 a year is less than will be needed to help houses in the very first rank of importance.
9. I cannot therefore recommend that if substantial extra money is available for preservation it should be spent on the temple.
10. Mr A.V. Bridgland, the Chairman of the Company which owns the site, has offered at his expense to re-erect the temple at ground level in one of the courtyards on the site. I recommended that this most generous and sensible proposal be accepted.
11. The appendix to this paper is a letter from Mr Nigel Nicolson MP, the only Member of Parliament who is on the Ancient Monuments Board for England.

MOW SE1 D. Eccles
Wednesday 29 September 1954

APPENDIX
House of Commons, SW1
Sunday 26 September 1954

Dear Eccles.

As I am the only Member of the House who is on the Ancient Monuments Board, I thought I would write you a note about my attitude to the preservation of the Cannon Street Roman Temple.

If you decided not to make any grant towards the huge cost of preserving the temple, I would entirely support you. All my instincts lead me to plead with you to save it, but I feel it would be wrong to do so, for the preservation of the temple, as distinct from its discovery, is really of little importance. Its archaeological value lies in its existence, its ground plan and the objects found in it. In itself it is not an object of beauty, and its dismembered stones would mean little to any but professional archaeologists. If it were preserved, few people would visit it, and even those that did would see it as part of a basement, surrounded perhaps by boilers and certainly by cement walls, which would kill any atmosphere of Roman London. If there is to be any additional grant for archaeology, there are a dozen better ways of using it, for instance in the excavation of other blitzed sites in the City. Indeed, one way of mollifying public indignation about the Mithraeum might be to make a grant for exactly that purpose.

I am of course speaking purely for myself, and I believe that most of the Members of the Ancient Monuments Board disagree with me. Although I went over the whole site with Grimes before it became news, I did not discuss the question of preservation with him.

If you have already decided to make a grant towards its preservation, I shall of course not oppose you, and I was very glad that you took such energetic action to allow the temple to be fully excavated.

Yours sincerely
signed Nigel Nicolson

At the meeting itself, the following points were highlighted and approved (CAB 128/27, C.C(54), no. 44, Friday 1 October 1954, 3pm)

Conclusions of a Meeting of the Cabinet
ROMAN TEMPLE IN THE CITY OF LONDON

3. The Cabinet had before them a memorandum by the Minister of Works (C.(54)301) about the possibility of preserving the remains of the temple of Mithras recently discovered on the Bucklersbury House site, Walbrook.

The Minister of Works said that, while the discovery of these Roman remains continued to arouse much public interest, the weight of the agitation in favour of preserving them had been reduced by the presentations made on behalf of the claims of other ancient monuments. His own advisers were of the opinion that any additional money which could be made available for the preservation of ancient monuments could be put to uses better than the preservation of this temple. The chairman of the property company which owned the site had now offered to re-erect the Mithraeum at ground level on a site adjoining Queen Victoria Street and to bear the cost of doing so, which was estimated at about £10,000. It seemed unlikely that the remains of the temple would greatly attract visitors if they were preserved *in situ* in the basement of an office building; whereas, if they were transferred to the site adjoining Queen Victoria Street, they would be in the open and visible to passers-by. The owner's offer was a generous one and he recommended that it should be accepted. He proposed that he should continue to lend his support to the Roman and Mediaeval London Excavation Council in their aim of investigating other exposed sites in London where ancient monuments might be found.

There was general agreement in the Cabinet that the offer made by the owner of the Bucklersbury House site to transfer the remains of the Mithraeum and preserve it on an open site adjoining Queen Victoria Street should be conveyed to the owner. While the aims of the London Excavation Council were meritorious, it was felt to be inexpedient that the Government should take any further measures of a special nature to promote their activities.

The Cabinet —

(1) Invited the Minister of Works to accept the offer of the owner of the Bucklersbury House site to transfer the remains of the Mithraeum to an open site at ground level adjoining Queen Victoria Street.

(2) Took note that the Prime Minister would write to the owner of the site expressing the Government's appreciation of the contribution which he was making towards the preservation of the remains of this Roman temple.

It is evident from this that the fact that the temple would be preserved was hailed with enthusiasm by the interested parties. The advantages for such a scheme for the purist were negligible but the news was greeted with praise from the press.

Fig 22 The machines move in on Monday 4 October (Ministry of Works/English Heritage)

But the interest in Mithras did not stop there. As the news that the temple was to be saved was being digested, the site began to reveal further art treasures which only strengthened the public's interest in Mithras and his temple. Photographs of the head of Minerva, followed by the discovery of the head of Serapis, Mercury and the hand of Mithras Tauroctonos, covered the daily newspapers. Finally, however, as the area available for excavation in the temple became exhausted (Grimes kept to his brief and excavated only those deposits related to the Mithraeum during his two-week extension), and press interest in the building focused solely upon the finds rather than any debate about the building's survival, the excavation came to a close on Sunday 3 October. On Monday morning, at the earliest time possible, machines began to 'dismantle' the temple and move it for safekeeping to a new site (Fig 22).

In 1962 eight years later, the reconstruction of the Mithraeum from the preserved fragments was completed and made available for display to the public. Unfortunately, the result, which is still accessible, bore only the slightest relationship to the original. In 1959 Baillie Reynolds, the Chief Inspector of Ancient Monuments, had refused a request from the contractors to supply skilled Ministry workmen to rebuild the monument on the grounds that the proposed location bore absolutely no relationship to that of the original.

The final word on this matter must go to Grimes:

> The decision of the owners to reconstruct the temple at their own charges was the last of a series of generous acts which...was accepted as the answer to the problems of preservation. Unfortunately, it has to be recorded that the final result, now visible on the Queen Victoria Street frontage of Bucklersbury House, falls short of what it ought to have been.
>
> My own part in this project ended in about 1959, when I was invited by the architects to comment on the proposals then being prepared. What happened after that I do not know, except that in the outcome my suggestions were completely ignored. The outline of the reconstruction is presumably accurate enough; apart from some irrelevancies (crazy paving, for instance, for all floors in the body of the building) the internal features, such as the variation in floor-levels, that gave the original such architectural quality as it possessed have been seriously maltreated. The result is virtually meaningless as a reconstruction of a mithraeum. (Grimes 1968, 234–5).

3 Period 1: the archaeology of the Walbrook valley up to *c* AD 240–50

Summary

Taken from from Grimes 1968 (95–8) with cross-references to this report and other annotations, in square brackets, added in 1995.

The sections [see Fig 23]... revealed this part of the Walbrook valley as a shallow basin 290–300 feet across [*c* 88–91m]: on the west its edge coincided generally with Sise Lane, on the east with the Walbrook street.The process of raising the levels by the artificial dumping of material began at an early stage and was particularly well illustrated on the west side of the main channel. Sections here presented a succession of artificial deposits with their associated timber elements, preserved because of the waterlogged nature of the area as a whole [the waterlogging was so bad in places that trenches had to be abandoned before natural surface could be reached]. The deposits consisted of layers of mixed and variable material, often containing much clay put down to provide fresh living-surfaces. [A major attempt to control the conditions in the valley at this point is probably represented by the laying down, probably at the same date, of clay dumps on both sides of the stream: see *Cutting F: Group III and Cuttings CA, CB and CD: Group IV* (see Fig 243).] The timber structures were mainly related to the floors themselves or to the various devices used for dealing with the wet conditions on site. These devices included a number of gutters whose construction followed a constant pattern [in particular, see *Cutting BB: Group VI,* and Figs 33 and 34 below]. They were flat-bottomed, up to about 2 feet [0.61m] wide and perhaps 6–8 inches [0.15–20m] deep, plank floored, with their vertical sides revetted with planks which were held in place by pegs driven into the ground against them on both sides. In several places were found wooden pipe-lines formed of bored lengths of timber, quadrangular in section, with iron collars [see *Cutting BB: Group V]*. One such, a few feet west of the temple, was still functioning and adding its quota to the continually accumulating water in the cuttings during the excavation [for this see below, *Cutting CD: Group VII,* Figs 41 and 42. For one of the collars from this pipe see *Chapter 5, The finds catalogue, Period 1 finds, VII.50,* Fig 167].

The...buildings were all of timber. It was at no time possible to recover the complete plan of any one of these buildings and interest concentrates therefore on the methods employed by their builders to ensure their stability on a not

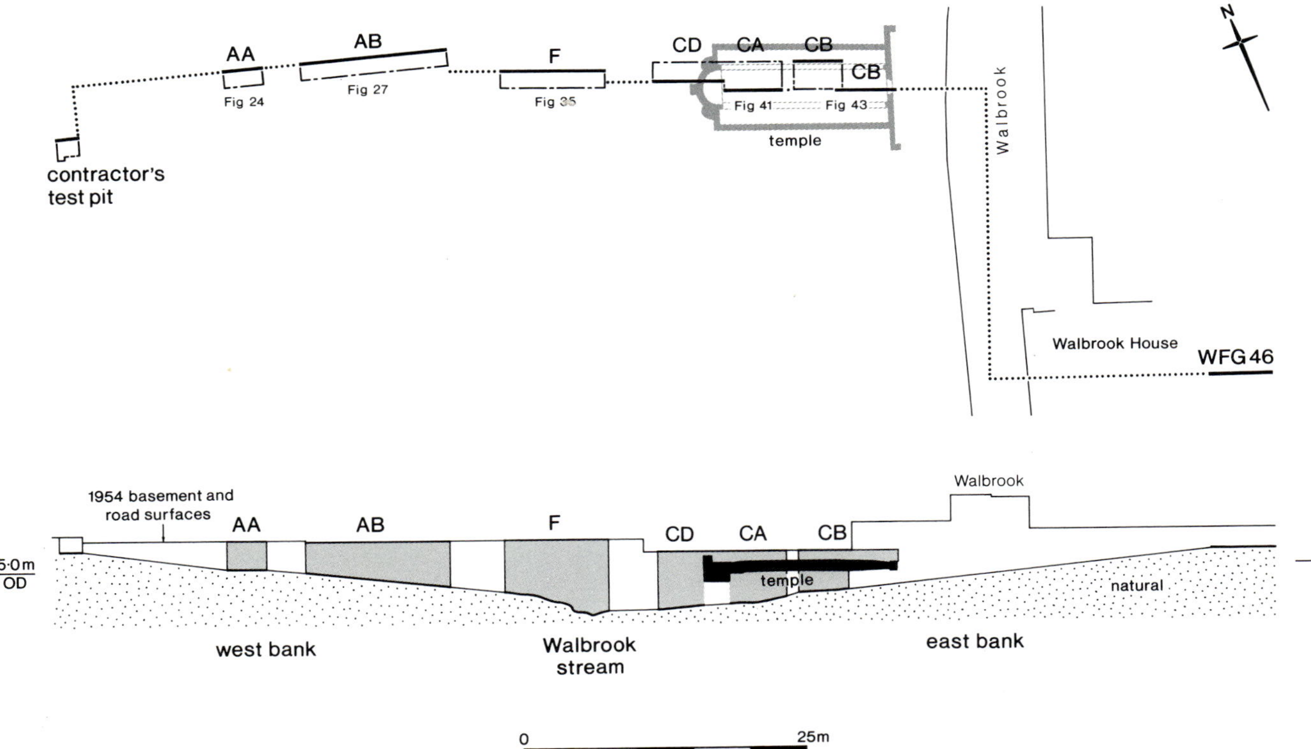

Fig 23 The positions of the trenches (top) and a composite profile showing the natural valley (bottom)

very satisfactory site [a number of incomplete plans, prepared from measured sketches in the site notebooks, have been reproduced below. See Figs 26, 29, 32 and 38]. On this, the wetter part of the area, underpinning was extensively employed to support the wooden floors on which some of the huts appeared to have been erected. Short (3–4 ft) [0.91–1.22m] closely set piles were driven into the ground in parallel lines to carry quite massive beams resembling modern railway sleepers [in particular, see Figs 37 and 38 below]. The beams seem to have been laid at right-angles with overlapping ends to form a framework, on which was laid in turn a plank floor. Some of the planks seen were up to 15 inches wide [0.38m]. As has already been said, it was impossible to recover a complete plan because, as usual, more ground could not be opened up: it would appear, however, that timber buildings were erected actually upon these floors, perhaps being assembled in prefabricated parts.

Away from the stream towards the north-west, there were indications of huts of a more normal kind, in an area which was not as waterlogged either in Roman or in more recent times. Here was a succession of hut-floors — or working floors — irregular in contour, at least one of which was overlaid by the remains of a collapsed thatched roof [unless the thick 'bark' deposits seen in *Cutting BB: Group V* (see below) and *Cutting F: Group III* (see below) were reinterpreted at some stage as being thatch, there is no record of this observation in the available archive]. In the cutting that produced these remains there were signs of leatherworking. One surface still bore the surviving portions of a skin held down by the pegs which had been used to stretch it for cutting up; and among the fragments of leather were recognisable parts of shoes [for this see below, *Cutting BB: Group V,* Fig 32].

The stream itself must, however, have been brought under control at quite an early date [the earliest activity in Cuttings CD and F dates to the Flavian period]. Immediately west of the temple the flow of water along the stream bed was controlled by revetments of planks held in place by fairly massive dressed uprights [for these see *Cutting F: Groups I–VI, Revetments 1 and 2,* and Figs 35 and 36]. There is an indication of two other revetments which had been destroyed during the Roman period by the cleaning of the stream.; and the building up of the surface as already described went on behind these constructions, which in time were often forced outwards over the stream by the growing pressure of the material behind them [see below, *Cutting F:* Revetment 1 and Platform D and Revetment 2, and Figs 35 and 36 below]. The period of the timber-revetted channel was succeeded by one in which the banks were less stable [this occurred during the first half of the third century. See below, *Cutting F: Group XIII],* though the process of raising the surface continued [for this see *Chapter 4]:* this state of affairs seems to have prevailed through late Roman and early post-Roman times.

The pre-temple groups

The stratigraphic groups associated with the pre-temple activity on the site are as follows.

Group I, east and west banks: Flavian
Group II, east and west banks: late first to mid second century
Group III, west bank: mid to late second century
Group IV, east and west bank: mid second to early third century
Group V, stream channel: late second to early third century
Group VI, west bank: first half of the third century
Group VII, east bank: third century but pre-dating construction of temple
Groups VIII–XI, Period 2 groups: see *Chapter 4*
Group XII, west bank, mid third century
Groups XIII–XV, Period 2 groups: see *Chapter 4*

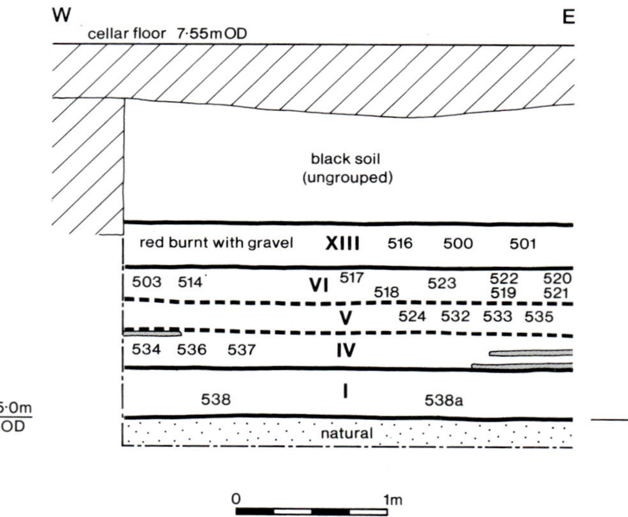

Fig 24 Cutting AA. Reconstructed section prepared from sketches in site notebooks

The west bank up to *c* AD 240–250

Cuttings AA and AB

Cuttings AA and AB were located in the basements of 18, 25 and 46 Mansion House Chambers (see above, Chapter 1, and Fig 10) and were separated by a large modern foundation.

The adverse groundwater problems which the excavators experienced across the entire site had their greatest effect on Cuttings AA and AB. Only in the extreme eastern end of Cutting AB were they able to excavate to any depth. Here, at *c* 3.60m OD they recorded the 'apparent surface of natural brickearth'. Elsewhere in the cutting the excavated level was *c* 4.60–4.67m OD. Flood water prevented any further work. In Cutting AA, the excavation reached *c* 5.00m OD on a brickearth layer which was believed to be natural.

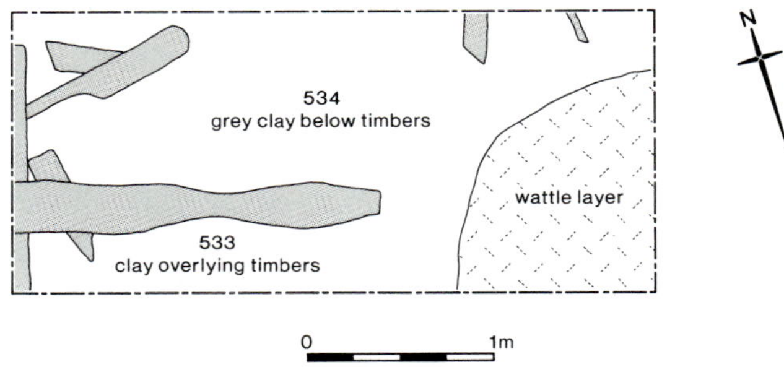

Fig 26 Cutting AA. Plan of Group IV timbers prepared from sketches in site notebooks

Cutting AA

Only a section sketch for the excavated deposits in this cutting is available for study (Fig 24). This shows a total depth of *c* 2.5m. The excavation of more than half the depth of this cutting was hampered by flooding.

The available records, the sketch and associated finds show that the lowest levels as excavated included material which can be included in Group I, ie the earliest recorded human activity on the site. The uppermost well recorded level equates with a thick dump of burnt, gravel material which is a western extension of the Group XIII horizon seen in the better recorded Cutting AB to the east.

Firm pale grey brickearth was identified at *c* 5m OD. Flooding and the short length of the cutting meant that it was not possible to identify a natural slope to this surface. It would appear, however, when this level is plotted on a composite section of the valley, that this surface most probably equates with the original natural land surface (Fig 23).

Fig 25 Cutting AA. Group IV timbers at the west end of the cutting (Grimes)

Cutting AA: Group I

This material consisted of a soft pale grey redeposited brickearth which was at least 0.33m thick. It lay directly upon the firm pale grey brickearth described above. The discolouration was caused by the inclusion of large amounts of organic material. This layer contained AA538 and AA538a. Its uppermost surface was almost horizontal.

Cutting AA: Group IV

Group I was sealed by a thick (*c* 0.40m) sequence of overlying timber layers, much decayed and poorly recorded. Each timber layer, of which there were at least three, was lying upon and sealed by dumps of grey/black clay. These contained AA534, AA536 and AA537. These equate with the timber layers seen in AB. One only of these horizons was recorded in any detail (Figs 25 and 26). This shows a number of planks laid horizontally with wickerwork lying around and adjacent to them. The majority of these were on alignments which would make some perpendicular and some parallel to the Walbrook stream course. These may have been intentionally laid or have been parts of collapsed structures.

Cutting AA: Group V

Similar grey/black clay dumps sealed the timber-rich deposits of Group II but these, Group V, were free of any timbers whatsoever. Even though the cutting at this level was still waterlogged this might suggest that no horizontal platforms existed in this area at this date. This conforms well with the record for the adjacent Cutting AB. Both Cuttings AA and AB, however, at this level OD contrast with the sequence recorded in Cutting F where timber platforms continued to be laid until the latest date in the Roman sequence. Group V contains AA524, AA532, AA533, and AA535.

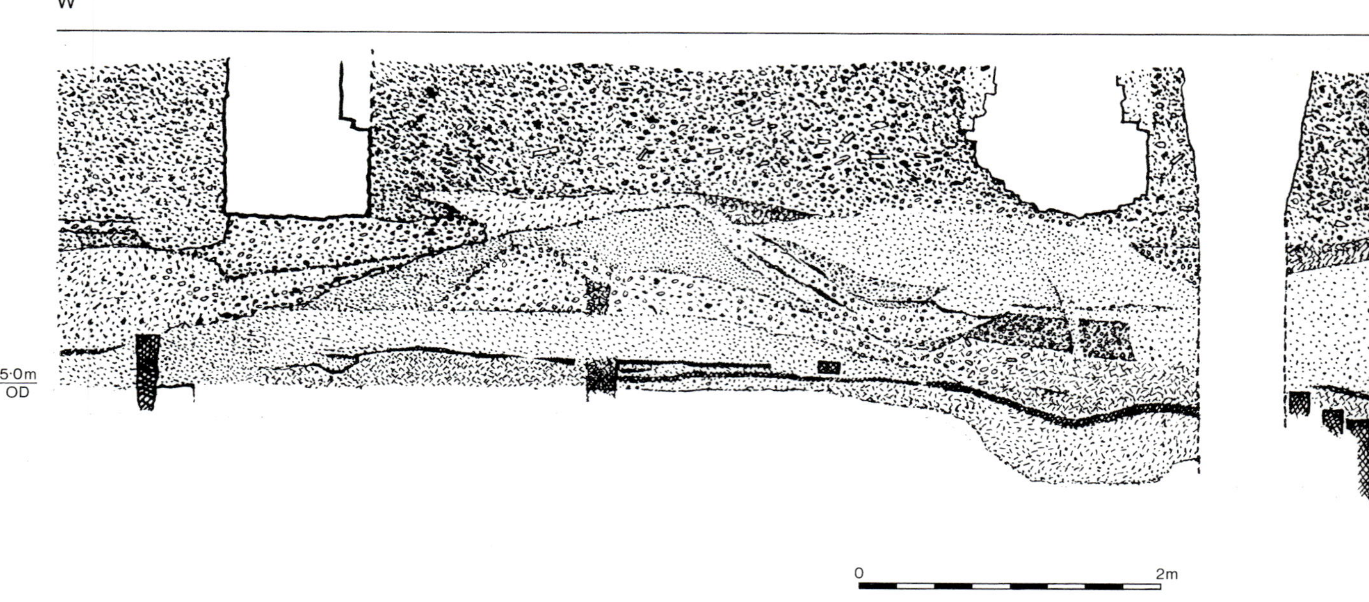

Fig 27 Cutting AB. Edited north section of cutting (original by Grimes)

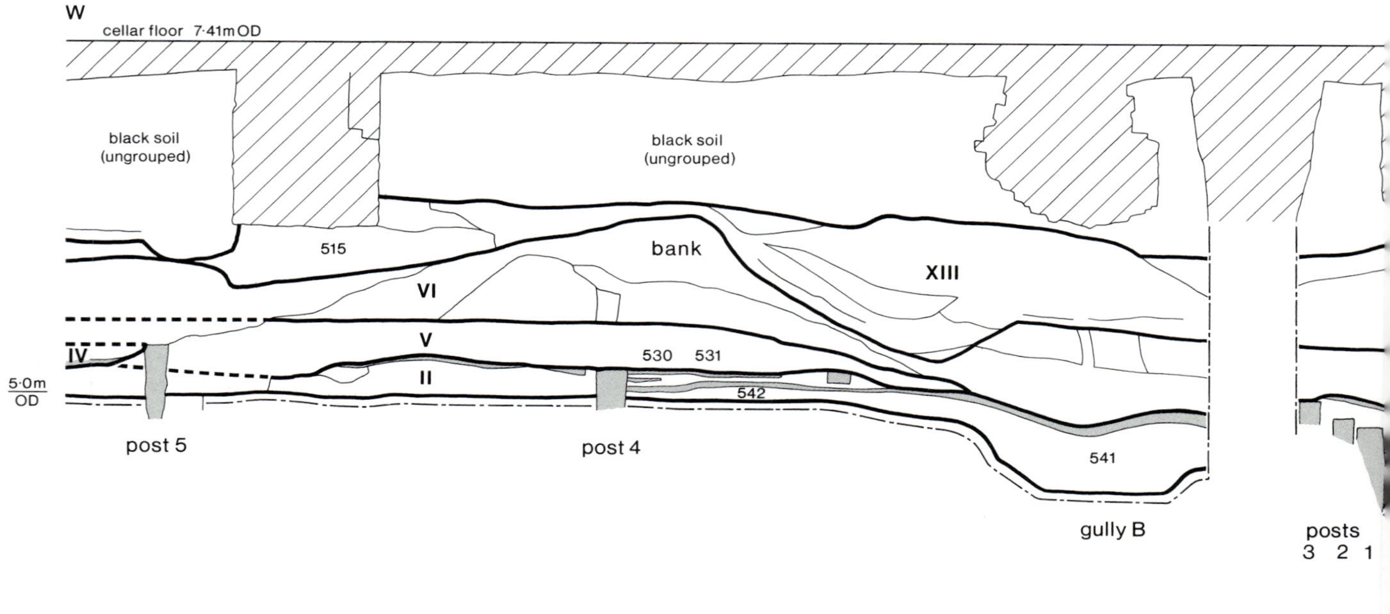

Fig 28 Cutting AB. Interpretive drawing of Fig 27

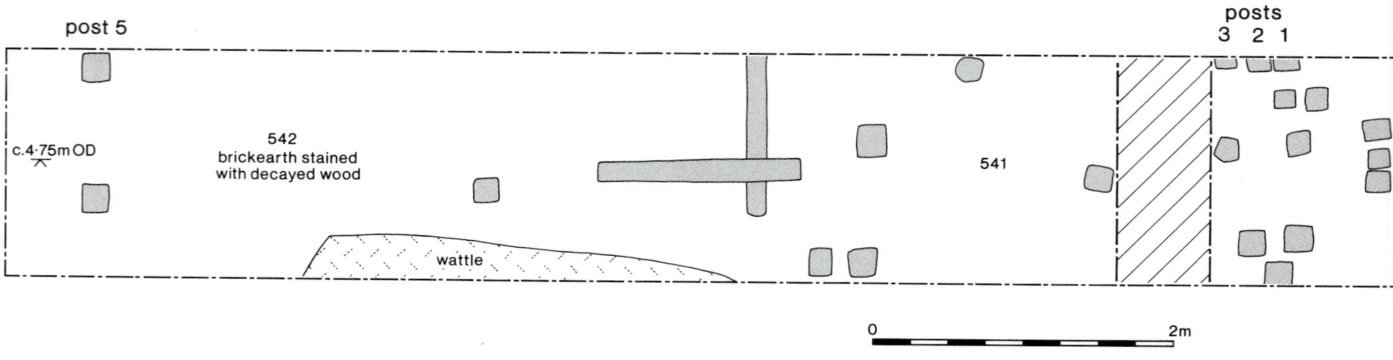

Fig 29 Cutting AB. Plan of Group II timbers prepared from sketches in site notebooks

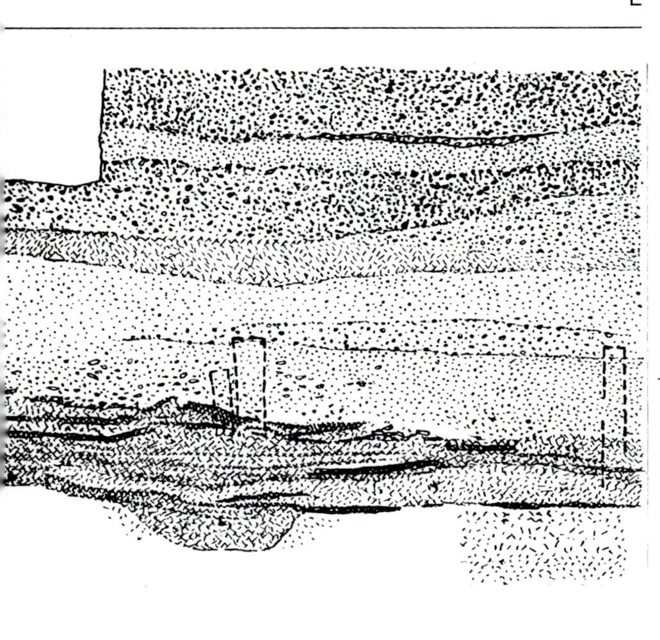

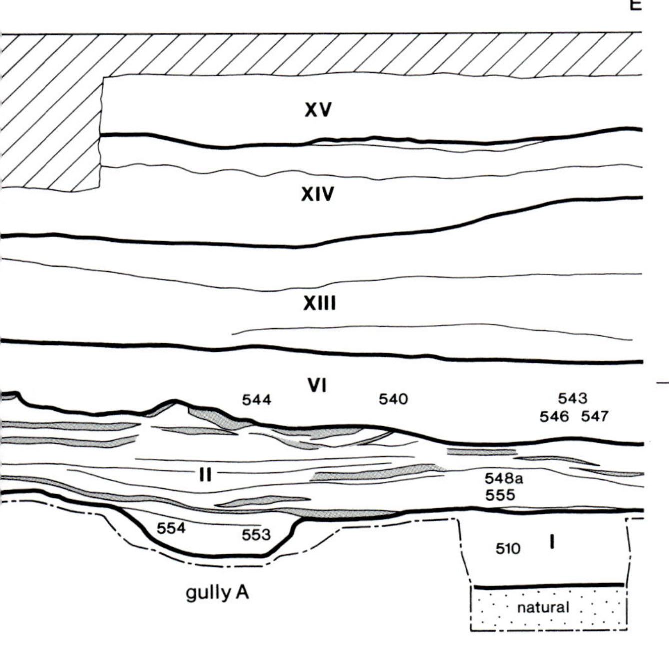

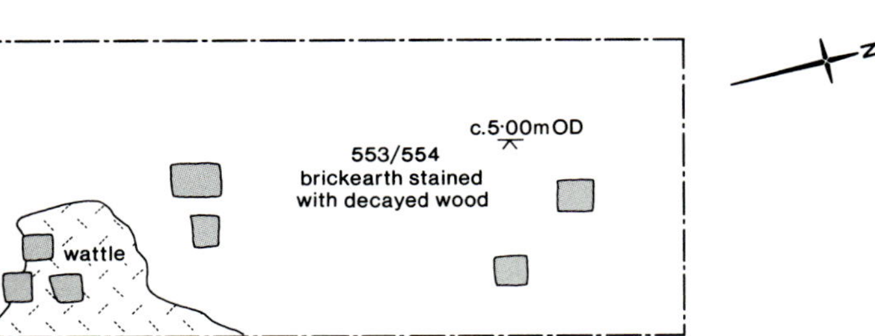

Cutting AA: Group VI

Another sequence of dumped material showed no actual evidence for any form of occupation or land use. The finds from this group, AA503, AA514, AA517, AA518, AA519, AA520, AA521, AA522 and AA523, belong to the first half of the third century.

Cutting AA: Group XIII

Group XIII layers, the highest in the recorded sequence, are described with other groups contemporary with the Mithraeum.

Cutting AB

A detailed section and notebooks are available for Cutting AB for study (Figs 27 and 28). However, only 16 uncontaminated finds groups survive. This therefore makes it difficult to interpret the full sequence in this cutting. A brief description of the available record is given below.

As noted above, the excavation of this cutting was severely affected by groundwater problems. As a result, and because of the pressures on the excavation on other parts of the site (especially in the Cutting C complex and Cutting F), natural was reached only in a small sondage at the extreme east end of the cutting. This, at *c* 3.60m OD, was described simply as brickearth.

Cutting AB: Group I

A layer of grey brickearth containing AB510, *c* 0.45m thick, speckled black with organic debris, rested directly on the surface of the natural ground level. This layer conforms with the Group I layer in both Cuttings AA to the west and F to the east. No floor surfaces, a feature of the Cutting F Group I deposit, were recorded here.

Cutting AB: Group II

Group II layers were identified across the entire length of the cutting. At the eastern end their descriptions and levels conform with Group II and III deposits in Cutting F and Group II and III deposits in Cutting BB. At the west end, however, they appear to thin out and are less well defined. It is of importance that no layer or finds group in Cutting AA could be satisfactorily placed in this group.

The group rested directly on the flat surface of the Group I brickearth deposit at the eastern end of the cutting. Across the remainder of the cutting, excavation ceased before the Group II layers could be totally identified.

In the main these layers consisted of dumps of grey or brown clay mixed with organic material. Between these was a succession of timber floor surfaces.

As already stated, these conform with Group II and III deposits in both Cuttings BB and F. The close proximity of the southern end of Cutting BB to the eastern end of Cutting AB should be emphasised here. It is probable that the floors and surfaces seen in the former are the same as those seen in the latter.

Two important features of the Group II deposits in Cutting AB are the cutting of two north–south aligned gullies and the general raising of the ground level of this group the further west one proceeds.

The two gullies are difficult to interpret but it is probable that they acted as drainage channels alongside the timber structures. The easternmost, Gully A, containing AB553 and AB554, would appear to be stratigraphically earlier than the western gully (Gully B). The first was sealed by timber surfaces which run up to a series of three vertically driven posts (Fig 28, Posts 1, 2 and 3). Gully B would appear to respect these posts, thus making it contemporary with those surfaces which sealed Gully A. It is possible that this represents a shift westwards, by *c* 3.5m, of a property boundary.

Gully B was also covered by a timber surface. A large post (Post 4) marking the western limit of that surface was *c* 4.5m from the group of three piles and, perhaps coincidentally, 3.5m west of the line of Gully B. It may, however, be of some significance that another large post (Post 5) recorded in the section at the west end of the cutting, driven during a later (probably Group IV) phase, was also *c* 3.5m from the single post just described.

Unfortunately only a single plan of the timber features during the later stages of Group II has survived for study (Fig 29). This shows a series of widely spaced vertical piles with overlying timber joists and planks. The density of the piles thins out towards the west end of the cutting, perhaps reflecting drier and more stable conditions in that part towards the end of this period of activity.

The general raising of the ground surface towards the west end of the cutting may have contributed towards this. It could, in part, have been due to the natural slope in this area. Additionally it could represent an attempt to raise this part of the valley deliberately, by means of a slight terrace, as a defence against groundwater and sporadic flooding. Note the similar raising of the ground surface during Group IV activity on the east bank of the Walbrook in Cuttings CA and CB (see below).

Cutting AB: Group V

Group V levels were seen only in the west end of the cutting. These consisted of a low mound of material which sealed the western end of the latest of the Group II structures. It was described as a 'fine light grey/yellow soil'. It was sealed at this end of the cutting by a dumped mound or bank of layers which were placed into Group VI. It is just possible, however, that these layers were the lowest in that mound and should therefore be treated as the earliest of the Group VI deposits.

Cutting AB: Group VI

Group VI layers covered the entire length of the cutting. At the eastern end these were horizontal with earlier groups and consisted of thick, homogeneous layers of grey soil mixed with gravel. Towards the west end of the cutting, the layers in this group made up a bank of material almost 0.60m in height, 0.90m if the underlying dump allocated by the excavators to Group V is included (see above).

This bank was not of one build, however. A mound of greyish mortary soil was first laid down and, to its east, a spread of gravelly grey soil covered the dump identified as Group V and the top of the latest timber buildings of Group II. The height of the bank was increased with a deposit of fine black soil, and between it and the accumulation of the homogeneous deposits towards the east end of the cutting a shallow gully *c* 0.30m deep was cut (not labelled on Fig 28).

This phase of activity is difficult to interpret at the east end of the cutting. Some timber piles were recorded at this level, suggesting that wooden structures had been constructed above them. Group VI layers in Cutting F record a major attempt to reconsolidate the edge of the stream bank and so these layers and the timbers probably represent the western end of this redevelopment. The bank, however, must have been an attempt to close off the western access to the streamside and the structures on its bank or, perhaps, a contingency against flooding. It is not possible to resolve this. It should be noted that contemporary levels in Cutting AA to the west were totally featureless. In which case the possibility that this bank represented some form of boundary, doubling as a flood barrier, must certainly be considered.

Cutting AB: Groups XIII to XV

Group VI levels were then sealed by a series of dumps, make-up layers and poorly preserved floor surfaces which, on stratigraphic and dating evidence, places them during the period of the life of the Mithraeum. These are Groups XIII–XV inclusive. These are described, along with contemporary deposits on the west side of the Walbrook, in Period 2 below.

Cuttings BA and BB

Cutting B, separated into BA and BB by a large Victorian foundation, was aligned approximately north to south at right-angles to the east end of Cutting AB. It was located in the basements of 46–8 and 58–63 Mansion House Chambers (Fig 10).

Cuttings BA and BB were also affected by groundwater problems and, as for Cuttings AA and AB, the lowest levels were not satisfactorily recorded.

The sequence in Cutting BB is complicated and not easy to interpret (Figs 30 and 31). Finds from this cutting were numerous, 73 finds groups being included in this study, but their ordering into groups or phases did not prove satisfactory. It is evident that the excavators and subsequent researchers had attempted precisely to equate the stratigraphy in this cutting as closely as possible with layers seen on the east bank of the Walbrook.

Cutting BA

Detailed written records for this cutting have been lost since Grimes allocated a number of Cutting BA finds groups to the stratified groups used throughout this report. These finds appear in the schedules below.

Cutting BB

In Cutting BB natural brickearth was seen over a third of the length of the cutting. At the extreme northern end of the cutting it was recorded at *c* 3.9m OD sloping southwards over 4.25m to a level of *c* 3.6m OD, the same as in the east end of Cutting AB. On the south side of the 3m unexcavated baulk in BB, unexcavated due to a fourth-century masonry platform, natural brickearth was also recorded at *c* 3.6m OD. At the extreme south end of Cutting BB, natural was taken to be brickearth scorched on the surface by fire.

Cutting BB: Group I (not on Fig 31)

At the extreme south end of the cutting a layer of buff grey brickearth rested directly upon the natural surface. This probably equates with a similar soil seen in the east end of Cutting AB. Unfortunately no finds were retrieved from this layer.

Cutting BB: Group II

The earliest datable layers recorded in this cutting were associated primarily with Group II deposits. At the south end these consisted of dark organic layers separated by thinner layers of grey clay, containing BB322 (Fig 31) and BB337. These are almost certainly the same floor surfaces as those recorded in the east end of Cutting AB. They run up to a wooden post driven into the underlying deposits, suggesting that this was part of a wall. Similar posts were seen in Cutting AB. Another similarity is the presence of a gully, in Cutting BB running east–west, which ran alongside these floors. This was lined with thin wooden planks emphasising its purpose as a drainage gully and contained BB338. It is possible that this gully met either Gully A or B in Cutting AB at right-angles just to the west of the cutting.

Other layers were BB349 on the north lip of the gully, BB343 and BB348 from the centre of the cutting, and BB350, BB356 and BB357 from thin horizontal platforms at the north end.

Cutting BB: Group IV

Layers that were probably contemporary with Group IV deposits in Cutting AA and, especially, Cuttings CA and CB overlay Group II layers at the north end of the cutting. They represented a continuation of the Group II activity seen in this part of the cutting, namely thin horizontal timber platforms separated by pale grey clay or brickearth. No layers from the south end of the cutting were placed into this group by the excavator, leaving a curious *lacuna* in the group sequence at that end. There it progressed straight from Group II to Group V, whereas at the north end these two Groups were separated by Group IV layers.

Cutting BB: Group V

Group V layers were recorded across the entire length of the cutting. As stated above, at the north end they rested upon layers allocated to Group IV but at the south end they rested directly upon the earlier Group II deposits. An analysis of the pottery has not helped to resolve this paradox.

The Group V layers are represented at the north end by a long series of overlying surfaces, similar in appearance to earlier phases of activity. However, when these were seen in plan they appeared to slope to the south-east. One of these showed staking out of leather (Fig 32). Six small wooden pegs had been driven into a sloping clay surface (Grimes 1968, 97). The latter was covered in an organic material thought at the time of excavation to be thatch material, probably reeds. In the south-east corner of the recorded area were traces of a plank floor. Very little remained but it appeared to be oriented approximately north-east to south-west. The upper layers of Group V at the north end contained BB300, BB301 and BB303.

This group also contained, at *c* 5.2m OD sloping to *c* 5m OD, the decayed remains of a timber which had been bored through to act as a water-pipe. It was aligned approximately north-west to south-east with the general slope. An iron collar at the north-west end, used to fix it to the next pipe, was recorded but not retained for further study. A similar collar came from Cutting CD (VII.50: Fig 167).

Similar floor surfaces, in fact probably the same surfaces, were recorded on the immediate south side of the unexcavated baulk. These contained BB329, BB334, BB340, BB341 and BB342. At the south end of the cutting the Group V layers were not as well defined. The main layer, *c* 0.75m thick, was described as light brownish clay, very compact with many pebbles and stones. It contained BB320 and BB321.

This layer of compact material and the floor layers just described are separated by the intrusion of the timber-lined channel in use during the subsequent Group VI period of activity but filled with Group XII

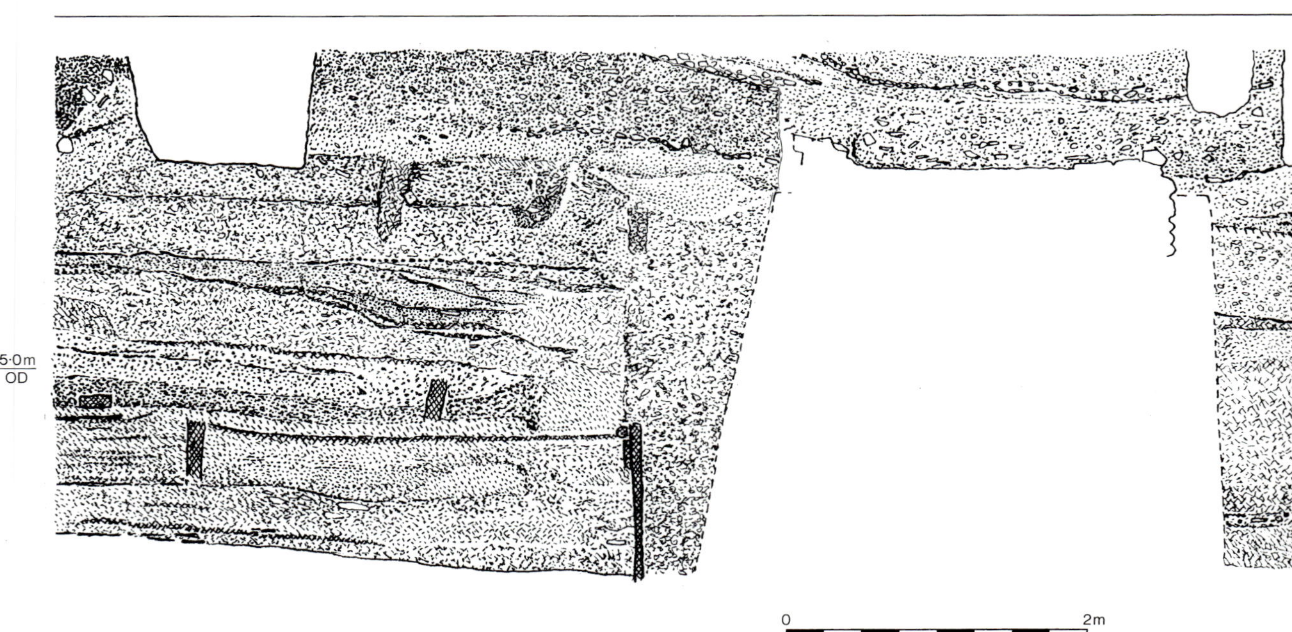

Fig 30 Cutting BB. Edited section of cutting (original by Grimes)

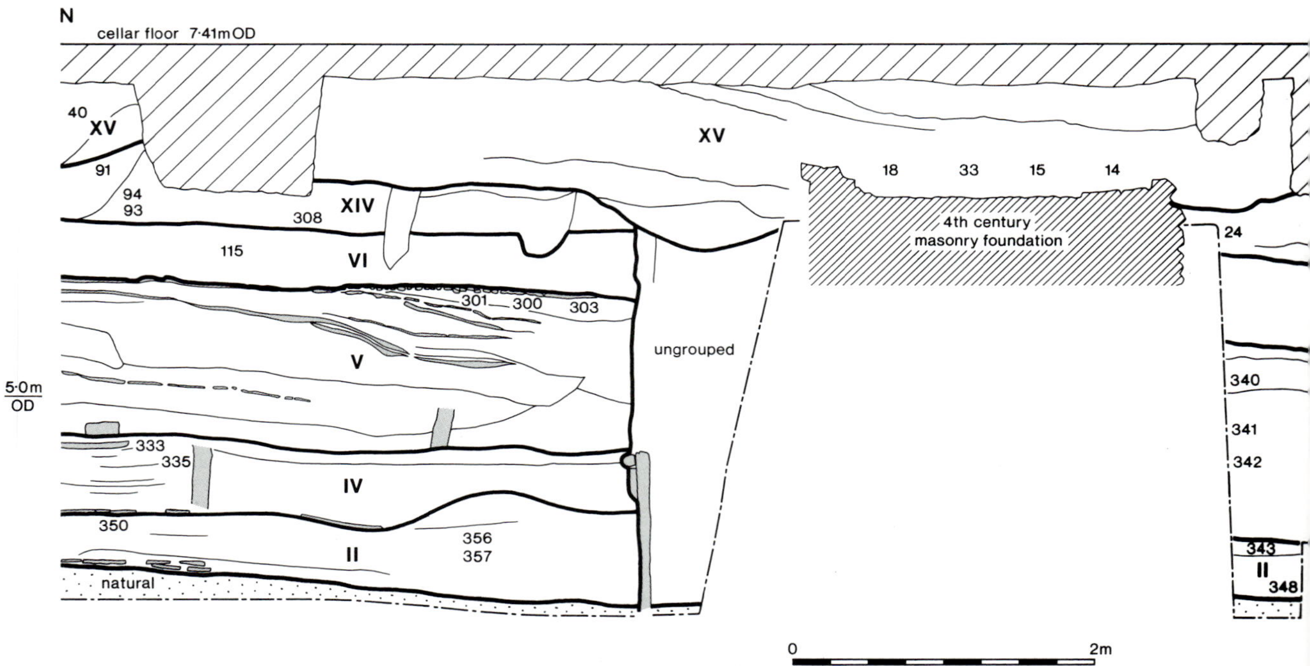

Fig 31 Cutting BB. Interpretive drawing of Fig 30

material. As will be seen, this gully had two phases of building. It is possible that an earlier phase is recorded here in Group V. A number of timbers were recorded just to the north of this channel but at a lower depth. The problems with groundwater prevented detailed recording but their position in the section would suggest that they belonged to the Group V period of activity. It is therefore possible that this water channel was the southern limit of the floor surfaces seen to its immediate north and on the north side of the unexcavated baulk.

Cutting BB: Group VI

Group VI layers were seen across the entire length of the cutting and covered the earlier Group V layers. They comprised layers of compact clay and organic material forming no coherent pattern. One floor surface consisting of timber planks could be discerned.

On the north side of the gully filled with Group XII material, which cut through these deposits, the Group VI layers were made up of a *c* 0.5m thick dump of burnt, loamy clay containing much tile and

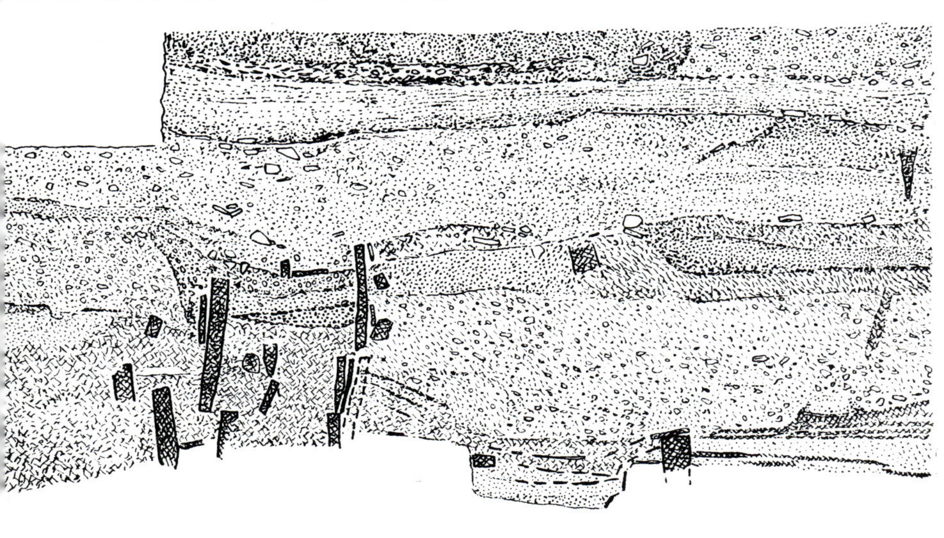

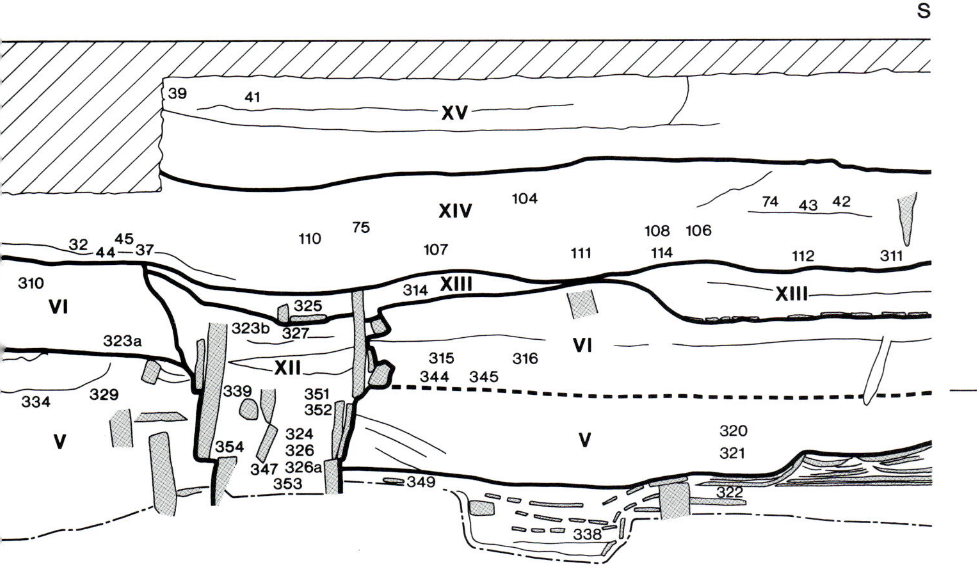

stones and capped by a rammed clay floor *c* 0.1m thick. The latter was probably a surface contemporary with the use of the latest of the water channels recorded at this point. This channel had at least two phases (Figs 33 and 34). The earliest channel was made up of squared vertical posts holding back vertically set planks against the gully cut (Fig 34a). Planks lined the gully floor. On the south side one upright, in the south-east corner, was used by the later gully. The others were not reused. On the north side, the posts were up to and higher than the later gully but appear outside the north side of it.

The later gully was built in the silted channel of the earlier (Fig 34b). Two boards, 0.28m and 0.33m wide, lined its base. The upright in the south-east corner, as indicated above, was reused *in situ* from the earlier gully.

Unfortunately it has not been possible to differentiate between the finds sealed between the two channel floors and the material which filled the latest channel. Both are included in Group XII.

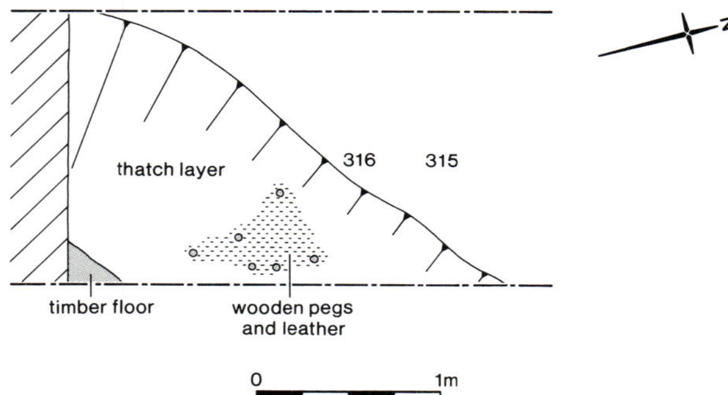

Fig 32 Cutting BB. Plan of Group V layers showing position of pegs and leather. Prepared from sketches in site notebooks

Cutting BB: Group XII

These layers were exclusively contained within the fills of the two superimposed channels described above. The fills were described as black or grey clay, mixed in places with gravel.

The upper fills of the latest channel were mainly gravel with some organic material. Their regular layering might indicate a gradual buildup of waterborne material. Their presence would suggest that the channel was no longer well maintained at this stage, a phenomenon represented by Group XII deposits in the stream bed itself in Cutting F to the east (see below).

Cutting BB: Groups XII–XV

Group XII layers, dating up to the middle of the third century, closed the pre-Temple phase of activity in Cutting BB. Chapter 4 describes Groups XIII, XIV and XIV, contemporary with the Mithraeum.

Cutting F

Cutting F (Figs 10 and 23) revealed a succession of superimposed Walbrook channels, each cutting the silted or backfilled channel of its predecessor, with a corresponding succession of timber revetments, platforms and dumps on the bank of the stream (Figs 35 and 36). Although these platforms were horizontal at the west end of the cutting they had slumped dramatically into the soft and unstable fills of the channel. It would appear that this creeping or slumping occurred throughout the Roman period and led on occasions to dramatic slumps, perhaps actual collapses, of the vertical revetments. This continued until the mid- to late third century after which the west bank was unrevetted. This led to dramatic erosion of the bank and rapid silting of the channel. While the course of the stream was revetted it would appear that it had been kept clean of choking silt by regular dredging. Such information makes this the most important cutting in this area of the Roman city for the nature and history of the Walbrook stream.

Cutting F was one of the first cuttings to be opened on the site in the early months of 1952. It was aligned approximately east to west in the rear basements of Nos 38–40 Mansion House Chambers. The basement level was at 7.41m OD. Flooding and the pressure of work for RMLEC on other sites in the City of London caused excavation in the cutting to be suspended during 1952 and not resumed until 1954. Site notes and finds for this initial period of excavation are therefore unfortunately few. They indicate that the 1952 season stopped at approximately 1.52m (5ft) below the cellar floor (*c* 5.89m OD).

Finds groups from this initial programme of excavation were prefixed 'W'. Many survive for study but their site locations are difficult to pinpoint precisely. The majority of these, in any case, contain very mixed Roman pottery including a few medieval sherds. These groups are not discussed in any detail in this report.

Work was resumed on Cutting F in February 1954 and was completed during the summer of the same year. Even with the addition by this time of a mechanical pump, supplied by the Corporation of London, the groundwater conditions continued to cause severe flooding. Consequently, when the excavations on this cutting were in an advanced state, a sump was rapidly excavated in the extreme east end of the cutting. This coincided with the course of the Walbrook channel itself, the deepest part of the site. Unfortunately the archaeological deposits there were not adequately recorded. As a result the deposits in the eastern part of the site to the east of the Group XII deposits (ie those in the bottom right-hand corner of the illustrated sections, Figs 35 and 36) were not sampled for finds and remain undated.

Fig 33 Cutting BB. The latest timber drain (Grimes)

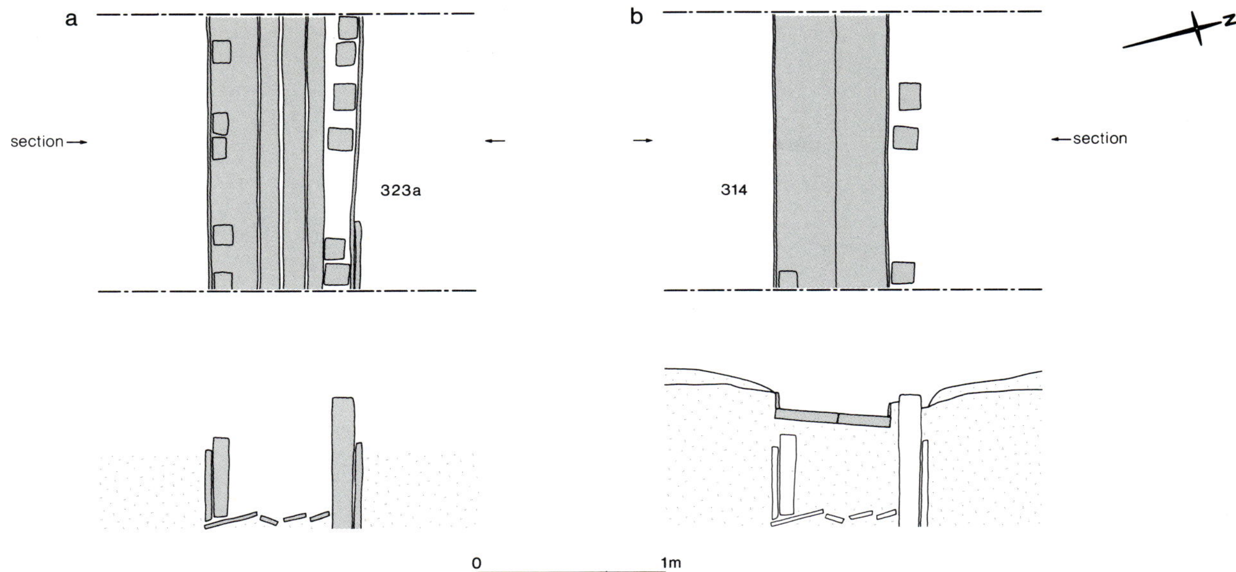

Fig 34 Cutting BB a) the first drain b) the latest drain. Plans and sections prepared from sketches in site notebooks

The information contained within the site records and finds can be divided into 13 distinct stratigraphic groups (Fig 36):

a) the first group contained all observations of the natural deposits. These were not numbered by the excavators.
b) there are nine numbered and stratified groups (I, II, III, V, VI, XII, X, XIII, XIV and XV). Groups I, II, III, V and VI correspond with similarly numbered groups in Cuttings AA, AB, BA, BB, CA, CB and CD. These pre–date the construction of the Mithraeum during the mid-third century. Group XII corresponds with VII in Cuttings CA, CB and CD, a pre-Mithraeum group, and with Group VIII in the temple itself. Groups XIII, XIV and XV are contem porary with the life of the temple.
c) the poorly recorded deposits in the position of the sump in the extreme east end of the cutting
d) the 1952 observations in the upper part of the cut ting from cellar floor to a level of approximately 5.89m OD
e) a medieval pit or ditch cut not seen in 1952 but examined in 1954 in the upper part of the cutting at the west end

Cutting F: natural deposits

The natural surface in Cutting F consisted of clean grey clay throughout. It was examined in detail across the entire length of the cutting (Figs 35 and 36). At the western end it was recorded at 2.55m OD and it sloped gradually eastwards, dropping 1m over 5.8m. At this point, 5.8m from the west end of the cutting, the grey clay was therefore at 1.47m OD. Here the slope broke almost vertically, dropping 0.6m to 0.86m OD. From this vertical break in the slope to the eastern extent of the cutting the surface of the natural deposits was approximately horizontal for *c* 3m. Only a shallow and irregular hollow, 0.15m deep and 0.6m wide, broke this surface midway between the vertical drop and the end of the cutting.

This channel, at least 3m wide as seen in this cutting, can be interpreted as one of the earliest of the Walbrook stream channels. It was filled on its west side and in the centre by Group V and XII deposits which date from the late second to third centuries. These groups are much later than the earliest deposits on the west bank of the stream. It is therefore probable that at least at this point along the course of the Walbrook the channel was well maintained and was regularly cleaned of choking silt and debris. This being so, the sudden 0.6m break in the slope of the surface of the natural ground level *c* 5.8m from the western edge of the cutting is probably a man-made profile caused by the recutting and cleaning of the channel close to the stream bank.

Cutting F: Group I

A number of fragments of planks and some unworked wood debris lay on the surface of the natural ground level. In one or two places thin layers of black occupation material were noted. No finds came from the latter.

Above these was a 5.5m-long accumulation of material which varied in thickness from 0.22m at the west end of the cutting to 0.3m at its eastern extent. At this point it had been truncated by the Group II/III revetment (Revetment 1: see below) and if it extended beyond this revetment it had been disturbed or removed by the stream and its maintenance. The top surface of this accumulation followed approximately the slope of the natural deposits. It contained F739 and F742.

This accumulation included both man-made and natural deposits. They consisted of an unspecified number of layers of dirty clay or buff clay speckled and stained with organic debris. At the time of excavation it was suggested that their deposition was the result of extreme but intermittent boggy conditions. These layers were interspersed with lenses of gravel and layers of broken wooden surfaces consisting of small planks, just a few centimetres wide, mixed with unworked wooden debris such as twigs, branches and bark. The worked timber elements were more frequent and more substantial towards the western end of the cutting.

These horizons were interpreted as insubstantial floors, working surfaces or treading surfaces on the bank of the stream. They were laid to consolidate an unstable and sometimes wet surface.

It is possible that some of the layers between these surfaces represent the upcast from the cleaning of the Walbrook stream channel. It is not known if these layers and surfaces on the stream bank were accompanied by revetting. The later Group II/III revetment (Revetment 1), driven through this Group I accumulation, must have been slightly set back from any earlier western stream bank. The maintenance of the channel contemporary with Revetment 1 would have removed any earlier containment of the stream bank.

It is of interest here to note that some broken and cracked-off timbers were recorded in the flat, 3m channel profile described above. These were in the vicinity of a quernstone recorded as lying on the natural surface. There, lying more or less horizontally, was a fallen or pulled–out pile. The source of this pile is not known but it lay against the shattered and splintered uprights of two piles which were still in their original positions. Their splintered upper portions were just exposed above the natural ground level. Unfortunately no other timbers were recorded due to the difficulties of excavation in this area.

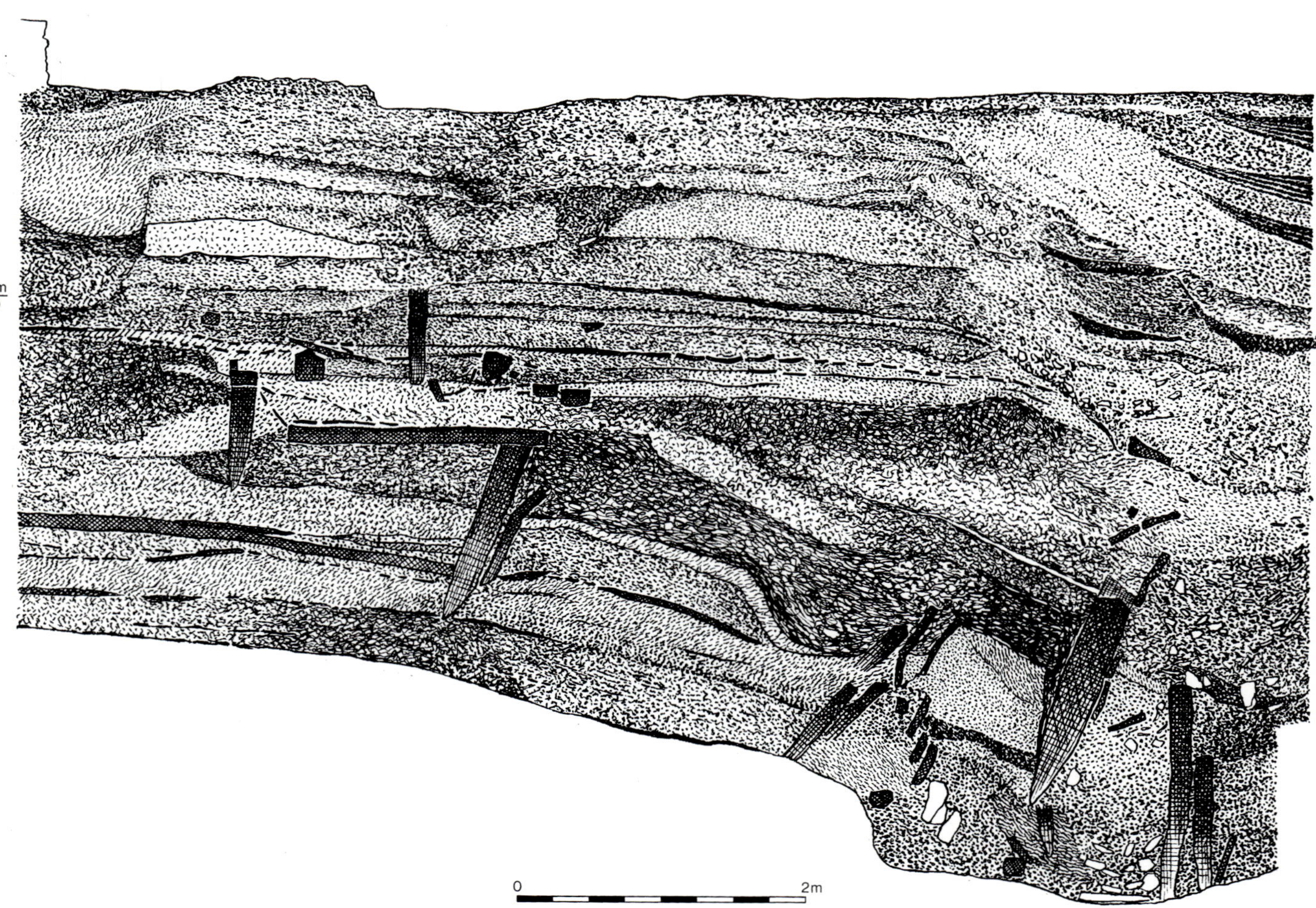

Fig 35 Cutting F. Edited section of cutting (original by Grimes)

It is just possible that these *in situ* piles represent part of a revetment which predated the Group II/III revetment. This had been removed during the maintenance of the channel alongside this revetment and, in time, became sealed by Group V and XII deposits.

Cutting F: Group II

The top of Group I deposits was sealed by a platform (Fig 36, Platform A) which was more substantial than anything which had been constructed before at this spot. It consisted of vertical piles driven into the earlier deposits with horizontal planks laid above them. The piles measured approximately 8–12cm square, but unfortunately no plans or details of their number survive. This platform was horizontal for most of the western part of the cutting, but as for the Group I accumulation it followed the natural slope eastwards.

A second platform (Fig 36, Platform B) was built on an intentional make-up, *c* 0.15m thick, of fairly dense buff clay make-up showing some signs of layering. This contained F740, F744 and F745.

Another deposit of buff clay varying in thickness a few centimetres to *c* 0.2m and containing F729, F730, F731, F734, F735 and F752 overlay Platform B. On this was laid a 2cm-thick layer of wattling and a woody material believed, at the time of excavation, to be tree bark.

This bark layer probably served as a temporary treading surface because immediately above it was built another platform (Fig 36, Platform C), itself more solid than any previous structure. It consisted of horizontal planks lying on a foundation of vertically driven piles. At the west end of the cutting the timbers were in a very good condition but towards the east, as they sloped towards the stream, the wood was more degraded and appeared almost peat-like in consistency.

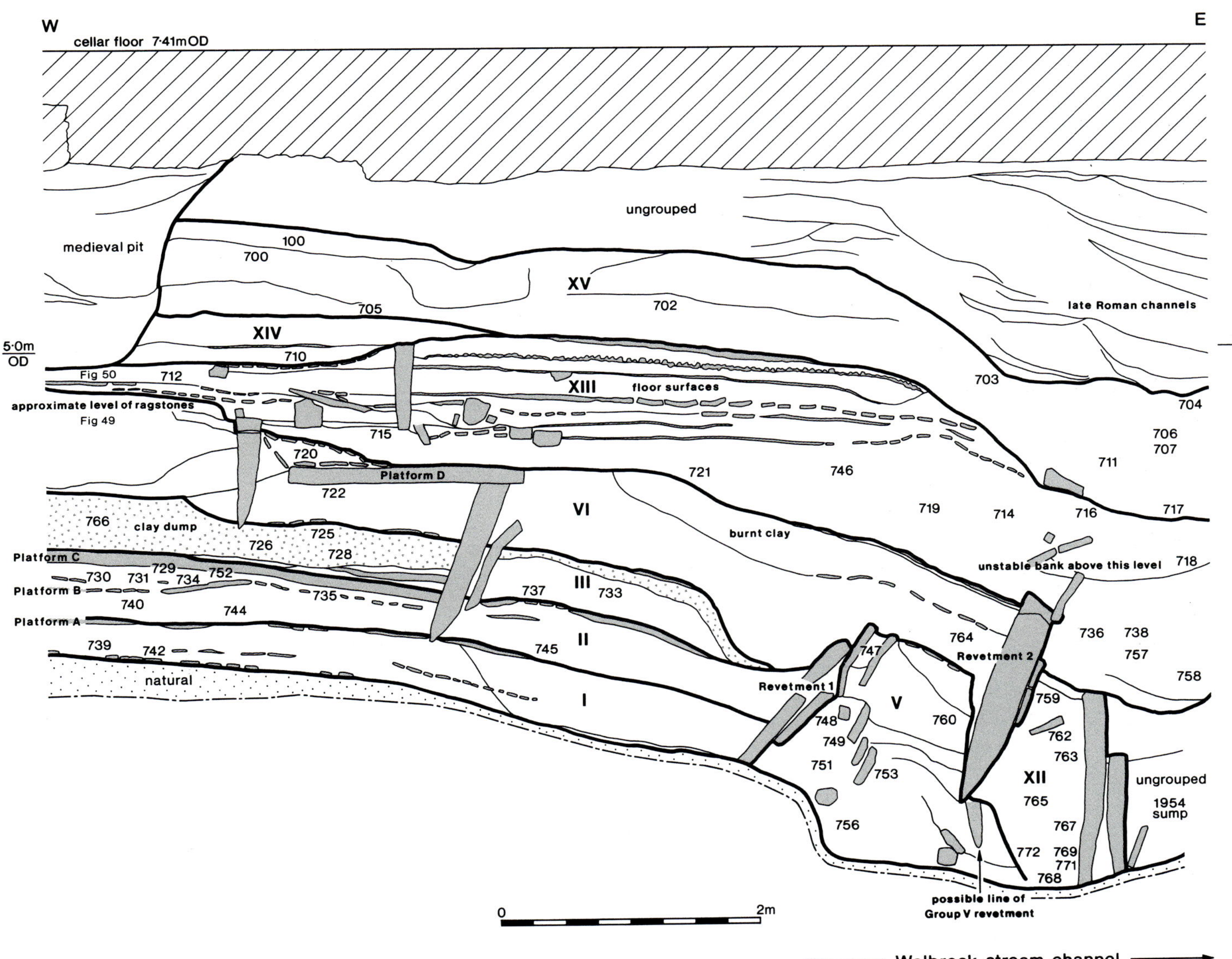

Fig 36 Cutting F. Interpretive drawing of Fig 35

These Group II platforms and their associated make-up deposits were associated with the westernmost of the large revetments (Revetment 1) recorded in the section. This section (Fig 35 and 36) shows clearly that the eastern limit of Platform C coincided with the original position of Revetment 1 (ie when it was upright) at a point 5.18m from the west end of the cutting.

Revetment 1 was made up of two rows of vertical timbers, set in pairs, driven deep into the underlying deposits with horizontal planks set on edge between them and additional planks secured against the outside face. It is not clear exactly how they were fixed in place. The full profile of the revetment as seen in the section, however, was not of one build. It would appear that as new platforms and dumps were laid on the stream bank, new timbers were driven immediately behind the back of the preceding timberwork. That profile therefore records a number of additions to the original line of the revetment. Its height increased as the bank behind it was raised.

Revetment 1 did not remain in a vertical position, as the section clearly demonstrates (Fig 36). It lay at approximately 45 degrees to the vertical and many of the horizontal planks, especially at the base of the revetment, later burst forward into the channel of the stream. In its final state the top of the revetment had moved *c* 1.2m eastwards, pivoting on the point where the vertical posts penetrated the natural subsoil. This final position, however, probably included a considerable amount of slumping after the revetment had been sealed by later accumulations. It will be seen that the later Group VI revetment (Revetment 2) also slumped into the stream channel causing its associated platform (Platform D) to subside at least 1m at its easternmost extent along with it (see below, *Cutting F: Group VI*).

This shift must have included a considerable amount of movement of the underlying stratigraphy. However, material immediately associated with Revetment 1 shows that some movement occurred while this revetment was still in use. Group III dumps, much earlier than Revetment 2, were laid to level up the surface of the Group II stream bank which had slumped and subsided behind the leaning Revetment 1.

Cutting F: Group III

Groups II and III were closely related and both represented further attempts to improve the condition of the west bank of the stream by means of horizontal platforms and a vertical timber revetment.

Group III consisted of two large dumps of material which sealed the final platform (Platform C) of Group II. The first of these, containing F733 and F737, was *c* 3m in length and varied in thickness from just a few centimetres to *c* 40cms (15ins). It infilled the hollow behind Revetment 1 which had been caused by that revetment slumping forward and the surface of Platform C subsiding. This dump of material, described as mixed, 'vaguely stratified' dirty loam, covered Platform C in the middle of the cutting but left the western end exposed. A number of horizontal timbers were laid on this dump of material, making a surface which corresponded with that of the exposed portion of Platform C in the west part of the cutting.

Soon after this new surface had been made the level was raised once again. This time a massive dump of dark-stained buff clay, practically stoneless, covered the entire surface of the west bank as exposed in this cutting from the western end of the cutting up to the lip of Revetment 1. This layer, which contained F725, F726, F728 and F766, was *c* 0.3m thick at the west and only a few centimetres thick at its east end. It was horizontal for *c* 3m but, like preceding layers and Group VI deposits above, it had subsided at its eastern end. There, where it would have met Revetment 1 when that revetment was still almost vertical, its top level was *c* 0.45m below its horizontal as recorded at the west end of the cutting. When Revetment 1 eventually moved forward the clay slumped forward into the void created by the collapse. This layer petered out *c* 0.30m from the revetment. This gap probably indicates the additional slump forward caused by the collapse of the Group VI Revetment 2.

This clay dump represents a major consolidation of the west bank in this vicinity. It is of importance to notice that a corresponding dump of clay appears on the east bank of the Walbrook stream at approximately the same level OD (see below, *Cutting CB: Group IV*).

Cutting F: Group V

The Group V deposits immediately overlay the cut of the channel of the western side of the stream and butted against Revetment 1. They also included many of the horizontal timbers of Revetment 1 which had burst into the stream with the weight of the dumps behind them. They reached almost to the full height of the slumped Revetment 1 and apart from some slight evidence of recutting it is probable that this Group represents a period when the stream had become choked with silt and the maintenance of its channel and the revetments was not being carried out as conscientiously as it had earlier or immediately after (see *Cutting F: Group VI* below).

Group V consisted primarily of shingle and coarse silt with at least two thick lens-like deposits made up of dense black organic material. The lowest of the shingle and coarse silt layers filled the angle formed by the vertical side and horizontal base of the stream channel (F756). It was sealed by a layer of dense buff clay mixed with shingle (F748, F749 and F751) on its west side. This material butted on the west against the horizontal planks of Revetment 1. It is tempting to suggest that the clay component of this layer derived from Group I and

II dumps which had burst through the revetment, forcing the planks into their final horizontal position.

On the east side of these planks, and also overlying the shingle and silt layer F756, was another shingle layer, F753. A number of squared ragstone blocks, some with mortar adhering to them, were recorded at the interface between these two layers.

Both F753 and F756 had been scoured on their east sides. The crescent-shaped profile of the scourings was filled with the first of the dense black organic layers. This layer, from which unfortunately no finds were retrieved, was later itself scoured on its east side by the Walbrook channel. This was later filled with Group XII deposits. The top of the organic layer was also cut or eroded by later action which occurred during the deposition of these Group V deposits.

This organic layer contained the remains of an unspecified number of vertical piles broken off at the top of the layer in a similar manner to those piles seen protruding from natural and probably associated with the Group I stream bank. These might indicate the line of another revetment, postdating Revetment 1 but predating Revetment 2, which was destroyed or dismantled during later cleaning of the channel.

This truncated organic layer and the piles were sealed by another shingle layer, which was in turn sealed by yet another dense black organic layer. This sloped down to the east. Above this was another layer of shingle mixed with coarse grey loam (F747 and F760). This final layer reached the top of Revetment 1.

The Group V deposits therefore appear to indicate a period when the stream channel against Revetment 1 was probably not as well maintained as previously. They were not deposited at one time but represented a number of fillings of the channel with coarse waterborne material followed by the settling of organic debris. This occurred at least twice. After the first occasion a recutting of the channel may have completely destroyed a revetment.

Cutting F: Group VI

The Group VI deposits represent a major construction phase initiated in an attempt, once again, to consolidate the west bank of the stream. This time an encroachment towards the stream channel making use of the silted-up portion represented by the Group V deposits was undertaken.

One of the main components of this group was a large dump of material described as black loam and coarse gravel up to 0.75m thick. This contained F722 and F764. This material sealed the entire surface of the preceding Group III and the Group V deposits which had filled the earlier stream channel. At the time of its deposition the west bank was relatively flat across the greater part of the cutting, except in the centre where the top of Group III sloped down. As mentioned above, this dump filled a large hollow behind Revetment 1. This massive dump was intended to act as the levelling foundation for yet another timber platform and revetment. The size of this structure was much larger than any previous structure in this cutting.

It consisted of massive timbers, at least 1.7m long and 0.3m square, driven their full length into the surface of the bank. The easternmost of these was driven into the Group V deposits and was used as a revetment to the stream. Horizontal planks, varying from 0.15m to 0.38m wide, were fixed with nails against the eastern faces of these. This revetment was at least 0.9m high but, as with Revetment 1, was added to (in Group XII), giving a possible height of up to 1.5m, although it is unlikely that all of this was exposed at any single time. The lower planks were probably covered over by the earliest of the Group XII channel fills (see below).

The platform connected with this revetment was constructed of heavy wooden planks on a foundation of densely packed vertically driven piles (Figs 37–9). The large piles described above gave additional strength to this foundation. In places, large horizontal joists up to 1.8m long and 0.15m to 0.2m square were placed between these piles to support the plank floor.

The sequence at the west end of the cutting as described in the site documentation is confusing, but its special nature requires explanation. A dump of dirty buff clay, containing F720, covered the west end of the wooden platform described above and would appear according to the section drawing to fill a shallow hollow at the extreme west end of the cutting.

Fig 37 Cutting F. Group VI timbers of Platform D (Grimes)

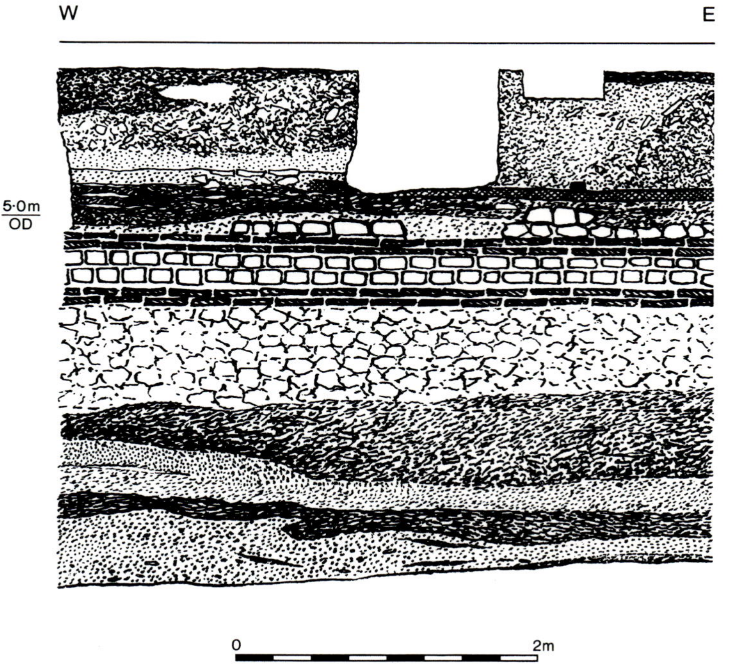

Fig 43 Cutting CB. Edited section of cutting (original by Grimes)

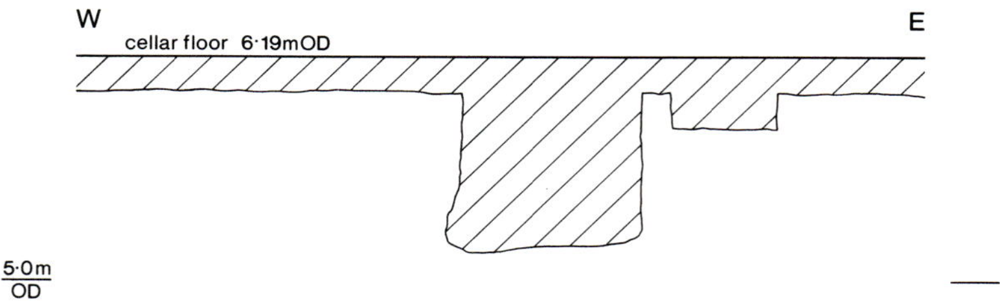

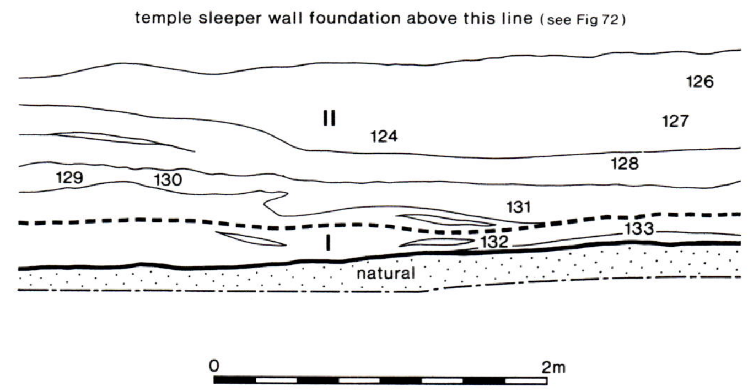

Fig 44 Cutting CB. Interpretive drawing of Fig 43

CD (CD222, CD219, CD218, CD223, CD221, CD224) covers the earlier period, with CD210, CD208 and CD209 at a somewhat higher level moving into the second century with CD213 and CD214 between. Throughout, there were horizontally discontinuous wattle floors with timber and upright stakes and posts. Few of these actually occurred in the section faces; those shown have been projected from the body of the cutting. In any case, not enough could be seen of either floors or timbers to produce a plan.

The surface of the peaty deposits was irregular, varying in depth from about *c* 3.83m OD at the extreme eastern end of Cutting CB to about *c* 3.19m OD on the west in Cutting CD. In Cutting CA, CA190 with Flavian-Trajanic samian came from this surface.

Over the length of the three cuttings as a whole correlation of the sequences was not possible because of gaps dictated by modern obstructions which could not be removed at the time the cuttings were made. Short as the distances were, the conditions over the area of Cutting CB must have been very different from those in CA and CD, but in the absence of an environmental study it can be said only that the evidence, for what it is worth, suggests relatively short-lived shack-like structures in a depressing, partly waterlogged setting, replaced and renewed as the surfaces built up in what must have been semi-natural conditions. The process took place during the second half of the first century AD and on into the early years of the second century.

Cuttings CA and CB: Groups IV and VII

Before describing the deposits which succeeded the peat, some explanation is required of the sections presented in Figures 41–4 with Cuttings CA and CB. Cutting CB was recorded in ignorance of what lay beneath the cellar floor. It was a matter of accident that, at *c* 3.75m OD, the section faces coincided with rubble foundations and the masonry faces of the west end of the north sleeper-wall, so that the upper deposits were recorded only in Cutting CA. Consequently only Groups I and II were visible in the east–west section of Cutting CB. The elevation of the sleeper wall recorded in Cutting CB is reproduced on Figure 72.

Above the irregular level of the Group II peat layers, all trace of organic layers had disappeared although some wooden features survived. The accumulations were mainly clay of a very mixed character, loamy in parts, with much stone and gravel; it was dirty and charcoal-stained, with abundant plaster fragments at the eastern end (CB120, CB121, CB123). There was some difference between Cuttings CA and CD, largely because of more varied human activity. Interpretation is rendered more difficult in that, in both cuttings, some features which were recognisable in the section faces could not be identified in the floor of the cutting because of the continually waterlogged conditions. The true stratigraphic positions of some finds from the body of the cutting — whether they came from within or beyond the 'disturbed' areas — is therefore uncertain. It does not, however, seriously affect the chronological succession, which (allowing for survivals) proceeds uniformly through the second century and into the third.

Cutting CB: Group IV

At the eastern end throughout Cutting CB, the dense peat deposit was overlaid by about 0.90m of stiff clay to the underside of the first floor of the north aisle of the temple. The clay was very wet when excavated; it was stony, containing some gravel, plaster fragments and dark charcoal discolourations. It was featureless, apart from a small occupation deposit near to its base on the north side. There were three piles, larger than usual: two on the north side, their tops at 2.18m below datum, and the third, apparently double (rather than split) at 2.00m down, which was probably not connected with the others. Pottery from these layers is dated to the mid- to late second century.

Cutting CA: Groups IV and VII

In Cutting CA, the vertical succession above the peaty layers was broken by features which complicate the section but were too incompletely seen to be capable of interpretation. One of these was a large pit or ditch which was recognisable in both sections but which was not seen in the 'treacly' mud of the floor of the perpetually waterlogged cutting. Its extent and shape as far as it was present in the excavated area were therefore not recorded. This feature, about 0.60m deep, appeared to have been dug from a surface about 0.30m below the building level of the temple, *c* 4.06m OD. Extensively decayed timbers suggested a plank floor.

Cutting CA: Group VII

Towards the east, the mixed filling of this feature had been cut into to create a plank-lined channel or gully, CA164. The corollary of this is that the material to the east of the planks in the section is the filling of the later channel. The floors of the two features coincide, that of the later channel being more irregular, but the fillings are quite different. In the earliest feature, there appears to have been a gradual build-up of various loams with a vaguely horizontal stratification and one pronounced clay layer; in the channel, the tipped layers suggest deliberate infilling. That the channel had been open was indicated by the presence of dressed uprights against its south side. This channel was 0.55m deep from the top edge of the plank lining on the west. This consisted of two planks; on the north side the single plank was 0.28m deep.

Little more can be done with these features than to record their presence. The stratification was indistinct and confused, particularly in the neighbourhood of the apse foundation, with indications of a much disturbed plank floor on a foundation of tiles which overlay the large pit but might have related to the timber-lined box, though it stopped short of it. It is, however, clear that they all preceded the temple, with the broad offset of the apse foundation, which was no more than mortar overspill on the lip of the construction trench, cutting through the above-mentioned floor and all sealed by the built-up material for the western steps or by the nave floor.

Among the pottery associated with these features there was as usual a good deal of residual material, with the significant groups belonging to the early third

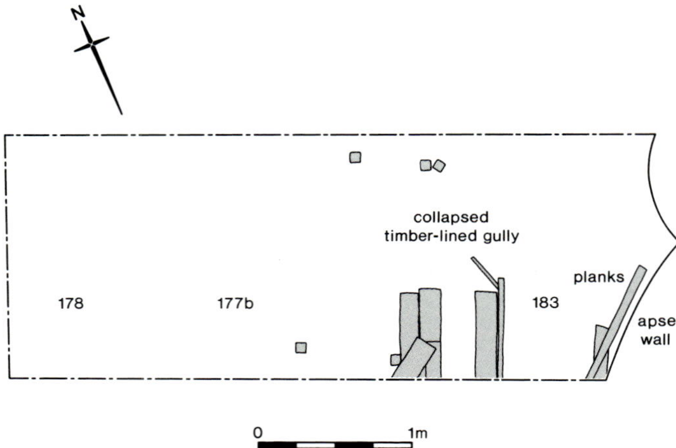

Fig 45 Cutting CD. Plan of Group VII timbers. Prepared from sketches in site notebooks

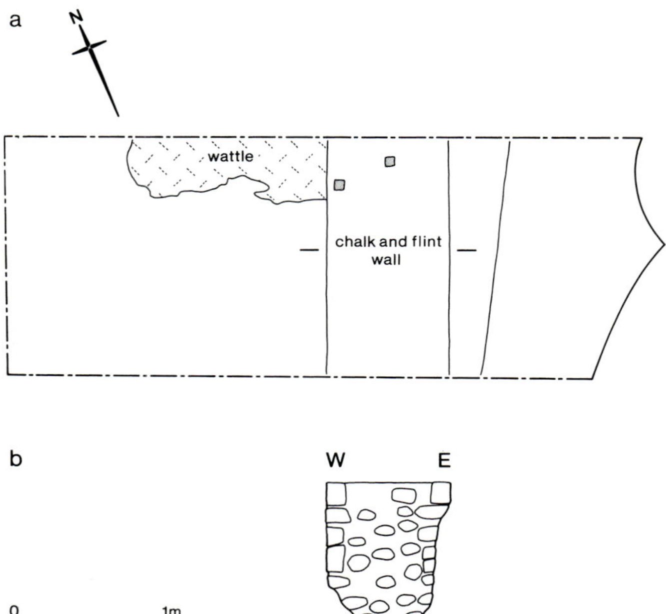

Fig 46 Cutting CD. Plan of chalk and flint wall to west of Mithraeum. Prepared from sketches in site notebooks

century (CA149, CA144, CA143, CA150) all below the mixed surface which carried the build-up of the temple floors.

The last feature to be noted here was a line of piles set roughly parallel with and a few centimetres in from the sleeper-wall foundation. They were of fairly uniform size (around 0.16 by 0.10 or 0.11m) and averaged 0.76–0.80m in depth. All except one at the west end were topped with tenons. The exception was at a somewhat higher level. They were spaced centre-to-centre between 0.75–0.90m apart, and evidently provided support for sleeper beams and a boarded floor of the type met with in Cutting F, or, though this is less likely, for a wall. It is remarkable that, whatever the structure represented, its alignment was very close to that of the temple, but with the tops of the piles at *c* 4.00m OD (0.30m below the 'offset' of the apse foundation) the two were not connected.

The evidence suggests the presence of an elaborate timber structure or structures on the site in the early third century, immediately preceding the building of the temple. Not enough could be seen of the different parts to decide whether they were related to one another in any way.

Cutting CD: Group VII

In Cutting CD, as in Cutting CA, the peaty deposits were succeeded by almost 0.60m of clay which displayed the usual variation in colour and constituents (Group IV). At the base of this deposit (3.25 m OD) an oblong-sectioned wooden water pipe ran obliquely across the cutting. It continued to produce a trickle of water, making its own contribution (in spite of attempts to plug it) to the general saturation. Above this, there were traces of wattling at various depths but they were scrappy and indeterminate. More definite was the surface which capped this mixed clay deposit at *c* 3.49m OD to 3.68m OD. At that level, the wattle was more continuous; there were other fragments of timbers and a few small pegs indiscriminately distributed and not planned. Just below this surface, *c* 1.10m west of the apse wall, there was a collapsed timber-floored and timber-lined gully (CD187 on Figs 42 and 45). This accumulation continued the chronological succession extending through the second century into the early part of the third (CD180, CD186, CD187, CD207) with CD179, of late second- or early third-century date at floor level.

Above this floor, there was a mixed black clayey soil about 0.30m deep, featureless but containing small stones, shells and pieces of wood. This material was sealed at *c* 4.06m OD by a surface, well prepared in its western part with a wattle floor. The floor was broken by a chalk and flint foundation *c* 0.90m out from the apse wall (Figs 42 and 46 and see below). The surface was not recognisable in the mixed grey black clay between the two walls but its level coincided with that of the top layer of a plank lining the foundation trench. It was probably the external building level of the temple. CD177b, CD178 and CD183, with CD182 and CD 177 (at a slightly higher level), ranging down to the mid-third century, are consistent with this interpretation.

4 Period 2: the archaeology of the temple and the Walbrook valley from *c* AD 240–50

Summary

The following summary is taken from Grimes (1968) with cross-references to this report and other annotations, in square brackets, added in 1995:

> The Temple of Mithras was...set in an area which had a character markedly different from what would have been expected so near to the known centre of Londinium. There was no concentration here of stone buildings of quality but a shallow somewhat depressing valley with a tendency to wetness, and a scatter of timber huts and a sporadic industrial activity. When the temple was built...deposits up to 8 feet deep [2.43m] had accumulated on the eastern side of the stream [see below, *The pre-temple topography]*.
>
> Lying east-to-west the building itself projected pier-wise into this raised ground; but at its east end with its vestibule would almost certainly have confronted a street, the predecessor of the modern street, which may be guessed to have followed the lip of the basin. [For details of the temple, its construction and phases and 1954 state of preservation see below, *Modern disturbance of the temple; The construction of the temple; The Phase 1 temple; The narthex.]*
>
> The waterlogged nature of the site had its problems for the modern excavator...; but one overriding advantage at least was that the wet conditions were admirable for the preservation of organic materials, so that the wooden features survived, not as flimsy elusive ghosts, but as their solid original selves [For the changes to the interior layout of the temple see below: *The Phase I temple; The Phase IIa temple; The Phase IIb temple; The Phase III temple; The Phase IV temple.*]

The temple groups and phases

The stratigraphic groups associated with the temple are as follows:

East bank groups
The surface of Group VII — site preparation phase
Group VIII — Construction and temple Phases I, IIa and IIb (Floors 1–4)
Group IX — temple Phase III (Floors 5–7)
Group X — temple Phase IV (Floors 8 and 9) and abandonment
Group XI — pit cut into Floor 9 at west end of temple

Contemporary west bank groups
Group XIII — Platforms, buildings and unstable stream bank
Group XIV — as for Group XIII, poorly preserved
Group XV — the latest recorded Roman material on west bank
Group XII — a west bank, Period 1 group (see above)

The west bank from *c* AD 240–50

Cuttings AA and AB

The groups which pre-date the construction of the Mithraeum have been described above (*Chapter 3, The pre-temple groups*; see Figs 24, 27 and 28 for the positions of these stratigraphic groups). Those groups which were contemporary with the temple are described here.

Cutting AA: Group XIII

A 0.15m- (6in) thick dump of material described as red burnt gravelly soil sealed the underlying Group VI (Fig 24). This included layers AA500, AA501 and AA516. It equates with a similarly described dump in AB to the east.

Cutting AA: ungrouped layers

The entire cutting was sealed by a *c* 1.2m–thick layer of black stony soil which corresponds with a similar thick layer which sealed Cutting AB to the east. No finds were kept from this layer. Hardcore and the concrete basement slab (7.55m OD) for 18 Mansion House Chambers completed the recorded section.

Cutting AB: Group XIII

The surface of the Group VI deposits was almost horizontal at the east end of the cutting (Figs 10, 23, 27 and 28). Towards the west, a gully separated these from a raised bank. The Group XIII layers, in effect, filled the eastern end of the cutting up to the top of this bank. The gully contains a number of different fills suggesting that some silting and erosion of the material from the bank probably happened over a period of time. However, during the period when the stream was no longer being revetted (see Cutting F below), the need for the bank was also discounted.

Those layers at the east end of the cutting were, as the recorded section clearly shows, homogeneous deposits in which it was not possible for the excavators to find any definite surfaces. These consisted in the greater part of light grey or yellowish grey loamy soils.

The absence of recognisable surfaces in Cutting AB compares dramatically with the profusion of contemporary timber surfaces which were recorded in Cutting F.

It will be seen, however, that these surfaces in Cutting F appear to have been platforms and buildings immediately alongside the bank of the stream, with a possible open area, indicated by a layer of ragstone and other building materials, at the extreme west end of the cutting. It is therefore probable that this Group XIII activity in Cutting AB is not of the same nature as that in Cutting F. There the Group XIII layers represented timber platforms and light buildings alongside an unrevetted stream with more solid external surfaces on the west side of these buildings. In Cutting AB the deposition of layers suggests merely an open area in which little appears to have been attempted.

It is interesting to note that at the western end of Cutting AB, a deposit of red burnt gravelly soil (containing AB515), also seen in Cutting AA at exactly the same level, rests directly upon the earlier group. On the very bank of the stream in Cutting F (see below), burnt material was among the last of the deposits to be laid before the Group VI revetment collapsed. The infilling at the stream edge at an early stage in the deposition of Group XIII layers to compensate for this collapse also included some burnt debris. It is possible that this layer and the Cutting AA and AB layers came from a common source and were dumped around the same time.

Cutting AB: Groups XIV and XV

Unfortunately, the latest levels in this cutting produced no finds groups of value which are still available for study, but considering the close proximity of the east end of this cutting to the south end of Cutting BB it is possible to suggest that some layers seen here are contemporary with the better recorded layers to the north. These layers, however, were featureless and represented build-ups of light grey gravelly material, sometimes separated by layers of finer, gravel-free soil. The western end of the site was covered by a thick layer of homogeneous black soil.

No medieval occupation was identified. In fact the entire length of the cutting was free of any medieval intrusions. Deep Victorian foundations in the form of a horizontal foundation of mixed hardcore and a concrete slab, the basement floors of 25 and 46 Mansion House Chambers, completed the recorded sequence.

Cutting BB

The groups which pre-date the construction of the Mithraeum are described above *(Chapter 3)*. Those groups contemporary with the temple are described here. Groups XIII, XIV and XV are represented in this trench (Figs 10, 23, 30 and 31).

Fig 47 Cutting BB. Late Roman masonry platform (Grimes)

Cutting BB: Group XIII

This group, containing BB314 and BB325, filled the depression left in the surface of the final water channel once it had gone out of use (see above). The fill consisted of black mixed loam containing many burnt clay fragments.

Cutting BB: Group XIV

Group XIV covered the entire trench and sealed the top of Group VI. It is evident that the interface between these two groups must have contained other material contemporary with Groups XII and XIII, filling the water channel. However, it was not possible to discern these.

This group mainly consisted of a single layer at the south end of unstratified loam mixed with stones, some burnt clay and other sparse building debris. It contained a great many finds, including BB24, BB32, BB37, BB42, BB43, BB44, BB45, BB74, BB75, BB104, BB106, BB107, BB108, BB110, BB111, BB112 and BB311. Only at the extreme south end were there possible signs of a floor with a single posthole.

The soil at the north end of the trench was very similar except that a floor surface was more obvious. Finds here were sparser and included BB91, BB93, BB94 and BB308.

A feature of this phase of activity was a large masonry platform built into or upon Group XIV layers (Fig 47). It comprised a solid raft of mortared ragstone.

Its function is not at all certain. No other masonry structures were recorded on the west bank of the Walbrook during these excavations. The only other stone feature was the loose ragstone platform, a Group VI/XIII feature, seen in Cutting F. This, as will be seen, was covered by four tiles mortared together. This platform contained one of the Bacchus torso fragments (*Chapter 5, The finds catalogue, Period 2 finds,* XIV.42).

Cutting BB: Group XV

Layers from this group covered the entire length of the trench sealing the enigmatic ragstone foundation briefly described above. At the north end of the trench they appeared as banded loam layers separated in places by thin layers of black organic material. These may represent accumulations of surface water over a period of time. This was sealed by a layer of stones. At the south end of the trench, from over the masonry foundation southwards, the layers of this group consisted of black, stony layers mixed with tile fragments and gravel.

The recorded section was sealed by Victorian foundations, hardcore and the cement basement slab of 46–8 Mansion House Chambers.

Cutting F

The preceding section described in detail how the Walbrook stream channel was well maintained with timber revetments, except for one short period during the late second or early third century (Group V) (Figs 10, 23, 35 and 36). These were associated with horizontal timber platforms raised on piles driven into earlier layers made up of timber floor surfaces and artificial dumps of clean, quarried clay and brickearth, mixed material from made-up ground, and upcast material from the dredging and cleaning of the Walbrook channel itself. Small hut-like or shed-like buildings were set back from the stream edge, allowing the platforms themselves to act as walkways or working surfaces over the west bank of the stream.

The unstable nature of the ground, and perhaps over-vigorous cleaning of the stream channel, led to at least two collapses of the revetments. These caused the subsidence on a number of occasions of the horizontal platforms but these were soon raised and levelled.

However, at some time during the first half of the third century, a major collapse and landslip marked the end of this tradition, at least for the channel itself. From that moment onwards the channel was not well maintained even though regular maintenance of the west bank continued well into the fourth century. The stream bank was left unrevetted, no doubt causing considerable erosion of the bank, and the channel subsequently became choked with silt deposits and, occasionally, intentionally dumped debris.

As discussed above, this change in the treatment of the stream channel probably occurred shortly before the temple was constructed, but since so much of this phase occurred during the life of the Mithraeum, from the mid-third century onwards, it is discussed in detail below.

Cutting F: Group XIII

Towards the western end of the cutting, between the raised ragstone surface described above in Group VI and the point at which the platform had slumped, the extant horizontal surfaces of the platform had a series of north–south aligned horizontal beams and base-plates. The pile and base-plate which appeared to retain the Group VI dump, described above, probably belonged to this series. Indeed, the ragstone layer itself may have been associated with the earliest of these structures. This was one of only two of these groups of timbers which was recorded in any detail.

Figures 48 and 49 show the west bank at 4.6m OD. The ragstone spread is visible on the west side of the cutting with a single triangular pile driven into it. The north–south beam (A) visible in the section resting on a pile butts against this spread (Fig 36). Two similar beams (B and C) ran parallel with it *c* 1.85m to the east and two smaller timbers, one possibly a displaced pile (D), protruded from the south face of the section. All of these timbers lay on top of a long timber at least 5.75m in length (F). At first this appeared to be a plank but further excavation showed it to be at least 0.15m thick with chamfered sides, the narrowest face showing upwards. When turned over the timber was hollowed out for use as a drain or gutter. Though no longer functioning as such, the presence of this

Fig 48 Cutting F. Group XIII timbers with ragstone platform at the rear (Grimes)

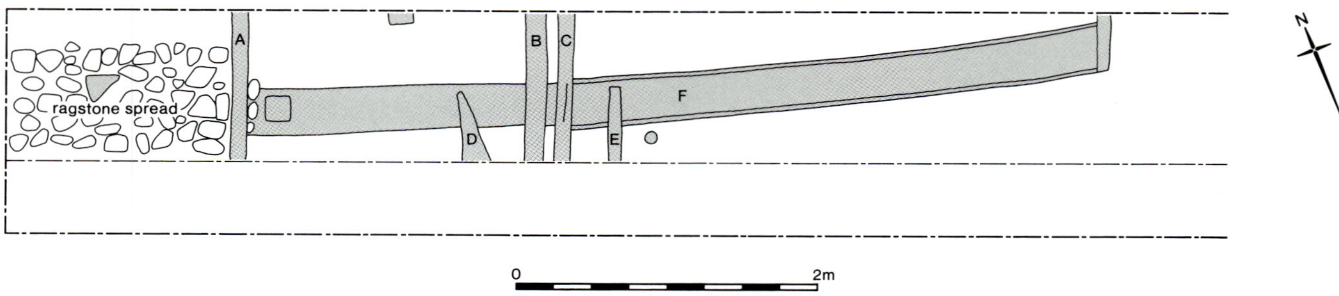

Fig 49 Cutting F. Plan showing Group XIII timbers and ragstone platform. Prepared from sketches in site notebooks

drain emphasises that drainage of the west bank was a constant consideration.

It is probable that these north–south beams, at *c* 2.4m apart, represented the west and east walls of a succession of narrow timber buildings. The coarse ragstone layer to their west might represent an external surface. To the east of these beams, between the easternmost beam and the channel of the stream, there was simply a succession of at least eight superimposed plank and clay floors. These, it can be suggested, were working or treading surfaces in front of the narrow wooden shed or hut-like buildings. These surfaces led directly to the unrevetted Walbrook stream.

Other reused timbers were noted in a second, well recorded group of timbers. Figure 50 shows the west bank at 4.8m OD. The ragstone spread had been covered over by a layer of grey clay which sloped from the north to the south. On this were set two timbers aligned east to west (A and B). Timber A curved north towards the north side of the cutting. A loose sandy fill lay between them. It is possible that these too represented a drain flowing into the Walbrook. At the east end of this group of timbers were a number of squared piles. Protruding from the south face of the cutting, and resting upon piles, were three planks (C, D and E). One of these had a rectangular tenon cut into it.

It would appear that this time the shed-like buildings had been dismantled and the ragstone surface covered over. Nevertheless, the bank was still maintained and boarded over to facilitate access to the stream and to provide a stable working surface.

While these floor surfaces were in use, the Walbrook itself, in an unrevetted channel, silted rapidly. At the start of the period represented by Group XIII the stream channel was *c* 1.8–2.4 m deep. At its close it was scarcely more than 0.6–0.9m deep. This in itself was probably one reason for raising so often the surface level of the west bank. The filling of the channel most probably led to occasional flooding.

At the base of the Group XIII channel deposits was a lens of almost stoneless silt. This rested directly on the earlier Group XII channel fill. F736, F738, F757 and F758 came from a 1.2m-thick layer of coarse silt with gravel, oyster shell, stone, tile and other debris, which was deposited on top of this layer. The nature of much of this particular fill would suggest that it had been deliberately dumped into the stream. Above this was a 0.45m layer of mixed silt with lenses of clay and gravel. Among this layer were two large planks, one 2.4m wide, the other 1.8m wide. The source of these planks is not clear, but they do rest immediately above the collapsed Group VI revetment. They may have been part of a revetment superstructure at this point. This, however, cannot now be confirmed. It is of course possible that they came from one of the many timber structures on the west bank of the stream.

Cutting F: Group XV

The layers in Group XV continued the sequence seen in previous periods on the west bank of the stream, namely a succession of timber platforms consisting of timber piles and horizontal planks. There are two immediately apparent differences. First, whereas the Group XIII deposits described above contained up to eight individual timber surfaces measuring 1m thick, the Group XV deposits were made up of, at the most, just three surfaces in a similar thickness of build-up.

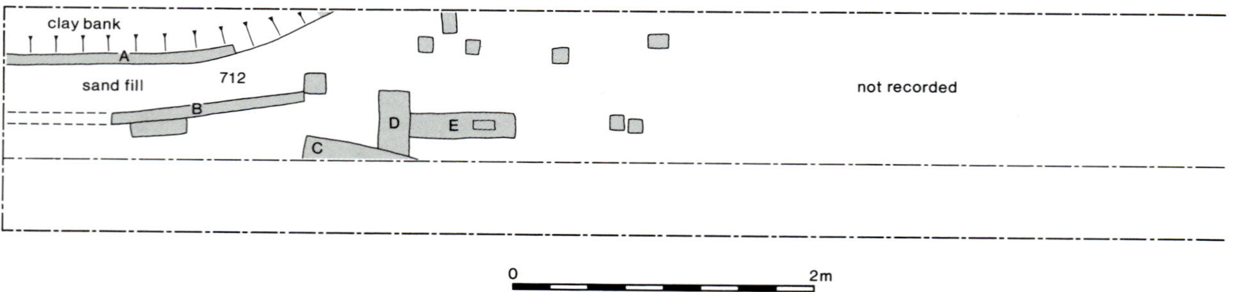

Fig 50 Cutting F. Plan showing Group XIII timbers. Prepared from sketches in site notebooks

Each of the three surfaces was described as spreads of decayed wood and horizons of stones on a make-up of clean clay. Secondly, fewer piles were used and the timber planking where present had decayed. Whether this indicates that the conditions were drier in antiquity or have dried since cannot be determined.

The stream bank itself had, by this time, become very unstable. All of the earlier revetments had long since disappeared from view and the maximum depth of the channel was probably never more than 0.9m. Also, the bank showed signs of eroding so badly that the width of the channel at the top began to increase while the depth became reduced. Whereas the west side of the channel was *c* 2.15m from the east end of the cutting at the time of the Group VI revetment, the lip of the eroded bank of Group XV was *c* 2.75m to 3m from the same point.

Probably as a result of the erosion of the unstable banks, the channel filled rapidly with mixed dark coarse-grained loam, gravel, small stones, oyster shells and bone. Much of this material may have been intentionally discarded into the channel.

The Group XV deposits were the latest identified by the excavator in Cutting F for which detailed records have survived. The top of this group coincided approximately with the lowest level of the 1952 excavations when this cutting was first opened. The section drawing of 1954, however, shows a further 0.6m of stratigraphy described as mixed loam, dark coarse grained and containing bits of clay and stones. It was 'vaguely stratified'. All of the surviving pottery groups from this layer contained only pottery of Roman date but none included more than a few abraded sherds.

The stream channels contemporary with these accumulations over the west bank indicated that the course of the stream was erratic. The succession of dark loam lenses with profiles indicating settlement into channels, separated by thicker bands of coarse gravel and silt, tended to meander from east to west and back again. This erratic course followed the thick silting of the channel during the period represented by the Group XV deposits.

Eventually it would appear that the course of the stream channel settled in one place with its central axis coinciding almost exactly with the extreme east end of the cutting. Here three distinct lenses of dark coarse loam banded with thin layers of yellow silty sand completed the long succession of Walbrook stream channels sealed beneath the basement slab of No 8 Walbrook. Considering their levels relative to the late Roman deposits, it is probable that these represented the course of the early medieval stream.

Finally, at an unspecified date, a pit was dug into the extreme west end of the cutting from a level higher than the very top of stratified deposits to a depth of 1.5m. It was intentionally backfilled with a *c* 0.3m plug of dense dark chocolate-coloured clay.

Modern building debris, hard core and the basement slab completed the section of Cutting F.

The temple on the east bank from *c* AD 240–250

Cuttings CA, CB, CD and CE

The pre-temple topography, modern intrusions into the temple, the construction of the temple and its fabric, the main alterations to the interior layout and the succession of floors in the nave are described below (Figs 10, 11 and 23). The sources for this section are varied and are as follows:

- **modern intrusions:** information here has come from contractors, die-line drawings, excavator's photographs and site notebook entries, and Ministry of Works survey notes, drawings and scale model
- **pre-temple topography:** information from manuscript notes by the excavators, site notebook entries and other site documentation
- **the construction and fabric of the temple:** information from numerous sources, in particular Grimes 1968, unpublished lectures by Williams, site notebooks and other documentation, photographs, and the Ministry of Works survey notes, plan, elevation drawings and scale model
- **a description of the temple in its original (Phase I) form:** information here has come from published and unpublished material by both Grimes and Williams
- **the five main phases of the temple:** information from Grimes 1968, unpublished lectures by Williams and Grimes, site notebooks and other site documentation, draft texts on the floor sequence by Grimes, unpublished research notes by Grimes and Williams
- **the narthex:** information from site notebooks and other site documentation

There are some areas of the temple for which details of the archaeological sequence are very poor. The details for the original aisles in the first phase are reasonably comprehensive (see *The Phase I temple: internal details*, below) but the later sequence contemporary with Floors 2–4, before the aisles and nave became one, are sparse: only individual elements such as timbers or piles were noted in detail. This was, in part, due to the difficulties of excavating these areas late in the excavation. The removal of the modern intrusions at this time affected especially the areas of the aisles.

In order to allow the reader to differentiate the Roman from later masonry in the illustrations and photographs which accompany the following text, the modern intrusions are described in some detail. These accounted for the flat nature of the remains of the temple and the absence of any medieval occupation on the site, except for the well on the south side of the building. The easternmost of three deep foundations which cut into the floor surfaces in the north part of the nave was the probable findspot for three sculptures discovered in 1889 (*Chapter 5, The finds catalogue, Period 2 finds, IX.44, 45 and 46:* see *Modern disturbance of the temple*, below).

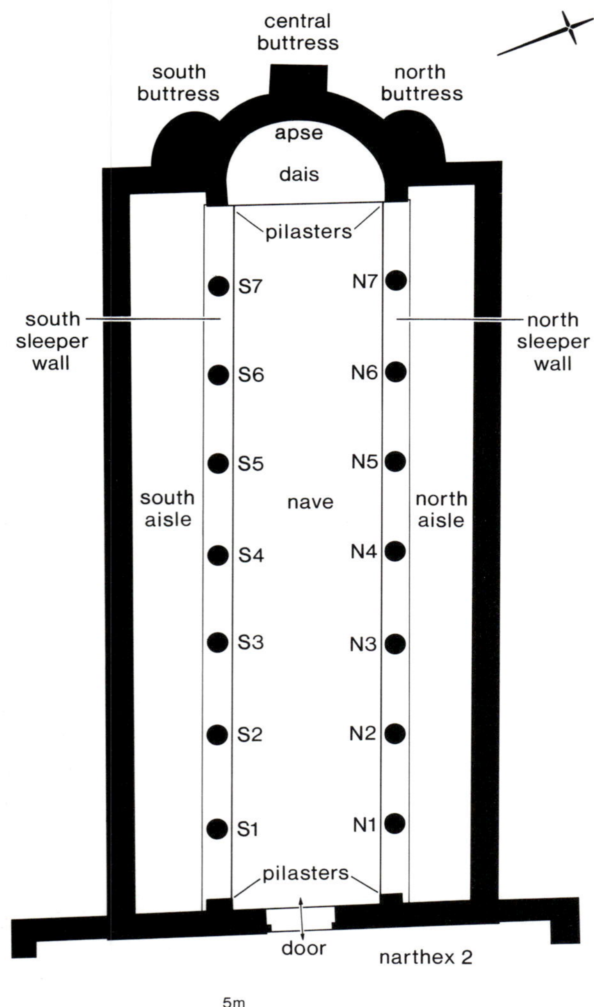

Fig 51 Terms used in this report

Figure 51 shows the main terms used throughout the following descriptions of the temple, its construction and internal alterations. Figures 62 and 90 locate the elevation drawings and section drawings respectively.

Modern disturbance of the temple

The temple lay immediately beneath the foundations and basement slabs of 7–9 Walbrook (Fig 52). The north wall of No 9 Walbrook overlay the south aisle of the temple and a central load-bearing wall of 7–8 Walbrook was located on the north side of it, just resting upon the north edge of the north wall. A north–south aligned load-bearing wall in the same property passed over the north aisle and the nave at the east end of the temple to connect with the north wall of No 9 Walbrook. A similar wall crossed the north aisle and the nave approximately halfway along the length of the temple.

All of the basements were of a single depth and no doubt the excavations for these in the Victorian period had removed much post-Roman stratigraphy. They had certainly truncated the tops of the Mithraeum walls. This accounted for the flat appearance of the extant remains of the building (Fig 53). The original heights of the walls before their truncation are therefore not known. It is probable, though, that the temple stood as an open ruin for a considerable time after its abandonment.

Only one post-Roman feature not associated with the Victorian buildings had cut into the building. This was a well which was in use during the post-medieval period. Its lowest fill included wire mesh and other post-medieval debris, the nature of which was not specified by the excavators (Figs 54 and 55). This material was probably thrown into the well during one of the post-medieval building-programmes on the site. The well itself, however, was probably of late medieval date and is of a type which has often been recorded in the City of London. It consisted of four courses of squared chalk blocks resting upon a ring of timber. The maximum height of the well, from the base of the timber ring to the extant height, truncated by the Victorian basements, was *c* 0.75m. Its construction shaft cut into the south face of the south wall of the temple and penetrated through the thickness of the wall. Due to its circular shape, only a very small part of the interior face of the south wall was destroyed.

The most serious damage to the temple and the deposits associated with it, however, was caused by the stanchion foundations for the load-bearing walls briefly described above (see Figs 53 and 55).

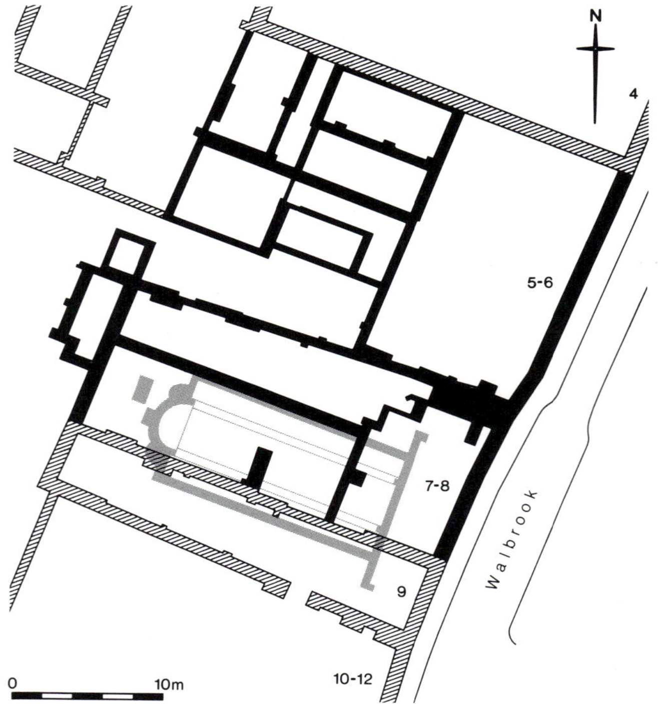

Fig 52 Modern (Victorian) foundations over the temple. Those in black belong to the 1889 redevelopment

Fig 53 General view of the temple looking west (Grimes)

The northern wall of No 9 Walbrook had two deep foundations which destroyed part of the temple superstructure. The first, at the west end, cut into the apse, the south buttress, and the west face of the west wall of the temple (Fig 55, A). The second was a deep stepped foundation which penetrated deep into the Roman stratigraphy at the east end of the south aisle (Fig 55, B). This foundation was not removed until very late in the excavation. Its removal disturbed any stratified remains beneath it, thus accounting for the lack of information for the south-east corner of the building.

The central east–west load-bearing wall of 7–8 Walbrook rested upon four deep foundations. At the west end, a square stanchion cut into the north-west corner of the temple to a level *c* 0.6m above the Roman foundation level (Fig 55, C: see also elevations Figs 57 and 60). Alongside this to the east a long narrow foundation with a deep stanchion at its east end destroyed approximately 5m of the temple wall to a similar level (Fig 55, D). At the east end, two shallower foundations cut into the top of the wall by *c* 0.4–0.6m (Fig 55, E and F).

The load-bearing wall which crossed the temple halfway along its length rested upon part of the long foundation (Fig 55, D) which cut the north wall and a second foundation on the north side of the central axis of the nave (Fig 55, G). The latter cut into the top of the Roman floor sequence. Its depth was not recorded. There was a small stanchion base to the east of this (Fig 55, H). It is not clear how this related to the building destroyed in 1941.

Two shallow drains disturbed the upper levels of the Roman layers in the building. At the north-east corner one truncated the external face of the northern wall of the narthex (Fig 55, I). The second passed right through the temple at a slight angle to its central axis (Fig 55, J). This cut into the south side of the north buttress and the apse wall and, fortunately, left the site of the building through the temple entrance.

Of particular importance here is the north–south load-bearing wall at the east end of the temple. This was supported on both deep and shallow foundations and formed the eastern limit of the excavations until the site was opened up for redevelopment during 1954. (See frontispiece. This photograph was taken before the wall in question had been demolished.) The shallow foundation joined the stepped foundation of No 9 Walbrook over the south aisle (Fig 55, K). The northernmost of these two penetrated deep into the Roman floor levels (Fig 55, L). This foundation was to the immediate west of the pit which contained three of the sculptures and it was here that the excavators in 1954 believed that sculptures had been found in 1889 (*Chapter 5, The finds catalogue, Period 2 finds, IX.44, 45 and 46*).

In 1889 these sculptures came into the possession of a London dealer, James Smith, who claimed that they had been found in that year near the middle of the Walbrook, near Bond Court (on the east side of Walbrook), 'at a time when deep sewage works were in progress'. Mr Smith had sold these sculptures soon after their discovery to Mr W Ransom of Hitchin, who ultimately donated them to the London Museum in 1915.

Fig 54 The medieval well on the south side of the temple (F F James)

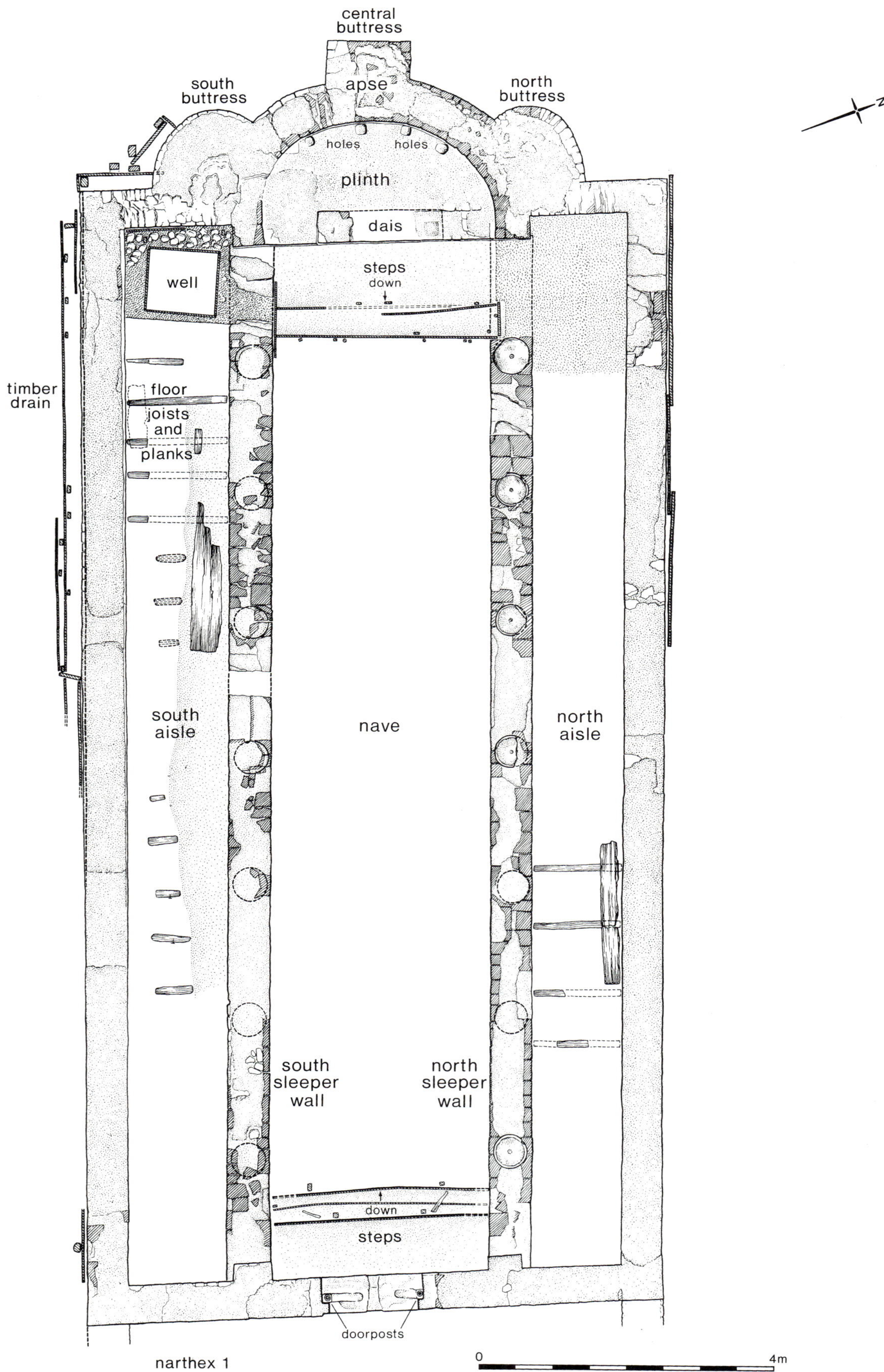

Fig 61 The Phase I temple, c *AD 240–50*

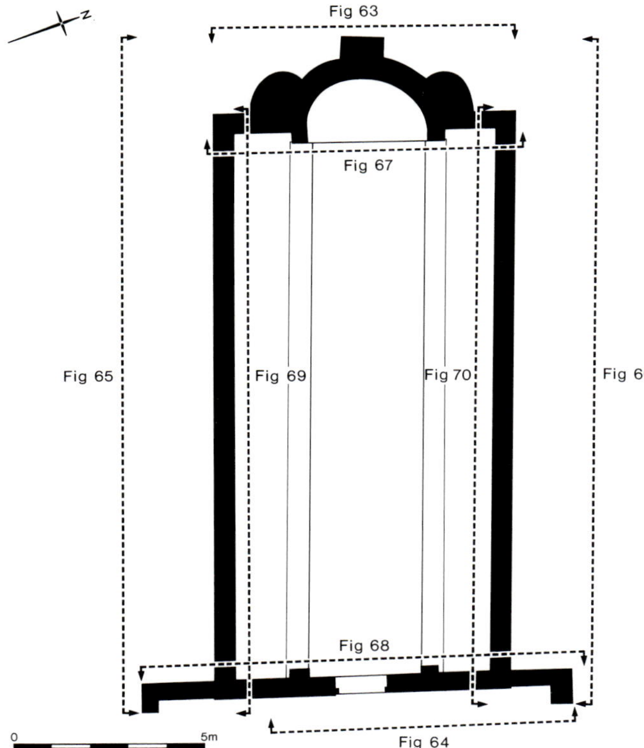

Fig 62 The location of the elevation drawings

IIb below) retained the build-up of floor surfaces (especially Floor 4) and not the build-up in the aisles.

In the following section, Grimes's text is indicated by his initials (WFG), Williams's by hers (AW). The cross-references and annotations in square brackets were inserted in 1995 to complement this report.

Figures 63–72 are edited elevations of the building. The positions of the elevations are shown on Figure 62. The originals were prepared by architects of the Ministry of Works.

The Walbrook Temple of Mithras: Phase I (Group VIII)

(WFG)...the main body of the temple (was) a rectangular building 58.5ft [17.83m] long by 26ft [7.84m] wide, entered from the east end, with a semi-circular apse or sanctuary at the west [Figs 61 and 73: see above, *The construction of the temple*]. The building was remarkably free from later disturbance; and though there had been some inevitable destruction not the least surprising feature of this aspect of the site was the way in which even modern foundations had not seriously damaged it [see above, *Modern disturbance of the temple*]... attached to the east end was a narrow room or narthex, the ends of which projected beyond the

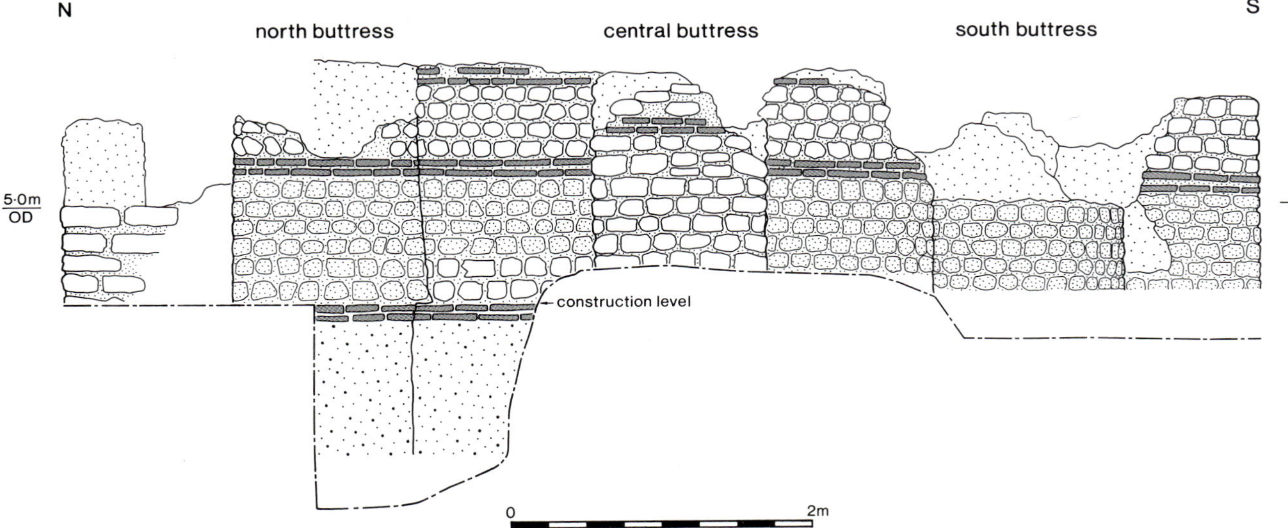

Fig 63 External elevation of the west end showing the west wall, apse and buttresses

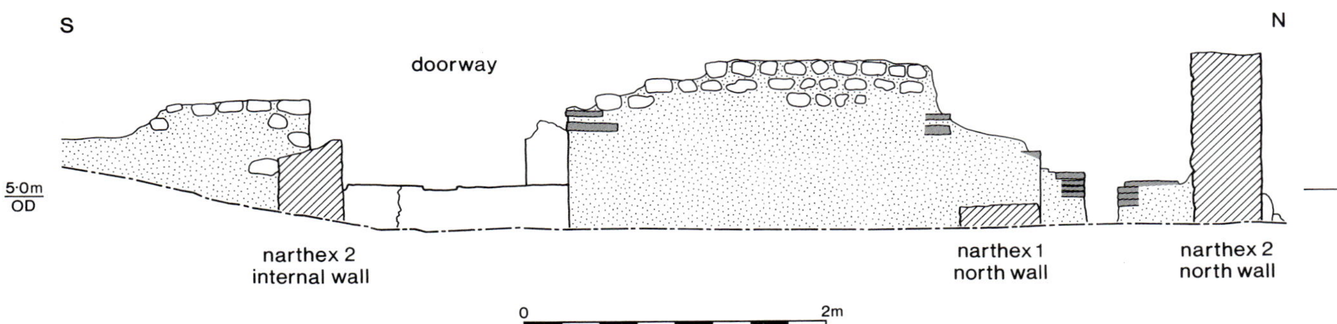

Fig 64 External elevation of the east wall with the internal face of narthex 2 on the right

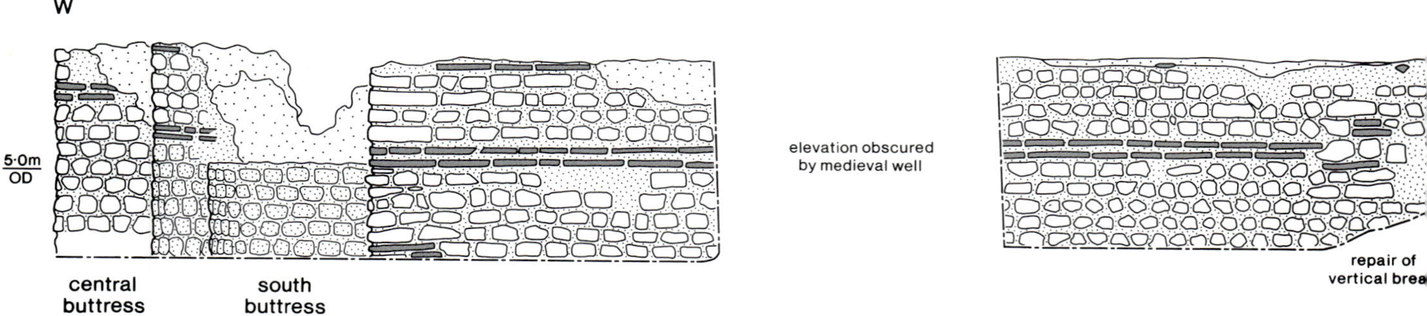

Fig 65 External elevation of the south wall

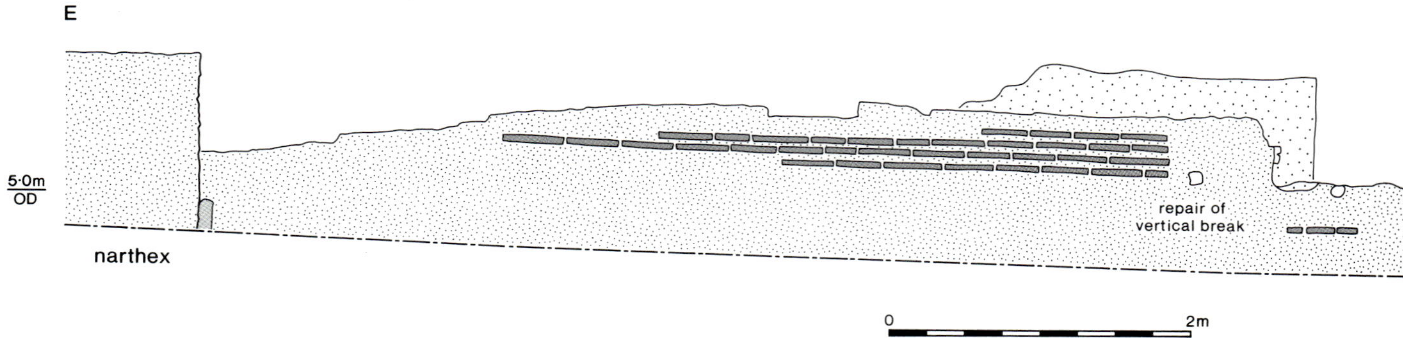

Fig 66 External elevation of the north wall

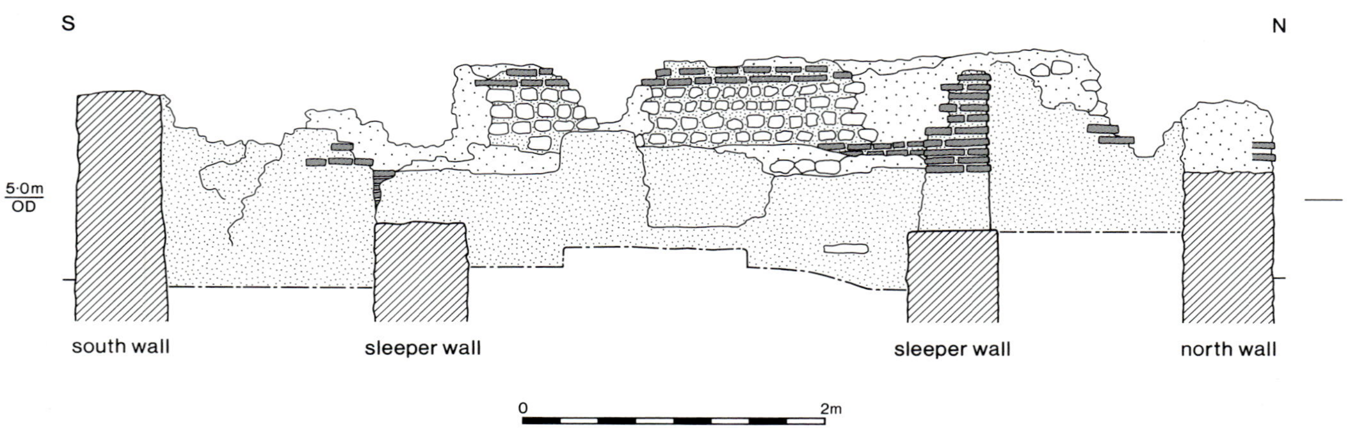

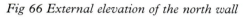

Fig 67 Internal elevation of the west end of the temple showing the west wall, the rear of the apse and the dais face

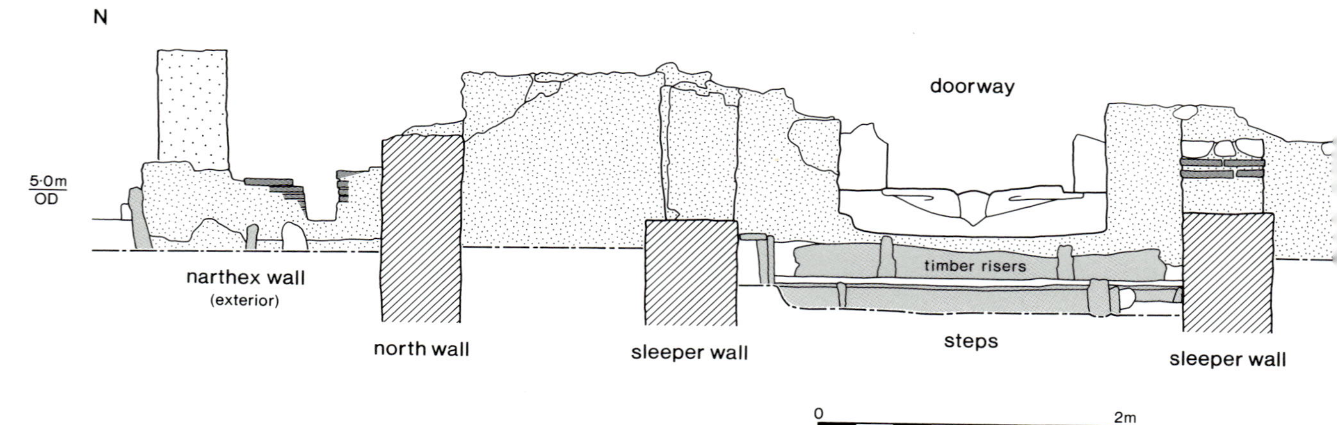

Fig 68 Internal elevation of the east end showing the external faces of narthex 2 on the left and right

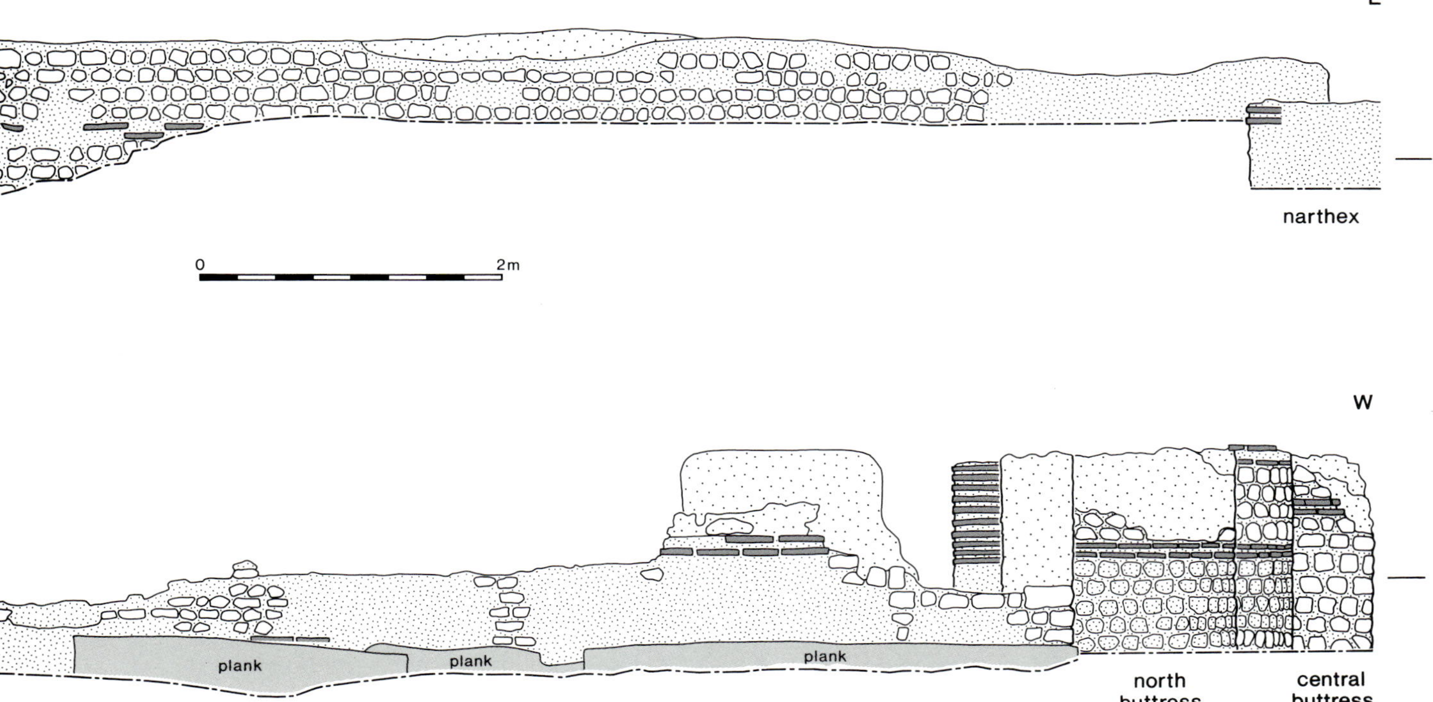

side-walls of the main building to give it an overall width of 36.5ft [11.12m]. The complete building would thus have been T-shaped in plan; but some part of the narthex lay — and still lies — under the modern street. Its full depth from front to back remains unknown [see above, *The specifications of the temple*].

(AW) (The walls of the temple) were of small squarish blocks of Kentish ragstone and well-coursed (Fig 74). Except at the west end they had no regular tile-courses, but short lengths of tilling occurred intermittently and the quoins were turned in tile. Any external plastering there may have been had perished — except at the west end and low down the walls above the foundation.

(WFG) Externally the most impressive feature of the building must have been the apse with its massive buttresses, themselves an indication of the unstable nature of the ground on which the temple had been built. The convex buttresses in the re-entrant angles of apse and west wall seen from the outside would have suggested that the temple had a triple apse; but the buttresses were solid [Figs 75 and 76, see *The construction of the temple*].

(AW) The buttresses and the apse still stood 6ft [1.82m] above the original building-level. They had regular tile courses and were faced with a pinkish mortar, particularly hard and impervious to water. These buttresses were not at first of one build with the apse wall [Fig 60]. To a height of nearly 3ft [0.91m] above the footings they had been carried up separately: above that they were bonded in [see above, *The construction of the temple*].

(WFG) Entrance to the temple by way of the narthex was through a double doorway, the original features of which were remarkably well-preserved [Figs 77 and 78]. The sill was a single block of stone making a double step down, with much-worn margins on the inner side. In the door rebates the sockets still retained the iron collars for the door-pivots. Immediately within the door, double steps downwards, their wooden risers in place, gave on to the sunken floor of the central body of the temple [see below, *The Phase I temple: internal details*].

(AW) Very little wood remained on their treads, just enough to indicate their having been boarded.

(WFG) Internally the building was revealed as of basilican plan, with nave and side-aisles defined by sleeper-walls which had carried the stone-columned arcades [Fig 79]: the positions of the columns were marked only by their settings; their number, seven aside, probably symbolised the seven grades of the cult [see above, *The construction of the temple*].

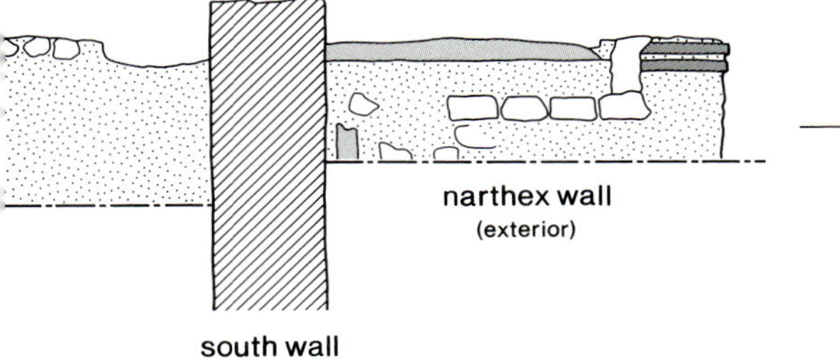

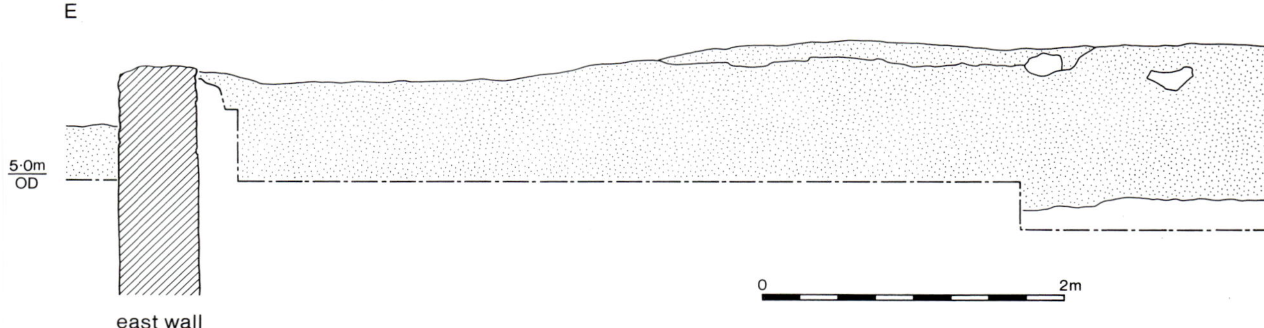

Fig 69 Internal elevation of the south wall

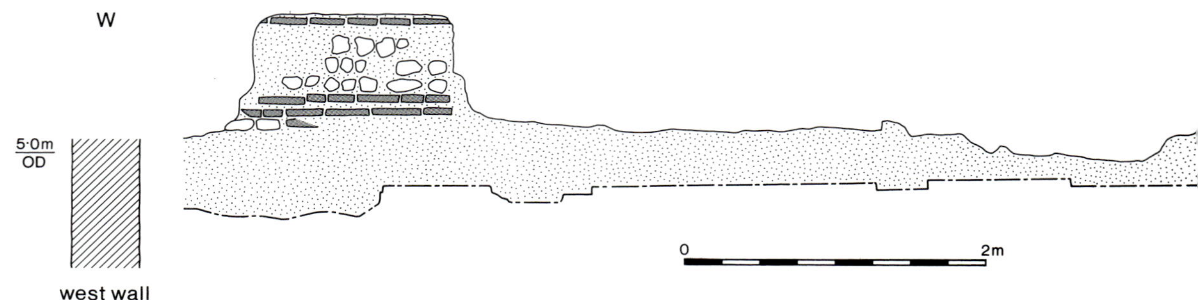

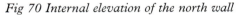

Fig 70 Internal elevation of the north wall

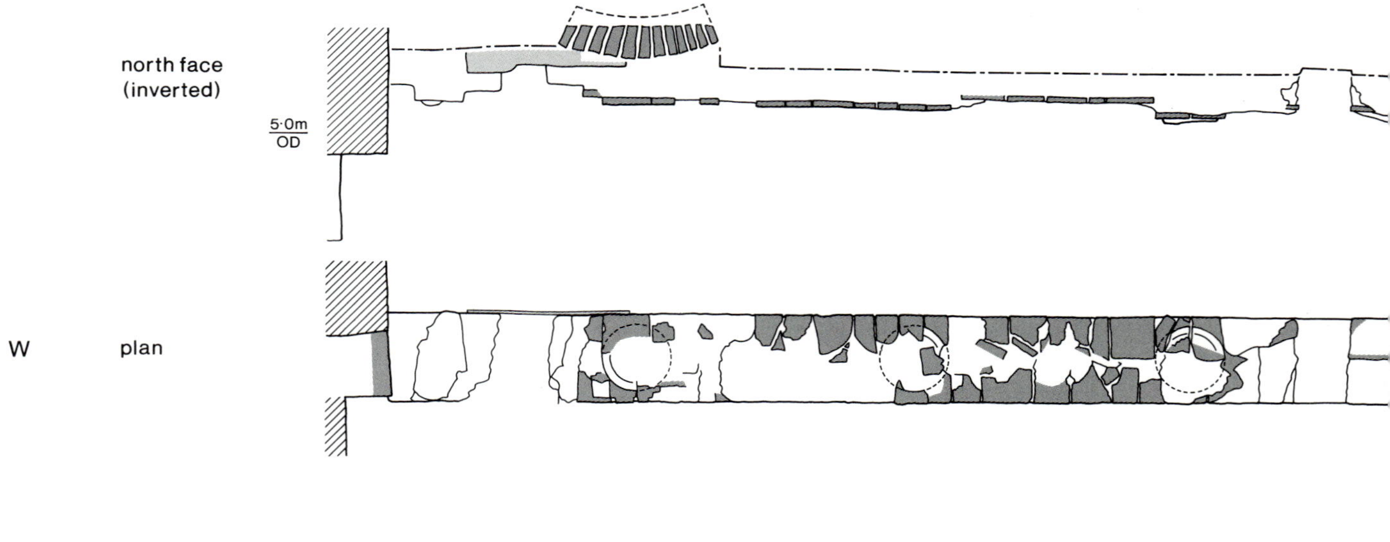

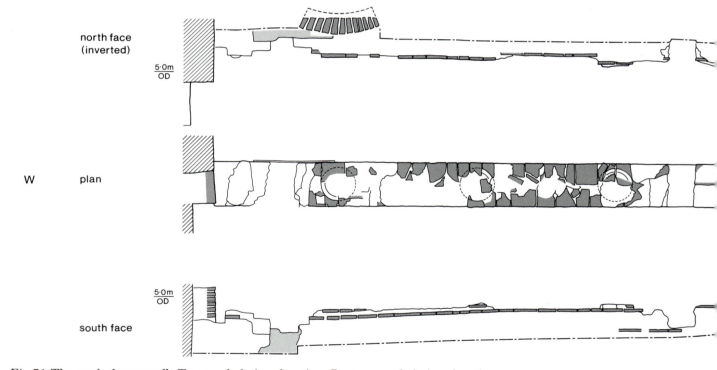

Fig 71 The south sleeper-wall. Top: north-facing elevation. Bottom: south-facing elevation

(AW) The column pads [settings] looked like round platters with straight sides. Made of pinkish concrete they were roughly 18in [0.45m] in diameter: and each had a central boss or dowel [Figs 80 and 81]. Part of one column base was found lying on its side on one of these settings [Fig 82].

(WFG) There were indications that the [first] floor of the nave had originally been boarded, though the one or two boards which survived were no longer in their original positions. The aisle floors were at a higher level, and here the signs of timber fittings were more definite. On both north and south transverse joists supporting occasional planks had survived; and there were vertical earth-set uprights also which might have carried fixed benches [Figs 83 and 84: see below, *The Phase I temple: internal details*].

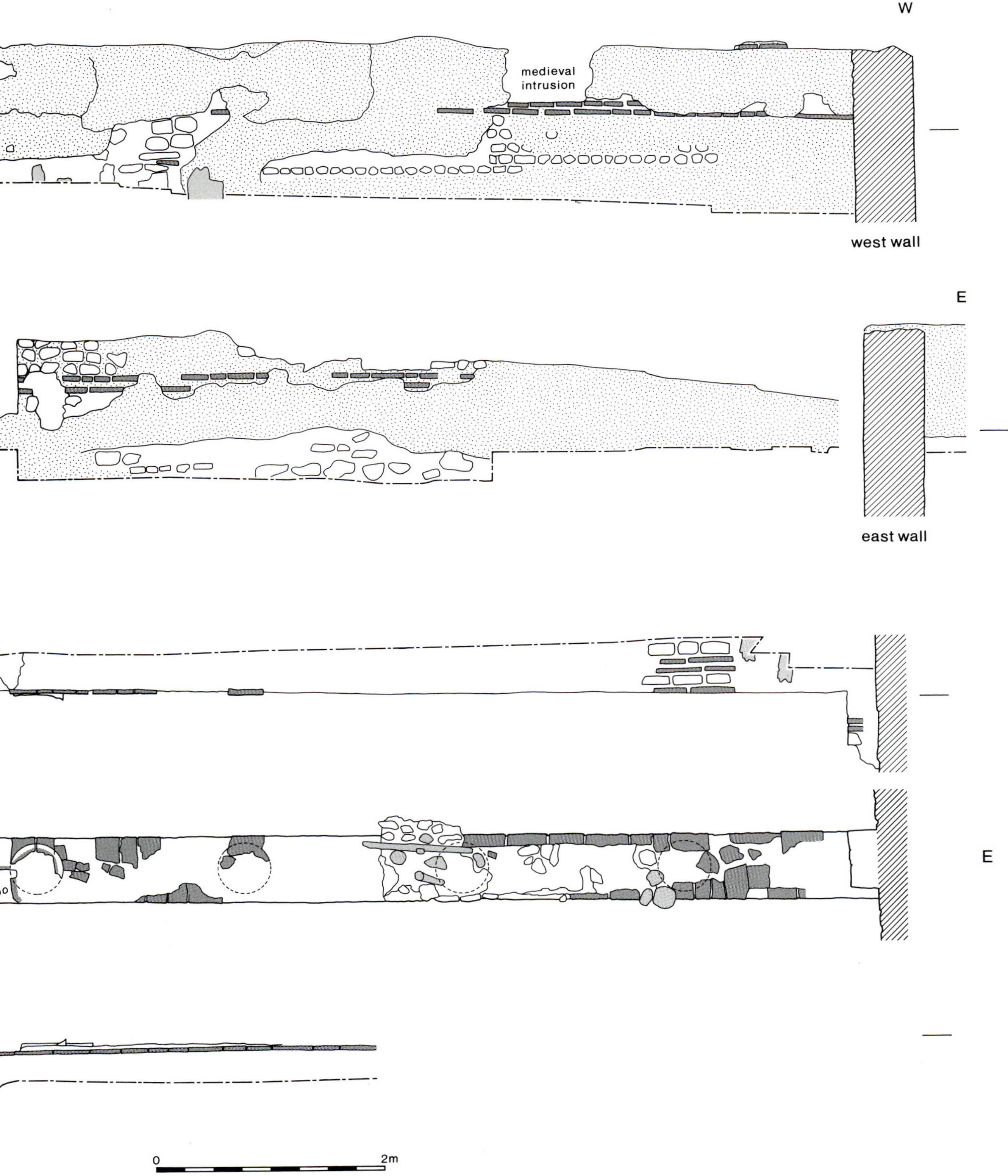

Such equipment was a normal part of the aisles of a mithraeum, since on them members of the community would have gathered to witness the ritual performed before the altars at the west end.

(AW) Two of these timbers [in the south aisle] had a nail driven into them from the side. Between the slots and the sleeper wall was a mortary floor. All this suggested wooden bench supports, with a passage left between the benches and the colonnade. [See Figures 61, 83 and 84.]

While the mortar floor continued westwards the slots were in that direction, replaced by joists which overlay the passage floor. They sloped slightly from the bottom of the rendering on the sleeper-wall to the base of the plaster on the outer wall. This meant that the wooden floor of the aisle lay 9in [0.22m] below

Fig 75 Multi-phase view of the west end

Fig 77 The Phase I entrance and steps (Grimes)

Fig 76 Detail of the apse wall and the central buttress (Grimes)

Fig 78 Detail of the Phase I entrance (Grimes)

used in the rest of the building and had evidently been decorated — though only one black stripe on a cream ground survived. It is suggested [in 1955] that the plinth carried a pair of slender columns supporting an epistyle or architrave from which would hang curtains intended to conceal the shrine. The upper part of a column of equal size was discovered among building rubbish outside the temple [It is probable that the plinth was the base of the main Mithras Tauroctonos scene. It is also probable that the recess in the face of the dais originally contained the Ulpius Silvanus Mithras Tauroctonos relief as, perhaps, a dedicatory stone]. A small gap had been left on either side of the plinth [on the dais] to allow access to the shrine. Against the wall of the apse were four small holes, uniform in size and shape and more or less evenly spaced out [Figs 61 and 75]. They may have held posts supporting some additional furnishing of the shrine or, perhaps, ritual vessels.

(WFG) Finally, in the south-west corner beside the apse was the shallow timber-lined well which through the early years of the temple's history provided the water required for ritual purposes [see below, *The Phase I temple: internal details*].

(AW) The well had been most carefully constructed and set in a hole big enough to allow for it to be packed with impervious clay [Fig 87]. There may have been an earlier way of providing a water supply for the sanctuary. This was suggested by a cut through the sleeper-wall near the well, and at the same point in the north sleeper wall [Fig 88]. Nothing survived to show the nature of this feature.

Fig 79 The south sleeper-wall between columns S2 (top right) and S6 (bottom left). Note the channel cut between columns S3 and S4 (RMLEC)

Fig 81 Column pad N7 (Grimes)

Fig 80 Column pad N6 (Grimes)

Fig 82 Column pad N7 before the removal of the only surviving piece of original column base from the site (see Chapter 5, The finds catalogue, Period 2 finds, VIII.43) *(Grimes)*

(WFG) But the building did not retain its original basilican features: long before the end of its useful life it had undergone many changes which in part at least were a reflection of the local ground conditions. The wet nature of the site must from the first have given trouble with standing water. The floor-level, first of the nave, then of the body of the temple as a whole, was gradually lifted through a succession of surfaces [Fig 89]. The final result was to raise the general level to that of the apse (a matter of about 3ft 4in [1m] above the original surface of the nave); but the changes were not carried out at the same rate everywhere because different parts of the building had their own special functions to fulfil and were therefore treated differently. There were nine successive floors in all in the nave, and before the last had been reached the door-sill had already been covered, making necessary a different arrangement for working the doors, with a wooden frame taking the place of the original socket-and-pivot device. [For the changes to the interior layout of the temple see below, *The Phase IIa temple, The Phase IIb temple, The Phase III temple, The Phase IV temple.*]

The internal sequence of the Phase I temple: nave floors 1–9

The main Phase I temple plan was to alter very little during the life of the building. It is possible that this may be of significance in the interpretation of the building because it would appear that it was a perfectly planned mithraeum from the outset. Within the building, however, many alterations were to take

Fig 83 Detail of the Phase I south aisle with the well at the west end. Note the channel cut between columns S3 and S4 (Grimes)

Fig 84 General view of the east end of the south aisle during Phase I showing timber bench settings (Grimes)

Fig 85 Cutting CA in 1952-3 showing the two Phase I steps at the base of the trench (Grimes)

place which were to transform entirely the character of the building. The most important of these, and the best recorded, were the nine superimposed floor surfaces. Indeed, it may be argued that the alterations could have encouraged the change in function of the building, changing it from a model mithraeum into a standard hall.

Below are set out the details of these internal alterations beginning with a description of the Phase I internal layout. This is followed by similar commentaries for the four other discernible phases of the temple, IIa, IIb, III and IV. The framework for the following descriptions comes from an unpublished preparatory text compiled by Grimes and Williams soon after the completion of the excavation. This contains, in the form of a later outline draft, additions and amendments by Grimes alone making use of information produced by the detailed study of the finds by his research assistants. To this has been added (in 1995) data and information from the many unprocessed records and research notes kept in the Grimes London Archive.

Attention is drawn to Figures 91–6 which locate the floor levels and the relative locations of the numbered finds groups referred to in this report. The positions of these sections are located on Figure 90. It should be pointed out that north-facing sections in the temple (Figs 91–2) have been reversed to place west on the left. (Compare the frontispiece, Figs 12 and 41.)

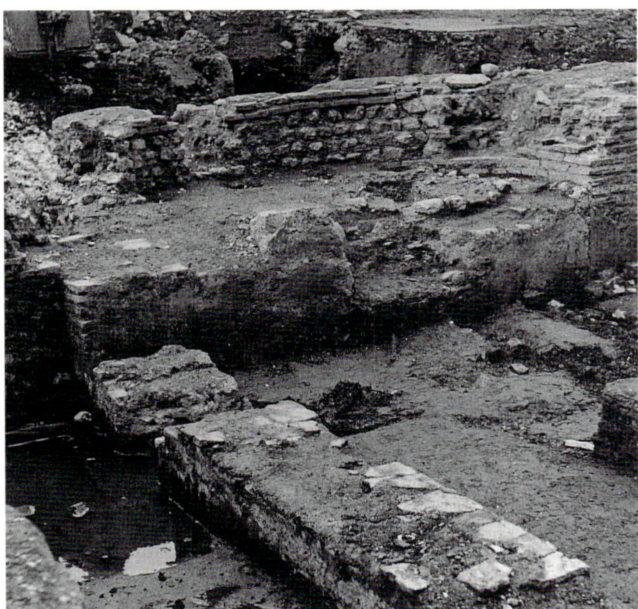

Fig 86 Detail of the apse and the dais at the end of the excavation. The Phase I steps have been removed. Note the relieving arches just visible in the sleeper walls, the hole in the face of the dais and the remains of the plinth above it (Grimes)

Fig 87 The Phase I timber well in the south-west corner of the temple. Note the stone packing or tumble at the rear (Grimes)

The Phase I temple: internal details (Group VIII)

The aisles

The general description of the aisles and their timber fittings is given above (Figs 61, 83 and 84), but it should also be noted that the well in the south-west corner and the cuts through the sleeper-walls described by Grimes and Williams above in connection with the water supply coincided with that part of the site which originally had a water channel or drain passing north–south through the site in the pre-temple Group VII phase. This feature probably dictated the need for the relieving arches in the sleeper-walls. It is possible that an earlier water supply to this area was adapted for use in the temple.

The nave

Floor 1

The original surface of the nave, at *c* 4.3m OD, coincided with the lower layers of the bottom steps at both east and west, and with the bottom of the plaster rendering on the inner face of the colonnade sleeper-walls (Figs 93–6).The floor itself had not survived, but may well have been of timber, since a number of pieces of boarding were lying on it, though none in an undisturbed position. The material beneath the floor was very mixed (CB319). This had been dumped into the hollow caused by subsidence of the Group VII channel. A large pine cone (*Chapter 5, The finds catalogue, Period 2 finds, VIII.54,* (CB361)) was found on this floor in the south-east corner of the nave.

Fig 88 The Phase I timber well showing the timber-lined channel cutting through the south sleeper-wall. Note the crack in the wall behind the well caused by the later subsidence of this part of the building (Grimes)

It has already been seen that the mixed deposits which made up this level, and into which the offset of the apse foundation had been set, were of the first half of the third century. The much worn *sestertius* of Hadrian (coin no 3: CA156) is consistent with such a date, which provides a *terminus post quem* for the first building of the temple.

For the building itself datable material came from the filling of the western steps (CA198 and CA199), from the base (CA146, CA153, CA154 and CA193) and from the mixed loamy filling that made up the body of the steps within the risers. The pottery from these

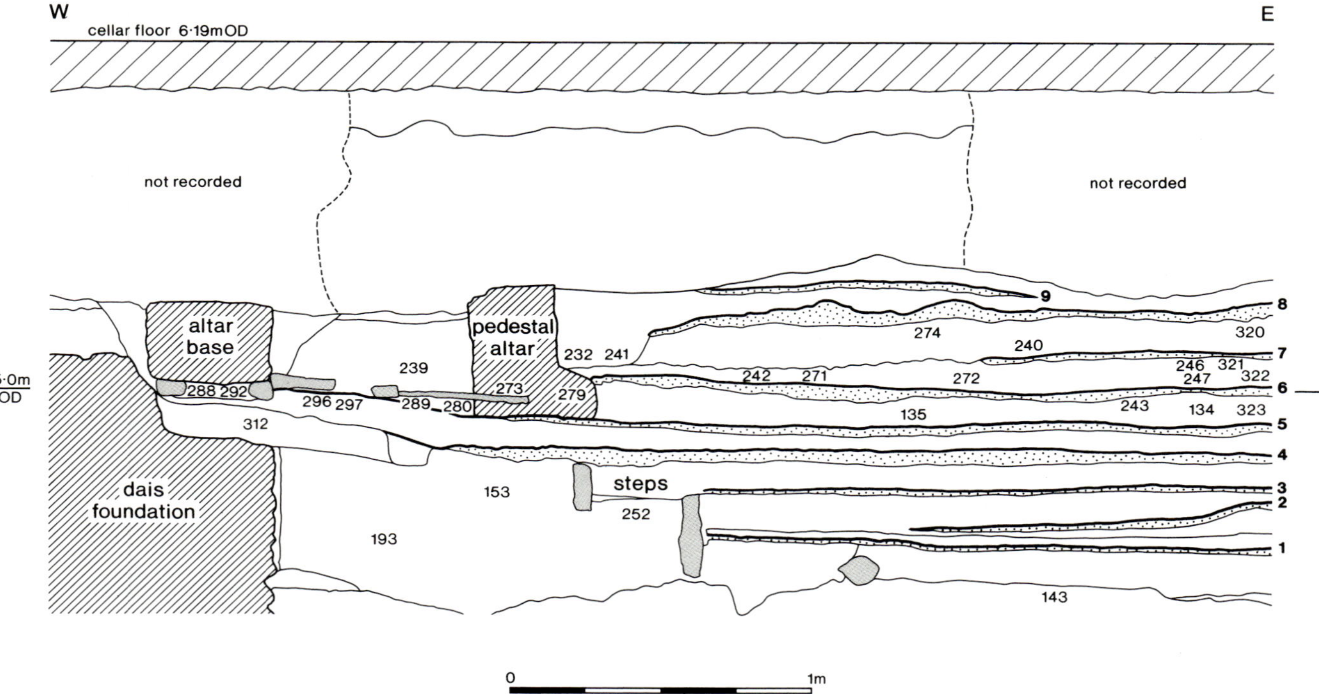

Fig 95 Cutting CA. Details of floors in the west end of the temple. Interpretive drawing

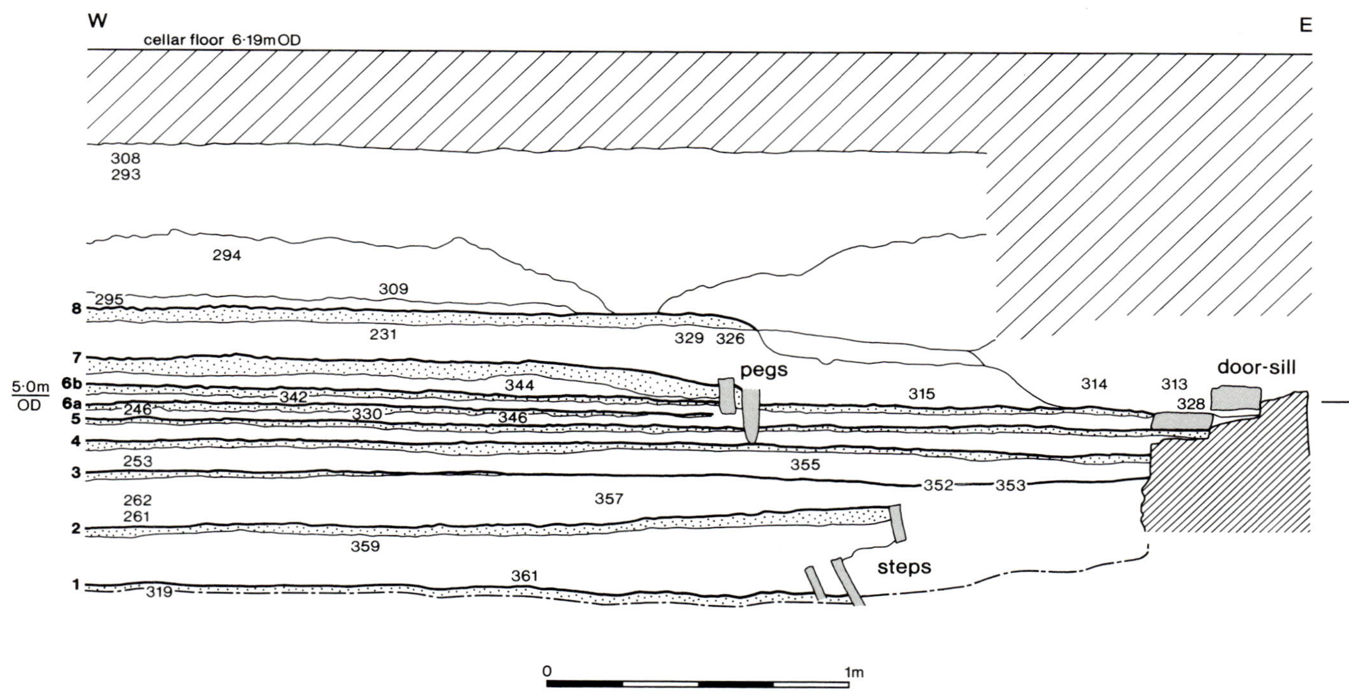

Fig 96 Cutting CB. Detail of floors in the east end of the temple. Interpretive drawing

A coin of Marius, who ruled briefly in AD 268 (coin no 6, CB355), also from the floor surface, provides an approximation to a fixed point. The pottery from below the floor, in the make-up (CB262, CB357, and from the top of Floor 2 CB261), from the floor itself (CB352, CB353), and from above it, in the filling of Floor 4 (CB253), should be viewed in relation to it. In fact, the general range of types is very similar through all this series, with forms which first appear in the late second century and continue apparently with little change, but there is a growing number of types which become common from the late second century onwards as well as some which more positively belong to the second half of the third century. Taken in conjunction with the coin they suggest a date for Floor 3 of *c* AD 280.

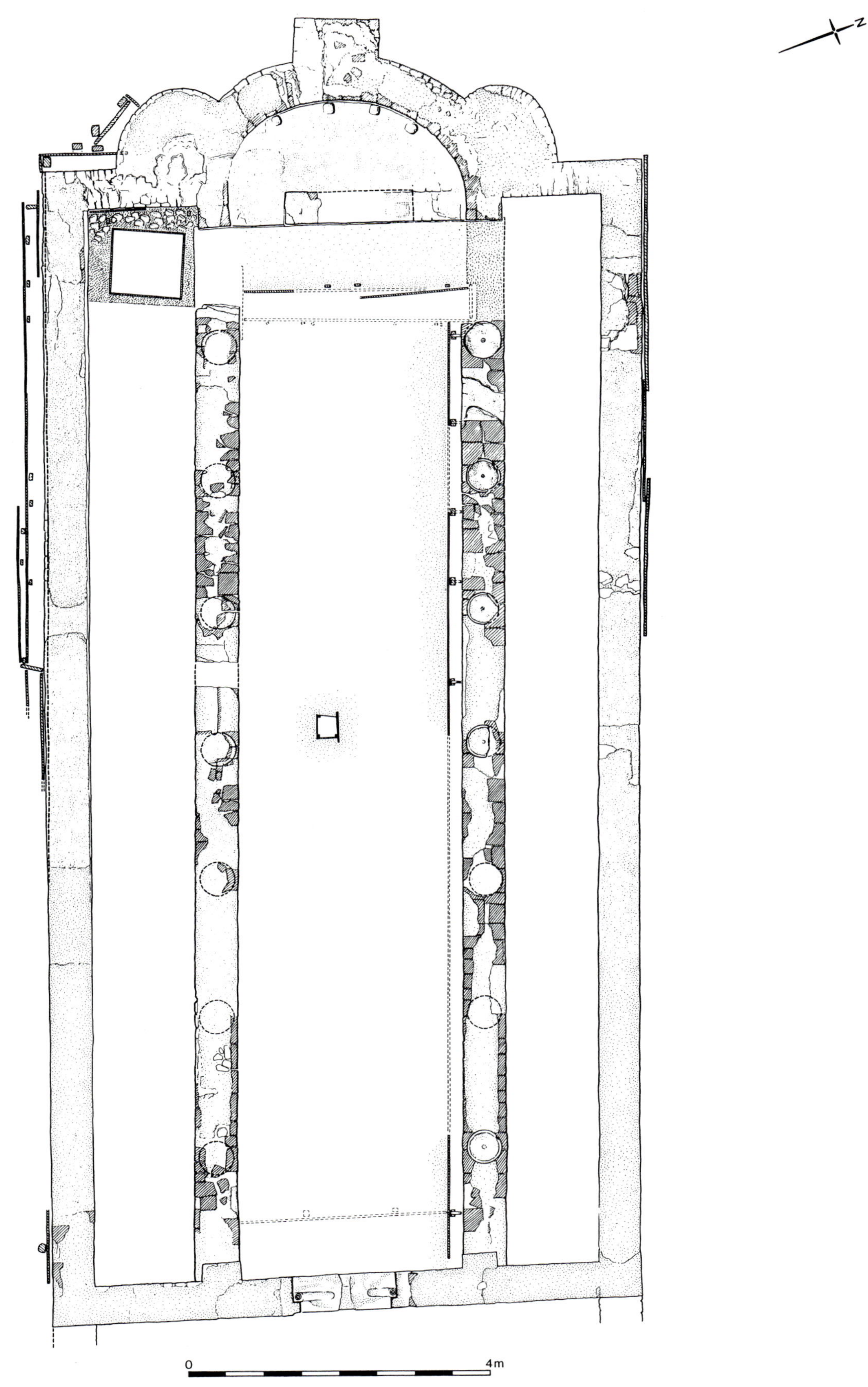

Fig 97 The Phase IIa temple

Fig 98 Floor 3 with the wooden channel cutting the Phase I entrance steps alongside the north sleeper-wall (Grimes)

Fig 99 Detail of the wooden drain near column pad N1 (Grimes)

Phase IIb temple: internal details

See Figure 100.

Floor 4

Floor 4 was about 0.1m above Floor 3 (Figs 93–6). It was made of yellow clay and mortar, 0.05m thick at the west end, rather thinner to the east, where it faded to a greyer colour. The floor overlay a loamy filling containing horizontal layers (CB253), interlocking in places, which appeared to be surfaces rather than structural floors. At the east end Floor 4 was about 0.08m below the lower ledge of the stone door-sill. To the west it rose over the upper step to end slightly below a 'pad' of grey loamy material which projected from a rough recess cut into the face of the apse apparently at this time.

With the laying of Floor 4 the nave acquired a one-level floor, with the steps finally eliminated at the west as well as at the east end. Also at this time, the nave floor became higher than the tops of the sleeper walls, thus requiring the addition of squat retaining walls between the columns. This feature is described in association with Floor 5 and the removal of the colonnade below.

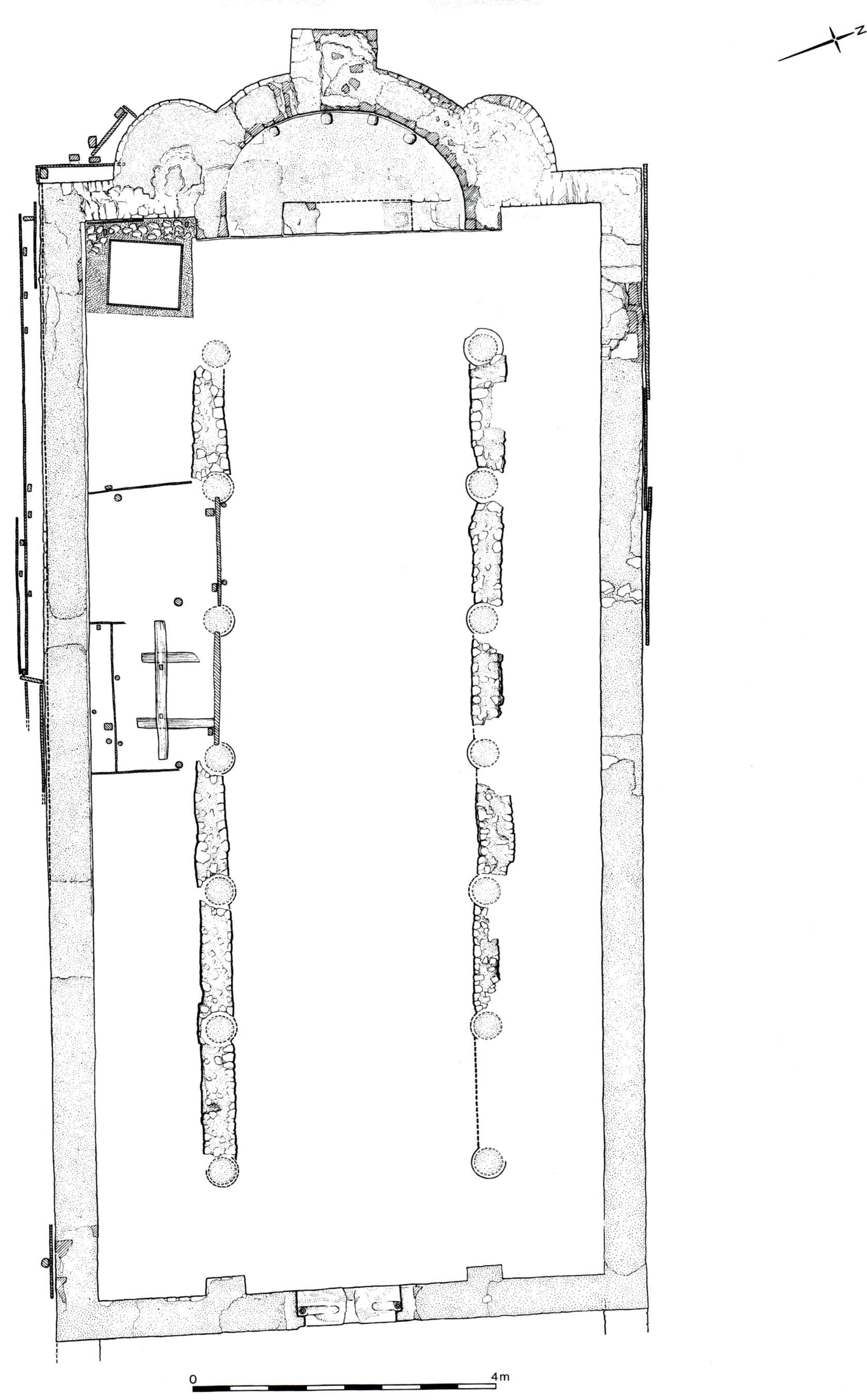

Fig 100 The Phase IIb temple

At the same time there were what appear to have been major changes in the apse arrangements. While Floor 4 was in use, before Floor 5 had been laid, a recess was created in the face of the dais. Crude as it was, it is possible to suggest that it was used to take an altar or cult base, as happened late in the floor sequence (see below, Floor 8). However, it is possible that this hole originated as a result of the removal of the Ulpius Silvanus Mithras Tauroctonos relief (*Chapter 5, The finds catalogue, Period 2 finds, IX.46;* Figs 196-200) which, though not as deep, is approximately the same size as this hole. The positioning of small reliefs, usually dedicatory, in such positions in front of the main cult scene is known elsewhere, eg Dura Europos (Rostovtzeff *et al* 1939). The recess may therefore not have been made to take an altar but may have been utilised following the removal of the Tauroctonos relief.

The effect of this change on the original arrangements in the face of the dais is probably closely related to the changes in the dais area which accompanied the use of the next floor (Floor 5). This included the setting up of at least one curious altar or pedestal, possibly part of a canopy. It was also into this floor that the sculptures including the Mithras Tauroctonos relief, if the theory suggested above is correct, were buried. It is argued in the section on Floor 5 that these alterations, while Floor 4 was exposed and after the laying of Floor 5, represent the redesign of the interior of the building to accommodate a new deity, probably Bacchus.

An additional feature contemporary with Floor 4 was a large timber frame which appeared to respect the positions of columns S4 and S5 creating a bay in the south aisle. Indeed, whereas squat masonry walls had been placed between all of the columns in the rest of the building, the spaces between S4 and S5 and between S5 and S6 were filled with timber planks set on edge. It is interesting to note that the only surviving fragment of column base from the site which was found *in situ*, on column pad N7 (Fig 51), had a vertical groove suitable for holding such planks. There was a masonry squat wall against it, which implies that similar timber planks acting as retaining walls may have been in position throughout the entire building before they were converted to stone. Perhaps whatever it was that filled the bays between columns S4 and S6 prevented the building of squat walls. The true function of this frame is not known, but unless it supported a piece of temple furniture it could have been the base for other cult statues (Figs 101 and 102). Perhaps it supported a composite sculpture of the kind suggested by Oikonomides (1975) (Fig 103).

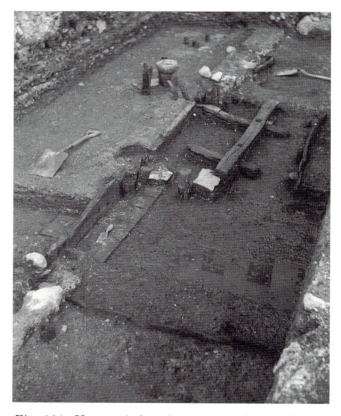

Fig 101 Heavy timber frame over the south aisle associated with Floor 4. Note the timber planks on edge slotted between columns S4 and S5, and S5 and S6. The squat altar at the top belongs to a later phase (Grimes)

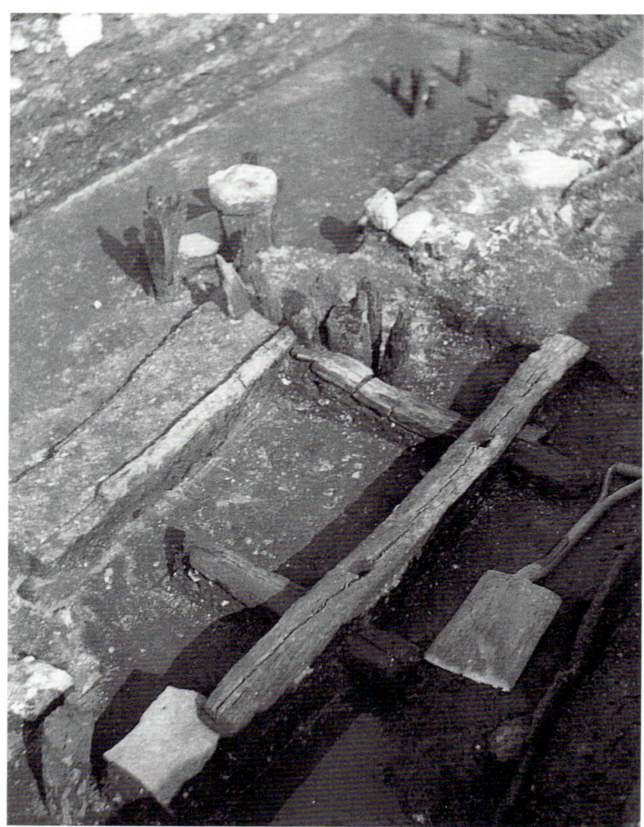

Fig 102 Detail of the timber frame between columns S4 and S5 over the south aisle. The squat altar comes from a later phase of activity (Grimes)

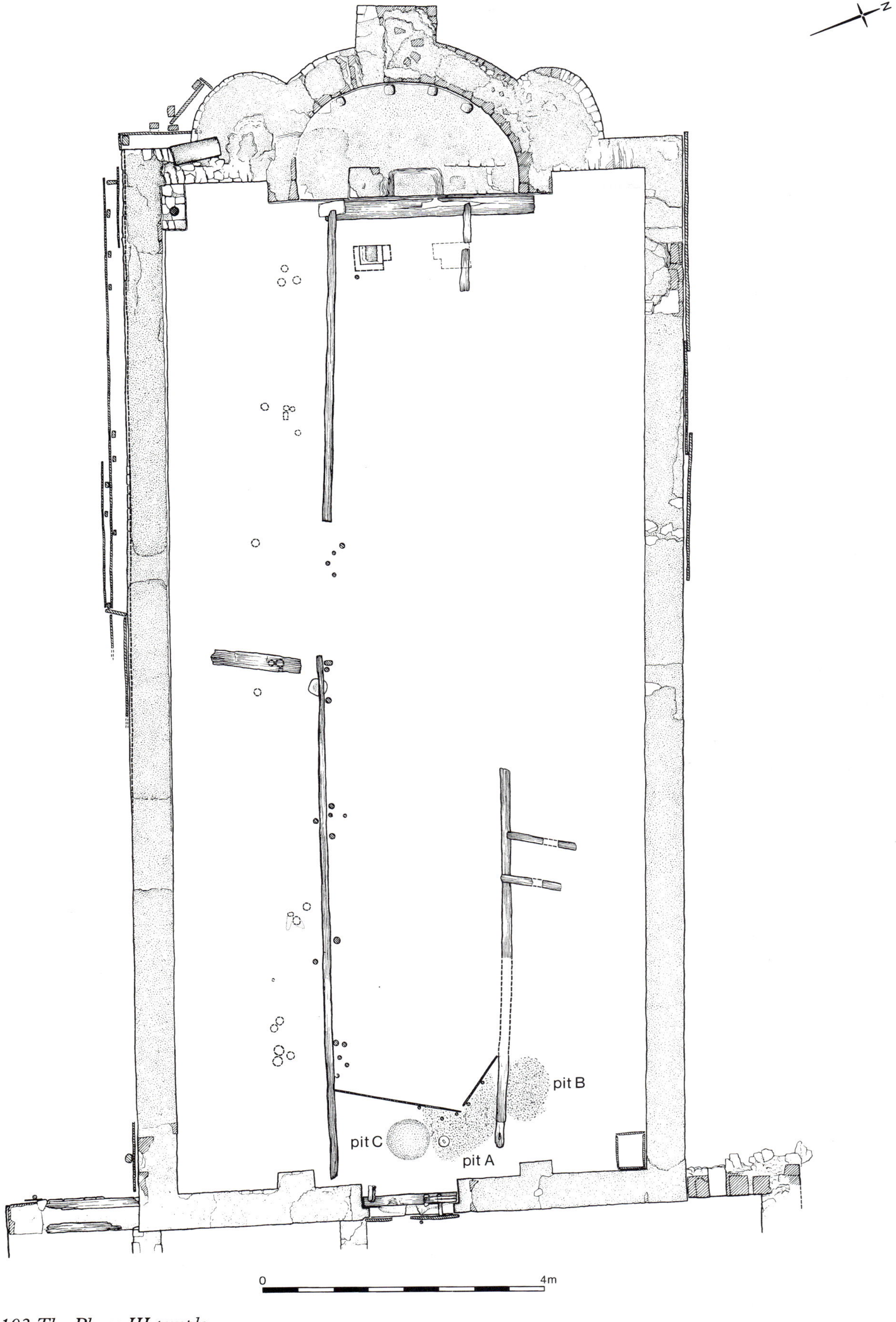

Fig 103 The Phase III temple

Fig 104 General view of the west end of the temple showing the south wall with, behind it, the accumulation of floors in the nave. The altar to the left (IX.48) rests on Floor 5. The well in the foreground is medieval (Grimes)

The Phase III temple: internal details (Group IX)

see Figure 103

Floor 5

Floor 5 succeeded Floor 4 over a 0.08–0.15m make-up (Figs 93–6). The floor was of mortar, slightly pink at the west end, changing to grey towards the east. At that end Floor 5 was level with the upper ledge of the stone door-sill; at the west it began to rise gradually about 1.2m back from the apse and appeared to be unbroken to the wall face. It overlay the mortar pad in the recess to end with the rough timber frame beneath the final altar support. There was no significant dating material from the make-up of Floor 5. The stone altar, pillar or pedestal 0.55m out from the apse face was set on Floor 5 (Fig 104). This curious object, for which it is difficult to find a suitable name, seems to have been one of a pair (its companion having been removed: see below, Floor 9), symmetrically placed on each side of the main axis of the nave.

The stone was not a normal altar, but since its upper part was broken and missing it is difficult to decide its purpose (Figs 105 and 205). Its back is plain; its base is offset and chamfered on the outer side and forward faces. On the inner side there is a low shoulder-like projection which is narrower than the main block. A votive offering had been laid in the outer re-entrant so formed. Two pegs had been set side by side in the recess, 0.22m and 0.11m high respectively. They provided support for a fragmentary greyware *olla* (CA279) which, set on a fractured edge, was held in place by two small lumps of mortar (Fig 108). The pot protected a deposit of greyish soil on which were some small bones, including a tiny patella and neck bone (said to have been set aside for detailed examination and subsequently lost, but to have included chicken bones; see *Chapter 6, Bones related to temple use*). This pedestal or altar stayed in place throughout the later life of the temple, being slowly buried as the floor levels rose (Fig 106). In this respect it resembled the main altar at Dura Europos, which in its final stage was buried to the full depth of its shaft (Rostovtzeff *et al* 1939: see also the Carrawburgh altars, Richmond *et al* 1951). It may be significant to note that the top level of this altar or pedestal was the same as the top of the plinth on the dais. In plan, the two ends of this plinth match the positions of this object and the projected position of its partner making a square *c* 1.6m across. It is possible that this was the base for a canopy, or *baldachino*, set on four posts or columns.

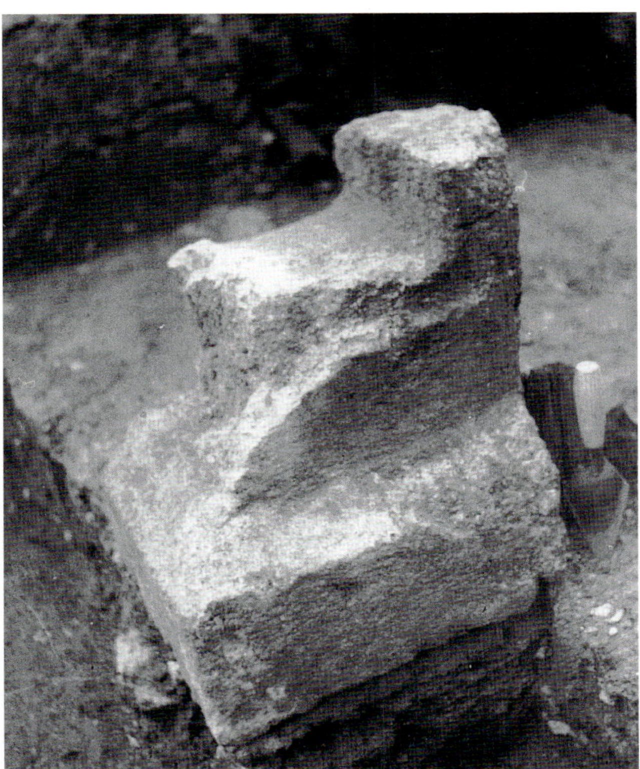

Fig 105 The pedestal or altar resting on Floor 5 (Grimes)

Fig 106 Multi-phase view of the west end of the nave showing the Phase I steps at the base, the pedestal or altar on Floor 5, the accumulations of Floors 6–8 against it and the stone block inserted in the face of the dais towards the end of the life of the temple (Grimes)

It may be of further significance to note that the column and capital fragment (X.64), which Professor Grimes and Williams interpreted as one of a pair which stood on the plinth on either side of a main Mithras Tauroctonos sculpture, came from the building debris over the final floor of the temple (Fig 103). In that context it is more likely that it came from the final phase of the building and that it belonged to the canopy structure which, as will be discussed below, replaced the main Mithraicon.

In the neighbourhood of the 'pedestal' there were several upright but broken stones which may also have been intended to carry votive offerings. CA245 and CA346 came from the surface of this floor.

Between the 'pedestal' and the apse wall was an additional layer of stony soil with some mortar, about 0.08m thick, with a well marked sloping surface which could not be recognised beyond the 'pedestal' to the east. A fragmentary wooden panel lay face downwards on this surface (Fig 107). Slightly higher a 0.25m-wide plank lay along the face of the apse, overlapping the north end of the opening by about 0.23m and falling short of the south end by about the same amount (Fig 108). It seems unlikely, in view of the shallowness of the deposit, that this sequence was appreciably later than the main Floor 5. It produced a number of coins which are therefore of particular value for the dating of an important phase in the history of the temple.

The main group of sculptures was buried in Pit A in Floor 5, a fact which, taken in conjunction with the reorganisation of the area of the apse, must have been

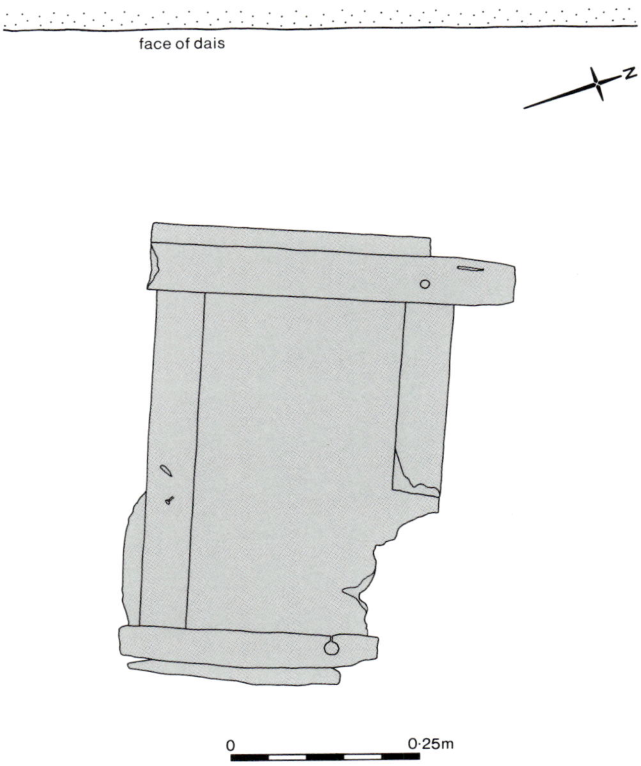

face of dais

N

0 0·25m

Fig 107 Wooden panel found on Floor 5 in front of the dais. Drawing prepared from sketches in site notebook

Fig 108 The pedestal/altar, votive deposit and wooden panel resting on Floor 5 in front of the dais. The stone block in the face of the dais is a later insertion (Grimes)

Fig 109 The surface of Floor 5, which originally covered the column pad (N1) and the site of the sculpture pit (Pit A). The base of the stone laver (Chapter 5, The finds catalogue, Period 2 finds, IX.37) *is visible top left (Grimes)*

of great significance for both the liturgical functioning and the architectural character of the building in its later history. Pit C, located in the entrance to the building, was probably dug from a slightly higher level and so was not contemporary with the two pits which contained the sculptures.

Before taking this aspect of the matter further it is necessary to examine the changes that by this time had taken place in the main colonnades, for it is clear that they had already been dismantled when the images were concealed; the disturbed area (Pit B), a hollow rather than a real pit (Figs 109 and 110) towards the east end of the nave extended across the north colonnade sleeper-wall, and that part of it which produced separately the neck of Mithras and the head of Minerva actually overlay a column pad, N1 (Fig 51). The head of Mithras almost certainly came from the same location but had been disturbed from its original site in the course of the removal of the modern foundations nearby. Obviously these pieces could not have been placed where they were found had the column been in place. The removal of the colonnades must have involved the almost total reconstruction of the superstructure of the building.

Here consideration must be given to the stretches of rough walling which on the north and south had been built on top of the original sleeper-walls between the columns (Figs 111 and 112). Details are shown of the walls around column pad N6 (Fig 113) and a wall and wooden plank set on edge against the column pad S6 adjacent top the Floor 4 wooden structure described above (Fig 114). The original height of this additional masonry is uncertain, for nowhere had it a finished top; its maximum height as preserved was 0.15m. It must in any case be admitted that owing to a misunderstanding of the sequence in the aisle the interpretation set forth in the interim account (1968) reverses the true order: the inserted masonry was intended to revet the accumulating deposits in the nave, not those in the aisles. Unfortunately the disorderly manner in which the excavation developed reduced the opportunities of studying the relationships. Along the north side, where the additional stonework was better preserved, the sleeper-wall lay down the middle of the first cutting, and the stratification was destroyed in deepening the cutting. On the south side, however, near the south-east corner, Floor 4 could be seen to make contact with the masonry near its surviving top. From this it would appear that the colonnades, still in place with Floor 4, had been removed by Floor 5. Once removed, the resulting voids were packed with rubble (Fig 115). At this time, or shortly afterwards, groups of posts, none more than 0.15m in diameter, were pushed into the surface of Floor 5 (or had the material of Floor 5 laid around them), either to support the old roof during its dismantling or, perhaps, to support the new roof during its construction (Figs 103 and 116). The posts followed the line of the south sleeper-wall, suggesting that they respected a purlin parallel with it above.

Fig 110 Pit A and its contents looking west (Grimes)

Fig 111 View west looking down the north sleeper-wall showing the squat walls between the columns which were subsequently removed (Grimes)

Fig 112 View of the south sleeper-wall showing the squat walls between the columns and, in the centre, the remaining wooden plank set on edge between column pads S5 and S6 (Grimes)

Fig 113 Column pad N6 and its squat walls (Grimes)

Fig 114 Column pad S6 and its squat wall and wooden plank (Grimes)

Fig 115 Stone packing in the void left by the removal of column S4 (Grimes)

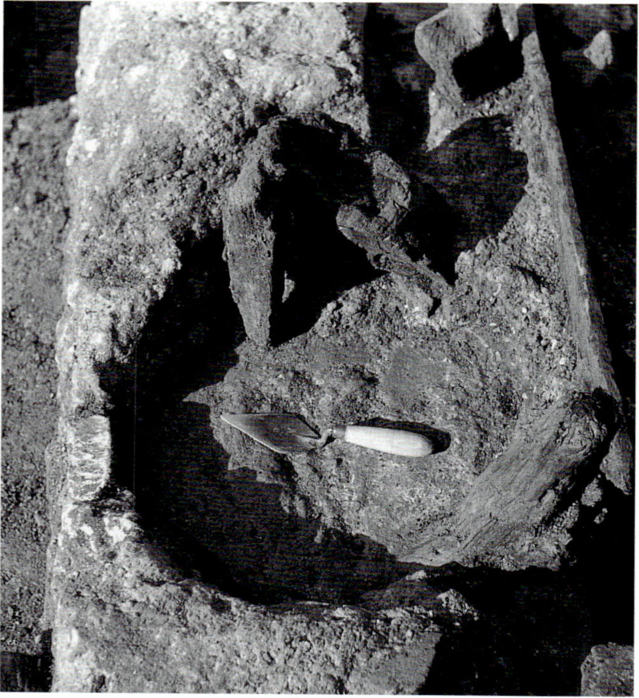

Fig 116 Small timber posts inserted to support the roof structure above column pad S1 (Grimes)

With one floor covering the entire interior of the temple, the well in the south-west corner had become covered (Fig 117). It is possible that this happened during an earlier phase but this cannot be determined. During this or the subsequent phase, a stone box was constructed in the same corner (Fig 118). This had a single posthole built into it. Near this was found the

Fig 117 Phase I/II well sealed by Phase III layers. The stone box was probably constructed towards the end of Phase III. Note the crack in the wall caused by the subsidence of the south-west corner (Grimes)

horseman roundel (*Chapter 5, The finds catalogue, Period 2 finds, IX/X.1,* Fig 216).

The reason for these changes is no doubt to be ascribed to the unstable character of the building, to which the poor nature of the ground must have contributed. This is best seen at the south-east corner, where the wall leaned outwards, causing a deep fissure in the wall at the west end of the south aisle. To repair this the south semicircular buttress was partially dismantled and a column drum inserted at ground level into the resulting gap (Fig 119). It is not possible to assign a date to these changes but the movement of the south-west corner of the temple was severe and could have resulted in the partial collapse of part of the structure there, including the internal colonnade. More evidence of stress to the building, which may have occurred at the same time, can be seen in the elevations of the north and south walls (Figs 65 and 66). These both show a marked change in the fabric of the building mid-way along their lengths. On the north wall, a tile course expanded to four courses and then abruptly ended. On the south side, an area of ragstone blocking broke a regular double tile course which ran along the length of the building. At a corresponding point on the interior, ragstone blocks had been used to seal an area where the rendering had collapsed. These details suggest that at some time the subsidence at the west end may have caused the building to break its back. In fact, the west end of the building as recorded was lower than the east end (see elevations Figs 65, 66 and 69–72).

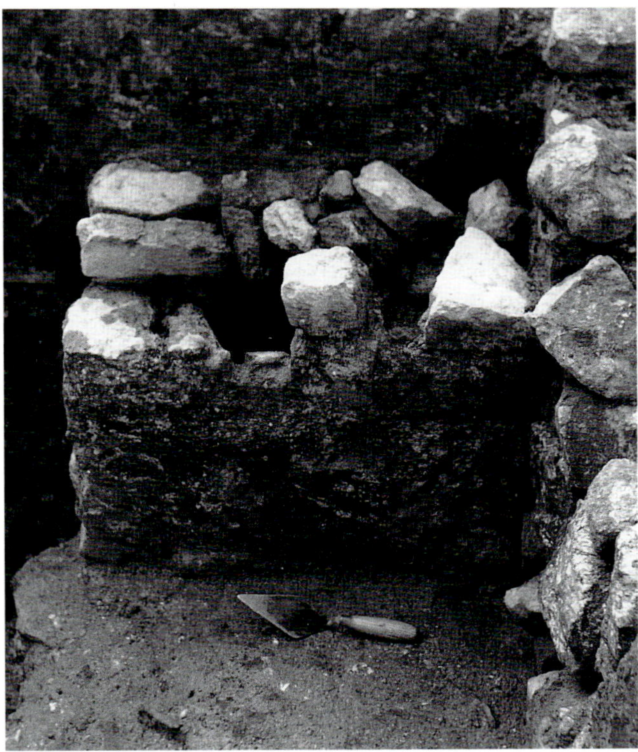

Fig 118 The Phase III/IV stone box in the south-west corner of the temple (Grimes)

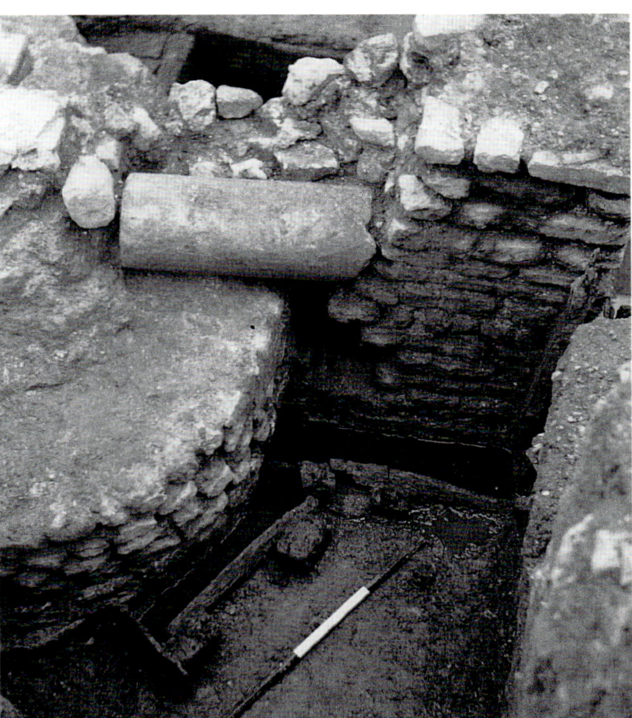

Fig 119 A column drum used as packing in the damaged south-west corner of the temple. Note the crack in the foundations below the drum (Grimes)

Floors 6A and B

Above Floor 5, Floors 6A and B were in effect one (Figs 93–6). CB330 constitutes part of the make-up for Floor 6. The two floors were separated only by a thin black layer (CB342), Floor 6B being clearly present only towards the east end. Their behaviour there was difficult to determine. They appeared to end on two obliquely set upright boards at their nearest point *c* 1.2m from the doorway, which was held in place by vertical pegs against their eastern face (these are visible in Figs 93 and 94). Beyond the boards a further floor continued at about the same level to end on the upper offset of the stone sill. There seemed to be no way of deciding whether this floor belonged to Floor 6 or Floor 7, though the fact that the planks on edge ended on the longitudinal beams that were contemporary with Floor 7 (below) might be thought to favour the view that they belonged to Floor 7 also.

It was at this stage, at the earliest, that the stone sill of the entrance-way was replaced with a wooden construction (Fig 120). No doubt this was due to the floor levels encroaching upon the sill and leaving an irregular ledge.

The main floor, Floor 6A, was about 0.12m above Floor 5. To the west it rose gradually to cover the chamfered base of the 'pedestal'. Over its eastern part it was burnt tile-red but became paler towards the west, with paler grey make-up below. In front of the 'pedestal' it had been quite heavily burnt and had the appearance of *opus signinum*. It was difficult to decide how Floor 6A behaved in the space between the 'pedestal' and the face of the apse. The pit dug for the removal of the (presumed) second 'pedestal' had destroyed the section on the north side. The evidence on the south side, slight as it was, suggested that the floor may have continued, beginning the process whereby the 'pedestal' was gradually buried by the building up of the later floor. A stony layer may have related to either Floor 6 or Floor 7.

The *INVICTO* ('Four Augusti') slab (*Chapter 5, The finds catalogue, Period 2 finds, IX.47,* Figs 201–2) lay on Floor 6B. The date of this inscription is AD 307–8 (Fig 121).

Floor 7

Floor 7 was 0.1–0.15m above Floor 6. It was made of a creamy cement, broken and irregular in places, and containing large quantities of broken tile towards the west (Fig 122). The make-up for Floor 7 incorporated much more stone and tile than usual, including a number of complete *tegulae* (CA344) (see Fig 92). In front of the 'pedestal' the underlying tile had 'come through' the worn cement so that floor and make-up appeared to be the same. It is unlikely that the tiles and stones in the make-up could have come from the dismantling of the colonnades because the interval of time between Floors 5 and 7 would have been too long. The tiles and stones must have been introduced in a single process when the floor was laid for the introduction of the longitudinal beams.

Fig 120 Phase III/IV wooden sill in the entrance (Grimes)

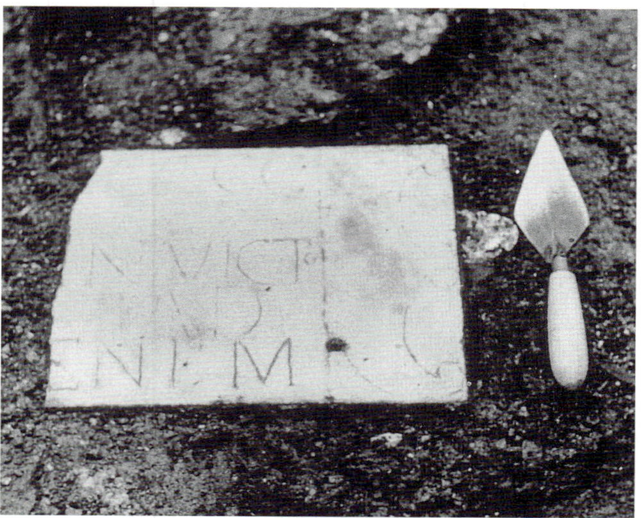

Fig 121 The Four Augusti inscription (IX.47) in situ *(Grimes)*

Fig 122 Wooden plank alongside the face of the apse lying on Floor 5. The east–west timbers and the tiles are Floor 7 features (Grimes)

Fig 123 East–west wooden beams on Floor 7 (Grimes)

At the east end the cement floor thickened and dipped to end on the obliquely set boards already referred to in connection with Floor 6. At the west end the floor sloped gradually to the face of the 'pedestal' almost making contact with the underlying Floor 6. The longitudinal beams rested on this floor on lines similar to the inner faces of the now completely buried sleeper-walls (Fig 123). These new alignments, however, were probably determined by the squared pilasters at the west and east end of each sleeper-wall. These remained visible throughout the life of the building.

The surface of the floor was cambered to meet the beams. Of the two, that on the south side was better preserved, surviving as two lengths: one on the east which was 7.6m long and the other on the west which was 4.57m long, with an interval of 1.95m between. The two were not quite on the same alignment, perhaps indicating separate structures. The eastern portion in particular was reinforced by stones packed under its sides; it was further supported by a makeshift altar consisting of a small column capital set in the floor, the shaft of which had been dressed to a tapering square section (Figs 124 and 125). Set where it was, along the inner face of the sleeper-wall, the altar may well have been in its original position, sunk into the preceding floor, Floor 6.

Fig 124 The squat altar supporting an east–west beam of Floor 7 (Grimes)

Fig 125 The fully exposed squat altar (Grimes)

Because of the presence of the modern foundations, a beam on the northern side of the axis of the temple was less completely seen. The eastern portion was partly under the concrete. Its overall length was 1.75m. A mortise in its east end showed that it was a reused timber. To the west all that remained were two broken fragments, not *in situ,* one of which rested on the plank which fronted the apse (Fig 92). This apparently deliberate arrangement was the result of disturbance. The beam was several inches above the level of the plank where undisturbed, and on the south side where there had been no interference the two were quite separate.

The Phase IV temple (Group X)

See Figure 126.

Floor 8

There was a vertical interval of about 0.15m between Floor 7 and Floor 8 (Figs 93–6). The floor itself was made up of a creamy cement which varied in thickness and had an irregular surface which was broken over the middle part of the site. The make-up was black soil, gravelly in places (CB231). Immediately under the floor there was a practically continuous layer of horizontally laid oyster shells. At the west end the floor was practically level with, or slightly below, the floor of the apse (Fig 127), and there was no doubt that the surface had been continuous around and behind the 'pedestal'. In front of the 'pedestal' there was a shallow pit with a featureless loam filling containing fragments of tile and mortar. The floor though broken was continuous across the pit.

Floor 8 was continuous across the north-western part of the building, covering in one piece both nave and aisle. All the earlier features, including the remains of the longitudinal beam, were completely buried. This surface extended eastwards for a distance of about 7.6m. Its limits were not clearly defined and some part of the loss may have been due to more recent destruction. On the other hand, the floor over the remainder of the nave though damaged in places had survived as a cambered surface which ended on the longitudinal beams, which were still in place at the east end. This surface was now higher than the floor in the entrance by about 0.3m. To accommodate this change in level two irregular steps were inserted up from the entrance.

A timber box was constructed in the north-east corner of the temple (Fig 128). This had been set into a pit lined with clay, making it watertight. The Bacchic group (*Chapter 5, The finds catalogue, Period 2 finds, X.59,* Figs 221–2) was found close by lying on Floor 8.

It is assumed that the south side of the temple replicated the north. It must, however, be admitted that the justification for this assumption is very slight, since a modern foundation laid along the inner face of the main temple wall and taking up practically the whole width of the aisle had effectively destroyed the upper levels. It appeared, however, that for the same distance as on the north the floor had extended across the line of the longitudinal beam on this side, presumably as far as the outer wall. It would appear that the body of the temple was now divided into two parts; a western area in which the floor was continuous across the width of the building, and an eastern one in which the longitudinal beams continued to maintain the distinction between nave and side aisles.

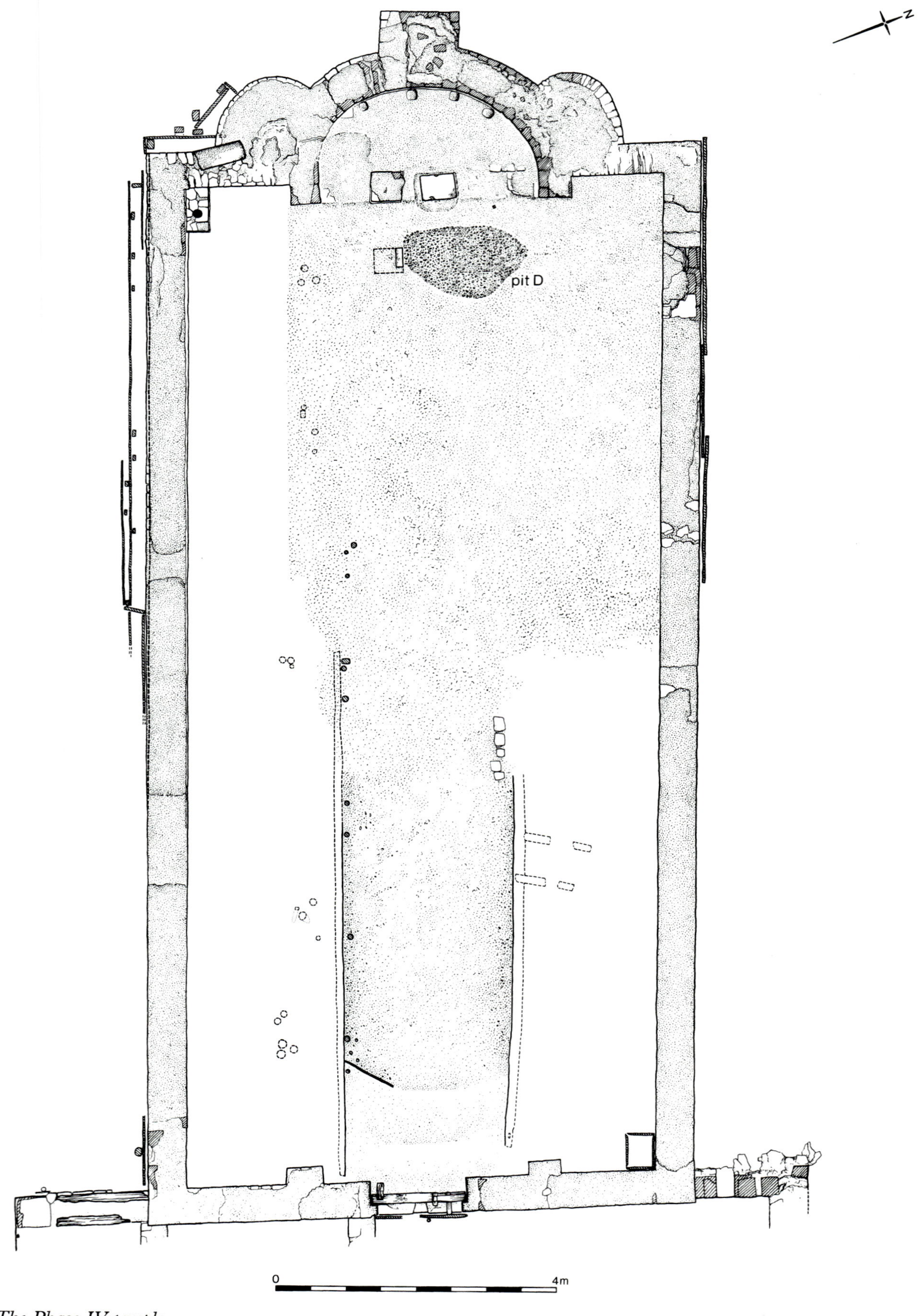

Fig 126 The Phase IV temple

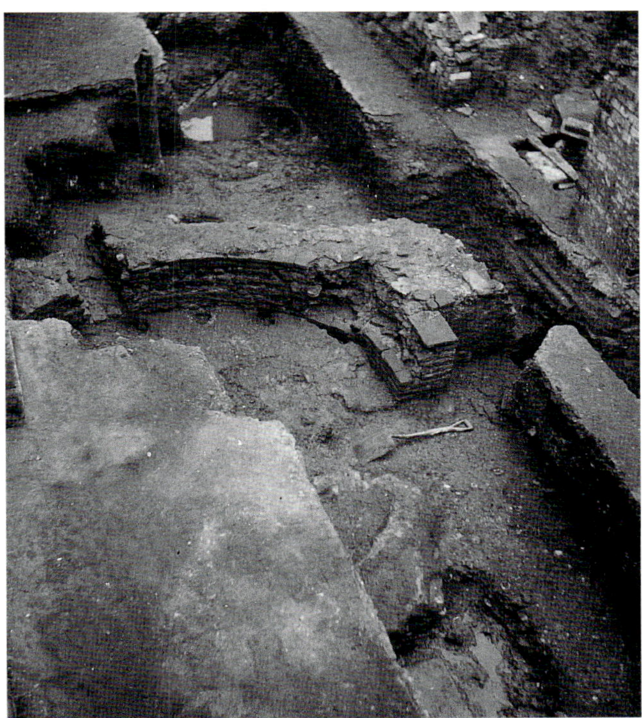

Fig 127 Floors 8 and 9 looking towards the apse. Floor 8 is level with the dais floor. Floor 9 is the irregular opus signinum *patch next to the blade of the shovel (Grimes)*

There are several questions here to which answers cannot be provided, in particular perhaps relating to the method by which the change from the single compartment on the west to the triple compartment on the east was achieved.

Floor 9

Floor 9 was represented by a fragment of *opus signinum* which overlay Floor 8, 1.4m back from the face of the apse (Fig 95). There were broken fragments elsewhere (Fig 127).

The two final events in this sequence were the setting in the apse of the block for the final altar and the digging of the pit for the removal of the object, assumed here to be another 'pedestal', which balanced the surviving 'pedestal' on the north side. Either or both of these happenings could have related to either Floor 8 or Floor 9.

As already noted, the recess in the face of the apse was an earlier feature cut apparently in relation to Floor 4. The altar, if this is what occupied this position (after the removal of the Mithras Tauroctonos relief?), had been removed and there is no way of knowing what took its place. It would appear, however, that a pit had been dug or redug through the make-up of the final floor(s) to take the block for the final altar (Fig 129). The pit, about 0.3m deep, was floored with a thin layer of mortar on which were laid a number of pieces of wood to provide a base for the block (Figs 130–1). The timbers were arranged in a rough rectangle, but no attempt had

Fig 128 The Phase IV timber box in the north-east corner of the temple (Grimes)

Fig 129 The stone block in the earlier dais recess (Grimes)

Fig 130 The wooden frame in the recess which supported the stone block (Grimes)

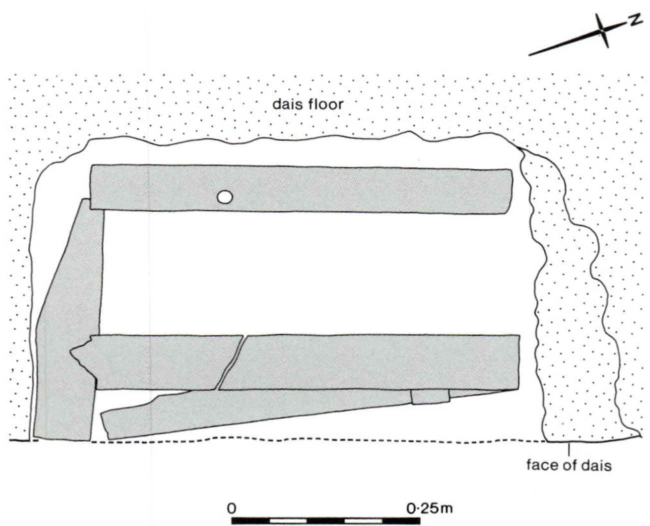

Fig 131 *Plan of the wooden frame prepared from sketches in site notebooks*

been made to fasten them together as a frame. Coins of Constantine I (AD 309–13: CA288) and Licinius I (AD 307–24: CA292), the latter adhering to one of the timbers, were found in the dark soil underlying the block; a barbarous radiate (CA296) came from the basal mortar layer. The block itself was a piece of reused stone bearing the fragmentary inscription ...*BENT*... (Period 2, X.62).

Pit D (Group XI)

A rubbish pit, an irregular oval in plan, impinged on the north face of the 'pedestal' (Fig 126). At a lower level it cut through the north-east corner of the wooden panel, tapering downwards to the surface of Floor 8. The filling was a mixture of stones, tile fragments and mortary soil, the coarse texture of which contrasted

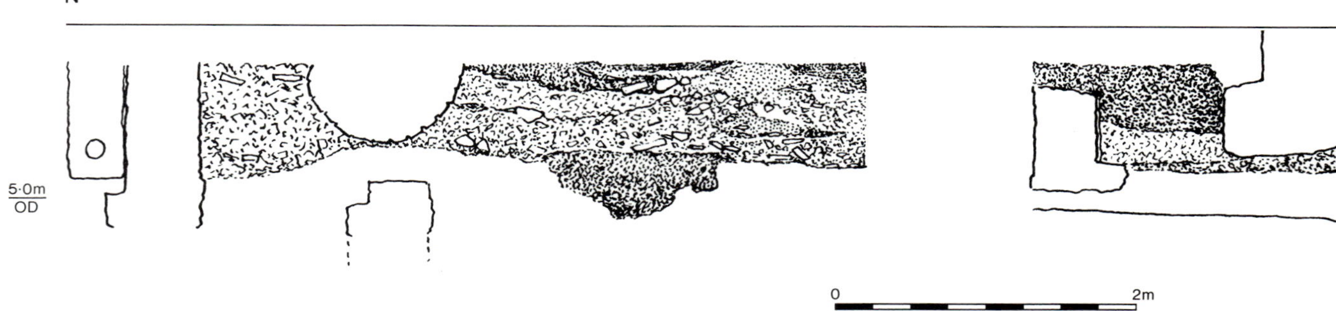

Fig 132 *Edited west section through the narthex area (original by Grimes)*

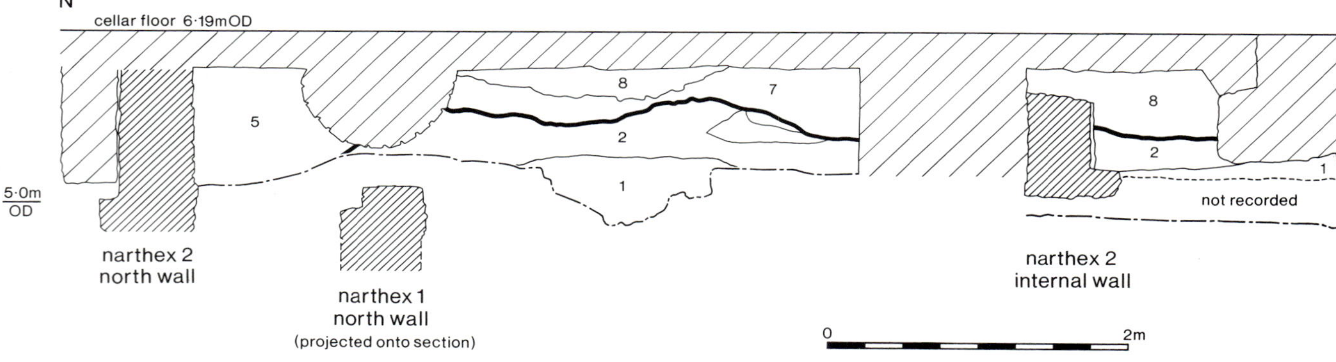

Fig 133 *Interpretive drawing of Fig 132*

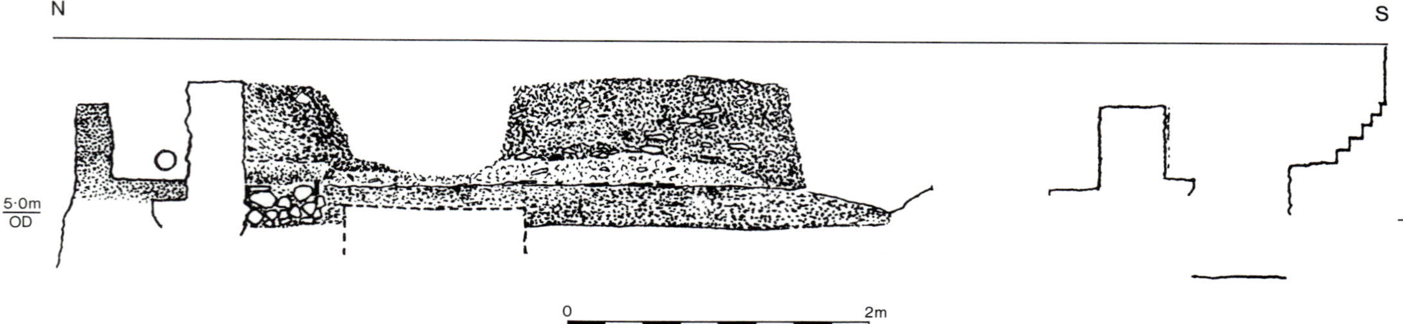

Fig 134 *Edited east section through the narthex area (original by Grimes)*

with the relatively smooth surface of Floors 8 and 9. CB241 and CB269 came from this filling. This pit was sealed by the general spread of building debris.

The narthex

The narthex could be only partially excavated due to its proximity to the edge of the site (Figs 132–7). As a result it is not possible to elucidate exactly the full sequence of events there.

It is evident, however, that the walls recorded there were not of one phase. At least two structures were present but it is not possible to relate them to the general sequence of events in the main temple, except that the wide narthex (Narthex 2) was in existence during the final phase of the building when, it can be argued, the building was no longer a mithraeum.

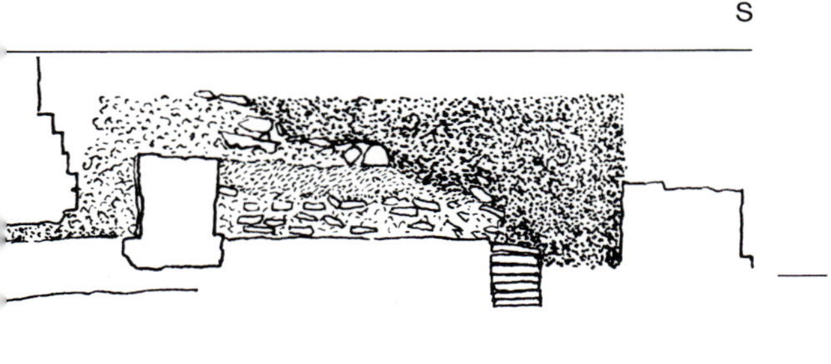

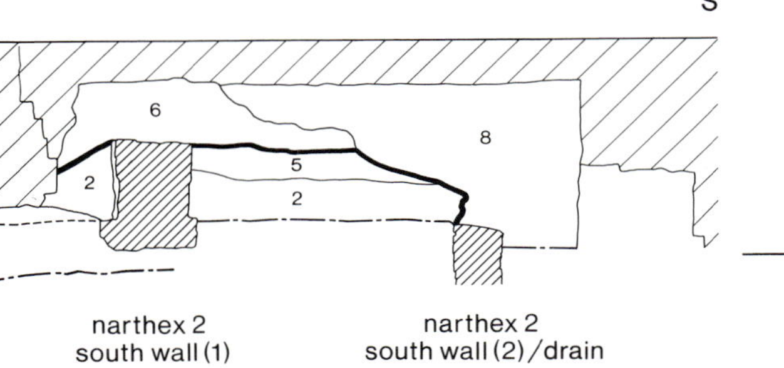

An approximate sequence is as follows:

Narthex 1

This structure is represented by two walls which extend from the north and south walls of the main building (Figs 61 and 132–3, Walls 1 and 2). The first, continuing the line of the north wall, was only ever built to foundation level. The face of the east wall of the temple above this foundation showed no signs of repair as if a wall attached to it had been dismantled. This plan, therefore, of a narthex of the same width as the temple, does not appear to have been completed. Technically these two foundations belong to Group VIII features.

Narthex 2

It is not clear whether Narthex 2 immediately replaced the planned Narthex 1 or if it was constructed at a later date (Fig 126). It was still in existence during the final years of the building. There is the possibility, therefore, that it does not belong to the Mithraeum at all but was constructed for the Phase III (Group IX) building.

Wall 1 of Narthex 1 was sealed by Layer 2 (Fig 133) which consisted of a coarse mixed black filling with no stratification. It was horizontal in general structure and contained charcoal stains, patches of grey clay and some gravel. This would appear to have been a levelling dump. On this were laid timber planks. These, presumably, were a floor surface.

This floor was contemporary with Wall 3, the northern wall of Narthex 2. This wall, built of tile and dressed ragstone, included a tile-lined culvert, which presumably led surface water away from the angle formed by Narthex 2 and the temple eastwards to drain away outside the entrance to the narthex. Its relationship with Wall 1 is not clear, but since that wall survived to a height above it, it is probable that they were, at some time, contemporary. This being the case, it is possible to envisage a narthex with the south wall on line with the south wall of the temple but the north wall extending north of the east face.

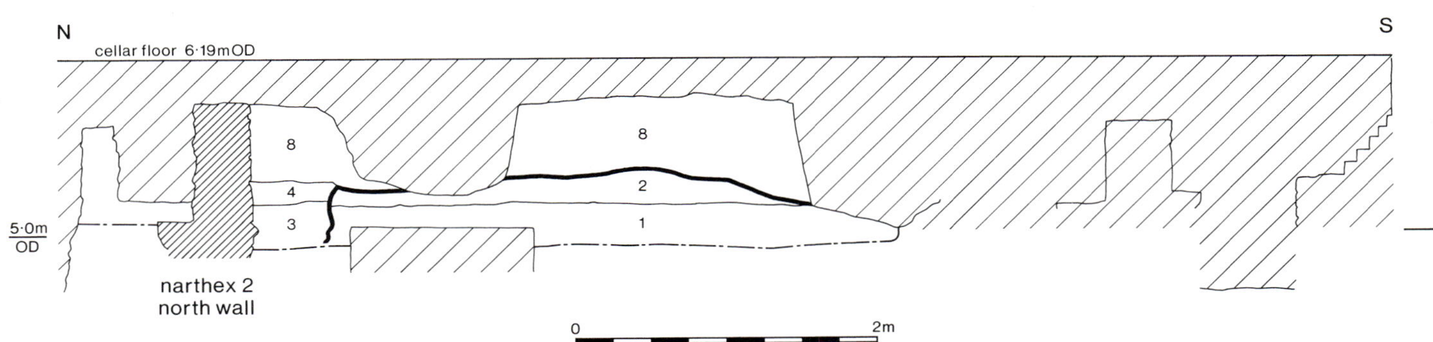

Fig 135 Interpretive drawing of Fig 134

Fig 136 The north wall of Narthex 2 seen from the outside. The north-east corner of the temple is on the right (Grimes)

A partition wall was constructed at some time between these two walls against the south jamb of the entrance-way (Wall 4), making a small room with Wall 2. The north face of Wall 2 and the south face of Wall 4 were rendered in hard pink mortar.

At the south–east corner of the temple, another construction was added which mirrored the plan of the Narthex 2 north wall (Wall 3). This was built of tile, dressed ragstone and timber and included another drain. This is almost certainly contemporary with the other three walls but its true function is not clear from the records. It was badly damaged by modern intrusions and the narrowness of the trench prevented a detailed record from being made.

The remaining observations for this area are few. The timber floor was covered with a layer of coarse white mortar with occasional tile fragments which appeared to be debris rather than a floor. This material was also recorded between Walls 2 and 4, sealing the rendered surfaces. It is possible, since these two walls did not survive as high as Wall 2 to the north and the remainder of the temple, that this mortar layer comes from the dismantling of these two walls.

A timber-lined box was constructed in a pit cut into this mortar debris layer in the internal angle of Wall 3. This had been packed with rough-hewn ragstones in what the excavators described as 'a curious red-brown matrix'. No explanation for this soil was given by the excavators.

These layers and features were then sealed by a succession of large dumps of mixed material. In the section furthest from the east wall of the temple (Figs 134 and 135) this was made up of mostly horizontal layers consisting of clay, loam and mortar with tile and stone. Closer to the temple, in the west section (Figs 132 and 133), the layer at the corresponding height consisted of building debris similar to the material which was piled up against the apse wall at the west end (Figs 95 and 96) and which covered the interior of the building. It is possible to reconstruct a similar mound of building debris banked up against the east wall of the temple and filling the narthex rooms.

Unfortunately no datable finds came from the floor or dumps associated with either Narthex 1 or 2. One of the Bacchus torsos (*Chapter 5, The finds catalogue, Period 2 finds, X.58*, Fig 220) overlay the building debris in the room made by Walls 2 and 4.

The end of the temple

The Group XI pit dug into the latest floor in front of the dais is the only evidence for any activity after the building had ceased to function as a temple. Exactly when this occurred, in the late Roman period or soon after, is not known. This pit was sealed by building debris. The latter consisted of 0.6m of irregular deposits made up of pink mortary debris (rendering?), stones, fragmentary tiles and building materials in a matrix of dense black soil. This was fairly level across the interior of the building. Similar material was also recorded spread across the area of the narthex and mounded up against the exterior face of the wall at the west end of the building (Figs 41 and 42).

The medieval chalk-lined well, cut from a much higher level, clipped the south wall of the temple by chance. It would appear that the ruin had become inundated and covered by Walbrook valley deposits, because the builders of the well appear to have been unaware of its existence and made no attempt to incorporate it into their structure. No other medieval intrusions were recorded. The 1889 foundation stanchions for 7–8 Walbrook cut into the walls and the floor surfaces of the temple. The construction of the basement slabs at that time truncated the tops of the temple walls and the lining of the medieval well to a common level. Following excavation in 1954 the temple was finally dismantled. Material from its fabric was used to reconstruct the ground plan of the temple on a new site on the south side of Queen Victoria Street close to Bucklersbury House.

Fig 137 View south along the narrow narthex cutting. The truncated north wall of Narthex 2 and the north-east corner of the temple is in the foreground (Grimes)

Coin 15, a radiate copy dated AD 270–80, came from the make-up of Floor 6 and was probably imported with the material for this deposit. Coin 12, dated AD 332–3, and associated with Floors 6 and 7, appears to be simply a lost coin but two other broadly contemporary coins also came from other parts of the temple at this time. Coins 13 and 14 came from Pit C in the floor of the nave in the temple entrance and sealed by the laying of Floor 7. The pit cut Floor 5 but the relationship with Floor 6 was not clear. There seems, however, no obvious reason for the deposit of these two coins in this pit. The three coins (12–14) cover the period AD 320–35.

The two coins (16 and 17) from Floor 7 make-up levels do not assist in dating Floor 7 since they are late third century in date and they too were probably redeposited in the material brought into the building for making the foundations for the floor. Similarly the coins (18 and 19) that came from Floor 8 can only indicate that Floor 8 is later than AD 335.

Four coins were found in Group X deposits in and around the timber sill of the entrance. Coins 22 and 23 are clearly residual but coins 24 and 25 are contemporary with the use of this part of the building. The timber sill was put in after the Floor 5 alterations had been effected and the coins dates of AD 341–6 and AD 321–3 or later bear this out.

Two other coins (26 and 27) were found in Group X deposits associated with the Bacchus group. Coin 26, a Carausian *antoninianus* is residual, probably from a make-up layer, but a copper alloy coin of Constantine II (AD 322–3) may be broadly contemporary.

Period 2 coins: Groups XIV and XV contemporary with the temple on the west bank of the Walbrook, coins 28–31

Coins 28–31 came from general dumps and surfaces on the west bank of the Walbrook opposite the temple. All coins date to the late third or early fourth century.

The remaining coins (32–7) cannot be directly stratified and are therefore not discussed.

Coin catalogue

Period 1 coins

Group IV

1 *As*, Vespasian; Ae 26mm; mint of Lyon; good/worn; AD 77–8; RIC 763
[BB333], MoL Acc No 92.30/41

Group VII

2 *Sestertius*, Trajan, Ae 31mm; illegible; very worn; AD 98–117 *[CA164], MoL Acc No 92.34/33*
3 *Sestertius*, Hadrian, Ae 32mm; illegible; very worn; AD 117–38
[CA156], MoL Acc No 92.36/25

Group XII

4 *As*, Domitian, Ae 28mm; worn; AD 85–96
Obv: IMP CAES DOMIT AUG GERM COS X (...CENS) PER PP. Laureate bust right
Rev: VIRTVTI AUGUS(TI) SC. Virtus standing right, holding parazonium and spear
[F768] from the Walbrook channel, lying on the base of the channel itself, MoL Acc No 92.32.31

Period 2 coins

Group VIII

5 *Sestertius*, Nerva, Ae 32mm; very worn; AD 96–8
Obv: Illegible, upper portion of bust right. just recognisable as Nerva
Rev: Illegible, standing figure
[CE264] from south aisle, MoL Acc No 92.33/6
6 *Antoninianus*, Marius, Ae 19mm; mint of Cologne; worn; AD 268; RIC 7
[CB355] from surface of Floor 3, MoL Acc No 92.50/6

Group IX

7 *Antoninianus*, Gallienus, Ar 20mm; worn and corroded; AD 260–8; RIC 207
[CA297] from make-up of Floor 5, under wooden panel, MoL Acc No 92.49/5
8 Radiate copy, Ae 15mm; worn; AD 270–80
Obv: Radiate head right
Rev: Altar
[CA296] from make-up of Floor 5, under wooden panel, MoL Acc No 92.127/52
9 *Follis*, Constantine I, Ae 19mm; mint of Trier; some corrosion; AD 300–15
Obv: (CO)NSTANTINVS PF AUG. Laureate and cuirassed bust left
Rev: SOLI INVICTO COMITI. In exergue (-)TR. Sol standing l. Chlamys (short cloak) draped over left shoulder, right raised, left holding up globe
[CE280] from surface of Floor 5, under wooden panel, MoL Acc No 92.61/2
10 *Follis*, Constantine I, Ae 23mm; mint of London; corroded; AD 310; RIC 120–7
[CE289] from surface of Floor 5, under wooden panel, MoL Acc No 92.61/1
11 *Follis*, Licinius I, Ae 22mm; mint of London; corroded; AD 310–17; RIC 117B
[CA273] from over the wooden panel on Floor 5, MoL Acc No 92.60/7
12 *Urbs Roma*, Ae 17mm; mint of Trier; corroded; AD 332–3; LRBC I, 65
[CA239] from layer over plank and wooden panel lying on Floor 5 Probably make-up of Floor 6 or 7, MoL Acc No 92.61/44
13 Constantine II, Ae 20mm; mint of London; good; AD 320–1; RIC 190
[CB325] from Pit C in east end of nave, MoL Acc No 92.63/5
14 Constantinopolis, Ae 17mm; good; AD 330–5
Obv: CONSTAN (TINOPOLIS). Helmeted bust of Constantinopolis left
Rev: Victory left on prow of galley

[CB325] from Pit C in east end of nave, MoL Acc No 92.61/57
15 Radiate copy, Ae 15mm; worn; *c* AD 270–80
Obv: Radiate head right
Rev: Bird standing left
[CB346] from make-up of Floor 6a over Floor 5, MoL Acc No 92.127/55
16 *Antoninianus,* Probus, Ae 22mm; mint of Ticinum; good; AD 276–82; RIC 517
[CB344[from make-up of Floor 7, over Floor 6b, MoL Acc No 92.56/19
17 Radiate copy, Ae 14mm; worn; *c* AD 270–80
Obv: Radiate head right, Claudius II type
Rev: Altar
[CB344] from make-up of Floor 7, over Floor 6b, MoL Acc No 92.127/53

Group X
18 Constantine II, Ae 17mm; mint of Trier; fair; AD 330–5; LRBC I,63.
[CA320] from make-up of Floor 8,over Floor 7, MoL Acc No 92.63/8
19 Radiate copy, Ae 17mm; worn; *c* AD 270–80
Obv: Radiate head right. ?double-struck
Rev: (P)A(X) AVG. Pax type. Female figure standing left, holding sceptre
[CA320] from make-up of Floor 8, over Floor 7, MoL Acc No 92.127/54
20 *Follis,* Constantine I, Ae 21mm; mint of London, good; AD 310–12; RIC 150–92
[CE288] from between timbers under block in face of dais, MoL Acc No 92.61/15
21 *Follis,* Licinius I, Ae 19mm; corroded; AD 310–17
Obv: (---)CINIVS(---)
Rev: (SOLI INVI)CT(O COMITI). Sol raising right hand and holding globe, standing left
[CE292] attached to east timber of frame under block in face of dais, MoL Acc No 92.60/12
22 *Sestertius,* Hadrian, Ae 32mm; very worn; AD 117–38
Obv: Illegible
Rev: Standing figure. ?Felicitas
[CB313] from layer over wooden sill of entrance, MoL Acc No 92.36/26
23 *As,* copy of Claudius I, Ae 24mm; illegible; ± AD 50
Obv: Base of head, left
Rev: SC
[CB313] from layer over wooden sill of entrance, MoL Acc No 92.127/11
24 Constans or Constantinus II, Ae 15mm; worn; AD 341–6
Obv: Completely illegible
Rev: Two victories type
[CB313] from layer over wooden sill of entrance, MoL Acc No 92.127/37
25 Constantine II, barbarous copy, Ae 19mm; mint of Trier; corroded; AD 321–3 or later
Obv: CONSTANTIN IVN NC. Radiate and cuirassed bust right
Rev: (BEATA TRANQVILLITAS) type but garbled. In exergue STR, altar with inscription (VOT)XXX
[CB328] from entrance area, MoL Acc No 92.63/17
26 *Antoninianus,* Carausius, Ae 17mm; worn; AD 287–93
Obv: IMP (CA)RAVSIVS (...). Radiate bust right
Rev (...) IIII(G). Female figure standing left, ?holding cornucopiae
[CB335] from north aisle, east corner. Near Bacchus group findspot, MoL Acc No 92.57/17
27 Constantine II, Ae 19mm; ?mint of London; corroded; AD 322–3; RIC 255
[CB335] from north aisle, east corner. Near Bacchus group findspot, MoL Acc No 92.63/2

Group XIV
28 Radiate copy, Ae 14mm; worn; *c* AD 270–80
Obv: Radiate head right. Very barbarous
Rev: Design derived from ewer with sacrificial accessories (PIETAS AVGUSTOR type)
[BB37] MoL Acc No 92.127/49
29 House of Constantine; AD 330–5
Obv: Illegible
Rev: GLORIA EXERCITVS. Two soldiers and standards
[BB37] MoL Acc No: not located in 1995

Group XV
30 ?coin blank for barbarous minim, Ae 15mm
[BB33] MoL Acc No 92.127/26
31 Radiate copy, Ae 12mm; corroded; *c* AD 270–80
Obv: Radiate bearded head right, very barbarous
Rev: Standing figure holding vertical sceptre
[BB18] MoL Acc No 92.127/48

Unstratified coins (Group 0)
32 Reduced *Antoninianus,* Tetricus II, Ae 16mm; probably irregular but good style and die; fair; *c* AD 270–80. RIC 254–7
[Cutting CB] from an unspecified temple floor between 4.70m OD and 5.00m OD (probably Group IX), MoL Acc No 92.52/19
33 House of Constantine, AD 330–5
Obv: Diademed bust right. illegible
Rev: GLORIA EXER(CITVS). Two standards between soldiers
[Cutting D], MoL Acc No: not located in 1995
34 Radiate copy, Ae 12mm; corroded; *c* AD 270–80
Obv: Radiate head right
Rev: Draped female figure standing left lower portion only
[Cutting E] from c3.90m OD, MoL Acc No 92.127/50
35 ?Radiate copy, Claudius II, Ae 16mm; corroded; AD 268–70 or later
Obv: Illegible. radiate head right
Rev: (GENIV)S EXER(CI). Genius standing left by altar holding patera and cornucopia
[Cutting E] from c4.00m OD, MoL Acc No 92.56/4
36 *Antoninianus,* Carausius, Ae 22mm; some corrosion; AD 287–93
Obv: IMP CARAVSIVS PF AUG. Radiate bust right

Rev: ?(PAX AVGG) type, inscription illegible. Female figure holding vertical sceptre left
[Cutting G] MoL Acc No 92.57/16
37 *Dupondius,* Nero; worn; AD 64–6
Obv: IMP NERO CAESAR (...). Laureate bust left
Rev: Seated figure right. Securitas type
[Unstratified] MoL Acc No 92.28/13

Chronological list of coins

Claudius I	Group X, no 23
Nero	Group 0, no 37
Vespasian	Group IV, no 1
Domitian	Group XII, no 4
Nerva	Group VIII, no 5
Trajan	Group VII, no 2
Hadrian	Group VII, no 3
Hadrian	Group X, no 22
Gallienus	Group IX, no 7
Marius	Group VIII, no 6
?copy, Claudius II	Group 0, no 35
Radiate copy	Group IX, no 8
Radiate copy	Group IX, no 15
Radiate copy	Group IX, no 17
Radiate copy	Group X, no 19
Radiate copy	Group XIV, no 28
Radiate copy	Group XV, no 31
Radiate copy	Group 0, no 34
Carausius	Group X, no 26
Carausius	Group 0, no 36
Constantine I	Group IX, no 9
Constantine I	Group IX, no 10
Constantine I	Group X, no 20
Licinius I	Group IX, no 11
Licinius I	Group X, no 21
Constantine II	Group IX, no 13
Constantine II	Group X, no 25
Constantine II	Group X, no 27
Constantine II	Group X, no 18
Constantinopolis	Group IX, no 14
House of Constantine	Group X, no 29
House of Constantine	Group 0, no 33
Urbs Roma	Group IX, no 12
Constans or Constantinus II	Group X, no 24
? coin blank for barbarous minim	Group XV, no 30

The pottery: general discussion

by J Groves

Previous work

Several unpublished reports have been produced on the Mithraeum pottery. Joanna Bird wrote the initial report in the early 1970s upon which all subsequent work is based. That document provides a very detailed descriptive account. It is arranged by context within trenches. Each sherd or group of sherds of the same type is described in detail (fabric, form, finish, decoration etc) and identifications are given if known. The unstamped and undecorated samian is also listed and dated. There are further sections on the decorated and stamped samian (by Joanna Bird and Brenda Dickinson respectively), and specialist reports by K Hartley (mortaria) and V Rigby *(Terra Nigra)*.

Bird's original report is accompanied by an illustrated type series in which virtually every sherd is referenced to an illustration. If another example of an already drawn vessel occurred it was not illustrated but recorded under the existing illustration number.

Another report by Joanna Bird, *The Mithraeum: summary of the dating evidence* (no date: writen in the mid-1970s), discusses the dating evidence by context and stratigraphical group. A report by Sarah Macready, *Walbrook coarse pottery* (no date: written in the late 1970s), is a rearrangement, by period, of Bird's initial report. Finally, an interpretive account of the material was produced by Macready, *Pottery from the Walbrook 1954* (no date: written in the late 1970s). The bulk of this report consists of discussions of the main fabrics/types and includes some statistical analysis. The material is also considered by site phase (pre-temple, temple and post-temple).

The assemblage is almost entirely composed of rim sherds, because body sherds, for the most part, were not retained. None of the above reports included any quantification by EVEs, weight or sherd count.

Subsequent work

For the purposes of this publication the non-samian pottery was re-examined against the text of Bird's initial report and the appropriate MoLAS pottery code appended to each entry. Some sherds are missing and therefore could not be checked. This accounts for many of the uncertain identifications. Previously unrecorded sherds were added to the record. The data were entered on computer in period groups. By using these data and Bird's early reports an effort was made to provide some record of quantification. This was achieved by counting the number of vessels represented in the report and the excluded material, ie mainly the number of rims. It was undertaken by 'context' and took account of sherd links recorded by Bird. Certainly not all the sherd links would have been recognised, particularly across 'contexts'. The total quantity of vessels is probably less than the total given. The figures are therefore an approximate guide only.

The samian was re-examined by Bird and an updated catalogue produced, *Walbrook: the samian catalogue* (1993), which is arranged numerically by context number. The report states the number of vessels represented in each entry, thereby providing a means of quantification.

The final report

The pottery is presented in the finds catalogues by stratigraphic group. The data are tabulated with each stratigraphic group having two main tables. The first lists the non-samian fabrics and forms; the second presents the samian forms by source/fabric. The quantity of each type is given in brackets if more than one vessel is represented.

Each set of group tables is accompanied by a commentary and a dating discussion. The percentages given in the text for non-samian wares are percentages of the non-samian wares only. A list of the contexts yielding pottery precedes the text for each group. An overall discussion of the pottery is given below *(General summary and discussion)*

The pottery section of each stratigraphic group provides details for certain categories of material, eg potter's stamps, decorated samian, unusual vessels, other vessels of intrinsic interest and graffiti. This pottery is also included in the group tables described above.

The dating of the late Roman assemblages depends to a considerable extent on the following publications: *Oxfordshire Roman pottery* (Young 1977), *The Alice Holt/Farnham pottery industry* (Lyne and Jefferies 1979) and *Roman pottery from the Nene Valley: a guide* (Howe, Perrin and Mackreth 1980). In order to avoid repetition these works will not be referenced in the following text.

The illustrations

The illustrated material has been selected to provide a representative sample of the non-samian wares for each group, including vessels which are considered to provide key dating evidence. Obviously residual material has been excluded. Additional illustrations of stamps and other material of intrinsic interest are presented in the appropriate sections in the latter part of the report. The illustrations are accompanied by a descriptive catalogue. The entries are minimal; more detailed expansions of the codes are given at the end of this brief introduction.

General summary and discussion

The dating of some of the groups (II, V and VI) is clearly problematical due to intrusiveness, the high degree of residuality and the generally mixed date of the pottery. These problems cast doubt on the integrity of all the groups and consequently make it difficult to date any of them with much confidence. This includes Group VII, which is crucial for dating the construction of the Mithraeum. Analysis of some groups is further limited by their small size (Groups I, III, IV and XI).

It is certain, however, that the latest assemblages lie well within the fourth century. It is possible that they may extend into the fifth century but this is difficult to determine because Roman pottery lacks diagnostic types which might help to recognise very late Roman deposits. Malcolm Lyne, however, has noted (cf archive notes) that the pottery from Mithraeum includes examples of 'Six Bells' ware, a late variant of the Alice Holt/Farnham industry, which he suggests may be fifth century. The curious unidentified vessel from Period 2 (X.52) adds to the possibility of fifth-century activity.

Samian is present in exceptional quantities, accounting for over half the pottery in several assemblages (see J Bird's comments below). This distortion almost certainly reflects the retention and disposal policy of material at the time of excavation and shortly afterwards in favour of samian. Most of the samian, including all the stamps, is residual and plays a limited role in dating the sequence.

One of the most interesting aspects of the pottery assemblage is the distribution of the C306. There is a total of 43 vessels of this type from the assemblage, 41 of which are confined to the sequence inside the Mithraeum (ie the Cutting C complex), with the greatest concentration (28) from Group X. This group, it should be noted, postdates the burial of the Mithraic cult icons and so is associated with the new cult (Bacchus?) which took over the temple.

The enigmatic nature of the C306 is described in detail by Symonds and Wade (forthcoming) but summarised here. It has an unusual distribution pattern, since it is largely confined to London and Colchester and has a tendency to occur in particularly large numbers on a few sites including the Butt Road Cemetery site, Colchester. Hull also noted its presence in the Colchester 'Mithraeum' assemblage (Hull 1958).

The function of these vessels is uncertain; it has not been established whether they are bowls or lids. Their poor finish possibly indicates that they were intended to have a limited life, perhaps even to be used on a single occasion only. The evidence tends to suggest that they may have played a part in ritual activities. Their occurrence in the London temple assemblage, irrespective of cult, corroborates this idea. The dating of the C306 is also uncertain but it seems to have been produced during the third and fourth centuries. It is clear that the C306 holds great potential for further research.

The 'frog pot' from Period 1 (VI.11–13) is another vessel type with probable religious or ritual associations. It is discussed by Bird in the finds catalogues below.

Industrial evidence from the pottery consists of three crucibles (Groups II, VII and IX) and one parting vessel (Group IX); those from Group IX are from trenches outside the Mithraeum. This material could be indicative of metalworking in the immediate vicinity or alternatively may have come from elsewhere in the City and been dumped as rubbish in the Walbrook valley.

Apart from the vessels discussed above, the late Roman groups seem to reflect fairly typical domestic usage. There appears to be no significant differences in this respect between deposits from within the Mithraeum and those outside it. There is a preponderance of types likely to be found in a kitchen for food preparation, cooking and storage: mortaria, and bowls and jars in reduced wares. The other main category of a domestic assemblage, namely tablewares in finer fabrics, occurs in smaller quantities. Beakers in Nene Valley colour-coated ware are the most common type but imported varieties such as Moselkeramik are also present. The other main element of the fineware repertoire, the bowl, is mostly represented by Oxfordshire red colour-coated ware.

Almost certainly, most of the pottery from the Mithraeum was not associated with its use but was presumably included in the material brought in for floor make-ups and other related construction purposes. This helps to explain the presence of an essentially domestic assemblage in a temple setting. Obviously there is a problem in trying to establish which elements of the assemblage, if any, were directly related to the building's function as a temple. The C306 seems to be the only vessel type which falls into this category.

Pottery codes and expansions

Pottery forms

Code	Expansion
I	Flagon
IA	Collared or Hofheim Flagon
IB	Ring-necked flagon
IB2	Ring-necked flagon with trumpet mouth and well defined rings
IB3	Ring-necked flagon with wide mouth and rings of equal diameter forming an upright neck
IB4	Ring-necked flagon with wide flaring mouth and fairly prominent rim
IB5	Ring-necked flagon with prominent rounded rim
IB7–9	Ring-necked flagon with cup-shaped neck/rim
IC	Pinched-mouth flagon
ID	Disc-mouth flagon
IE	Two-handled flagon with squat bulbous body
IF/G	Metal derivative flagons (MT3)
IJ	Two-handled amphora-type flagon
II	Jar
IIA	Bead-rim jar
IIB	Necked jar with rounded body
IIC	Necked jar with carinated shoulder and cordon at base of neck
IID	Necked, round-shouldered jar with 'figure-7' rim and decorated zone on shoulder delineated by cordon and grooves
IIE	Necked, round-bodied jar with decorated shoulder zone
IIF	Slightly everted-rim jar (BB1/BB2 type)
IIF1	Slightly everted-rim jar with burnished decoration on neck (BB1 type)
IIG	Necked jar usually with cordon or other division at neck/shoulder junction
IIJ	Simple neckless jar (sometimes called unguent jar)
IIJ1	As IIJ but small
IIM	Storage jar with rolled rim and decorated zone on shoulder
IIR	Narrow-necked jar/flask
III	Beaker
IIIB	Ovoid beaker
IIIB1	Ovoid beaker with barbotine ring and dot decoration
IIIC	Everted-rim beaker with sloping shoulder
IIIE	Everted-rim beaker without neck or shoulder having zone of decoration delineated by groove beneath rim
IIIF	'Poppy-head' beaker
IIIG	Carinated beaker with tall rim
IIIH	Round-bodied beaker with tall rim
IV	Bowl
IVA	Bowl with grooved flanged rim
IVF	Bowl with hooked or folded-over rim
IVG	Bowl with flat rim (BB1 type)
IVH1	Bowl/dish with triangular/rounded rim and lattice decoration (BB2 type)
IVH5	As for IVH1 but undecorated
IVJ	Dish with plain rim
IVK	'Surrey bowl'
V	Plate
VA	Plate with plain exterior profile
VI	Cup
IX	Miscellaneous, eg triple vase

Pottery decoration

Code	Expansion
BAD	Barbotine (no examples)
BDD	Barbotine dot (no examples)
BFD	Barbotine figure (no examples)
BUD	Burnished decoration
BR	Bead rim
BX	Castor box
CA	Carinated bowl
CDR	Copy of Dragendorff samian form (eg CDR27)
CMB	Combed
CR	Cornice rim
CRT	Copy of Ritterling samian form (eg CRT12)

CRUC	Crucible
C306	Camulodunum type 306 bowl
ER	Everted rim (beakers only)
ERJ	Strongly everted-rim jar (BB1 type)
FB	Flanged bowl (BB1 type)
FN	Funnel-necked flagon
FOB	Folded beaker
G226	Gillam type 226: incipient flanged bowl
G238	Gillam type 238 mortarium
HPD	Hair-pin barbotine
INDE	Indented
LMPH	Lampholder
MORT	Mortarium
MORT BEF	Bead and flange mortarium
MORT HAM	Hammerhead mortarium
MORT HOF	Hooked flange mortarium
MORT WAL	Wall-sided mortarium
MOTTO	Motto beaker
NCD	Incised decoration
NE	Necked bowl
NJ	Necked jar
OL	Obtuse lattice
PR	Plain rim
RC	Rough-cast
ROD	Rouletted
SCD	Barbotine scale
SJ	Storage jar
STD	Stamped decoration
STRA	Strainer
TZ	Tazza
WPD	White-painted

External typologies

Code	**Typology**
C	Camulodunum (Colchester) Hull 1958
G	Gillam 1970
MT	Marsh 1978, London finewares
P	Fulford 1975, Porchester 'D' ware
Various	Young 1977, Oxfordshire wares

Dates/phases

Code	**Expansion**
ANTO	Antonine
E2	Early second century(*c* AD 100–130)
E/M3	Early to mid-third century(*c* AD 200–250)
FLAV	Flavian (*c* AD 70–100)
FLTR	Flavian–Trajanic (*c* AD 70–120)
L2/M3	Late second to mid-third century (*c* AD 170–250)
M/L1	Mid- to late first century (*c* 50–100)
NEEF	Neronian–early Flavian (*c* 55–80)
NERO	Neronian (*c* 55–70)
PREF	Pre-Flavian (*c* 40–70)

Fabrics

Code	**Expansion**
AHFA	Alice Holt/Farnham ware
AHSU	Alice Holt Surrey ware
AMPH	Misc Amphora Types
ARGO	Argonne ware
BB1	Black-burnished 1 ware
BB2	Black-burnished 2 ware
BB2F	Black-burnished 2 ware fine
BBS	Black Burnished Style wares
BHWS	Brockley Hill white-slipped ware
C186	Camulodunum Type 186 Amphora
C189	Camulodunum Type 189 Amphora
CALC	Late Roman calcite-gritted ware
CC	Miscellaneous colour-coated wares
CCGW	Copthall Close grey ware
CGBL	Central Gaulish/Lezoux black colour-coated ware
CGOF	Central Gaulish colour-coated ware: Other fabrics
COAR	Miscellaneous coarse wares
COLC	Colchester colour-coated ware
COMO	Colchester mortaria
DR20	Dressel 20 amphora
DR28	Dressel 28 amphora
EIFL	Eifelkeramik
ERMS	Early Roman micaceous sandy ware
ERSA	Early Roman sandy A ware
ERSA/B	Early Roman sandy A/B ware
ERSB	Early Roman sandy B ware
FINE	Miscellaneous fine wares
FMIC	Fine Micaceous black/grey ware
GROG	Miscellaneous grog-tempered wares
HOO	Hoo-type ware
HWB	Highgate Wood 'B' grog-tempered ware
HWB/C	Highgate Wood B/C grog/sand-tempered ware
HWC	Highgate Wood 'C' sand-tempered ware
HWC+	Highgate Wood 'C' ware with added coarse sand
KOLN	Cologne colour-coated ware
L555	London Type 55.5 amphora
LOMI	Local/?London mica-dusted ware
LONW	London ware
LOXI	Local oxidised ware
MARB	Miscellaneous marbled wares
MHAD	Much Hadham ware (oxidised)
MICA	Miscellaneous mica-dusted wares
MOSL	Moselkeramik
NFF	North French flagon fabric
NFSE	North French/Southeast England wares
NKGW	North Kent grey ware
NKSH	North Kent shell-tempered ware
NVCC	Nene Valley colour-coated ware
NVWW	Nene Valley white ware
OXCC	Oxfordshire colour-coated ware
OXID	Miscellaneous oxidised wares
OXMO	Oxfordshire mortaria

OXPA	Oxfordshire parchment ware
OXRC	Oxfordshire red colour-coated ware
OXWS	Oxfordshire white-slipped redware
OXWW	Oxfordshire white ware
PE47	Pelichet 47/Dressel 30 amphora
PORD	Portchester 'D' ware
PRW	Pompeian red ware
RDBK	?Verulamium region 'Ring and dot' Beaker fabric
RHMO	Rhineland mortarium (other than Soller)
RHOD	Rhodian-style amphora
RVMO	Rhone Valley mortaria
RWS	Miscellaneous white-slipped red wares
SAND	Miscellaneous sand-tempered wares
SHEL	Miscellaneous shell-tempered wares
TN	*Terra Nigra*
TNIM	*Terra Nigra* imitations
TSK	Thameside Kent ware
VCWS	?Verulamium region coarse white-slipped ware
VRG	Verulamium region grey ware
VRMA	?Verulamium region marbled ware
VRW	Verulamium region white wares
VAR	Variant

The samian

by J Bird

Much of the samian from the Walbrook excavation was residual in later levels, and for this reason only those stamped and decorated pieces relevant to the dating of the site, and a small number of other vessels of particular interest, have been illustrated and described in the text. Such a large assemblage does, however, merit consideration as a whole, and this discussion is based on all the samian recovered.

General summary and discussion

The overall dating of the samian is shown on the graph, Figure 138, which is based on 305 stamped and decorated pieces. The general outline follows the usual pattern for British sites, which as Marsh (1981) has demonstrated is apparently governed by variations in samian supply; however, comparison between Figure 138 and the graph for London as a whole (Marsh 1981, fig 11.8) does show differences in detail which are presumably to be explained by the history and development of the site. The most notable of these differences is the relatively low level — approximately half that shown by Marsh — of early to mid-Antonine material, but the comparatively high level of samian dating into the first half of the third century should also be noted.

By far the largest amount of samian, 63% of the stamped and decorated pieces, is from South Gaul, and almost all of this is likely to have originated at La Graufesenque. There is one decorated sherd and a very few plain vessels that may have come from

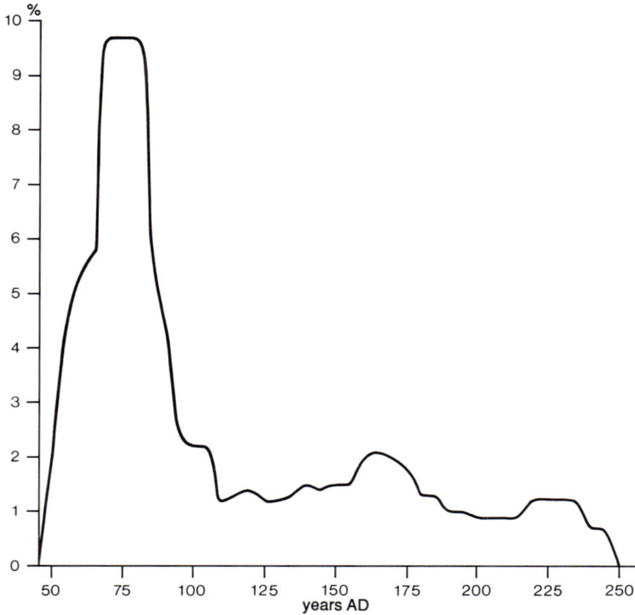

Fig 138 Distribution of the samian by date

Montans. As the graph shows, the peak of this first-century material lies *c* AD 70–85, and there are many decorated vessels, both Dragendorff Form 29 and 37, having stylistic links with the Pompeii Hoard samian. The decoration includes designs and motifs associated with such potters as Meddillus, Mommo, Pontus, Severus and Vitalis; there are also three plain-ware stamps each of Pontus and Severus, and two of Vitalis. Two Dragendorff Form 29s are stamped by Meddillus (II.22 and II.41), and there is a fragment of a Dragendorff Form 37, unfortunately unstratified, signed in the mould by Censor (0.4). Slightly later Flavian potters such as M Crestio, Crucuro and Germanus are represented, and late Flavian–Trajanic wares are present in some quantity. Relatively few of the Neronian decorated bowls could be assigned to specific styles: they include decoration associated with such potters as Bassus and Coelus (represented also by single plain-ware stamps of Bassus and of Bassus-Coelus), Licinus, Masclus, Murranus and Niger. The plain wares include one marbled piece (VII.19) and an unusual spouted and handled bowl (IV.10); of the commoner types, there is a relatively low proportion of such specifically pre-Flavian forms as Ritterling Forms 8 and 9 and Dragendorff Form 24/25.

The central Gaulish wares originated from Les Martres-de-Veyre and Lezoux (5% and 18% respectively of the stamped and decorated pieces). The decorated ware from Les Martres includes two bowls each of Drusus I, X-12 and X-13, and there are five identified plain-ware stamps. Apart from second-century types, the Lezoux products include a small group of vessels in the 'micaceous' ware of the first century: a Flavian Dragendorff Form 37, an undecorated Form 35, and examples of Forms 18/31, 27 and 33. The relatively low level of Antonine samian is emphasised by the low numbers of bowls by the largest factories: the Cinnamus group is responsible for only 7–9 pieces, and the slightly later workshops of Paternus II and Doeccus-Casurius for only 3 or 4 and 3–7 bowls respectively. Apart from mould-decorated wares, there are several sherds of Déchelette Form 72 jars with applied motifs and barbotine, and a small number with incised decoration.

East Gaulish wares are hardly present at all until the later second century: earlier pieces include a bowl of the Satto-Saturninus workshop and one of Gesatus of Lavoye. The later factories at Rheinzabern and Trier were responsible for most of the East Gaulish products (10% and 3% respectively of the stamped and decorated wares). These wares date up to the middle of the third century, and bear comparison with the late material from the waterfront at St Magnus House (Bird 1986a). The Rheinzabern vessels include decorated bowls of Julius II–Julianus I (5–7 bowls) and Primitivius (4), both of whom were active well into the third century (cf Bittner 1986). There are two bowls, of Firmus II and Primitivius IV, with mould-stamps (VII.31 and VII.32). The Trier products include late vessels by Criciro and Afer, one of them with a 70mm-deep rim band. The plain forms from both centres also include late types dating from the first half of the third century (cf Bird 1996): Dragendorff Form 53 (VII.40), Ludowici Form SMb with barbotine decoration, Ludowici Form Th, flagon and jar forms. The cup (VII.43) is probably also a late East Gaulish product.

Acknowledgements

The initial work on this report (1970) owed much to Brian Hartley, who gave generously of his time and expertise in advising and teaching a newcomer to the subject; it is a great pleasure to thank him now for all his help. I would also like to thank Brenda Dickinson for her comments on the potters' stamps, and for her prompt revision of her 1970 report.

Samian codes

Fabrics/Source

Code	Expansion
ARGO	Argonne ware
CG	Central Gaul
EG	East Gaul
LG	La Graufesenque
LR	Le Rozier
LZ	Lezoux
MARB	Marbled (slip)
MLEZ	Micaceous Lezoux
MONT	Montans
MV	Les Martres-de-Veyre
RZ	Rheinzabern
SG	South Gaul

Typologies

(codes for general form categories are listed above)

Code	Expansion
CH	Chenet 1941
CU	Curle 1911
DE	Déchelette 1904
DR	Dragendorff 1895–6
KN	Knorr 1952
LD	Ludowici 1912
RT	Ritterling 1913
WA	Walters 1908

The sculptures: general note

by J Hall

For a full discussion of all these sculptures, see Toynbee (1986), from which the brief catalogue descriptions are taken, and below (Groups IX, VIII/IX/X, IX/X, X AND XIV). Additional information has been provided by Susan Walker, Martin Henig and Tom Blagg. In 1995 samples were taken of the marbles for isotopic analysis. The results, which question the original visual identifications made by Professor Toynbee and S E Ellis, are presented after this note.

The breaking down of the corpus of sculptures into their respective stratified groups reveals many of the misconceptions which have accrued over the last 40 years (Fig 139). For instance:

- the limestone hand and forearm of Mithras Tauroctonos (IX.43) comes from the fill of the pit which contained Serapis, Mercury and the oversized hand. It is not certain if it is a primary deposit or a random find in the backfill.
- the roundel (IX/X.1) comes from the phase of the temple which postdated the burial of the Mithraic icons and was therefore placed in the temple when it had perhaps passed into the possession of the

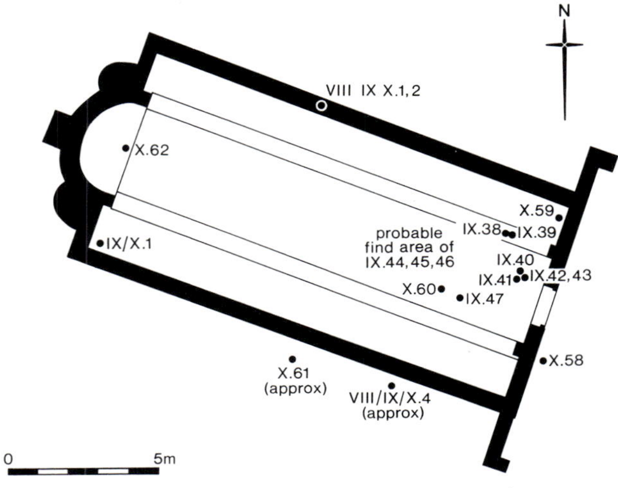

Fig 139 The location of the sculptures

followers of another cult. There is no need to attempt to find a Mithraic connection for it.

- the Dioscurus relief (VIII/IX/X.5) was found at some distance from the temple and does not appear to havebeen directly associated with it. Indeed, it is suggested below that it came from a separate shrine in the valley.

The stable isotope analysis of the marble sculptures

by K Matthews and S Bowman

Experimental procedure

The experimental procedure is based upon the work of McCrea (1950), although it was not applied to the provenancing of classical white marble until the 1970s (see, for example, Craig and Craig 1972, Coleman and Walker 1979, and Walker and Matthews 1988).

Eleven marble sculptures and one inscription were sampled (Table 1). One artefact was unsuitable for analysis: the roundel was carved from a very thin (*c* 4mm) sheet of marble, and it was felt that drilling into the edge of it would undoubtedly cause severe damage to the object. Two samples were collected from the statue of Mercury, one from the statue itself, and one from the detached base on which the statue stands.

Powder samples were collected from the sculptures by using a 4mm tungsten-carbide-tipped masonry drill. The samples were taken from an already damaged area of each object which is not normally visible when the object is on public display. The initial drillings were discarded to eliminate any material affected by the weathering process. The grain size of these sculptures was also noted. From the powder thus obtained, 10mg were reacted with 100% orthophosphoric acid *in vacuo*. The carbon dioxide evolved was isotopically analysed using a VG Micromass 602D mass-spectrometer.

The isotopic (∂) obtained is given in parts per mil (‰ ie per thousand) relative to the PDB standard (Craig 1957) where

$$R={}^{13}C/{}^{12}C$$

or

$$R={}^{18}O/{}^{16}O$$

The standard error on these measurements is typically ± 0.05 ‰.

Results

The analytical results are presented in Table 1 together with details of the sculptures. It was noted that, with one exception, these sculptures were all carved from fine-grained marble. The exception was the inscription panel, the marble of which was very coarse-grained.

The isotopic ratios have been plotted $\partial^{13}C$ versus $\partial^{18}O$ (Fig 140): also on the plot are the 90% ellipses (Leese 1988) of isotopic signatures obtained from quarry data very kindly made available by Professor Norman Herz of the University of Georgia, USA (see also Herz 1987), and supplemented by data from quarry samples measured by the Department of Scientific Research of the British Museum. The ellipses selected include those for some of the more important marble quarrying areas in antiquity, and for which data are available, albeit limited. The ellipses represent those areas which produce fine-grained marble. However, also on the plot is the ellipse representing the Proconnesus quarries, which produced coarse-grained stone.

Table 1 Isotope analysis of marbles

Number in diagram	*Description*	*MoL Acc No*	*BMRL No*	*$d^{13}C$ ‰*	*$d^{18}O$ ‰*
1 (IX.44)	Water-deity	A 16931	52421T	2.18	-1.63
2 (IX.45)	Genius	A 16932	52422R	2.47	-3.20
3 (IX.46)	Relief of Mithras Tauroctonus	A 16933	52423P	1.83	-2.29
4 (XIV.42)	Bacchic torso	18015	52424Y	2.61	-2.69
5 (IX.39)	Minerva	18491	52425W	2.64	-2.98
6 (IX.42)	Mithraic hand	18492	52426U	2.35	-1.73
7 (IX.41)	Figure of Mercury	18493	52427S	2.63	-2.81
8 (IX.41)	Base of the figure of Mercury	18695	52428Q	2.13	-2.11
9 (IX.40)	Serapis	18494	50997U	2.54	-3.26
10 (X.58)	Bacchic torso	18495	52429Z	2.37	-3.25
11 (X.59)	Bacchic group	18496	50998S	1.75	-3.98
12 (IX.47)	Inscription panel	18499	52430R	3.46	-1.62
13 (IX.38)	Mithras	20005	50996W	2.19	-3.49

Note that the standard error on these measurements is typically ± 0.05 ‰

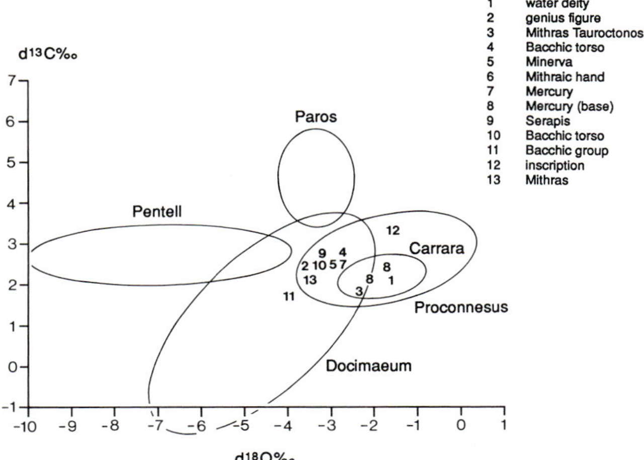

Fig 140 Isotopic analysis of the marbles from the temple

Discussion

Examination of the plot reveals that the marble used for the fine-grained sculptures, ie not the inscription panel (12), appears to have originated in the Docimaeum (or Afyon) quarries in Asia Minor or in the quarries at Carrara. It is known that both of these quarries were being exploited in Roman times (Susan Walker pers comm).

Two of the sculptures, the water-deity (1) and the Mithraic hand (6) appear to have originated from Carrara. Eight seem to be from the Docimaeum quarries: the genius figure (2), the two Bacchic torsos (4 and 10), Minerva (5), Mercury (7), Serapis (9), the Bacchic group (11), and Mithras (13). There are also two results (3 and 8) that fall within an area of overlap of the ellipses representing Docimaeum and Carrara. Unfortunately, stable isotope analysis cannot distinguish between the two sources in such instances, ie these two sculptures could have come from either of the two sources.

One of these (8) is the base for the statue of Mercury (7). The base has been carved in such a way that the statue fits into it, giving the appearance that the whole ensemble was of just one piece. A cursory study of the two pieces suggests that it would be very difficult to cut one block of stone to give such a joint. It seems more likely that the base was carved separately to fit around the bottom of the statue. Isotopically, the results are different, even when experimental errors are considered: 0.5‰ in the carbon ratios and 0.7‰ in the oxygen ratios. The study of the association of fragments of stone has been reported by Coleman and Walker (1979) and also by Matthews (1988). It has been demonstrated that for these types of marble, variations of the order of about 0.1‰ can be expected if the fragments were originally from a single larger block. In the case of the statue of Mercury, despite the apparent visual similarity of the stone, it seems unlikely that they were both from a single larger piece of stone.

The isotope ratios for the inscription panel (12) correspond only to the Proconnesus ellipse. Such a provenance is entirely consistent with the stone's grain size, which is fairly coarse.

It was noted that the roundel, which was not analysed, was of a coarser-grained marble, and therefore is unlikely to be from any of the fine-grained marble quarries that are represented on the plot. The marble was also much greyer in colour than the other sculptures.

Conclusion

Twelve sculptures, plus the base of one, were analysed. Of the 12, 8 are of marble likely to have originated in the Docimaeum quarries in Asia Minor, and 2 are of Carrara marble from Italy. A further two pieces, one of which is the base for the statue of Mercury, could have originated in either of these two locations. The inscription panel was found to be Proconnesian marble. These identifications are consistent with the grain size of the stones.

Comments on the isotopic analysis of the sculptures

by S Walker

In her publication of the sculptures of the Walbrook Mithraeum, the late Professor Jocelyn Toynbee suggested that all the marble sculptures forming the basis of the present investigation were carved in Carrara marble, a view then supported by an examination of the stones under ultraviolet fluorescent light by the late S E Ellis (Toynbee 1986, 64–5).

However, in the programme of stable isotope analysis reported here, only two of the sculptures fell unequivocally within the ellipse representing samples from the Carrara quarries (Fig 140), the reclining water-deity (Sample 1, IX.44) and the colossal hand of Mithras Tauroctonos (Sample 6, IX.42). The base of the statue of Mercury (Sample 8, IX.41) and the relief representing Mithras Tauroctonos, dedicated by Ulpius Silvanus (Sample 3, IX.46), fell within both the Carrara and the Docimaean ellipses.

Another seven sculptures exhibit lower oxygen ratios and, for the most part, higher carbon ratios than those mentioned above. They form a miscellaneous group in terms of subject matter, quality and date, ranging from the very fine head of Serapis (Sample 9, IX.40) to the cruder heads of Minerva (Sample 5, IX.39) and Mithras (Sample 13, IX.38), the figure of a Genius (Sample 2, IX.45), the statuette of Mercury (Sample 7, IX.41, notably different from its base), and the two Bacchic torsos (Samples 4, XIV.42 and 10, X.58). All these results fall within the Docimaean ellipse. However, though fine-grained, the stone for these sculptures does not resemble Docimaean marble in its appearance. It is very grey in tone and, in most cases, exhibits irregular patches of dark blue colouration, sometimes confined by the sculptors to the back of the figures. In appearance the marble is not unlike that of the samples that fall within the Carrara ellipse, particularly the colossal Mithraic hand and the base of the statue of Mercury. The latter may be reasonably considered the same stone as that used for the figure though not, apparently, from the same block despite the miniature scale. The reason for the discrepancy in isotope readings remains puzzling.

The results of the inscription (Sample 12, IX.47) and the Bacchic Group (Sample 11, X.59) are distinct from these. The former falls outside the Carrara ellipse but within that of the Proconnesian quarries. Visually the marble resembles Proconnesian in its medium to large glittering crystals and in the blue grey bands of colour traversing the block.

The Bacchic Group, like the inscription, is cut from a very thin slab of marble, in this case fine-grained, sugary and honey-toned. Reddish blue blotches on the torso of Bacchus suggest that the group may be carved of Docimaean marble from Phrygia, better known in its coloured version of pavonazzetto. This was, along with Proconnesian marble, imported to London for use as veneer (Pritchard 1986, 186, fig 13: the third-century contexts offer the highest number of instances of use of both marbles). In composition the group resembles other small-scale sculptures known to have been made by sculptors based at the Phrygian quarries in late antiquity. Both Docimaeum and Proconnesus are listed amongst those quarries whose prices were regulated by the edict of Diocletian (Lauffer 1971, 192, frag 33, lines 7–8). It is of some interest, then, to note that the inscription and the Bacchic group are associated with the fourth-century use of the Mithraeum, perhaps as a shrine of Bacchus, and that in material they are quite distinct from the Mithraic group.

The small objects

by A Wardle

The finds from the Mithraeum excavations were originally studied by Joanna Bird and the initial report completed in 1972. The catalogue entries have subsequently (1993) been revised by Joanna Bird and reordered by the editors in accordance with recent work on the original archive. In view of the nature and date of the excavations, it was decided to adopt a traditional arrangement of the objects, by material rather than function.

General summary and discussion

The material from Period I, particularly finds from the spreads and dumped deposits of Groups I and II, can be seen as an addition to the large assemblages of finds from the Walbrook stream and banks. It can be compared, for example, with the dumped assemblages from the nearby Bucklersbury House excavations, particularly Guildhall Museum Excavation Register no 268G and Excavation Register no 268H, which date from the early second century and came from the stream bed (Wilmott 1991, 128–32). These produced a similar mix, with a few military items, personal possessions, and a range of iron tools and fittings in a good state of preservation. Groups I and II contained a limited number of military objects (see below), several items for personal adornment and use, two brooches, a brooch chain, finger ring, pins, shoes, various cosmetic implements, several objects used in a domestic context, chiefly fittings and utensils, several items with a possible religious connection, and various iron tools and fittings, including several styli. The preservation of these is, as with the Walbrook iron in general, generally good, but the range and quantity do not appear to be as extensive as that from other published groups. The number of finds from these groups is too small for valid statistical analysis by function, as attempted by Wilmott (1991), although further work on the entire Walbrook assemblage might prove of interest.

The contrast with the material from the Period II groups is principally one of scale, the smaller number of finds recovered reflecting changes in the pattern of occupation in this part of the Walbrook valley (Wilmott 1991, 179). There is, not surprisingly, little material from the Mithraeum itself, and it is impossible to establish with certainty the association of finds from Period II contexts outside the Mithraeum with the temple. Many objects from such contexts, some located on the other side of the Walbrook stream, are clearly or probably residual.

The finds of greatest interest are those with a religious, specifically Mithraic association. The significance of the sculptures from the Mithraeum has been discussed elsewhere (Toynbee 1986) as have the silver canister and strainer, which undoubtedly had a place in Mithraic ritual. Other objects were also originally from the temple. One laver (IX.37) came from the building with one of the groups of sculpture, and another, much larger stone vessel was found outside (VII/IX/X.3). Such lavers would have undoubtedly have served a ritual purpose and have been found in other mithraea (Harris and Harris 1965, 4). The jet dagger grip and scabbard mount (VIII.55 and IX.53) could have belonged to a sculptural group, they may have been votive objects or they could have been part of the cult paraphernalia. There has been some discussion of the use of such lead alloy vessels as X.57, which came from the narthex of the temple, and it is quite possible that they were votive offerings (Henig 1984, 132). The identification of the iron dagger (XIII.20) as a 'ritual object' or perhaps part of sculptural group must remain less certain. It is not clear whether this is the object described by Grimes (1968, 114) as being found with the jet handle within the temple. Its context description places the findspot in Cutting F, at some distance from the Mithraeum itself. Similarly, a fragment of gilded leather may be part of the temple furnishings (X.67), but a second fragment (VII.53), perhaps from a couch, was found in a Walbrook deposit that pre-dated the construction of the Mithraeum.

Other objects from the site may have a religious connotation, but because of their stratigraphic position have no connection with the Mithraeum. Most notable among these is the 'frog pot' (VI.11–13), the frog being associated with the worship of Sabazios. Although the cults of Sabazios and Mithras are often linked (see *Appendix 1: A fourth-century* bacchium *or* sacrarium, by Martin Henig), the 'frog pot' sherd was found in a Period I group (Group VI) and its use was earlier than the Mithraeum. It may be significant, however, that this cult was also closely associated with Dionysus (see *Appendix 1*). Similarly, the lamp (VI.14), of a type sometimes found on temple sites, came from a Period 1 context (Group VI), and other sherds found in later groups could be residual (XIV.38, XV.21, 0.3). A broken fragment of a Venus figurine (VII/IX.6), found outside the Mithraeum, may have come from a local or domestic shrine and such material should be seen in the context of similar finds from throughout the Walbrook valley.

The site produced several items with a military association, but they are from diverse groups and contexts and cannot be linked in any way. They do, however, extend the general Walbrook assemblage, which will be examined together with the evidence with the rest of the evidence from the rest of London by M C Bishop *et al* in a corpus of military finds (forthcoming). The antler ear laths from composite bows (II.125 and IX.51) are of particular interest, as they comprise two of only three examples from London.

The finds catalogue

Period 1 finds

Group I – Flavian

The finds catalogued and discussed below come from the following layers:

Cutting AA: 538, 538a
Cutting AB: 510
Cutting CA: 215
Cutting CB: 132, 133
Cutting CD: 228, 234
Cutting F: 739, 742

These layers represent the first attempts to consolidate the west bank of the Walbrook stream. The east bank (Cutting CD) was covered with a deposit which could be interpreted as foreshore material. The west bank layers rested directly upon the natural profile of the valley. Features took the form of wooden plank walkways, floors and treading surfaces in association with lightweight shed-like or hut-like buildings. The wet conditions close by the stream became extreme on occasions — almost marshlike. Some of the make-up dumps between successive floors may be upcast from the clearing of the stream channel. Any timber revetments associated with these surfaces would have been destroyed by later cleaning of the stream channel.

The pottery is of Flavian date, including Highgate Wood sand-tempered ware (HWC) and a base fragment from an early Flavian samian Dragendorff Form 37. Diagnostic second-century types are absent.

The small finds from this group are few, comprising a little domestic debris (needle I.19, spoon I.20) and two wooden objects, writing tablets (I.22 and 23) and a barrel bung or stopper (I.24). In addition, the group contained a harness pendant (I.21), one of the small number of military items from the site. With the exception of the writing tablet fragments, which came from the west bank in Cutting F, all of the finds came from the east bank of the Walbrook in Cuttings CA, CB and CD.

The vessels

Pottery

Tables 2 and 3

A Flavian date is probable for this small assemblage. The presence of Highgate Wood 'C' sand-tempered ware and the samian Dragendorff Form 37 provide the date of after *c* AD 70. There is also an absence of types diagnostic of the second century and a predominance of fabrics and forms typical of the first century. All the samian is from South Gaul, with most vessels falling within the Neronian/early Flavian period. Samian constitutes 33% of the assemblage, which is an exceptionally high ratio for the City of London. The combined Flavian samian assemblages from the city average at 8% EVEs.

Table 2 Group I pottery excluding samian

Fabric	*Forms*	*No of vessels (approx)*
AHSU	IIA; IID	2
AHSU?	NJ	1
FMIC	IIIG/H	1
GROG	IIA	1
HWB	IIA; IVF; LID(2)	4
HWB?	VA	1
HWC	IVA	1
HWC?	NJ	1
OXID	III	1
NKSH	IIM	1
RDBK	IIIB; IIIB1	2
SAND	NJ	1
VRW	II	1
Total		18

Table 3 Group I samian

Source/Fabric	*Forms*
SG	DR15/17; DR18(8); DR15/17 or 18(3); DR24/25(2); DR27(7); DR29(10); DR30; DR37; ?RT8 or 9; RT12; VI
Total no of vessels (approx)	36

Catalogue of illustrated pottery vessels
For code expansions see above, *Pottery codes and expansions*
Fig 141

I.1. Grog-tempered ware bead-rim jar (GROG IIA). *[AA538]*
I.2. Highgate Wood 'B' Grog-tempered ware bead-rim jar (HWB IIA). *[CB132]*
I.3. Alice Holt/Surrey ware bead-rim jar (AHSU IIA). *[CD228]I*
I.4. Alice Holt/Surrey ware necked jar with zone of burnished decoration on shoulder. *(AHSU IID) [CB132]*
I.5. Highgate Wood 'C' sand-tempered ware bowl (HWC IVA/F). *[CB132]*
I.6. Sandy ware (possibly) Highgate Wood 'C' ware necked jar (HWC? NJ). *[CD228]*
I.7. Unidentified reduced sandy ware necked jar (SAND NJ). *[CD228]*
I.8. Verulamium region white ware jar (VRW II). *[CA215]*
I.9. Ring and dot Beaker fabric ovoid beaker (RDBK IIIB). *[CB132]*
I.10. Unidentified oxidised ware beaker (OXID III). *[CD228]*

Selected samian

I.11. Joins I.12. Dragendorff Form 29, South Gaul. Upper zone straight wreath with chevron leaves, flanking a large rose motif. The rose is on a bowl stamped by Manduillus (Knorr 1952, Taf 33, F), on bowls attributed to him (Knorr 1952, Taf 33, G, H) and on a bowl in a style associated with stamps of Modestus (Bird and Marsh 1978, fig 28, no.15). The wreath is on a bowl whose lower zone recalls the work of Murranus (Bird and Marsh 1978, fig 28, no.1). *c* AD 50–70. *[AA/AB538] no 1a*
I.12. Joins I.11. *[AA/AB538a] no 1*

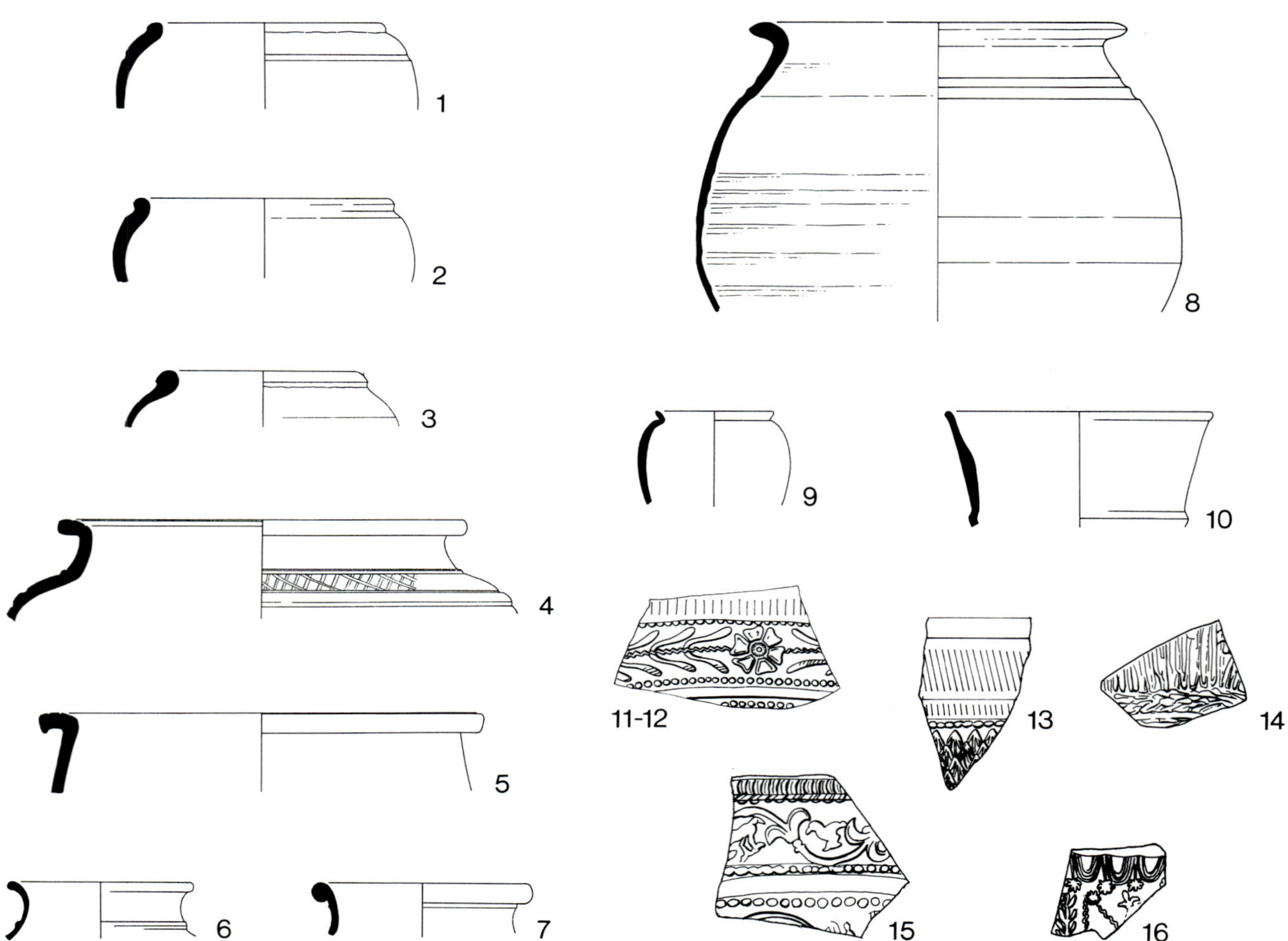

Fig 141 Period 1, Group I pottery vessels (nos 1-8 scale 1:4; nos 11-16 scale 1:2)

I.13. Dragendorff Form 29, South Gaul. Arrowheads in upper zone: cf Knorr 1952, Taf 23, A, stamped by Felix. Probably pre-Flavian. *[CB132] no 1*

I.14. Dragendorff Form 29, South Gaul. Gadroons and basal wreath: the wreath is recorded at La Graufesenque on bowls stamped by several Neronian potters. *c* AD 55–70. *[CB132] no 2*

I.15. Dragendorff Form 29, South Gaul. Scrolls in both zones. The leaf in the upper occurs with the same tendril binding and one of the birds on Knorr 1952, Taf 34, B, stamped by Licinus; a second Licinus bowl has both birds with more elaborate leaves (Knorr 1919, Taf 46, D). The shallow relief suggests use of the mould by a later potter; the style dates *c* AD 50–65. *[CD234] no 2*

I.16. Dragendorff Form 30, South Gaul. The fine conical ovolo with large rosette is recorded from a number of 30s but is not yet associated with any individual potter; it was also used on Dragendorff Form 11. Panels with ears of grain (cf Hermet pls 73, no 13, 74, no 11, 75, nos 3, 4), and saltire with bud. *c* AD 50–65. *[CA215] no 1*

Samian ware stamps

I.17. Primus iii, LG (b), 33a, Dragendorff Form 15/17 or 18, *c* AD 60–75. *[CB132]*

I.18. Unidentified, CO, Dragendorff Form 15/17 or 18, NEEF. *[CB132]*

The small objects
Fig 142

Copper alloy

I.19. Needle with plain tapering shaft; the eye is partly broken. Cf LRT pl xlii, 2–5. Length 93mm. *[CB132] MoL Acc No 18227*

I.20. Spoon with plain shaft tapering to a point; the squarish bowl is broken. Length 97.5mm. *[CB132] MoL Acc No 18198*

I.21. Drop-shaped pendant with two small *peltae* cut out and a knob at the base. The attaching rivet is still in place, with a washer on the underside. Such pendants are military, and were attached to riding harness; the drop-shaped type is of first- to third-century date (Bishop *et al* forthcoming, IK 13). Length 51mm. *[CB133] MoL Acc No 18214*

Wood

I.22. Writing tablet. Part of one leaf with a slot for the seal string in the raised border on the long side. *Abies* (silver fir) 137 x 56mm. *[F739] MoL Acc No 18211*

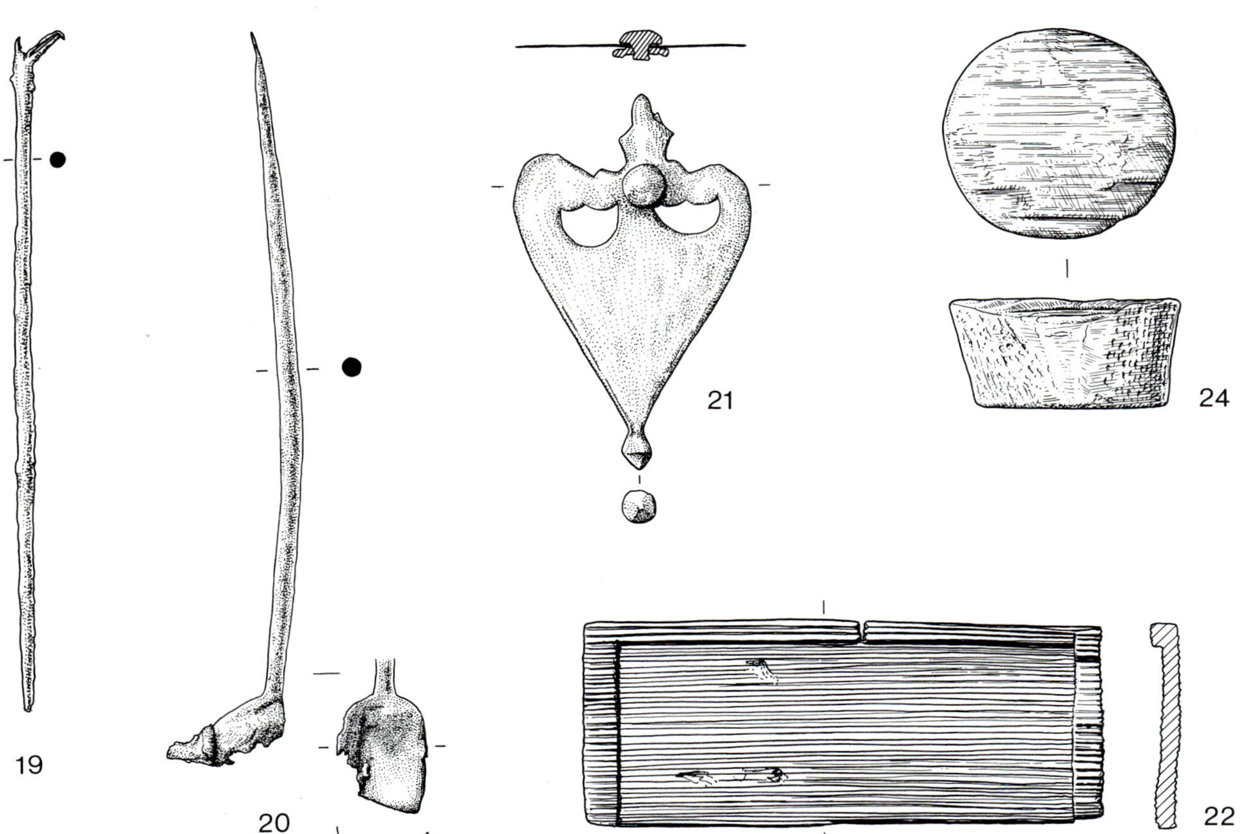

Fig 142 Period 1, Group I small objects (scale 1:1)

I.23. Fragment of writing tablet. *Abies* (silver fir). *[F742] MoL Acc No 18212. Not illustrated*

I.24. Round barrel bung or stopper, tapered; the underside is coated with pitch or resin. Similar to example from Guildhall Museum work on this site (Wilmott 1991, 151, no 604 and fig 111). Diameter 58mm, maximum thickness 28mm. *Abies* (silver fir). *[CB132] MoL Acc No 18197*

Group II: late first to early second century

The finds catalogued and discussed below come from the following layers:

Cutting AB: 541, 542, 548a, 549, 553, 554, 555
Cutting BB: 322, 337, 338, 343, 348, 349, 350, 356, 357
Cutting CA:162, 189, 190, 197, 205, 206, 211, 212
Cutting CB: 124, 126, 127, 128, 129, 130, 131
Cutting CD:209, 210, 213, 214, 218, 219, 221, 222, 223, 224
Cutting F:729, 730, 731, 734, 735, 740, 744, 745, 752

The consolidation of the west stream banks continued, and began in earnest on the east bank. This was on a much larger scale than before, making use of clean dumps of fresh soil and dirty material. The latter was probably derived from the cleaning of the stream channel. Rather than simple timber surfaces, the first of a number of stout timber platforms with piles, planks and sometimes joists were constructed. Again, evidence for lightweight buildings was recorded but none could be seen in plan. These were associated with the first of the identifiable revetments. This tilted forward, causing subsidence behind it, leading to renewed consolidation of the banks and creating even greater pressure on the revetment.

Although the pottery assemblage from this group contains a few sherds dating from the late second or early third century to the fourth century, these are likely to be contaminations from higher levels. The bulk of the material dates from the late first century up to, and including, the Antonine period. The pottery is very mixed, which may partly reflect the nature of its deposition, ie in upcast dumps.

The 33 small finds from Group II are similar in character to the material from Group I. Although nothing here is closely datable, the objects are consistent with a depositional date in the second century. Domestic material includes copper alloy and iron needles (II.111 and II.115), a lead handle mount (II.109), a shale platter (II.110), and probable furniture fittings, studs (eg II.113) and a bone hinge (II.124). There are several well preserved iron tools and implements – two styli (II.116 and II.117), tweezers or forceps (II.118), a gouge (II.119), a pruning hook (II.120) and miscellaneous fittings, part of a lock (II.121), and a T-clamp (II.122). The styli (II.116 and II.117), lock (II.121) and tweezers (II.118) came from the C complex of trenches on the east bank of the stream; the others were from west bank deposits.

Two objects have military associations, an antler ear lath from a composite bow (II.125), one of two found on the site (see IX.51 from Period 2), and a stud (II.112). A number of fragments of glass belonging to types common in the late first and early second centuries were recorded. In addition, however, there was a small group of glass from a single context which included glassworking debris. An almost complete lid-moil, a rare find, was recorded (II.134).

The waterlogged conditions again favoured the preservation of organic materials, with two more wooden stoppers (II.131 and II.132) and several shoes and fragments of leather, the latter coming from below the Mithraeum in Cutting C. Although the group contained waste, it is not the evidence for leatherworking noted by Grimes, which came from the western side of the Walbrook (1968, 98). The glassworking debris may indicate the presence of a glassworker in the vicinity. No evidence for furnaces of any type was found on any part of the site.

The vessels

Pottery

Tables 4 and 5

The dating of this group is very problematical. There is some obviously intrusive mid-third- to fourth-century material: three Alice Holt/Farnham ware vessels [F 740, CB 128, CA 189]; a black-burnished-style flanged bowl [BB 337] and an Oxfordshire red colour-coated ware bowl [CD 223]. If those sherds are discounted the dating of the assemblage is derived from the samian. The vessels concerned are a few Central Gaulish vessels of Antonine date, namely a Dragendorff Forms 31R [CD 209], 33, 36 [AB 541] and two Déchelette Form 72s [AB 541 CA 190], and, from East Gaul, a Dragendorff Form 37 [F 730] (rim only), a Form 45 [CD 209] dated to the second to mid-third century, and another Form 37 of Antonine or possibly early third-century date. As a group these vessels seem indicative of the late second century. The remainder of the assemblage, however, tends not to support such a date. In a typical late second-century group black-burnished ware would be one of the dominant wares, but in this assemblage only three vessels are present, a BB1 lid [CA 189] and two BB2 bowls (IVH1) [BB 337].

The main fabrics represented are Alice Holt Surrey ware (20%), Highgate Wood 'C' sand-tempered ware (16%) and Verulamium region white ware (11%). The production of these is considered to end *c* AD 160. First-century wares are also well represented; for example, most of the samian is South Gaulish, and Highgate Wood grog-tempered 'B' ware constitutes

Table 4 Group II pottery excluding samian

Fabric	*Forms*	*No of vessels (approx)*
AHFA	IVJ(2); IV/ERJ?	3
AHSU	IIA(15); IIC(6); IID; IIC/D; NJ(22); IVF?; IVK(2); LID	49
AHSU?	IV	1
BB1	LID	1
BB2	IVH1(2)	2
BBS	FB	1
CC	III HPD	1
CCGW	IV	1
CGOF	III RC	1
CGOF?	III RC	1
C186		1
ERSA?	IIA BUD	1
ERSB	IIA(3) II; NJ	5
ERSB?	IIA BUD; NJ	2
ERSA/B	NJ	1
ERMS	IIB(2)	2
ERMS?	IIB?; NJ; II/III	3
FINE	IIIB; IIIC; VA(2)	4
FMIC	IIIB BAD; IIIB ROD(2); III BDD(5); III(4)	12
GROG	IVF; IVF?; SJ; LID(2)	5
HOO	III? WPD	1
HOOVAR	NJ	1
HWB	IIA(3); SJ(2); IVF(7); LID	13
HWB?	SJ; IVF	2
HWB/C	IIA; IVF(3)	4
HWC	IIA(2); II; NJ(4); IIIF(7); IVF(17); IV; LID(7)?	40
HWC?	IIE?; IVF; LID(2)	4
KOLN	III BFD; III RC; III ROD	3
LONW	IV CDR37? NCD ROD	1
LOMI	IV CRT12	1
LOXI?	IVA	1
MICA (1241?)	III; IV	2
OXID	IB; IIG; ?	3
OXRC	IV	1
PE47		1
RDBK	IIIB1(2)	2
RHMO		1
RHOD		1
RVMO		1
SAND	IIA(2); IIE(2); NJ(3); IVA(2); IVF(8); VA; CRUC; LID(4); LMPH?	24
CCGW?	II	1
SHEL	IIA(2); NJ; IVF; LID	5
TN	V	1
TN/TNIM	V	1
VCWS	TZ	1
VRG	IVA(2)	2
VRW	IA; IB2(3); IB3?; ID; IE; IVA; IVF(2) MORT HOF(15); LID; TZ	27
VRW?	LID	1
Total		243

5% of the non-samian fabrics. A wide range of other early fabrics is present, such as Early Roman sandy micaceous ware, Fine micaceous black/grey ware and Hoo ware.

Clearly Group II contains very mixed material which is difficult to date. If the Antonine to mid-third-century samian (no II.7) is not regarded as intrusive it seems likely that the assemblage is mid- to late second-century. As in Group I the samian constitutes a very large part of the assemblage (59%) and includes 30 stamps. All these stamps belong to first-century potters and are, therefore, residual.

None of the standard vessel types from this group is illustrated.

Catalogue of illustrated pottery vessels
Fig 143

II.1. Hoo Ware (variant) necked jar. The fabric is as Hoo ware but with a red slip which is a previously unknown variant. The vessel has an everted rim and a high rounded shoulder. There is a very similar jar in Hoo ware in a Neronian assemblage from the King Street excavation in the City (KNG85, context 587, Corpus No 33102), which is more complete and shows that this form has a bulbous body. *[CB128]*

II.2. Hoo Ware beaker with (?)white painted decoration. Body sherd of a beaker with carination and broad cordon, possibly of the same form as Monaghan's class 2F, girth beakers (1987, 68–90). The white slip on the exterior is burnished.

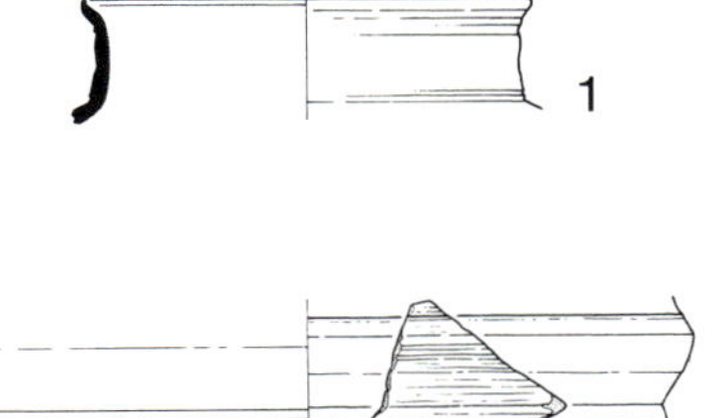

Fig 143 Period 1, Group II Hoo Ware vessels (scale 1:4)

Table 5 Group II samian

Source/ Fabric	*Forms*
SG	CU11(5); CU11?; DE67; DE67?; DR15/17(15); DR15/17R(10); DR15/17 or 15/17R; DR16; DR18(78); DR18R(4); DR18 or 18R(6); DR15/17 or 18(15); DR15/17R or 18R(6); DR22(2); DR24/25; DR27(93); DR30(3); DR33(3); DR35(4); DR27 or 35DR36(7); DR29(36); DR37(28); DR30 or 37; DR42; RT8(2);RT9; RT12(2); RT13;
SG	MARB DR15/17
SG?	DR33
MLEZ	DR18/31; DR27; DR33
MV	DR18/31
CG	CU11(2); DE72(2); DR27?; DR31R; DR18/31(3); DR33(3); DR36
EG	DR37(2); DR45
Total no of vessels (approx)	353

The cordon has zig-zag decoration which may be white painted or, alternatively, unburnished white slip. There is possibly further decoration beneath the carination but abrasion makes this uncertain. This type of decoration and finish is previously unknown on Hoo ware. *[CB127]*

Mortarium stamps

II.3. Verulamium region white ware hooked flange mortarium. The stamp is damaged but is probably from Die A of Doinus, reading DOINVSF, *c* AD 70–100. He was one of the foremost potters of the Verulamium region; his stamps have a wide distribution throughout Britain. *[CD209]*
II.4. Verulamium region white ware mortarium. DOINV(SF), as above. *[F740] Not illustrated*

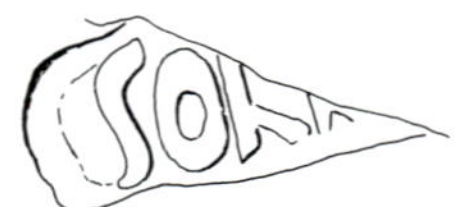

II.5. Verulamium region white ware mortarium. Broken stamp of Sollus from one of the three dies used by him. Stamps by Sollus have wide distribution and his commonest die is one of the finest made by a mortarium potter. This die, however, is semi-illiterate and badly executed and the stamps from it have a remarkably confined distribution (London and Wickford in Essex). *c* AD 70–100/110. *[BB343]*

Mortarium graffito 'stamp'

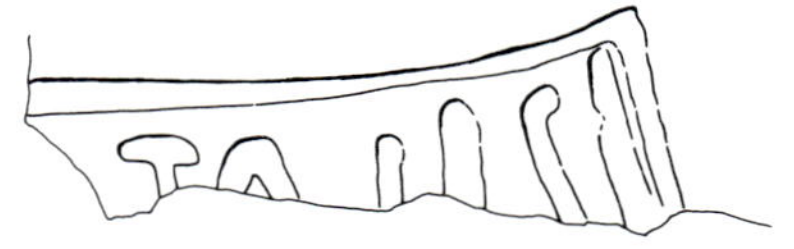

II.6. Verulamium region white ware mortarium. The vessel is not stamped but marked with retrograde, pre-firing graffito, a rarely used technique. It is damaged but probably reads BILAT( ); the B and T are clear, the other letters less certain. (From note by Mr R P Wright.) *[AB541]*

Terra Nigra *stamp*

II.7. Camulodunum 16. Platter base with a slight offset; although functional, the footring is unworn.The fragmentary stamp is placed centrally on the base inside a broad incised circle. It is possibly from the same die as one on a similar platter from Old Winteringham, Lincolnshire, which this piece closely resembles in fabric and technique. Hard fine white fabric, with occasional dark flecks; the dark blue black interior surface is highly polished, the exterior varies from dark blue black to silver grey and is less well burnished. This combination of fabric and form is typical of *Terra Nigra* in the late Claudian–early Flavian period and occurs frequently on military sites. *[CB124]*

Selected samian
Figs 144–7

II.8. Dragendorff Form 29, South Gaul. Upper zone scroll, finely modelled but slightly smudged. The terminals are a bud and probably a cordate leaf (cf Hermet 1934, pl 39, no 30). *c* AD 55–75. *[AB541] no 1*
II.9. Dragendorff Form 29, South Gaul. Central palmette wreath above scroll. *c* AD 60–80. *[AB541] no 2*
II.10. Dragendorff Form 29, South Gaul. Scroll in upper zone with poppy buds and rosettes; the motifs are common, eg Knorr 1952, Taf 62, B, stamped by Virtus. Burnt. *c* AD 60–80. *[AB541] no 3*
II.11. Dragendorff Form 29, South Gaul. A similar daisy motif is on Atkinson 1914, pl 5, no 28, stamped by Vitalis. *c* AD 65–85. *[AB555] no 1*
II.12. Dragendorff Form 29, South Gaul. Lower zone festoons with spurred leaves and trifid pendants, below a blurred trifid wreath. Similar leaves and pendants occur on bowls stamped by such potters as Meddillus (eg Knorr 1952, Taf 40, B). *c* AD 70–85. *[BB349] no 1*
II.13. Dragendorff Form 29, South Gaul. Upper zone scroll with spurred leaves, palmettes and spirals: Knorr 1952, Taf 50, A, stamped by Pontus, has closely similar leaves and beaded bindings. For the general style, cf Knorr 1952, Taf 44, B, by Murranus.

Fig 144 Period 1, Group II samian (scale 1:2)

The lower zone may have panels and tendrils, but is very fragmentary. *c* AD 55–75. *[BB356] no 1*

II.14. Dragendorff Form 29, South Gaul. Scroll in the upper zone: the small six-branched leaf is on a bowl stamped by Seno (Knorr 1919, Taf 78, B). *c* AD 55–70. *[BB356] no 2*

II.15. Dragendorff Form 29, South Gaul. Lower zone scroll with spurred leaves and berries. *c* AD 60–80. *[BB356] no 12*

II.16. Dragendorff Form 29, South Gaul. Eagle, probably Hermet 1934, pl 28, no 8, and small bird, cf Hermet 1934, pl 28, no 64. *c* AD 50–70. *[CA190] no 2*

II.17. Dragendorff Form 29, South Gaul. The straight wreath in the upper zone, and its rosette terminals, are on Atkinson 1914, pl 5, no 26, stamped by Vitalis; this bowl also has small circles in the field. *c* AD 70–85. *[CA190] no 1*

II.18. Dragendorff Form 29, South Gaul. Arrowheads in a panel. *c* AD 70–85. *[CA205] no 3*

II.19. Dragendorff Form 29, South Gaul. The general style of the upper zone scroll recalls stamped bowls of such Neronian potters as Murranus and Celadus. Hermet 1934, pl 42, no 39, is close, with acorns instead of palmettes flanking the trifid leaf. The lower zone contains gadroons. *c* AD 50–70. *[CA206] no 1*

II.20. Dragendorff Form 29, South Gaul. Basal arrangement of leaf-tips, probably arranged in panels, with rosettes and spirals. *c* AD 55–75. *[CA206] no 6*

II.21. Dragendorff Form 29, South Gaul. Upper zone scroll: the pointed leaf is on Knorr 1952, Taf 80, B, attributed to Senicio. *c* AD 60–80. *[CA211] no 15*

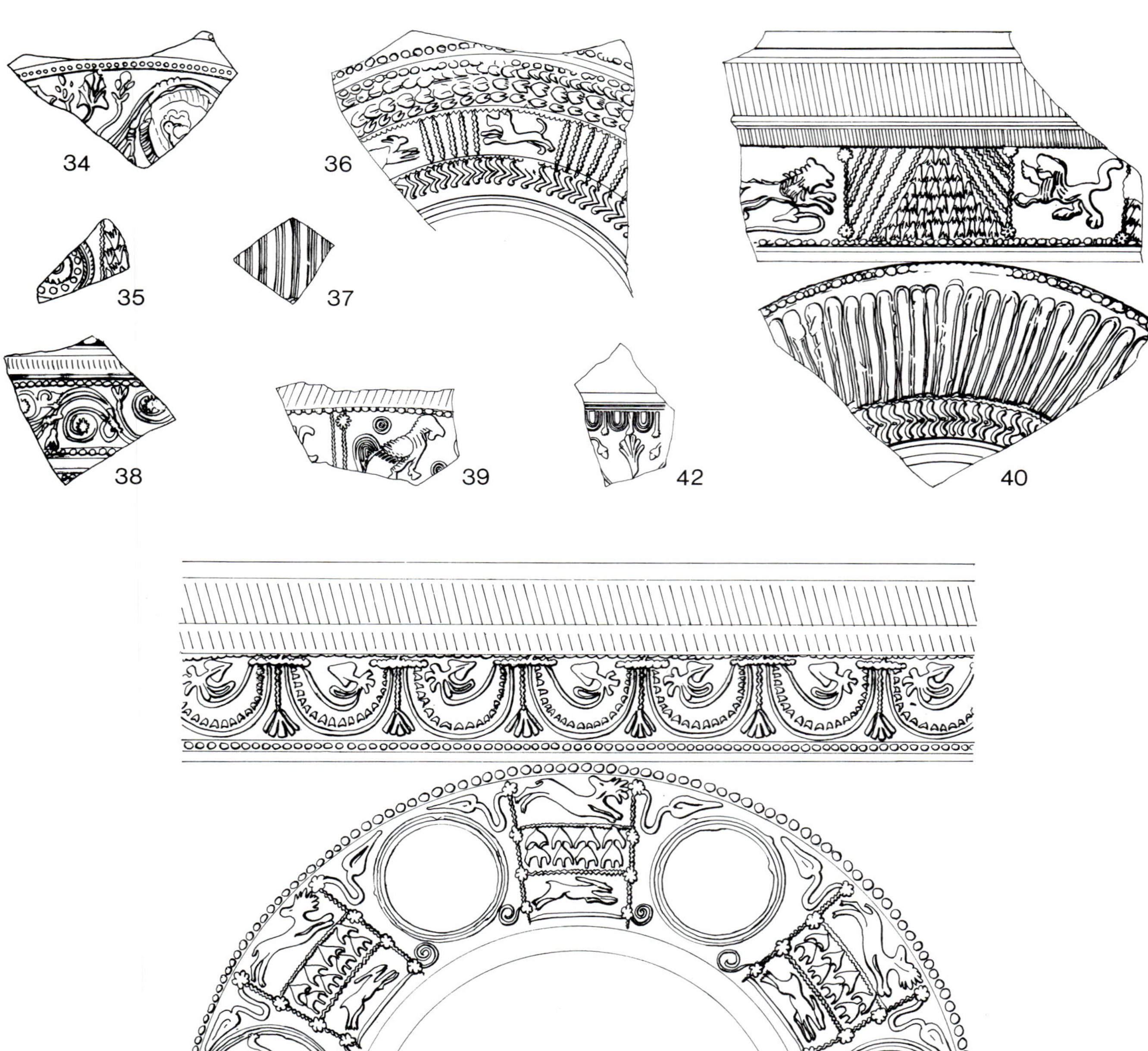

Fig 145 Period 1, Group II samian (scale 1:2)

II.22. Dragendorff Form 29, South Gaul. Lower zone band of short gadroons above festoons with spurred leaves: as Knorr 1952, Taf 40, B, stamped by Meddillus. Burnt. *c* AD 70–85. *[CA211] no 11*
II.23. Dragendorff Form 29, South Gaul. Upper zone scroll with curled cordate leaf: cf Hawkes and Hull 1947, pl 25, no 9. Burnt. *c* AD 50–65. *[CA212] no 6*
II.24. Dragendorff Form 29, South Gaul. Upper zone divided by groups of corded verticals into panels with corded medallions and rosettes. for similar designs, cf Hermet 1934, pl 50, nos 3, 8; cf also the designs on the Neronian–Flavian cup form Hermet 9, Hermet 1934, pl 91, no 18 etc. *c* AD 65–85. *[CA212] no 26*
II.25. Dragendorff Form 29, South Gaul. Panels at the base, including fine wavy lines and cordate leaves on tendrils. Neronian–early Flavian. *[CB124] no 1*
II.26. Dragendorff Form 29, South Gaul. Short gadroons in lower zone. *c* AD 65–85. *[CB126] no 2*
II.27. Dragendorff Form 29, South Gaul. Lower zone scroll with arrowheads in the arcades and buds above. Rather smudged, probably on removal from the mould. *c* AD 60–80. *[CB127] no 11*
II.28. Dragendorff Form 29, South Gaul; rather soft fabric. Upper zone scroll: cf Knorr 1919, Taf 82, B, stamped by Vitalis, for the bud and scrollery, but in a reversed arrangement. *c* AD 65–85. *[CB127] no 10*

Fig 146 Period 1, Group II samian (scale 1:2)

II.29. Dragendorff Form 29, South Gaul. Lower zone wreath scroll, with long narrow buds, too broken to identify. *c* AD 50–65. *[CB128] no 2*

II.30. Dragendorff Form 29, South Gaul. The hare (Hermet 1934, pl 26, no 55) in the upper zone occurs frequently on bowls assigned to Bassus-Coelus (eg Knorr 1952, Taf 10, G, H). The palmette and corded motif in the lower zone were used by numerous potters. The frilled leaf was used on stamped bowls of Niger (Knorr 1952, Taf 47, D), while the wreath is close to one on Knorr 1919, Taf 12, D, stamped by Bassus. *c* AD 50–70. *[CB128] no 3*

II.31. Dragendorff Form 29, South Gaul. Swan (Hermet 1934, pl 28, no 37) in neat upper zone festoon. Pre-Flavian. *[CB131] no 19*

II.32. Dragendorff Form 29, South Gaul. Large arrowheads grouped horizontally in upper zone. Neronian–early Flavian. *[CB131] no 20*

II.33. Dragendorff Form 29, South Gaul. The straight wreath and rosettes are on a stamped bowl of Mommo (Atkinson 1914, pl 4, no 18). *c* AD 70–85. *[CD210] no 2*

II.34. Dragendorff Form 29, South Gaul. Lower-zone scroll with berries and palmate leaves, over corded medallions with a bird (cf Oswald 1936–7, 2289). Similar leaves were used by several potters: for the style, cf Hermet 1934, pl 55, especially nos 16, 33. *c* AD 55–75. *[CD214] no 2*

II.35. Dragendorff Form 29, South Gaul. Panels with arrowheads, and cordate wreaths with large rosettes and hollow roundels. Early to mid-Flavian. *[CD214] no 3*

II.36. Dragendorff Form 29, South Gaul. The lower zone has a blurred trifid wreath above a band of panels, including a dog, Hermet 1934, pl 26, no 28, and hare, Oswald 1936–7, 2079, divided by vertical wavy lines. cf Atkinson 1914, pl 2, no 2, stamped by Mommo, for the wavy lines and generally similar style.

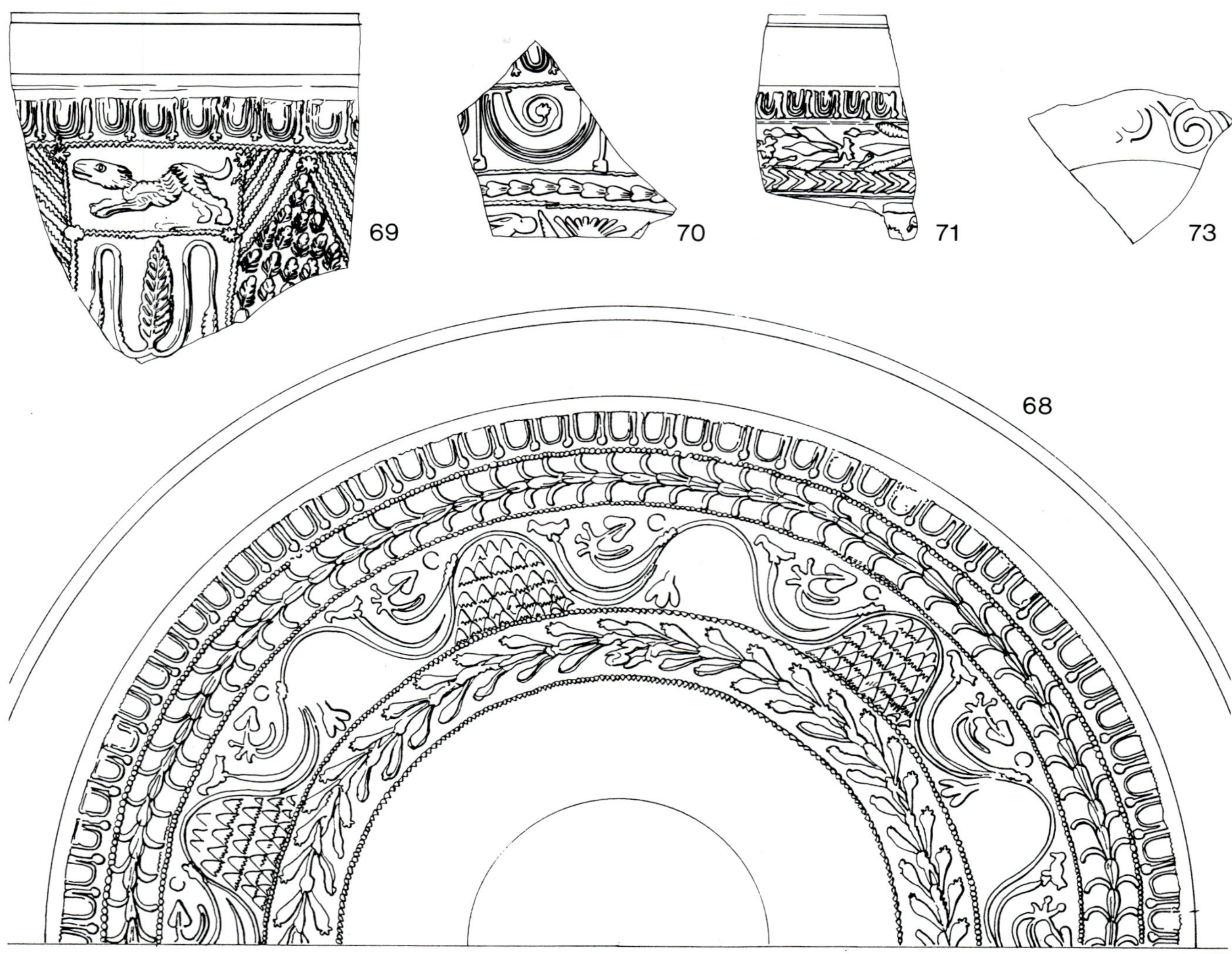

Fig 147 Period 1, Group II samian (scale 1:2)

The basal chevron wreath is a common motif in the Pompeii Hoard. *c* AD 70–85. *[CD218] no 4*

II.37. Dragendorff Form 29, South Gaul. Gadroons in lower zone. Pre- or early Flavian. *[CD221] no 3*

II.38. Dragendorff Form 29, South Gaul. Neat upper zone scroll with small trifid terminals and beaded bindings: cf Hermet 1934, pl 39, no 1. Similar designs occur on bowls stamped by such potters as Aquitanus (eg Knorr 1952, Taf 3, B, with a longer trifid motif). *c* AD 55–75. *[CD223] no 1*

II.39. Dragendorff Form 29, South Gaul. The cockerel, trifid motif, wavy lines and roundel are all in the same arrangement on Knorr 1952, Taf 33, E, stamped by Labio and perhaps from the same mould. *c* AD 55–70. *[F731] no 5*

II.40. Dragendorff Form 29, South Gaul. Upper zone panels, including lions (Oswald 1936–7, 1447 and 1497Q) with leaf tendrils, and arrowheads with wavy lines. Both lions are on stamped bowls of Mommo (Atkinson 1914, pls 2, no 2, 4, 15), as are the leaf tendrils (Atkinson 1914, pl 4, no 14). The lower zone has gadroons above a chevron wreath (also on Mommo bowls: Atkinson 1914, pls 2, nos 2 and 7, 4, no 15). For the general style, cf Atkinson 1914, pl 2, no 3. *c* AD 70–85. *[CD218] no 1*

II.41. Dragendorff Form 29, stamped by Meddillus of La Graufesenque (a). The stamp reads Meoillvus: die 5a. Most of the motifs are previously recorded on Meddillus' bowls. The upper zone has toothed festoons with alternating spurred leaves and palmette pendants: the palmette and spurred leaves are on stamped bowls from London (Knorr 1952, Taf 40, B, D). The lower zone has medallions with a lion (Hermet 1934, pl 28, no 9) and with an eagle and hare (cf Hermet 1934, pl 28, no 1), with a long leaf and tendril; the surviving medallions are apparently all separated by a stack of three panels, with a stag (Hermet 1934, pl 27, no 15), arrowheads and a hare (Oswald 1936–7, 2079). The eagle and hare and the second hare are on a stamped bowl from Rottweil (Knorr 1919, Taf 54, A), the distinctive arrowhead on Knorr 1952, Taf 40, B, and the stag is Knorr 1919, Taf 54 no 10. *c* AD 70–85. *[CD221] no 1, [CD223] no 1 and 3 and 4. MoL Acc No 19812*

II.42. Dragendorff Form 30, South Gaul. Small ovolo with trident tongue, fan-shaped leaf (cf Hermet 1934, pl 12, no 79) flanked by tendrils with a small ivy-like leaves. Neronian–early Flavian. *[BB337] no 1*
II.43. Dragendorff Form 30, South Gaul. Saltire motif. Pre- or early Flavian. *[CA189] no 9.*
II.44. Dragendorff Form 30, South Gaul. Panels including saltire with frilled leaf, and long ears of grain. The frilled leaf is too incomplete to identify, but is clearly one of the smaller versions. The ear of grain is on Hermet 1934, pls 73, no 13, 74, no 11, and 75, no 3. *c* AD 55–75. *[CA212] no 25*
II.45. Dragendorff Form 30, South Gaul. Panels with tendrils. *c* AD 55–70. *[F745] no 2*
II.46. Dragendorff Form 37, South Gaul. The trident-tongued ovolo recorded by Mercator and Cobnus *c* AD 80–100. *[AB549] no 4*
II.47. Dragendorff Form 37, South Gaul. The ovolo is recorded on bowls in the style of Calvus. The lattice, rosette and a similar dog are on a Form 29 from Camulodunum (Hawkes and Hull 1947, pl 37, no 10), dated pre- to early Flavian. *c* AD 70–90. *[AB555] no 3*
II.48. Dragendorff Form 37, South Gaul. Basal wreath of S-gadroons. *c* AD75–95. *[AB555] no 4*
II.49. Dragendorff Form 37, South Gaul. Broken trident-tongued ovolo, spurred leaf in festoon. Flavian. *[CA162] no 3*
II.50. Dragendorff Form 37, South Gaul. Part of wreath of foliage motifs. Flavian–Trajanic. *[CA189] no 7*
II.51. Dragendorff Form 37, South Gaul. Bird in a small medallion, above panel with panther and grouped vertical wavy lines. *c* AD 70–85. *[CA189] no 8*
II.52. Dragendorff Form 37, South Gaul. Panel design, including Minerva (Hermet 1934, pl 18, no 14) and a saltire, separated by asymmetrical vertical wreath; below is a heavy basal wreath. The grass, wreaths and saltire are all characteristic of later bowls (cf Hermet 1934, pl 87, no 4). *c* AD 80–100. *[CA189] no 4*
II.53. Dragendorff Form 37, South Gaul. Basal wreath with part of second wreath above. *c* AD 70–95. *[CA190] no 3*
II.54. Dragendorff Form 37, South Gaul. Neat single-bordered ovolo with small hollow rosette or ring tongue, above a wreath of leaves. The foliage motif below was used by a number of Flavian potters, including the M Crestio-Crucuro group. *c* AD 70–90. *[CA205] no 4*
II.55. Dragendorff Form 37, South Gaul. Lion or panther in a panel. Flavian. *[CA206] no 4*
II.56. Dragendorff Form 37, South Gaul. Band of s-gadroons above small panels including a griffon (cf Hermet 1934, pl 25, nos 4, 6) and grouped arrowheads. The general style would fit with the Pompeii Hoard. *c* AD 70–85. *[CA212] no 27*
II.57. Dragendorff Form 37, South Gaul. Similar wreath festoons occur on stamped bowls of Quintus (Knorr 1952, Taf 51), while the spurred leaf motif was used by a number of potters. For the lance-shaped gadroon, cf Hermet 1934, pl 84, no 3, with a mould-stamp of Crucuro, and Knorr 1952, Taf 31, D, stamped by Iucundus. The palmette pendant is unusually elaborate. *c* AD 70–90. *[CB126] no 1*
II.58. Dragendorff Form 37, South Gaul. The upper surviving frieze probably consists of panels, including a small medallion with leaf tendrils. The lion in the lower frieze is probably Knorr 1919, Taf 65, no 1, assigned to Pontus; the leaf tendrils and foliage motif are in a similar arrangement on Knorr 1952, Taf 83, A, with mould and bowl stamps of Severus. The basal wreath of S-gadroons is characteristically Flavian. *c* AD 75–95. See also II.59. *[CB128] no 1*
II.59. Dragendorff Form 37, South Gaul. Basal wreath of S-gadroons, below running animal. Flavian. Probably from the same vessel as II.58. [CD223] no 2
II.60. Dragendorff Form 37, South Gaul. The dog (probably Oswald 1936–7, 1924), grass motif and S-shaped gadroons are on Hermet 1934, pl 84, no 1, by Crucuro; the grass motif and leaf tendril are on Knorr 1952, Taf 83, A, by Severus. *c* AD 75–90. *[CD209] no 1*
II.61. Dragendorff Form 37: See II.66. Joins CA189.5 and CA211.3. *[CD213] nos 1 and 2*
II.62. Dragendorff Form 37, South Gaul. Lower zone scroll with lobed leaves over a formal arrangement of triple leaf and leaf tendrils: for the arrangement, cf Atkinson 1914, pl 3, no 13, in a saltire scheme. Burnt. *c* AD 70–85. *[CD218] no 8*
II.63. Dragendorff Form 37, South Gaul. Panels, including arrowheads and a lion (probably Oswald 1936–7, 1397). *c* AD 75–95. *[CD221] no 2*
II.64. Dragendorff Form 37, South Gaul. It is unclear whether the blurred ovolo has one or two borders; the tongue has a small rosette at the left side. Below is a chevron wreath, in the general style of the Pompeii Hoard material. *c* AD 70–85. *[CD209] no 3*
II.65. Dragendorff Form 37. Bifid wreath, short gadroons, basal wreath of chevrons: none of the motifs is diagnostic, but the style is close to that of the Pompeii Hoard (Atkinson 1914). *c* AD 70–85.*[F740] no 8*
II.66a–c. Dragendorff Form 37, South Gaul. The ovolo is probably one used by M Crestio and Crucuro; the panels below include a pair of gladiators (Hermet 1934, pl 21, nos 139 and 140), a saltire, and grouped arrowheads and wavy lines, with vertical wreaths separating the panels. The vertical wreath and arrowhead panel are on Wheeler 1923, fig 74, no 54, with the same hollow arrowhead motif. *c* AD 70–90. a: *[CA189] no 5*, b: *[CD213] no 1 and 2*, c: *[CA211] no 3*
II.67a–b. Dragendorff Form 37, South Gaul. The ovolo occurs on a Form 37 from Canterbury from a stamped mould of Frontinus, and with the cordate and trifid leaves on a signed Frontinus bowl (Hermet 1934, pl 85, no 2). The arrowhead panels and the saltire with cordate and trifid leaves are all common Flavian motifs; the fan-shaped leaf in the vertical wreath is less common, but there are similar ones on contemporary bowls. The cupid is Hermet 1934, pl 18, no 37. *c* AD 75–95. a: *[CA205] no 1 and 2*, b: *[CA206] no 2 and 5*

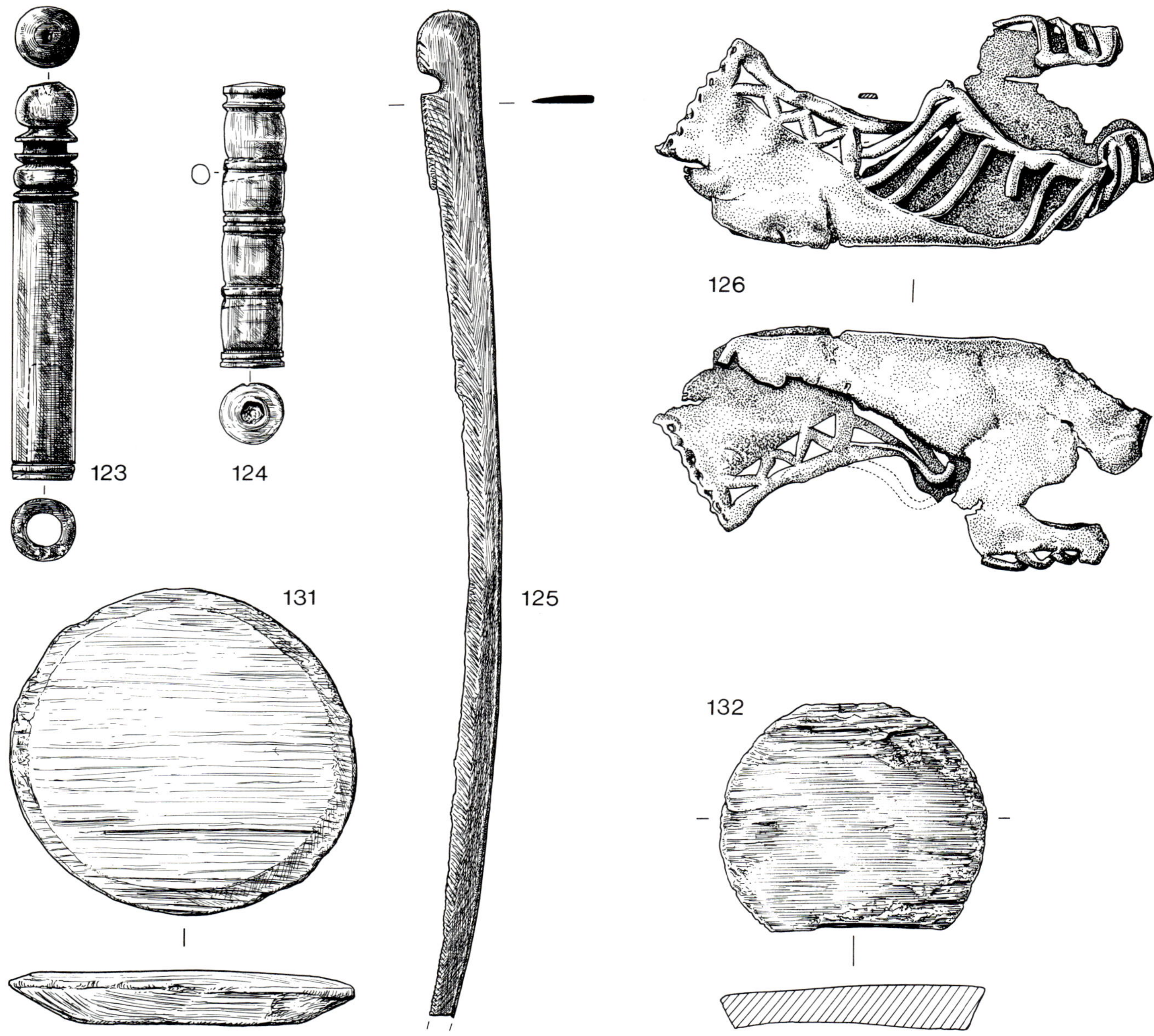

Fig 150 Period 1, Group II bone, antler, leather and wood objects (no 126 scale 1:2; rest scale 1:1)

Bone
Fig 150

II.123. Handle, elaborately turned and highly polished. The socket is bordered by two grooves and the knob finial has a shallow hole in the top; cf Cunliffe 1971, fig 67,12. Length 65mm. *[F729] MoL Acc No 18199*

II.124. Perhaps an unusual hinge (cf No 3, MoL Acc No 18171 below), turned from solid bone and highly polished (cf Waugh and Goodburn 1972, fig 54, no 191). One end is rounded and was probably a terminal, the other has a shallow socket. There are five equally spaced mouldings, with a hole beside the second and fourth. Length 63mm. *[AB553] MoL Acc No 18123*

Antler

II.125. Ear lath from a composite bow, broken at the lower end. The upper end is rounded, with a nock for the bowstring; the nock itself is slightly damaged. The convex face is scored along the nock edge, while the outer edge and spine are mainly smooth; the flat face has heavy scoring. The composite bow is fully discussed by Marsden (1969, 8) and is shown in use on Trajan's Column (Rossi 1971, 189, fig 102). Two other stiffeners have been recovered from the Walbrook: IX.51 above and MoL Acc No 13942, from the 1928–34 Bank of England site. Recent accounts of these bows have included the Walbrook examples (MacGregor 1985, 157, fig 83; Bishop and Coulston 1993, 135 and fig 95, 1, 4; Bishop *et al* forthcoming, no 4C01). Length 325mm. *[BB343] MoL Acc No 18268*

Leather

II.126. Child's *carbatina,* a type of shoe made in one piece and seamed at the heel, with a front thong fastening. The scalloped edge of the heel seam suggests pulling of the threads by wear. The upper is decoratively cut. For a description of this and other types of shoe (nos 4–8), see Ross 1972. Length 156mm. *[CA206]*
II.127. Incomplete adult's shoe with a double row of hobnails round the sole margin. *[CA206] Not illustrated*
II.128. Incomplete adult's insole with marks of a single row of hobnails round the sole margin and a row along the centre to a rough circle on the fore tread. *[CA162] Not illustrated*
II.129. A counter, the roughly crescent-shaped piece used to reinforce the heel of a shoe. The edges are very sharply cut, and it has probably never been used. 3mm thick; maximum height and width 56 x 53mm *[CA206] Not illustrated*
II.130. Complete piece of thin leather (56 x 19 x 0.5mm thick) attached to a thicker fragment by fine stitch-holes. Possibly a reinforcement to a heel seam. *[CA206] Not illustrated*

Wood

II.131. Round bung or stopper with a pronounced chamfer; the underside is coated with pitch or resin; diameter 108mm. *Abies* (silver fir). *[AB541] MoL Acc No 18155*
II.132. Round bung or stopper, chamfered; maximum diameter 83mm, now warped. *Abies* (silver fir). *[CA212] MoL Acc No 18210*
II.133. Spindle or peg, length 210mm, tapering from 8 to 4mm. *Buxus* (box). *[CD224] MoL Acc No 18225 Not illustrated*

Glassworking debris
Fig 151

II.134. A lid-moil. Free-blown; natural green blue glass. The blowing-iron end shows traces of staining by iron oxide. The vessel end has been flared and cracked-off. D of vessel *c* 75mm.

This moil (waste glass from the end of a blowing-iron) is the most complete to come from the glass-working assemblages of Londinium. It was found together with five fragments of moils from the blowing-iron end, one fragment of lid-moil from the vessel end, three distorted fragments of waste and a single thread. All are in natural green blue glass. Also associated were 72 fragments of glass from the bodies of a variety of vessels (square-sectioned and cylindrical bottles, flasks, beakers). It is probable that this small group represents part of a larger cullet dump dating to the late first or early second century. Glassworking evidence in London of this date has been found at Old Bailey (Shepherd and Heyworth 1991, 14) and Guildhall Yard (GYE92, context 14319), both much farther to the west of the Walbrook. It is possible that this small assemblage represents another addition to the growing corpus of London glassworking sites. There is no evidence, however, that glass was being worked on this site, merely that debris from the process was being dumped there. *[CD222] MoL Acc No 20743*

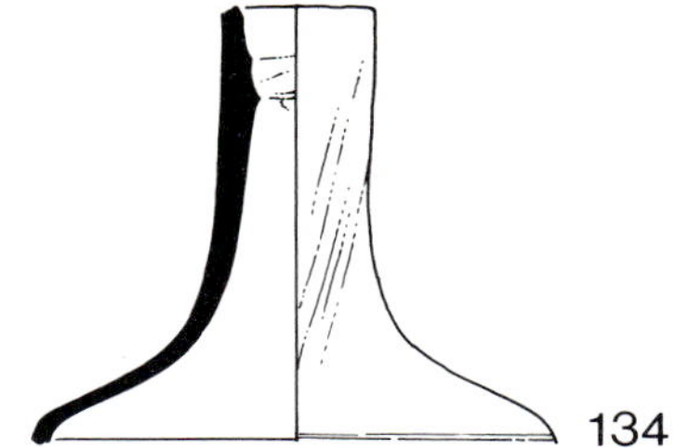

Fig 151 Period 1, Group II glass lid-moil (scale 1:2)

Group III: mid- to late second century

The finds catalogued and discussed below come from the following layers:
Cutting F: 725, 726, 728, 733, 737, 743, 766

This Group includes only layers in Cutting F. These represent a repair to the surface behind the stream revetment following its partial collapse. This was followed by a massive dump of clay which would appear to correspond with similar dumps at the top of Group IV deposits in Cuttings CA, CB and CD.

The pottery shows similar features to the material from Group II but is unfortunately too small a group to permit accurate dating. Stratigraphically it is likely to belong to the mid- to late second century.

Only four small finds were recorded. These included a leather shoe sole (III.12), a fine awl of iron and bone (III.11), a ligula (III.9), and a possible furniture fitting (III.10).

Table 6 Group III pottery excluding samian

Fabric	*Forms*	*No of vessels (approx)*
AMPH		1
AHSU	IID; II	2
BB2	IVH1	1
CC	III RC	1
HWB	IVF	1
HWC	IIA; III; IIIE BDD; IVF(2)	5
HWC+?	IIA	1
OXID	III?	1
VRW	IB; IE; IVA NCD(2); IVJ; TZ	6
VRW?	NJ	1
SAND	NJ(2); IVF	3
Total		23

Table 7 Group III samian

Source/ Fabric	*Forms*
SG	CU11; DE67; DR15/17; DR18(8); DR18R; DR27(12); DR29; DR33; DR35; DR37(6); VI(3); KN78
MLEZ	DR35
CG	DR18/31; DR30; DR33; DR37
EG	DR37
Total no of vessels (approx)	43

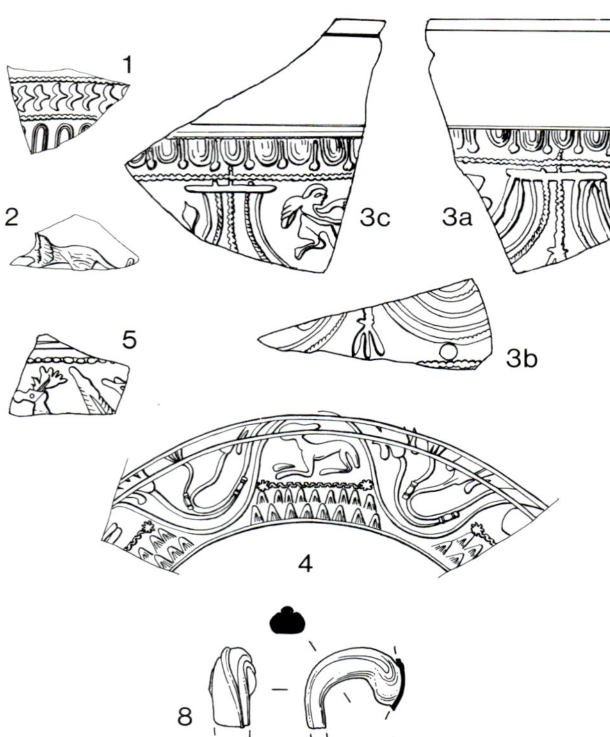

Fig 152 Period 1, Group III samian and glass vessels (scale 1:2)

The vessels

Pottery
Tables 6 and 7

This assemblage is too small for accurate dating. As in Group II black-burnished ware is poorly represented (one vessel). Samian accounts for 65% of the pottery.

Selected samian
Fig 152

III.1. Dragendorff Form 37, South Gaul. From same vessel as II.65. *[F728] no 26*

III.2. Dragendorff Form 37, South Gaul. Part of animal, probably a dog (cf Oswald 1936–7, 2013). *c* AD 70–100. *[F728] no 8*

III.3a–c. Dragendorff Form 37, South Gaul. Trident-tongued ovolo above a frieze of fine festoons containing spurred leaves, probably arranged in alternating pairs, and figures, including a cupid (Hermet 1934, pl 18, no 36). The festoons are separated by a trifid pendant, and have small roundels below. *c* AD 70–90. a: *[F743] no 1,* b and c: *F 733] nos 2 and 7*

III.4. Déchelette Form 67, South Gaul. Scroll with ?palmate leaves (damaged in the turning of the top), over a hare (Oswald 1936–7, 2103) on arrowheads. For a similar arrangement, cf Hermet 1934, pl 91, no 4 *c* AD 75–100. *[F728] no 1*

III.5. Knorr Form 78, South Gaul. Stag (Hermet 1934, pl 27, no 16) with formal leaf and grass tuft. Burnt. *c* AD 75–95. *[F737] no 4*

Samian ware stamps

III.6. Calvus, La Graufesenque (a), 2a, Dragendorff Form 27, *c* AD 75–90. *[F728]*

III.7. Unidentified, OFFCANN?, CG, Dragendorff Form 18/31, Early second century. *[F726]*

Glass

III.8. Fragment from the handle of an oil-flask *(aryballos)*. Applied to a free-blown form; natural blue glass. Dolphin-like handle attached to the neck of the vessel. Late first or second century. *[F725]*

The small objects

Fig 153

Copper alloy

III.9. Instrument, bent and broken at one end where it is flattened for a spatula-type head. The plain shaft has a small bead approximately one-third of its length from the head, with a probe bulb at the other end. Length 125mm. *[F726] MoL Acc No 18169*

III.10. Heavy peg with short faceted shaft and large ornamental finial. Probably from a piece of furniture, or from a litter. Length 55mm. *[F728] MoL Acc No 18209*

Iron

III.11. Awl, set in a bone handle. The handle is broken; since the hole retaining the awl runs the whole length, it is probably reused. Length 100mm. *[F726] MoL Acc No 18168*

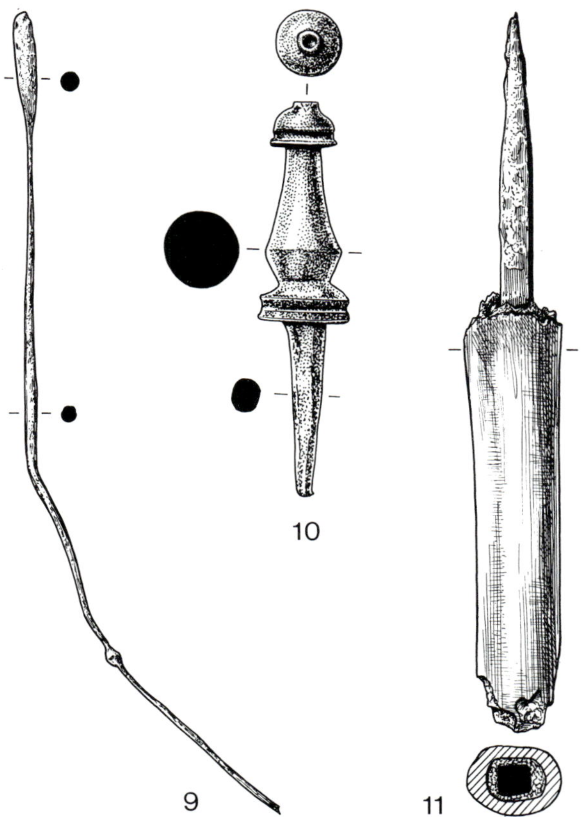

Fig 153 Period 1, Group III small objects (scale 1:1)

Leather

III.12. Fragmentary adult's shoe sole with five parallel rows of hobnails along the sole. The insole is still in place. *[F725] Not illustrated*

Group IV: mid- to late second century

The finds catalogued and discussed below come from the following layers:

Cutting AA: 534, 536, 537
Cutting BB: 333, 335
Cutting CA: 161, 196, 202, 203, 204
Cutting CB: 120, 121, 123

This group includes the extensive dumping of a clay raft across both the west and east banks of the Walbrook stream and can be equated with the clay dump in Cutting F (Group III). At the extreme east end of the site, on the east bank, there appears to have been a raised terrace. Drains were laid on the lower terrace of the east bank, probably acting as land drainage channels. On the west bank, lightweight clay and timber buildings were erected set back from the stream bank.

The small group of pottery dates to the Hadrianic or early Antonine period.

The few finds are typical of a domestic context, and include various personal possessions; a brooch (IV.19) of mid-first-century date, either residual or a survival, a bracelet (IV.20) and a ligula (IV.21).

Table 8 Group IV pottery excluding samian

Fabric	*Forms*	*No of vessels (approx)*
AHSU?	IIA	1
CC	III	1
HWC	IVF(2)	2
HWC+	IIF	1
LOMI	IV MT26	1
LOXI	LID	1
RVMO(2)		2
SAND	II/III AL; IVA; IVF	3
VRW	IB; IB4; IB5; IVA	4
AMPH/VRW		1
Total		17

Table 9 Group IV samian

Source/ Fabric	*Forms*	
SG	CU11; DR15/17R(3); DR15/17 or 18; DR18(5); DR24/25(4); DR27(5); DR29(4); DR36(4); DR37(7); DR30; DR30 or 37; RT8(2); VI	
CG	DR18/31; DR27; DR33; DR35; DR36; DR46	
Total no of vessels (approx)		45

The vessels

Pottery
Tables 8 and 9

A small group dated to the Hadrianic to early Antonine period by the Verulamium region white ware ring-necked flagon with a thickened rim (IB5) and the Highgate copy of a black-burnished ware jar (IIF). Samian is the dominant fabric (73%) but it mostly consists of first-century South Gaul material. The small collection of Central Gaulish vessels is composed of early second-century types apart from a Dragendorff Form 36 which is Hadrianic.

Catalogue of illustrated pottery vessels
For code expansions see above, *Pottery codes and expansions*
Fig 154

IV.1. Highgate Wood 'C' sand-tempered ware bowl (HWC IVF). *[CA161]*
IV.2. Highgate Wood 'C' ware (with added sand) slightly everted-rim jar (HWC+IIF). *[BB333]*
IV.3. Verulamium region white ware flagon with flaring mouth (VRW IB4). *[CA203]*

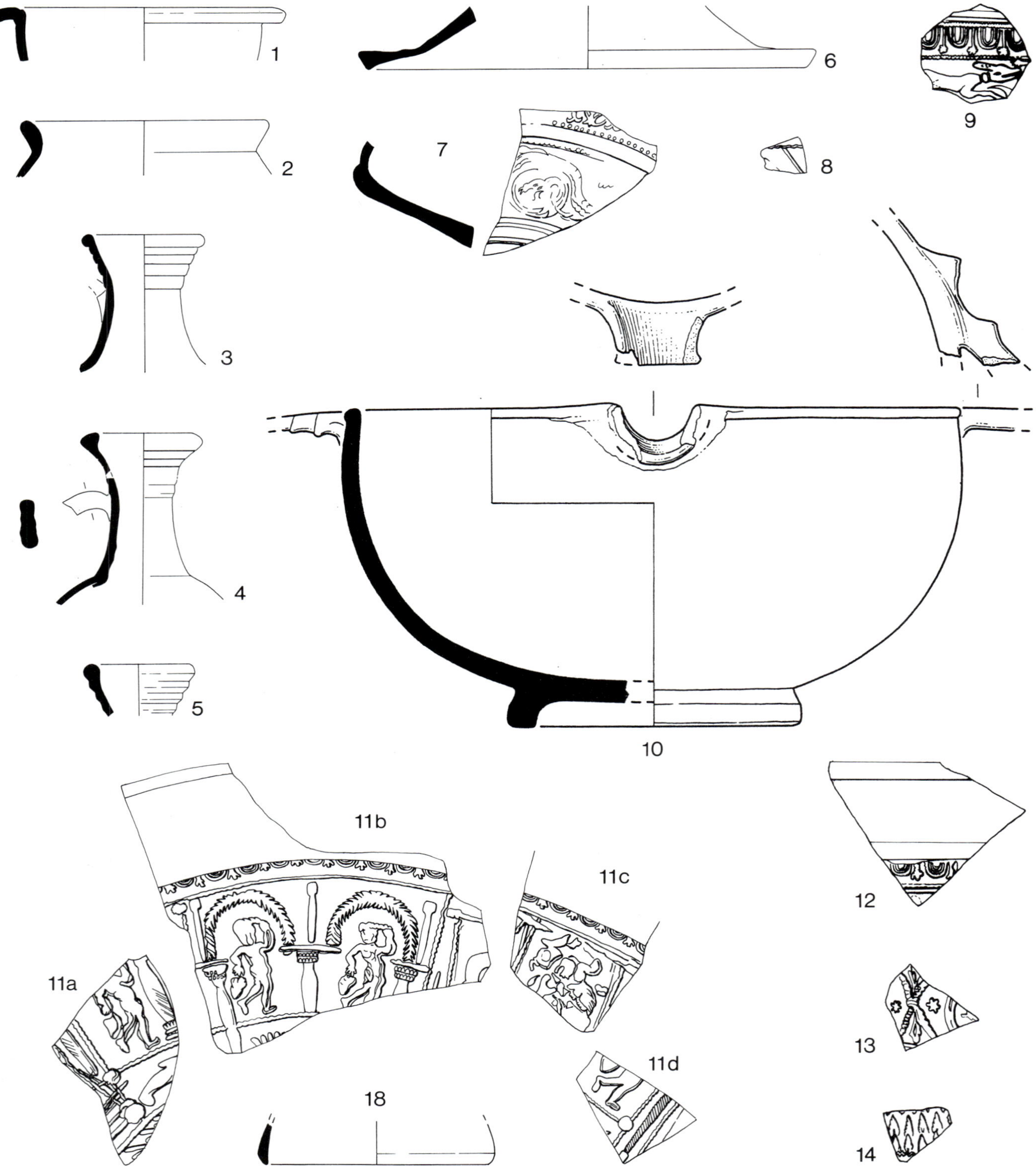

Fig 154 Period 1, Group IV pottery, including samian, and glass vessels (nos 1-6 scale 1:4; nos 7-18 scale 1:2)

IV.4. Verulamium region white ware ring-necked flagon with prominent rim (VRW IB5). *[CA203] [CA204]*

IV.5. Verulamium region white ware ring-necked flagon (IB) with affinity to the IB7–8 which has a cupped-shaped neck/rim and is of Antonine date. *[BB333]*

IV.6. Local oxidised ware (LOXI) lid. *[CA202]*

Selected samian

IV.7. Dragendorff Form 29, South Gaul. The profile has an unusually sharp carination. Upper zone scroll, probably; the lower zone has a scroll with medallion containing a bird, but has been badly smeared during manufacture. *c* AD 55–70. *[AA536] no 1*

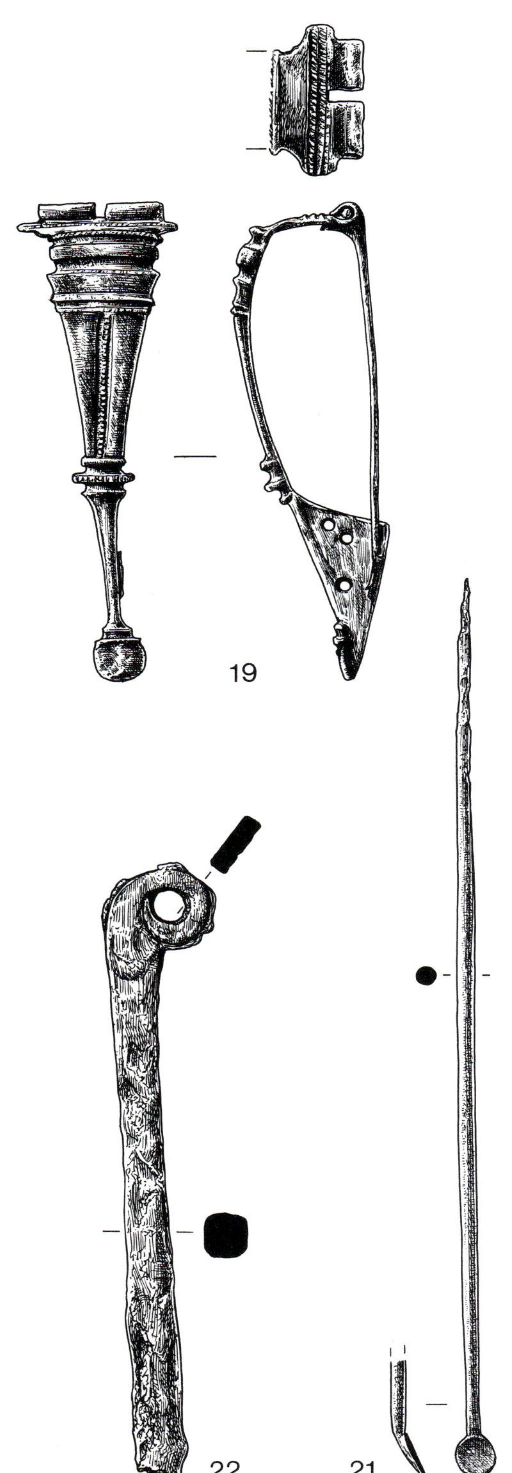

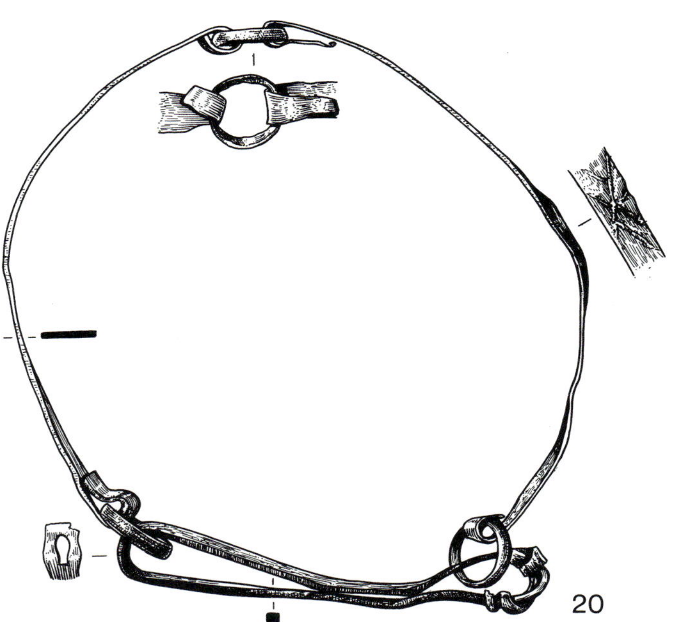

Fig 155 Period 1, Group IV small objects (scale 1:1)

IV.8. Dragendorff Form 29, South Gaul. Scrap of border and plain line. Pre-Flavian probably. *[BB335] no 3*

IV.9. Dragendorff Form 30, South Gaul. The ovolo is one used with similar wavy lines on bowls in the style of Calvus. The dog is probably Hermet 1934, pl 26, no 18. The sherd has been cut down to make a counter. Early to mid-Flavian. *[CB120] no 1*

IV.10. Plain hemispherical bowl with spout and handles. The spout is of the type occasionally found on Dragendorff Form 37s and Form 30s (eg Dannell 1971, fig 130, no 49), but the handles are more elaborate: the flat upper portion is cut out and has a scalloped edge, while there are indications of a round skyphos-type handle applied to its underside (cf cup form Dragendorff Form 34). The fabric is apparently South Gaul, so an early to mid-Flavian date is likely. *[AA536] no 11 [AA535] no 6*

IV.11. Dragendorff Form 37, South Gaul. The trident-tongued ovolo is almost completely removed. The division of the design by columns with wreath festoons, coarse borders and knobbed sticks is typical of the latest South Gaulish bowls; cf Hermet 1934, pl 86, nos 1, 5, 6, 8–12; no 1 also has the small panel with grass tufts. The figures are a satyr (cf Hermet 1934, pl 19, nos 80, 81, which are larger), possibly the shoulder of a satyr with pipes (cf Hermet 1934, pl 19, no 90), Hercules and the Erymanthian boar (Oswald 1936–7, 790) and a hare (Oswald 1936–7, 2075). The Hercules type occurs on a bowl from La Graufesenque by the Trajanic potter L Cosius. The basal wreath is composed of trifid leaves. *c* AD 90–110. *[BB333] no 6, 13, and 14, [BB323A] no 9, 23, and 25, [BB324] no 42*

IV.12. Dragendorff Form 37, South Gaul. Blurred trident-tongued ovolo. *c* AD 90–110. *[BB333] no 15*

IV.13. Dragendorff Form 37, South Gaul. Triple leaf arranged in a cross, with small medallions and rosettes. *c* AD 70–90. *[CA196] no 3*

IV.14. Dragendorff Form 37, South Gaul. Panel of leaf-tips. Early to mid-Flavian. *[CB120] no 2*

Samian ware stamps

IV.15. Bassus ii, La Graufesenque (a), 3a, Dr24/25, *c* AD 45–65. *[AA536]*

IV.16. Lucceius i, La Graufesenque (a), 1a, Dr18, *c* AD 50–65. *[AA537]*

IV.17. Maternus (?) i, La Graufesenque (c), 1a, RT8, *c* AD 50–65. *[AA536]*

Glass

IV.18. Fragment from the base of, probably, a conical beaker (eg Isings form 21). Free-blown; colourless glass. Ground and polished to form a domed base-ring. Late first century. *[BB 335]*

The small objects

Fig 155

Copper alloy

IV.19. Brooch, complete except for the hinge-pin and part of the catchplate, in the style of the Aucissa-Hod Hill series. The head, vertical rib and central moulding bear hatched decoration; the lower half of the bow narrows unusually sharply to a knob at the foot. Probably Neronian. Length 65.5mm. *[CB 120] MoL Acc No18121*

IV.20. Bracelet composed of two strips joined by rings, with a roughly worked loop bound at one end by wire. The loop may have been added to enlarge the bracelet, or twisted to hold it in place. One strip has traces of possible decoration. Length of link 57.5m; approximate diameter 78mm. [CA 203] MoL Acc No 18230

IV.21. *Ligula,* with plain round shaft tapering to a point at one end; the circular head is flat and everted; cf LRT pl xxxviii, especially No 7. Length 124mm. *[AA 534] MoL Acc No 18163*

Iron

IV.22. Looped fitting: roughly square section, flattened and turned under one and a half times to form a loop. Length 84mm. *[BB 335] MoL Acc No 18165*

Ceramic

IV.23. Gaming piece cut from a samian sherd, South Gaulish Dragendorff Form 30. *[CB 120] Not illustrated*

Leather

IV.24. Part of a thong, 110mm long, 5mm wide and 4mm thick, cut to a diagonal point at one end. Unworn. *[CB 120] Not illustrated*

Group IV/V: mid-second to early third century

The following two objects come from a layer [BA332] which can no longer be precisely located in Cutting BA. Notebook details indicate that it belongs to either Group IV or V.

Iron

Fig 156

IV/V.1. Stylus (Manning type 2) with round shaft, off-set eraser and point. Length 112mm. *[BA 332] MoL Acc No 18173*

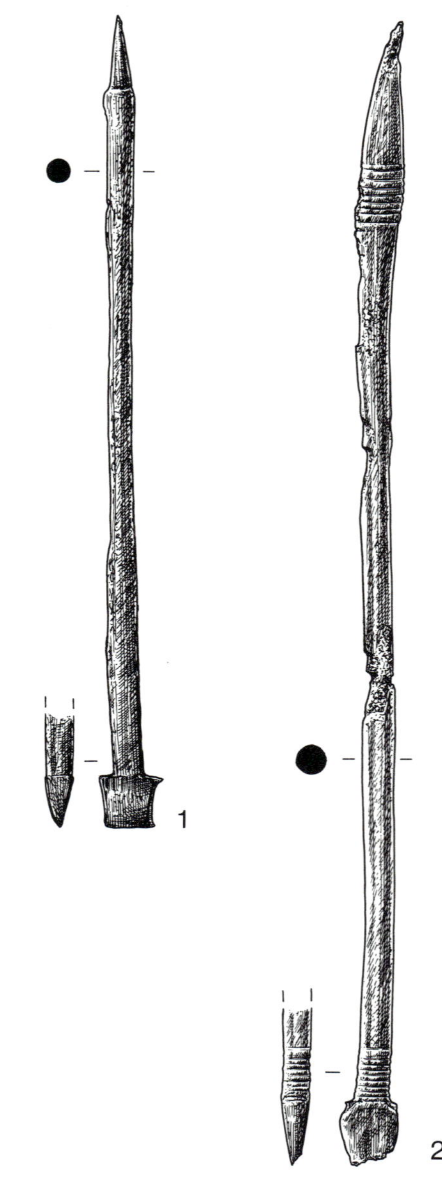

Fig 156 Period 1, Group IV or V small objects (scale 1:1)

IV/V.2. Stylus (Manning type 4) with offset eraser; the round shaft tapers to a simple point. The shaft is decorated with incised lines at each end. Cf LRT pl xxiv,1, for shape and decoration. Length 157mm. *[BA 332] MoL Acc No 18157*

Group V: late second to early third century

The finds catalogued and discussed below come from the following layers:

Cutting AA: 524, 532, 533, 535
Cutting AB: 530, 531
Cutting BB: 300, 301, 303, 320, 321, 329, 334, 340, 341, 342
Cutting F: 747, 748, 749, 751, 753, 756, 760

Table 10 Group V pottery excluding samian

Fabric	*Forms*	*No of vessels (approx)*
AHSU	IIA(2); NJ(3); III	6
AHSU?	IIC?	1
AHFA	FB	1
BB1	IVG; G226 BUD	2
BB1	IVG? AL	1
BB2	IVH1(5); IVH5	6
CALC	II	1
CC	III(2); III BAD	3
COAR	II	1
COLC	III RC	1
C186		1
DR20		2
ERMS	VA	1
ERMS?	?	1
ERSB	IIA	1
FINE	V	1
FMIC	IIIB; IIIG/H	2
GROG	II?; IVF; IVF NCD	3
HWB	SJ	1
HWC	NJ(2); III; IIIF; IVF(2); VI CDR27	7
HWC+	IIF(3)	2
HWC?	IVF	1
KOLN	III ROD; III RC	2
LOMI?	IVJ	1
L555		1
NFSE	MORT HOF	1
NKSH	IIM; SJ	2
NVCC		1
OXID	V/LID	1
RDBK	IIIB	1
RHMO?		1
SAND	LID	1
TSK	IIF	1
VRW	IA; IB7; II(2); IVA; IVF; MORT; MORT HOF; TZ(3)	11
Total		71

The Walbrook channel was allowed to silt up almost to the top level of the Group II and III Revetment 1 and the stream was allowed to find its own course through these silts. It is possible that a revetment was constructed in the old channel but later channel cleaning would have removed this.

Away from the stream bank, light clay and timber buildings and thin timber platforms were constructed, continuing the activity shown in Group IV.

The pottery from this entire group is mixed and does not form a cohesive group. This is due to intrusive material in the Cutting F layers of this group, from the deepest part of this almost permanently waterlogged trench. Excluding the obvious intrusions, however, a late second-century to mid- to late third-century date seems likely, with the emphasis on the late second and early third century.

Metal objects are well preserved in this group, including tools. An awl (V.41) and a punch (V.42) come from Cutting BB. The Group V layers in Cutting BB included much leather waste and a leather skin still staked out for drying (Grimes 1968, 97). Unfortunately none of these were kept for study.

Two dishes of tin alloy are the most notable finds coming from the accumulations in the Walbrook channel in Cutting F (V.34 and V.35). The only personal item is a braided copper alloy chain from Cutting BB which once linked a pair of brooches (V.37).

The vessels

Pottery
Tables 10 and 11

The pottery is of mixed date and does not form a cohesive group. The latest sherds are the Late Roman calcite-gritted ware jar (II), usually dated *c* AD 300–400 [BB 300] and the Alice Holt/Farnham ware flanged bowl [F 753], *c* AD 270–400, but most of the

Table 11 Group V samian

Source/ Fabric	*Forms*
SG	CU11(2); DR15/17R; DR18(19); DR18 or 15/17; DR15/17R or 18R; DR24/25(2); DR27(11); DR36(3); DR37(6); RT12; IV(2)
Mont?	DR37
MV	DR27; DR18/31; DR37
CG	DE64; DR27(4); DR18/31(9); DR31; DR31R; DR18/31 or 31; DR18/31R or 31R; DR33(6); DR35; DR36(2); DR37(6); DR38(2); DR45; VI
EG	DR38; IV
Total no of vessels (approx)	109

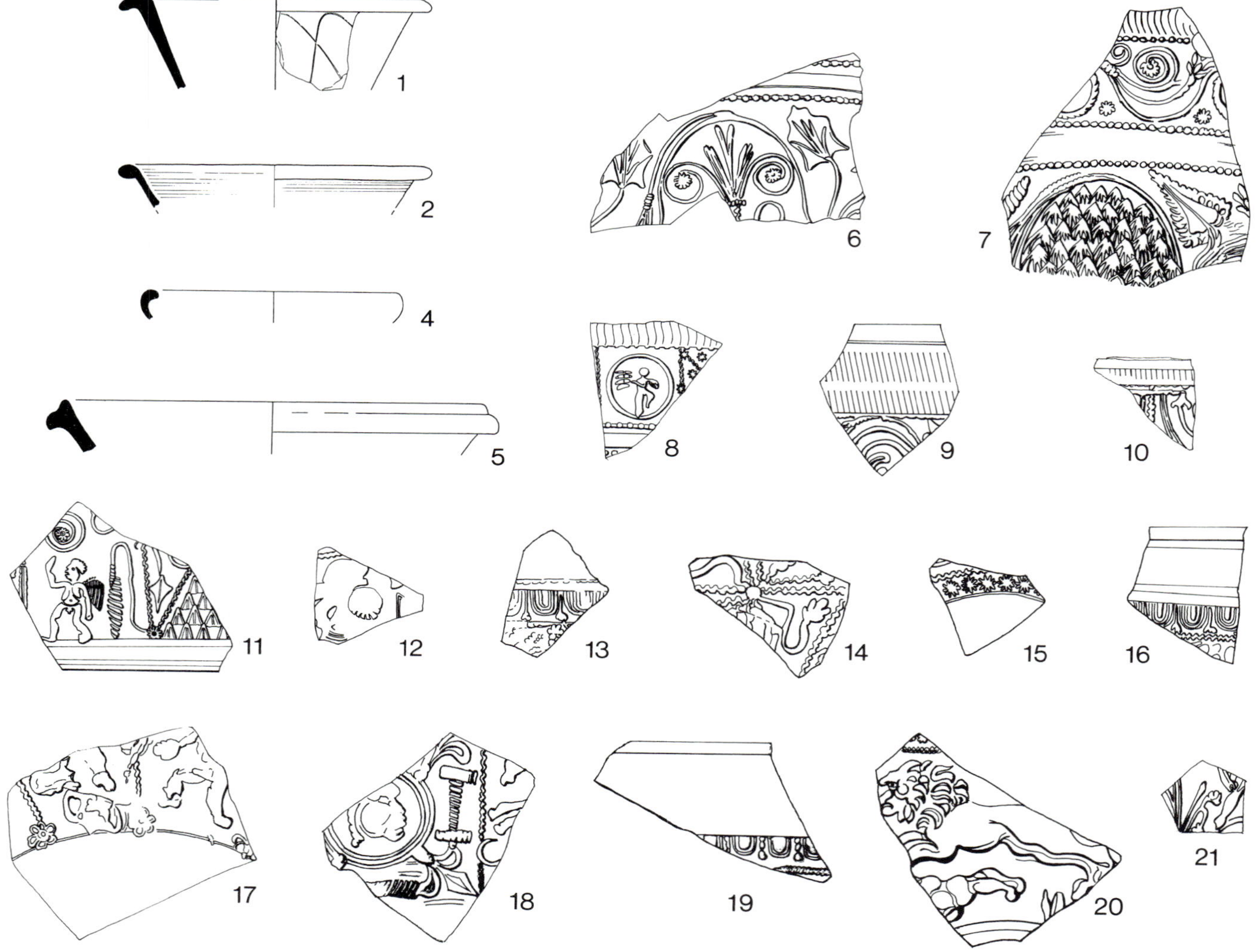

Fig 157 Period 1, Group V pottery vessels, including samian (nos 1-5 scale 1:4; nos 6-21 scale 1:2)

other material is considerably earlier, ie pre *c* AD 160. The exceptions are a BB2 (IVH5), a Thameside Kent ware everted-rim jar (IIF), a BB1 incipient-flanged bowl (G226), Nene Valley colour-coated ware and some of the Central Gaulish (Dragendorff Form 31, Form 18/31 or 31, one of the Form 33s, Form 38, Form 45) and eastern Gaulish samian (Dragendorff Form 37). These vessels as a group suggest a late second to mid–late third-century date, which would seem to be the most likely for the assemblage. If this is so a large proportion of the sherds are residual and Alice Holt/Farnham and Late Roman calcite-gritted ware vessels are probably intrusive. Samian (60%) is the most common fabric.

Catalogue of illustrated pottery vessels
For code expansions see above, *Pottery codes and expansions*
Fig 157

V.1. BB1 incipient-flanged bowl (G226) with burnished decoration. *[AB531]*
V.2. BB2 undecorated bowl (IVH5). *[F756]*
V.3. Thameside Kent ware everted-rim jar (TSK IIF). *[AB531] Not illustrated.*
V.4. Unidentified oxidised ware dish or lid (OXID V/LID). Same type from the New Fresh Wharf Excavations (Richardson 1986, p123 fig 1.160–1). *[BB329]*
V.5. Alice Holt/Farnham ware flanged bowl (AHFA FB). Intrusive. *[F753]*

Selected samian

V.6 Dragendorff Form 29, South Gaul. Lower zone scroll winding over 'spectacle' scroll and foliage motifs. Atkinson 1914, pl 6, no 34, stamped by Patricius, is a similar arrangement but with chubbier leaves and a different foliage motif. *c* AD 60–80. *[AA535] no 1*
V.7 Dragendorff Form 29, South Gaul. Upper zone scroll with beaded bindings and berries, over small corded medallions. The lower zone scroll has large frilled leaf and berries, over arrowheads; the frilled leaf, berries and binding occur on bowls stamped by,

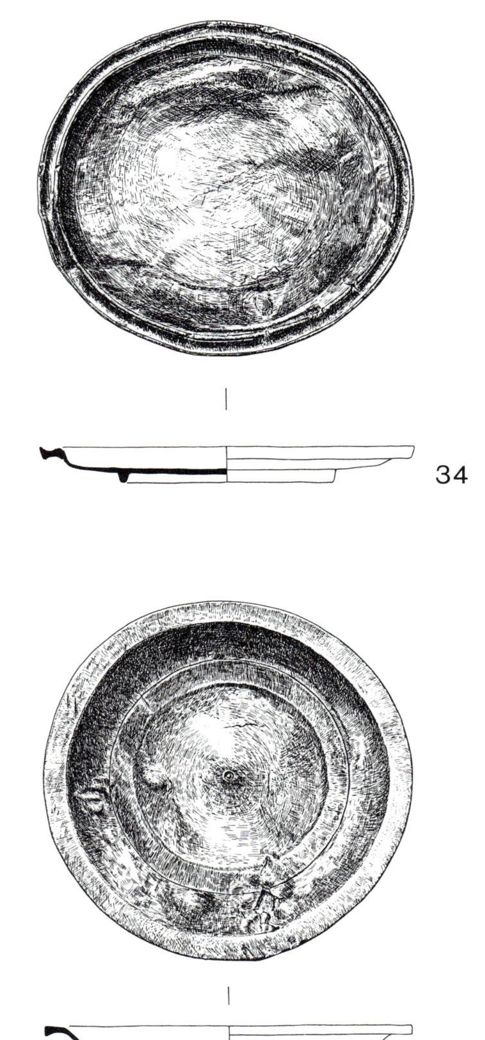

Fig 158 Period 1, Group V lead alloy vessels (scale 1:4)

or assigned to, Masclus (Knorr 1952, Taf 36, A, D). *c* AD 55–70. *[F756] no 1*

V.8. Dragendorff Form 29, South Gaul. The cupid is a smaller version of Oswald 1936–7, 409. For a similar arrangement of a wavy-line lattice and rosette, see Atkinson 1914, pl 5, no 28, stamped by Vitalis. *c* AD 65–80. *[AA535] no 2*

V.9. Dragendorff Form 29, South Gaul. Scroll in upper zone with spurred leaves and ?other leaves. *c* AD 65–85. *[BB341] no 2*

V.10. Dragendorff Form 29, South Gaul. Upper-zone festoon with small pointed leaf. *c* AD 70–85. *[BB341] no 3*

V.11. Dragendorff Form 30, South Gaul. A Form 30 from Verulamium (Hartley 1972, fig 83, no 4), assigned to Martialis, has the corded motif on a tendril, the pointed leaf and tendril, and similar borders. The cupid, pointed leaf, corded motif and spiral are in a rather earlier-looking arrangement from London (Stanfield 1930, fig 5, U). *c* AD 50–70. *[AA535] no 3*

V.12. Dragendorff Form 37, South Gaul. Gladiator is Hermet 1934, pl 21, no 139, normally placed with no 140. Rather shallow relief. *c* AD 70–90. *[AA535] no 4*

V.13. Dragendorff Form 37, South Gaul. The trident-tongued ovolo is recorded for Mercator and Cobnus. *c* AD 85–110. *[BB334] no 10*

V.14. Dragendorff Form 37; the fabric suggests origin at one of the later South Gaulish factories, such as Montans. Coarse saltire motif with berries. First half of second century. *[BB334] no 1*

V.15. Dragendorff Form 37, South Gaul. Basal band of rosettes below scroll. *c* AD 70–85. *[BB341] no 5*

V.16. Dragendorff Form 37, South Gaul. The four-pronged ovolo was used by M Crestio and Crucuro. *c* AD 75–95. *[BB341] no 1*

V.17. Dragendorff Form 37 in the style of Geminus of Lezoux. He is recorded as using the border and rosette on a bowl from Le Mans (B R Hartley pers comm), the shield (Simpson 1968, pl 85, no 56) and the astragalus (Stanfield and Simpson 1958, pl 66, no 16). There are links with the work of Acaunissa, who also used the border, rosette and astragalus (Stanfield and Simpson pl 80, no 21). The figure is Oswald 1936–7, 213. *c* AD 125–45. *[BB 300] no 3*

V.18. Dragendorff Form 37 in the style of the potter X-5 of Lezoux. The triple leaf and border are on Stanfield and Simpson pl 67, no 9, a similar composite column on pl 67, no 5, and the mask and medallion on pl 67, no 8. The animal is a horse, cf Oswald 1936–7, 1902–3. *c* AD 125–45. *[BB340] no 2*

V.19. Dragendorff Form 37, Central Gaul. The ovolo (Rogers 1974, B12) was shared by a group of potters, but the neat beads and the fabric suggest that this piece is by Sacer (cf Stanfield and Simpson pl 82, no 3). *c* AD 125–50. *[BB321] no 1*

V.20. Dragendorff Form 37, fabric of Les Martres-de-Veyre. The motifs (bear Oswald 1936–7, 1627, lion Oswald 1936–7, 1450, foliage Rogers 1974, L19) are common to the potter X-13 at Les Martres and to the Sacer-Attianus group at Lezoux. There are several bowls in this style in the London second fire ('Hadrianic') group (eg Dunning 1945, fig 9, no 15). *c* AD 110–30. *[BB340] no 1*

V.21. Déchelette Form 64, Lezoux fabric. The leaf is composed of at least two (probably three) impressions of Rogers 1974, J17, shared by potters of Les Martres and Lezoux; the figure is not identifiable. Probably Hadrianic. *[BB340] no 3*

Samian ware stamps

V.22. Complete but illegible, South Gaul, Dragendorff form 24/25, Pre- or early Flavian. *[AA535]*

V.23. Vitalis ii, La Graufesenque (b), 27h, Dragendorff Form 33, *c* AD 70–95. *[F747]*

V.24. Lic--- and Seve---, La Graufesenque (a), 2a, Dragendorff form 27, *c* AD 75–100. *[F751]*

V.25. Roppus ii and Rut---, Les-Martres-de-Veyre (a), 1a, *c* AD 100–25. *[BB334]*

V.26. Unidentified, MV, Dragendorff Form 27, early second century. *[BB334]*

V.27. Gongius, Lezoux (c), 2a, Dragendorff Form 31R, *c* AD 140–60. *[F748]*

Graffiti

V.28. Highgate Wood sand-tempered ware beaker. MIIR on underside of base. Reads: ...] MER. Previously published in *Britannia* 1971, 2, 300, no 63. *[BB301]*

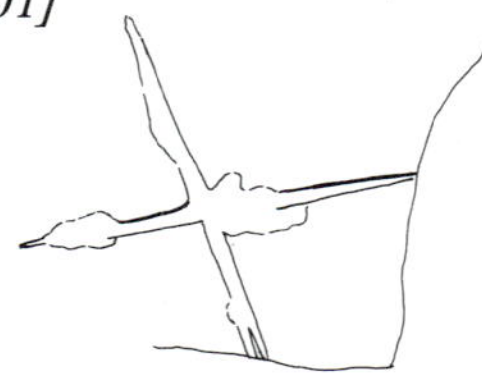

V.29. Samian Dragendorff Form 31R 'X' on base. Also stamped. *[F748]*

Amphorae stamps

V.30. L.A.M on the handle of a globular oil amphora, form Dressel 20; the stamp is not included in Callender (1965). Sandy drab cream fabric, paler slip, chalk and iron pyrites. *[535]*

V.31. SABINAM on the handle of a globular oil amphora, form Dressel 20; not in Callender 1965. Sandy drab cream fabric and slip, chalk and iron pyrite inclusions. Identified by J J Paterson. *[535]*

Tituli picti

V.32. Camulodunum Type 186. IVLI written in black ink on neck. *[AA535] (MoL Acc No 22248)*

V.33. London Type 55.5. Two characters written in black ink on neck. *[AA 533/535] (MoL Acc No 22247)*

Lead and lead alloy
Fig 158

V.34. Oval dish, with elaborately moulded rim and low footring. Badly battered: the drawing shows the restored section. Tin (Jones 1983, 54 fig 6 no 8). Diameter *c* 197mm. *[F748] MoL Acc No 18220*

V.35. Circular dish, with simple horizontal rim and deep concave wall; the footring is similar to that on No 1. The interior of the base is marked by the point of the lathe. Tin (BM; Jones 1983, 54, fig 6 no 9). Diameter 196mm. *[F748] MoL Acc No 18221*

The small objects

Fig 159

Copper alloy

V.36. Catch-plate from a brooch. Length 46.5mm *[BB 320] MoL Acc No 18158 Not illustrated.*

V.37. Braided chain, probably from a pair of brooches, attached to a loop and clasped by a decorative band. Cf LRT, fig 29, 35. Length 202mm *[BB 342] MoL Acc No 18208*

V.38. Stud, 18mm long, with hollow domed head and faceted pin. *[BB340] MoL Acc No 18203 Not illustrated*

V.39. Plain ring, 20mm in diameter, with semi-circular section. *[BB 340] MoL Acc No 18201 Not illustrated*

V.40. Plain ring, 18mm in diameter, with semi-circular section. *[BB 340] MoL Acc No 18202 Not illustrated*

Iron

V.41. Awl, tapering to a point at each end, as No 24. Cf LRT, pl xxxiii, 2. A handle may have been attached to one end. Length 82.5mm. *[BB 340] MoL Acc No 18224*

V.42. Short punch, with squarish head tapering to a point. Probably a carpenter's punch, used to drive nail

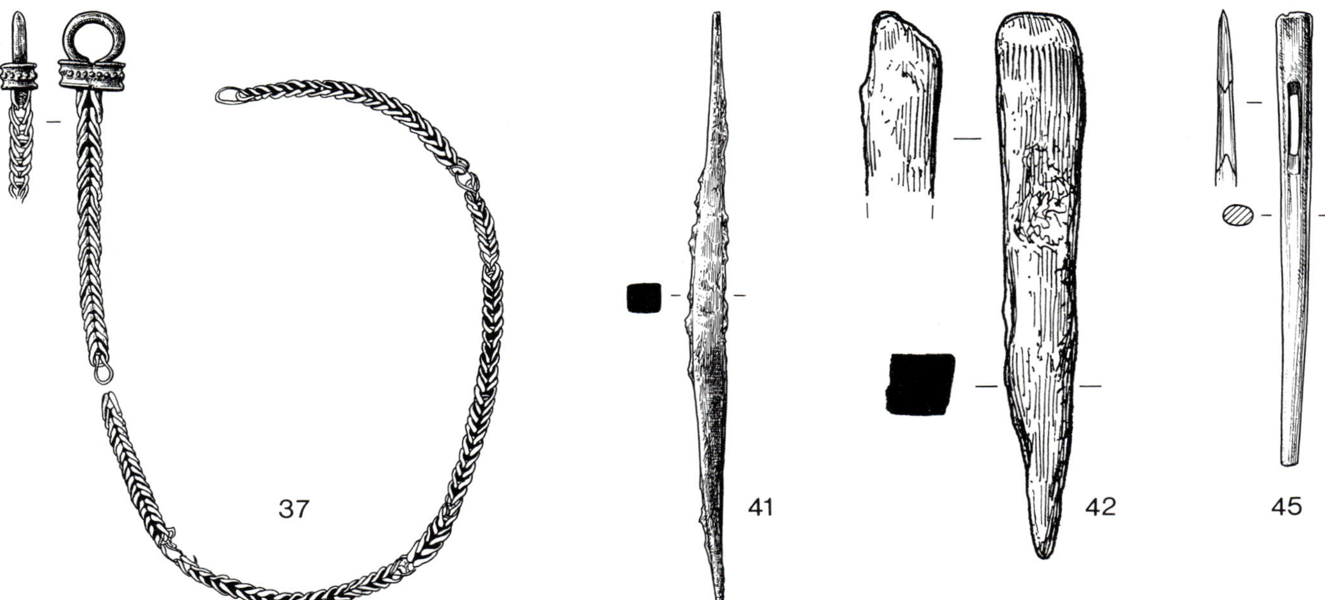

Fig 159 Period 1, Group V small objects (scale 1:1)

heads in, as it is well worn but not battered. The identification of various types of punches is discussed in Manning 1972, 163. Length 75mm. *[BB 341] MoL Acc No 18240*

V.43. Double-spiked loop, 47mm long; rectangular section. The arms are straight and parallel. [BB 321] *MoL Acc No 18298 Not illustrated: see XII.68 for illustration of type*

V.44. Double-spiked loop, 68mm long; rectangular section. The arms are straight and parallel. *[BB 334] MoL Acc No 18299 Not illustrated: see XII.68 for illustration of type*

Bone

V.45. Top of a needle, with plain shaft and chisel-shaped head; the rectangular eye is bevelled at each end. Cf LRT, pl xlii, 6; Crummy 1983, fig 70, no 1982. Length 63mm *[BB 320] MoL Acc No 18297*

Group VI: first half of the third century

The finds catalogued and discussed below come from the following layers:

> Cutting AA: 503, 514, 517, 518, 519, 520, 521, 522, 523
> Cutting AB: 540, 543, 544, 546, 546B, 547
> Cutting BB: 310, 315, 316, 323A, 344, 345
> Cutting F: 720, 722, 764

A new revetment with a timber platform was constructed on massive dumps, the most substantial of the revetments. The dumps were laid down to level the surface of the west bank following the collapse and subsidence of earlier revetments and surfaces. The line of this new revetment encroached by at least 1.5m into the earlier stream channel sealing the Group V silting of the stream.

Lightweight timber and clay buildings were constructed on the west bank but set back from the edge of the channel, leaving an exposed platform of at least 5m alongside the stream. This revetment collapsed into the stream channel, probably as a result of the pressure of material behind it slumping forward and from erosion at the base of the revetment by the stream channel.

The dating of this activity from the pottery is once again confused by intrusive material but a pre-*c* AD 250 date is the most likely. Stratigraphically this group belongs to the first half of the third century. This group therefore highlights a phase of activity on the west bank of the stream immediately before the construction of the temple. The size and scale of the revetment would suggest an increased interest in maintaining the stream channel and its bank sides.

The small finds from this group are generally similar in nature to those found in earlier groups. Many, for example a brooch (VI.48) of mid- to late first-century date are likely to be residual. Other items of personal use from the 'occupation' levels include a bone hairpin (VI.54), a *ligula* (VI.50) and the ring from a manicure set (VI.49). One iron chisel was found (VI.52).

The object of greatest apparent interest is a fragment of lamp chimney, of a type which is sometimes associated with religious sites (VI.14). This example comes from Cutting AB and has no connection whatsoever with the Mithraeum, which it predates. The 'frog pot' fragment (VI.11–13) was also found in this group in Cutting F and has therefore no direct association with the later Mithraeum.

Table 12 Group VI pottery excluding samian

Fabric	*Forms*	*No of vessels (approx)*
AHFA	IIF/ERJ	1
AHSU	I; II; IIA; NJ	4
AMPH		1
AMPH/NFF		1
BB1	IIF1; G226 BUD	2
BB2	IIA; IVH1; IVH5	3
BB2F	IVH5	1
BBS	IIF; FB BUD; IVJ	3
BHWS	IB	1
CC		1
CGBL	III BR ROD	1
CGOF	III	1
DR28?		1
FINE	IIIE BDD; IV CDR44	2
GROG	II	1
HOO	IA(3)	3
HWC	IIE; IIF; IVF(4); LID; IIIF; IIIB	9
HWC+	IIF(3)	3
HWB/C	IVF	1
KOLN		1
LONW	IV CDR37(2); IV	3
LOXI?		1
L555?		1
MOSL	III WPD motto	1
NFSE	G238; MORT; MORT HOF	3
NKSH		1
NVCC	III BAD; FOB	2
OXID	III; MORT	2
OXRC	IV STD ?C83	1
PE47		1
RHMO	MORT BEF?	1
RVMO(2)		2
SAND	NJ; NJ BUD; II 'frog pot'; C306?; CRUC	5
VCWS	IB	1
VCWS?	I	1
VRG	IVA	1
VRW	IA(2); IB2; IB5(2); IJ; IJ?; IIJ; II; NJ; IVA(2); MORT HOF(5); TZ(2)	19
Total		87

The vessels

Pottery
by J Bird, S Macready and J Groves
Tables 12 and 13

This assemblage also presents dating problems. The Oxfordshire red colour-coated ware bowl with stamped decoration (IV STD ?C83) [F 764] is post-*c* AD 345. The Alice Holt/Farnham ware jar (IIF/ERJ) and the black-burnished style flanged bowl (FB), both from [BB345], are unlikely to pre date *c* AD 250, and are types which continue into the fourth century. These sherds seem too late for the rest of the assemblage, for which a third-century date is more probable. This is because a cluster of types falls within a mid- to late second- to third-century date range: a BB1 incipient-flanged bowl (G226), a BB2 bowl (IVH5), a Central Gaulish/Lezoux black colour-coated ware beaker (III BR ROD) and a Moselkeramik 'motto' beaker (III), some of the Central Gaulish samian and all the East Gaulish samian. The Moselkeramik beaker provides the post-*c* AD 200 date. The Oxfordshire red colour-coated ware, Alice Holt/Farnham ware, and black-burnished style vessels described above are likely to be intrusive.

Table 13 Group VI samian

Source/ Fabric	*Forms*
SG	CU11; CU15; DE67(2); DR15/17 or 18; DR16; DR18(13); DR18?; DR18R; DR18 or 18R(5); DR22; DR27(24); DR29(9); DR30; DR33(7); DR35(2); DR36(4); CU11 or DR36; DR37(13); DR46; RT8; CU11 or RT12; RT13
MV	DR30; DR37
CG	DR27(2); DR18/31(15); DR31; DR18/31 or 31; DR33(3); DR37(4); DR30 or 37; DR42; DR45; IV
EG	CU21; DR18/31; DR30; DR31; DR30 or 37; DR38?; DR45; I/II/III?
EG?	DR18/31 or 31
Total no of vessels (approx)	133

A considerable proportion of the assemblage is composed of residual material. Verulamium region white ware, for example, accounts for 25% of the assemblage. Samian, as in previous groups, forms a large part of the assemblage (60%).

This assemblage includes sherds of a 'frog-pot' (VI.11–13 below), a type of vessel considered to be associated with religious cults (see *Chapter 7, Occupation in the valley at Bucklersbury House*).

Catalogue of illustrated pottery vessels
For code expansions see above, *Pottery codes and expansions*
Fig 160

VI.1. BB1 incipient-flanged bowl (G226) with burnished decoration. *[F720]*
VI.2. Fine BB2 ware undecorated bowl (BB2F IVH5). *[F764]*

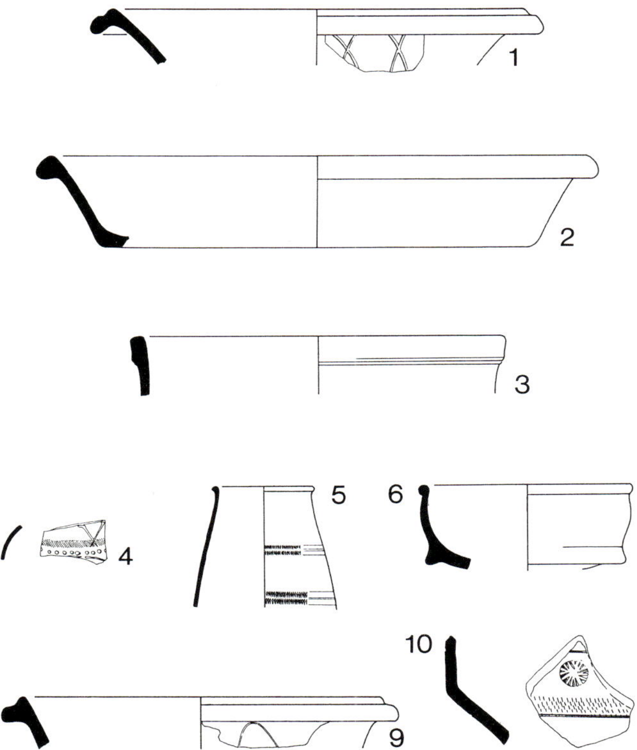

Fig 160 Period 1, Group VI pottery vessels, excluding samian (scale 1:4)

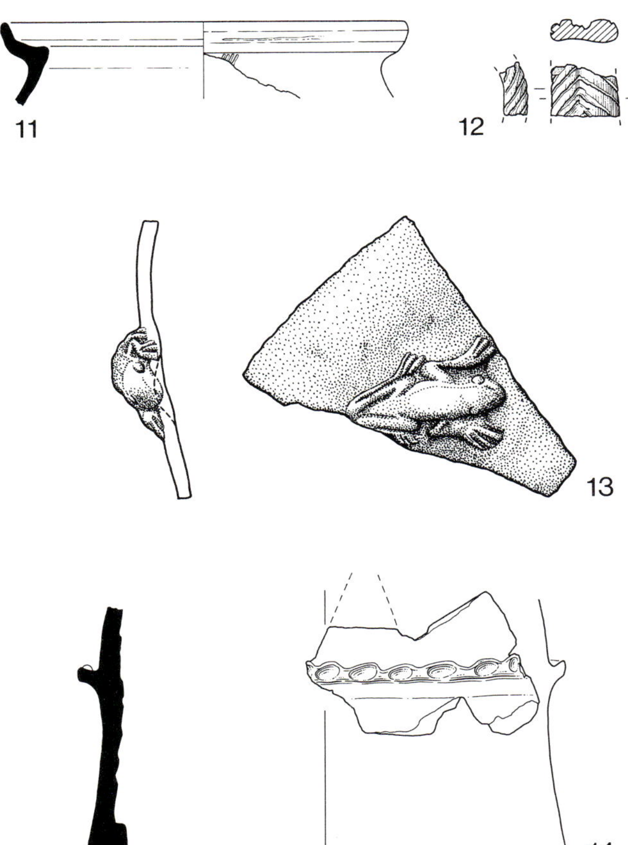

Fig 161 Period 1, Group VI 'frog' pot and chimney (no 13 scale 1:2; rest scale 1:4)

VI.3. Unidentified reduced sandy ware Camulodunum type 306 bowl. (SAND C306). *[BB345]*
VI.4. Moselkeramik 'motto' beaker (MOSL III). *[F720]*
VI.5. Central Gaulish/Lezoux black colour-coated ware bead-rim beaker with rouletted decoration (CGBL III BR ROD). *[AB540]*
VI.6. Unidentified fine greyware copy of a samian Dragendorff Form 44 (FINE IV CDR44). *[AA518]*
VI.7-8. Two Alice Holt/Farnham ware everted-rim jars (AHFA IIF). Probably intrusive. *[BB345] Not illustrated*
VI.9. Black-burnished style flanged bowl with burnished decoration (BBS FB BUD). Probably intrusive. *[BB345]*
VI.10. Oxfordshire red colour-coated ware bowl with stamped decoration, possibly Young type C83 (OXRC IV STD ?C83). Intrusive. *[F764]*

The frog pot fragments (JB)
Fig 161

VI.11–13. Sherds from the rim, body and handle of a wide-mouthed jar or crater; the sherds were not found together, but the unusual fabric and the treatment of the motifs indicate that they are probably one vessel, or at least from the same workshop. The diameter of the rim is 220mm; it has a plain upright rim with a broad flat ledge on the interior, and the wall below clearly turns outwards. The foot of an applied creature, a frog or possibly a lizard, survives just below the rim, and there are scars where two other applied features have broken away. The body sherd comes from a wider part of the vessel and carries a frog in relief; the frog was modelled separately and applied to the vessel wall, after which the details of eyes and feet were incised. The handle is a thick strap, its upper surface deeply cut in imitation of plaited work.

The fabric is reminiscent of Rhineland Granular Grey ware (RGGW). Detailed fabric description: moderate ill-sorted white quartz (SA, 0.25–0.5 mm), sparser black iron ore (0.1–0.25 mm) and sparse unidentified inclusions. Dark grey surfaces (7.5R 4/0), lighter grey margins (7.5R 6/0) and brown core (7.5YR 6/4). Burnished on exterior and all over rim and lid-seat and narrow bands of burnishing on interior.

A continental source is also suggested by the unusual inner ledge which is paralleled on two mithraic vessels from Cologne (Ristow 1974, Taf 13 and 16), on snake-decorated pots from Potaissa in Romania (Daicoviciu 1969, Taf 31) and Unterbaar in Bavaria (Ulbert 1963, Abb 2), and on the series of *Eifelkeramik* lid-seated jars and bowls (Gose 1950, Typen 505–7 and 540–7). The links with these vessels suggest a broad second- to third-century date for the Walbrook sherds.

The frog motif and its symbolism are discussed by Bird (1996), where the vessel is attributed to the cult of the oriental mystery god Sabazios, or possibly to a syncretistic cult linking the worship of Sabazios with that of Bacchus-Dionysus. The complete vessel

VI.42. Illit, NH.\VI, La Graufesenque (c), 117, Dragendorff Form 27, Flavian. *[F722]*

VI.43. Broken, probably illiterate, South Gaul, Dragendorff Form 27, Flavian or Trajanic. *[BB310]*

Graffiti

VI.44. Dragendorff Form 27, South Gaul. *[BB546]*

VI.45. Samian Dragendorff Form 27, South Gaul. On base. Also has a stamp. *[BB310]*

Glass

VI.46. Fragment from the rim and side of a shallow pillar-moulded bowl (Isings Form 3). Cast and sagged; natural blue-green glass. Two ribs extant, polished on the rim and interior. Mid- to late first century. *[F 722]*

VI.47. Fragment from the rim of a flask or bottle (eg Isings form 102, 120b, 126 or 127). Free-blown; natural green glass. Outsplayed, fire-rounded rim with an applied trail of the same metal immediately below the lip. Third or fourth century *[BB 310]*

The small objects

Fig 163
Copper alloy

VI.48. Brooch, complete. A heavy bar separates two panels with niello flowers; both panel borders and the bar bear milled decoration. The foot has a heavy waisted moulding. The form is difficult to parallel closely, though features such as the hinge type, the central bar and the shape of the foot suggest links with the Aucissa-Hod Hill series. Similar floral motifs appear on a brooch from Richborough (Bushe-Fox 1949, pl xxvi, no 14) and on a cruciform brooch from Aislingen (Ulbert 1959, pl 16, no 15). A Neronian, perhaps to early Flavian, date is likely. Length 43.5mm *[BB 316] MoL Acc No18122*

VI.49. Probable ring from a toilet set, made of folded sheet copper alloy and flattened at the ends for a hole to carry the cross-piece; cf Guildhall Catalogue, pl xxvi, 19; Wilmott 1991, 131, no 497). Height 19.5mm *[BB344] MoL Acc No 18204*

VI.50. *Ligula,* 123mm long. Faceted shaft tapering to a point; the circular head is mostly lost. *[BB310] MoL Acc No 18159 Not illustrated*

VI.51. Mounting or stud in the shape of a lion's head. The interior is hollow, but shows no trace of the method of attachment; cf LRT, pl xlvii, A, 5–6. Length 21mm. *[F720] MoL Acc No 18175*

VI.52. Chisel with offset pointed tang for a handle. The shaft is round, flattened out to form the chisel head, and has incised grooves just below the tang. Cf LRT pl xxxii, 4. Length 132mm. *[AB547] MoL Acc No 18161*

VI.53. Fragment of ring, 57mm in diameter; subrectangular section 6 x 5 mm. *[F764] Not illustrated*

Bone

VI.54. Top of a hair pin, shaped like a nail with plain shaft and flat round head (cf Crummy 1983, fig 22, Type 6). Length 19mm *[BB323] MoL Acc No 18780*

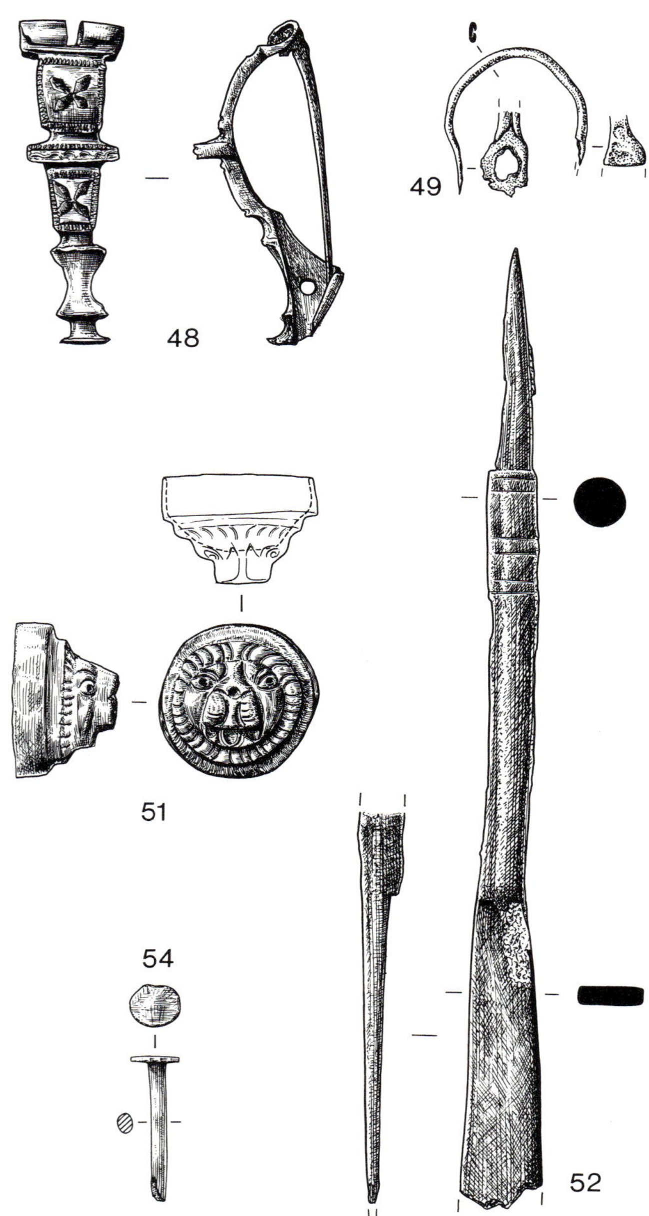

Fig 163 Period 1, Group VI small objects (scale 1:1)

Table 14 Group VII pottery excluding samian

Fabric	*Forms*	*No of vessels (approx)*
AHFA	ERJ	1
AHFA?	SJ	1
AHSU	IIA(2); NJ(4)	6
AHSU?	IIA	1
AMPH		1
BB1	ERJ(3); IVG BUD; IVJ BUD(5); IV BUD; FB BUD; G226 BUD(2)	13
BB2	IVH1(2); IVH5	3
BB2F	IVH5(7); IV	8
BBS	IIF; IVJ BUD	2
CC	ID; III	2
COAR	NJ	1
COLC	III(2)	2
COLC?	III	1
CGBL	III	1
CGBL/MOSL	III ; FOB	2
FMIC?	IIIF	1
HWC	IIF; NJ(4); IVF(4)	9
HWC?	IIF AL	1
KOLN	III CR BAD; III BAD; III(2)	4
KOLN?	II BFD	1
LOMI	IF/G MT3; IIIB; IVJ; IV MT26; IV MT28; IV MT35	6
MARB	I/II	1
MOSL	III?; FOB ROD	2
MOSL?		1
NVCC	III BAD; III BFD; III CR(2); III ROD; III(2) FOB SCD	8
NVCC?	III	1
OXID	MORT HAM; MORT; LMPH?	3
PRW	V	1
RHMO?	HAM	1
SAND	NJ(3); II; IVA; IVF; IV; C306; ?C306(2)	7
VCWS	IB; IB7-9	
VRG	IV	1
VRMA		1
VRW	IB5?; IIG(2); IVA; TZ	5
VRW?	IVF	1
Total		105

Group VII: third century but pre-dating the Mithraeum

The finds catalogued and discussed below come from the following layers:

Cutting CA: 143, 144, 149, 150, 153, 164, 193, 252, 258
Cutting CD: 177A, 177B, 178, 179, 180, 182, 183, 186, 187, 192, 194, 207, 208

Table 15 Group VII samian

Fabric/ Source	*Forms*
SG	DR15/17(3); DR18(6); DR15/17 or 18(2); DR27(2); DR29(3); DR30; DR33; DR37(3)
MONT?	DR27
MV	DR37(2)
CG	DE72(7); DR27(2); DR31(4); DR31?; DR31R; DR18/31(5); DR18/31R; DR33(2); DR36; DR37(5); DR45; LD TG; II; IV
EG	DR31; DR33(4); DR36 VAR; DR37(12); DR38(3); DR45; DR53; I; II; IV; MORT
EG?	DR38; VI
CG/EG	DR18/31
Total no of vessels (approx)	95

Following the sequence of consolidating the banks on either side of the stream, the activity on the east bank appears to have been more specialised. While Group VI activity on the west bank, contemporary with this phase, was in the form of better and larger revetments with associated platforms and buildings, a number of intercutting pits, tanks or drains/channels were cut into the surface of the east bank. These were dug at the foot of the terrace seen in Group IV. A 1m-wide flint and chalk structure was constructed later parallel to the course of the stream. These features were in existence when the decision to build the Mithraeum was made. The construction cut for the temple truncated the top of the terrace at the east end of the site and levelled the top of the clay and flint foundation. The hollow features were backfilled with loose soil and debris which subsided during the building of the temple.

The nature of this activity on the east bank is difficult to interpret. Considering the class and status of the temple which immediately succeeded it, it is possible that it represents some form of religious activity. The clay and flint foundation might be interpreted as a perimeter wall enclosing this.

The dating from this group, especially the material thrown back into the negative features, has the most important bearing upon the date of the temple. The pottery suggests a date from *c* AD 240–50 until the end of the third century. With Group VIII deposits, the first four floors of the Mithraeum, securely dated to the last half of the third century, a construction date for the Mithraeum of *c* AD 240–50 is most likely as the latest date. The second quarter of the third century is probably more acceptable.

There are few small finds from this group. Those which exist consist mainly of undatable miscellaneous personal objects and fittings, such as a leather shoe sole (VII.53), tweezers (VII.48), gaming pieces (VII.51 and VII.52) and a water pipe junction collar (VII.50). Of greater interest is a fragment of gilded leather (VII.53) which may have come from an upholstered couch (eg Liversidge 1955, 10 and pl 22), although other identifications are possible. This, along with a second fragment of gilded leather (X.67), has previously been discussed as part of the Mithraeum furnishings (Harris and Harris 1965, 4), but it is now apparent that it comes from a preconstruction deposit. The second fragment of leather is, however, from a Mithraeum context (Group X [CB295]).

The vessels

Pottery
Tables 14 and 15

Black-burnished 1 is the predominant fabric (12%), with the plain-rimmed dish decorated with intersecting arcs being the main form. Nene Valley colour-coated ware also features more strongly than in the earlier assemblages (8%). The Alice Holt/Farnham ware everted-rim jar (ERJ) and the BB1 flanged bowl (FB) indicate that the assemblage postdates *c* AD 250. The small quantity of Alice Holt/Farnham ware and the absence of Oxfordshire red colour-coated ware and other late types suggests that this group is unlikely to be much later than *c* AD 270. A date of *c* AD 250–70 to 300 is therefore suggested for the assemblage. A high degree of residuality is very evident among the other wares, with Verulamium and Highgate products well represented with other fabrics such as Local mica-dusted ware. The proportion of samian has declined to 47% but this is still an abnormally high percentage.

Catalogue of illustrated pottery vessels
For code expansions see above, *Pottery codes and expansions*
Fig 164

VII.1. Alice Holt/Farnham ware everted-rim jar (AHFA ERJ). *[CA143]. Not illustrated*
VII.2. BB1 strongly everted-rim jar (ERJ). *[CD177A]*
VII.3. As above. *[CD207]*

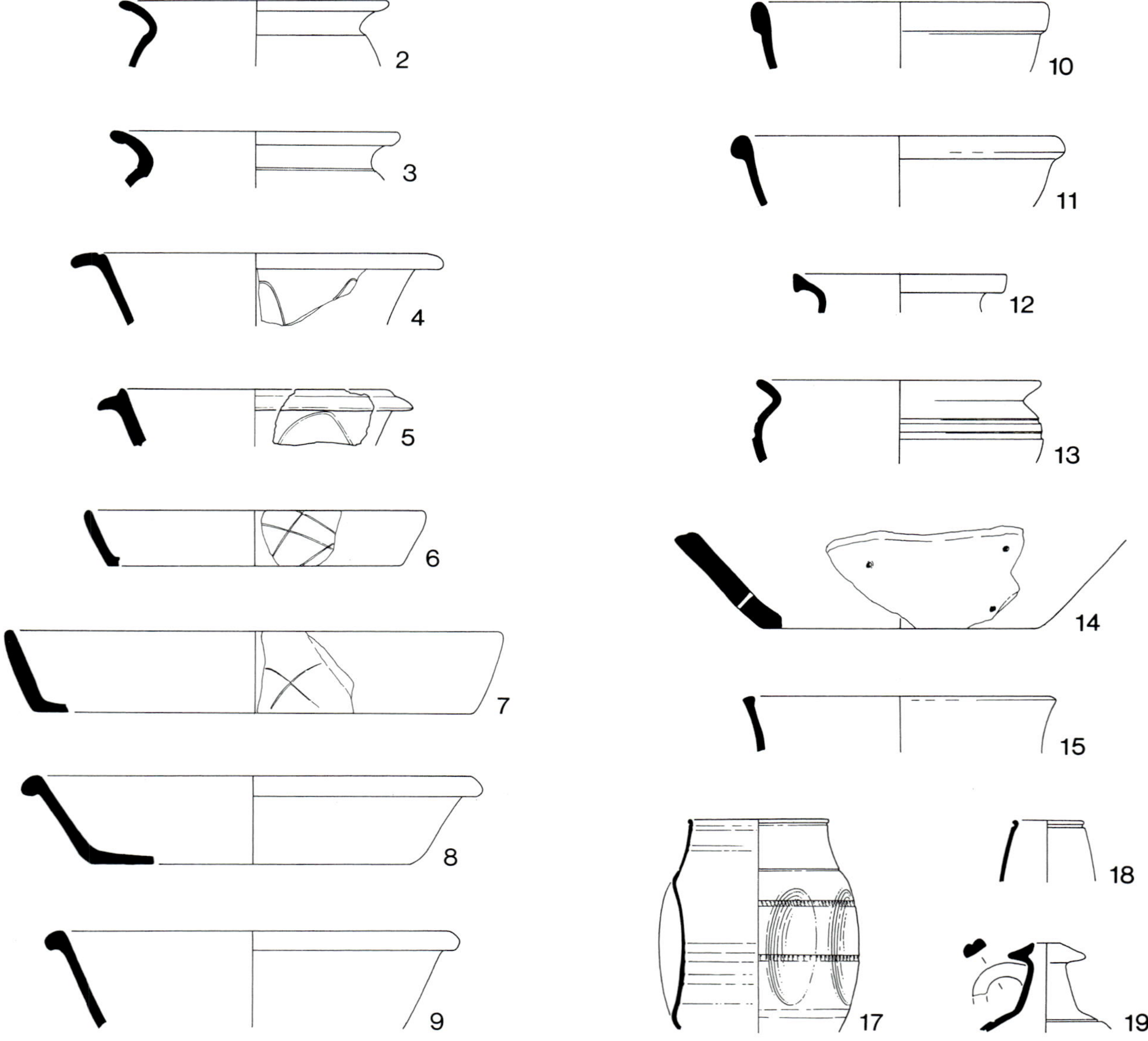

Fig 164 Period 1, Group VII pottery vessels, excluding samian (scale 1:4)

VII.4. BB1 incipient-flanged bowl with burnished decoration (G226 BUE). *[CD177A]*
VII.5 BB1 flanged bowl with burnished decoration (FB BUD). *[CA150]*
VII.6. BB1 plain-rimmed dish with burnished decoration. (IVJ BUD). *[CD178]*
VII.7. Black-burnished-style plain-rimmed dish with burnished decoration (BBS IVJ BUD). *[CD207]*
VII.8. Fine BB2 undecorated bowl (BB2F IVH5). *[CD179]*
VII.9. As above. *[CD180]*
VII.10. Unidentified reduced sandy ware Camulodunum type 306 bowl (SAND C306). *[CA252]*
VII.11. Unidentified reduced sandy ware bowl, possibly Camulodunum type 306 (SAND C306) or a black-burnished type (IVH). Very abraded. *[CD177A]*
VII.12. Reduced sandy ware necked jar (SAND NJ). *[CA193]*
VII.13. Reduced sandy ware jar (SAND II), cf Lyne and Jefferies type 3B.11. *[CD178]*
VII.14. Reduced sandy ware storage jar (base) with perforations in body wall, possibly Alice Holt/Farnham ware, cf Lyne and Jefferies 1979, type 10.1. This could have served as a beehive. *[CA252]*
VII.15. Unidentified reduced sandy ware bowl (SAND IV). *[CD178]*
VII.16-17. Moselkeramik folded beaker with rouletted decoration. *[CD177B] [CD178]*
VII.18. Nene Valley colour-coated ware beaker (NVCC III). *[CA150]*
VII.19. Unidentified colour-coated ware disc-mouthed flagon (ID), Buff fabric with brown colour-coat. *[CD177B]*

Selected samian
Fig 165

VII.20. Dragendorff Form 29, South Gaul. Upper zone panels with massed arrowheads both filling the panel and with wavy lines; lower-zone gadroons. *c* AD 65–80. *[CD208] no 1*
VII.21. Dragendorff Form 29, South Gaul. Basal chevron wreath, used by several potters, including those of the Pompeii Hoard (cf Atkinson 1914, pl 16, no 79). *c* AD 70–85. *[CD208] no 2*
VII.22. Dragendorff Form 29, South Gaul. Upper zone frieze with running hound and leaf on tendril: for the style, cf Knorr 1952, Taf 83, A, by Severus. *c* AD 70–85. *[CD208] no 8*
VII.23. Dragendorff Form 37, South Gaul. The ovolo and gladiators are on a mould-stamped bowl of Mercator from Southwark (Bird and Marsh 1978, fig 190, no 159), which also has a similar tendril but different terminal. The bird and bud are also recorded for Mercator: Knorr 1919, Taf 57, nos 14 and 23. *c* Ad 80–100. *[CD180] no 2*
VII.24. Dragendorff Form 37, South Gaul. Trident-tongued ovolo. *c* AD 70–85. *[CD208] no 9*
VII.25. Dragendorff Form 37, South Gaul. Panel of arrowheads and wavy lines above a basal wreath; the leaf composing the wreath was used by several potters (eg Knorr 1952, Taf 50, stamped by Patricius, and Taf 19, F, by M Crestio). Slightly burnt. *c* AD 75–95. *[CD208] no 4*
VII.26. Dragendorff Form 37 in the style of X-12 ('Ioenalis') of Les-Martres-de-Veyre. Stanfield and Simpson pl 41, no 483, has the vine scroll, star and wavy line borders; pl 41, no 475, has the beaded ring replacing the ovolo. *c* AD 100–25. *[CD180] no 1*
VII.27. Dragendorff Form 37 in the style of Albucius of Lezoux. The ovolo and leaf are both on Stanfield and Simpson pl 121, no 9. The surface is rather abraded. *c* AD 150–80. *[CD182] no 2*
VII.28. Dragendorff Form 37 in the style of Casurius of Lezoux. For the ovolo, rather heavy beadrows and curved gadroons, cf Stanfield and Simpson pls 135, no 34, 136, no 44. *c* AD 165–200. *[CD182] no 1*
VII.29. Dragendorff Form 37 in the style of Secundus I of Lezoux, who used the partially impressed dolphin on the panel border (cf Simpson and Rogers 1974, 1969, fig 2, no 4). The dolphin is similar to Oswald 1936–7, 2401, the Perseus is Oswald 1936–7, 234. *c* AD 150–80. *[CD192] no 2*
VII.30. Dragendorff Form 37, Central Gaul. The bold wavy lines suggest a late potter such as Servus II, but the incomplete and rather blurred ovolo cannot be matched. Mid to late Antonine. *[CA143] no 6*
VII.31. Dragendorff Form 37 stamped in the mould by Firmus ii (Firmus iv) of Rheinzabern(a), die 3a. The ovolo is probably Ricken and Fischer 1963, E42, not previously recorded for him; the Hercules (Ricken and Fischer 1963, M87a), column (Ricken and Fischer 1963, 0220) are on Taf 124, no 6. The horse, Ricken and Fischer 1963, T116a, is also apparently new to Firmus II's repertoire. The motif in the medallion with the stamp is not certainly identifiable: cf the masked figure, Ricken and Fischer 1963, M109. Late second to mid-third century. *[CD192] no 1*
VII.32. Dragendorff Form 37 stamped in the mould by Primitivus of Rheinzabern(a), die 15c. The style is that of Primitivus iv, who is recorded as using all the motifs: ovolo Ricken and Fischer 1963, E41, cupid Ricken and Fischer 1963, M111a, flautist Ricken and Fischer 1963, M166, small kneeling figure Ricken and Fischer 1963, M265a and beadrow Ricken and Fischer 1963, 0232. Ludowici and Ricken 1948, Taf 200, no 10, has the ovolo, flautist, stamp and beadrow in the same arrangement, and may be from the same, or closely similar, mould. The band between rim and decoration is 70mm deep. Early to mid-third century. *[CA143] no 2, [CA154] no 1, 2, and no 3, [CA157] no 1, [CA198] no 2*
VII.33. Dragendorff Form 37 in the style of Julius II-Julianus I of Rheinzabern. They are recorded for all the motifs: ovolo Ricken and Fischer 1963, E23, beadrow Ricken and Fischer 1963, O256, cross Ricken and

Fischer 1963, O53, and the medallions Ricken and Fischer 1963, K9 and K14, here arranged one inside the other, as on BB326.2 and 4; cf also CB115.3. Early to mid-third century. *[CA144] no 2*

VII.34. Dragendorff Form 37 in the style of Julius II-Julianus II of Rheinzabern. They are recorded for all the motifs: panther Ricken and Fischer 1963, T35, cockerel Ricken and Fischer 1963, T235, ornament Ricken and Fischer 1963, O178, and cross Ricken and Fischer 1963, O53; cf Ludowici and Ricken 1948, Taf 204, no 22, 208, no 24. Early to mid-third century. *[CA149] no 1*

Fig 165 Period 1, Group VII samian vessels (nos 20-42c scale 1:2; no 43 scale 1:4)

VII.35. Dragendorff Form 37, Rheinzabern. The rosette, Ricken and Fischer 1963, O39, was used by several potters but only Primitivus III appears to have used it between medallions (Ricken and Fischer 1963, Knorr 1919) in this way (Ludowici and Ricken 1948, Taf 196, nos 4, 8). Early to mid-third century. *[CA149] no 2*
VII.36. Dragendorff Form 37, in the style of Trier Werkstatt II. The cornflower is Fölzer 1913, type 845, the basal wreath of hollow leaves is Fölzer type 904. Antonine. *[CD179] no 2*
VII.37. Dragendorff Form 37 in the style of Janu II of Rheinzabern. The ovolo and square beads (Ricken and Fischer 1963, E70) and arcade are on Ludowici and Ricken 1948, Taf 19, no 7. Later second to early third century. *[CD194] no 1*
VII.38. Dragendorff Form 37, East Gaul. Border of squareish beads, with a sprig motif apparently impressed twice to give a bow effect. Probably from one of the earlier factories, such as Blickweiller or La Madeleine. Hadrianic-Antonine. *[CD208] no 7*
VII.39. Dragendorff Form 37 in the style of Dexter of Trier. he is recorded for the ovolo (Fölzer 1913, type 938; Gard 1937, R3/25), and also used the beadrow and the festoon (Fölzer Taf 15, nos 2, 7). Mid- to late Antonine. *[CD 208] no 5*
VII.40. Body and base of a two-handled jar Dragendorff Form 53. The body is decorated with dots and tendrils in barbotine; the surviving handle base was clearly applied to an incised surface, and masked with heavy barbotine in a v-shape (where fingermarks are still visible). The pedestal is solid above a grooved foot. The form is rare in Britain (see Bird 1996); East Gaul, and probably Rheinzabern. Early to mid-third century. *[CD183] no 1, [CD176] no 1*
VII.41. Déchelette Form 72, CG, with applied figure of Mercury; no 50 in Déchelette's (1904) applied types. Antonine. *[CA144] no 1*
VII.42. Rim and several sherds, Déchelette Form 72, possibly all from the same vessel but too fragmentary to be certain. The applied motifs are a figure of Minerva (no 15 in Déchelette's (1904) applied types), a dancer — probably a Maenad — with a tambourine, and a leaf (a smaller version of Déchelette's applied type 157). The body sherds also have barbotine tendrils. CG, Antonine. *[CA149] no 3,6 7,8, and no 9*

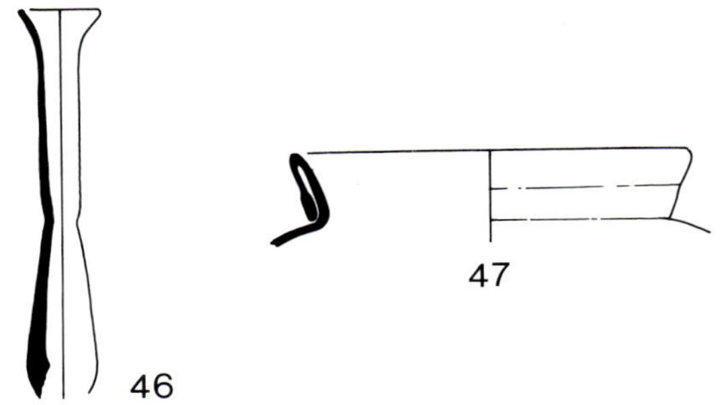

Fig 166 Period 1, Group VII glass vessels (scale 1:2)

VII.43. Cup rim from an undecorated vessel, probably East Gaul. There is apparently no close parallel for the form, which has a plain upright lip and rather sharply rounded shoulder; the diameter is approx 85mm. Probably early to mid-third century. *[CA252] no 1*

Samian ware stamps
by B Dickinson

VII.44. Firmus iv, Rheinzabern (a), 15c, Dragendorff Form 37, late second to mid-third century. [CD192]

VII.45. [Primitivus, Rheinzabern (a), 15c, Dragendorff Form 37, early to mid-third century. *CA143]*

Glass
Fig 166

VII.46. A small phial. Free-blown; natural green glass. Late first or second century. *[208]*
VII.47. Fragment from the rim of a bulbous-bodied jar (Isings form 67c). Free-blown; natural green blue glass. Rim folded over and down to form a collar. Late first or second century. *[208]*

The small objects
Fig 167

Copper alloy

VII.48. Plain tweezers, made in one piece. Length 71.5mm. *[CA150] MoL Acc No 18184*

Lead and lead alloy

VII.49. Strip, 120mm long, 4mm wide and 1mm thick. The upper surface is roughly bevelled, the lower flat. *[CA150] MoL Acc No 18185 Not illustrated*

Iron

VII.50. Collar for joining two sections of wooden water-pipe. The collar was driven into the wood up to the flange and provided a seal for the junction; cf LRT pl xii for collars in position. Diameter *c* 110mm; height 25mm *[CD207] MoL Acc No 18231*

Ceramic

VII.51. Gaming piece cut from a samian bowl, CG, Antonine. *[CA150] Not illustrated*
VII.52. Gaming piece made from a sherd of BB1. *[CD177A]*

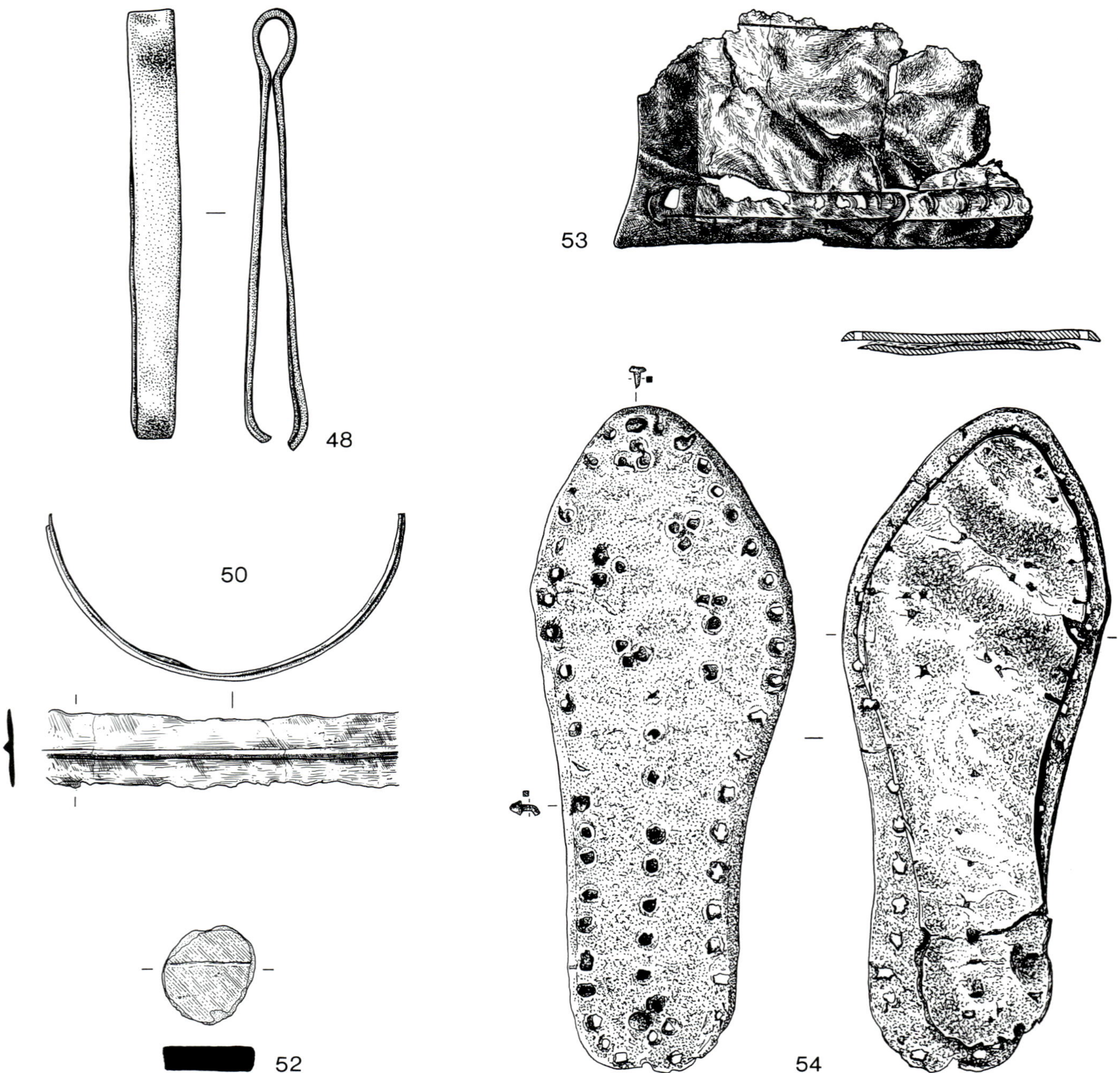

Fig 167 Period 1, Group VII small objects (nos 48 and 52 scale 1:1; nos 50, 53, 54 scale 1:2)

Leather

VII.53. Corner fragment, perhaps from the fore-part of a shoe (M Rhodes pers comm), a saddle or a piece of furniture. The surface is gilded, apart from a band along the two surviving edges. The decoration, defined by incised lines, is of spaced crescent-shaped stamps; there is also an incised line along the broken upper edge. The shaped corner is apparently deliberate, rather than caused by stretching; it has a rough hole, with the impression of a circular stud or nail head. Liversidge (1955, 10 and pl 22) suggested that this piece may have come from an upholstered couch. Length 120mm x 69mm. *[CA153] MoL Acc No 18449*

VII.54. Sole and insole of an adult's shoe; the hobnails are arranged in a decorative pattern and have worn into the insole. *[CA 258]*

Group XII: mid-third century

The finds catalogued and discussed below come from the following layers:

Cutting BB: 115, 313, 323B, 324, 326, 326A, 327, 339, 347, 351, 352, 353, 354
Cutting F: 759, 762, 763, 765, 767, 768, 769, 771, 772

Table 16 Group XII pottery excluding samian

Fabric	*Forms*	*No of vessels (approx)*
AHFA	ERJ; SJ	2
AHFA?	IVJ BUD	1
AHSU	IIC; IID; NJ	3
AMPH		1
BB1	IIA; IIF1; IIF; IIF AL;ERJ; III BUD;IVJ BUD(4); G226(2);FB BUD	13
BB1?	IVJ BUD	1
BB2	IIF; IVH(2); IVH1(5)	8
BB2F	IVH5(3)	3
BBS	FB BUD	1
BHWS	IE	1
CGBL	FOB	1
COAR	SJ?	1
HWC	NJ(3); IIIF; IVF(3)	7
KOLN	III BAD; III ROD(2); III	4
LOMA?	LID	1
LOMI	IVJ	1
LONW	IIR	1
LOXI	MORT BEF	1
LOXI?	IIG	1
MICA	IX MT6.1	1
MOSL	III FOB	2
NFSE	I	1
NKSH		1
NVCC	III BFD; III; FOB BAD	3
NVWW?	IC	1
OXID	IV CDR37 ROD; MORT HAM; MORT HOF	3
OXMO	M17(2); ?M22	3
OXWS	MORT BEF	1
OXWW?	IV	1
RHMO		1
RWS	IB7-9	1
SAND	IIE; NJ(2); C306; ?C306	5
SAND?	?	1
VCWS	IB; IB7-9	2
VRW	IC; IIG(4); IVA; TZ; MORT HOF(2)	9
Total		88

This group would appear to represent a period of neglect of the water channels in the vicinity. Both the channels in Cutting BB and the main course of the Walbrook stream were allowed to fill up with silt, shingle and dumped debris.

Pottery evidence suggests a date broadly contemporary with the construction of the temple, ie mid-third century.

Most of the finds in this group came from Cutting F and the assemblage (25 objects) is similar in general

Table 17 Group XII samian

Source/ Fabric	*Forms*
SG	CU11; CU11?; DR15/17(2); DR29; DR35; DR36(2); DR37(5); RT12?
MV	DR37
CG	CU21; DE72; DR27(3); DR31(3); DR31R(3); DR18/31(6); DR18/31 or 31; DR33(8); DR35; DR36(2); DR37(11); DR30 or 37(2) DR42; DR45; WA79(2); WA79?; II; MORT I/II/III
EG	DR30R; DR31(4); DR31R; DR18/31 or 31; DR33; DR37(10); DR38(2); DR45; DR45?; DR46; LD TG; I; I/II/III; IV; cf DR32; MORT
CG/EG	DR37; MORT
Total no of vessels (approx)	117

character to the earlier Walbrook groups. A bracelet (XII.47) is likely to be of third-century date, but many objects may be residual and a range of other personal items could date from the first and second to the third or fourth centuries. These include finger-rings in copper alloy (XII.48) and iron (XII.59), a buckle (XII.49), tweezers and a spatula-probe (XII.51 and XII.52), and a mixing palette (XII.70). An enamelled sealbox (XII.53) is of second-century date and two iron styli were found in Cutting B (XII.60 and XII.61). A lead candlestick (XII.57) is well preserved, but apart from several fittings, such as a hinge (XII.66), joiners' dogs and double-spiked loops, the only iron objects were two knife blades (XII.62 and XII.63).

The vessels

Pottery

Tables 16 and 17

Black-burnished 1 is the predominant fabric (15%) but the readings for other late Roman fabrics are low. Nene Valley colour-coated ware and Oxfordshire wares both register at 4% and only two Alice Holt/Farnham ware vessels are represented. A date extending beyond *c* AD 250 is indicated by the presence of Alice Holt/Farnham ware, Oxfordshire fabrics and black-burnished ware flanged bowls. It is unlikely, however, that the assemblage is much later than *c* AD 270 due to the absence of Oxfordshire red colour-coated ware and fourth-century wares such as Late Roman calcite-gritted ware and Portchester 'D' ware.

There is a high degree of residuality, with samian (57%) and a wide range of first and second century fabrics in evidence, for example Alice Holt Surrey ware, Verulamium region white ware, Highgate Wood 'C' sand-tempered ware, and London Ware.

XII.24. Dragendorff Form 37, South Gaul. Hollow-leaved plant motifs, lion (cf Oswald 1936–7, 1475). *c* AD 90–110. *[F767] no 2*

XII.25. Dragendorff Form 37, Central Gaul. The ovolo may be that on Stanfield and Simpson pl 90, no.1, by Birrantus II, which has the same fine beadrow. *c* AD 125–50. *[F765] no 3*

XII.26. Dragendorff Form 37 in the style of Cinnamus of Lezoux. Scroll as Stanfield and Simpson pl 161, no 51; the lozenge motif is on pl 160, no 46. *c* AD 150–80. *[F765] no 1*

XII.27. Dragendorff Form 37, Central Gaul. The hollow rosette suggests the work of Criciro or Divixtus (Stanfield and Simpson pls 116, no 8, 117, no 4). *c* AD 135–75. *[F768] no 2*

XII.28. Dragendorff Form 37 in the style of Paternus II of Lezoux. The goat (Oswald 1936–7, 1840), both borders, the festoon and astralagus are on Stanfield and Simpson pl 104, no 9, the ovolo, borders, festoon and astralagus on pl 105, no 13, and the Victory (Oswald 1936–7, 812) on pl 105, no 18. *c* AD 160–90. *[F768] no 1*

XII.29. Dragendorff Form 37 in the style of Cinnamus of Lezoux. The ovolo and scrollery are on Stanfield and Simpson pl 162, no 60. *c* AD 150–80. *[BB327] no 1*

XII.30. Dragendorff Form 37 in the style of Sissus II of Lezoux. The ovolo and corded motifs at panel junctions occur regularly in his work. The leaf is on a signed bowl from Caerwent (Stanfield and Simpson pl 77, no 1); unpublished bowls from Camelon and Wilderspool have the festoon with the corded motif and spiral, the ovolo, the naked figure (Oswald 1936–7, 569) and the squirrel (Oswald 1936–7, 2142) (B R Hartley pers comm). The warrior is Oswald 1936–7, 166. There are slight traces of a possible cursive signature at the base. *c* AD 130–60. *[F767] no 1*

XII.31. Dragendorff Form 37 in the style of X-12 ('Ioenalis') of Les Martres-de-Veyre. The ovolo is probably Rogers 1974, B185; the leaf and beads are on Stanfield and Simpson pl 41, no 480, the palmate leaf on pl 41, no 485, and the trifid bud and beads on pl 35, no 413. *c* AD 100–25. *[F769] no 1*

XII.32. Dragendorff Form 37, Central Gaul. There is no apparent parallel for the ovolo. Hadrianic-early Antonine. *[BB324] no 2*

XII.33. Dragendorff Form 37 in the style of Maiiaaus of Trier, who used this ovolo and the untidy wavy line borders (Gard 1937, Taf 15, no 13). from the same bowl as BB327.2. Later second to early third century. *[BB324] no 1*

XII.34. Dragendorff Form 37, Rheinzabern. Leaf Ricken and Fischer P26. Later second to first half of third century. *[BB324] no 26*

XII.35. Dragendorff Form 37 in the style of Maiiaaus of Trier: the ovolo and untidy borders are on BB324.1, which is probably from the same bowl. Later second to early third century. *[BB327] no 2*

XII.36. Dragendorff Form 37 by the anonymous Trier Werkstatt II. The two wreaths are Fölzer 1913, types 899 and 902. The use of multiple wreaths is common in the work of Werkstatt II: cf Fölzer Taf 12 — no 6 has the same wreaths but reversed, with a similar plain line between. Early to mid-Antonine. *[F763] no 1*

XII.37. Dragendorff Form 37, East Gaul. The ovolo is one used at Blickweiler: cf Knorr and Sprater 1927, Taf 36, no 2 (the Meister des grossen Figuren) and Taf 62, no 2, the potter stamping L.A.A. Antonine. *[F765] no 2*

XII.38. Déchelette Form 72, Central Gaul. Applied leaf, a larger version of Déchelette's (1904) applied leaf type 157. Antonine. *[BB324] no 6*

Samian ware stamps

XII.39. Pontus?, La Graufesenque (a), 8b, Dragendorff Form 27, *c* AD 65–90. *[BB339]*

XII.40. Genialis iii, Les-Martres-de-Veyre (a), 2a (?used at LZ), *c* AD115–50. *[F767]*

XII.41. Cucalus, Lezoux (a), 2f, Dragendorff Form 27, *c* AD130–55. *[F759]*

XII.42. Borillus i, Lezoux (a), 4a, Walters Form 79, *c* AD150–80. *[F762]*

XII.43. Habilis, Lezoux (b), 5d, Dragendorff Form 31, *c* AD 150–80. *[F762]*

XII.44. Illit, La Graufesenque (c), Dragendorff Form 27, Neronian to early Flavian. *[BB351]*

Graffiti

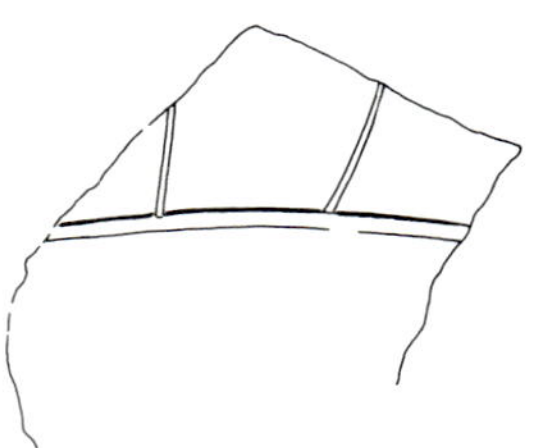

XII.45. Samian Dragendorff Form 33 (Central Gaulish). Scratched up to central groove. *[BB 324]*

Glass

XII.46. Fragment from the rim and side of a straight-sided, 'Airlie' beaker (Isings form 85b). Free-blown; colourless with a faint yellow brown tint. Rim thickened, fire-rounded and sloping slightly inwards. Late second or early third century. *[BB326]*

The small objects

Fig 170

Copper alloy

XII.47. Fragments, probably of a bracelet. The rounded upper surface is cut to resemble cord; cf Goodburn 1984, fig 10, no 66. Length 66mm. *[F763] MoL Acc No 18244*
XII.48. Finger-ring; the lozenge-shaped bezel is decorated with raised dots, probably cast in a mould. An identical ring was found at Verulamium, dated AD 75–85 (Waugh and Goodburn 1972, pl xxxviii, b). Dimensions 19 x 18mm. [F768] MoL Acc No 18252
XII.49. Semicircular buckle, with attached bar. The heavy bone tongue, decorated with notches, may be a replacement. Height 21mm; length of tongue 25mm. *[F765] MoL Acc No 18250*
XII.50. Pin with small conical head. Cf LRT pl xli, 5. Length 104mm. *[BB352] MoL Acc No 18223*
XII.51. Tweezers with incised lines round the edge; made in one piece. Length 49.5mm. *[F763] MoL Acc No 18246*
XII.52. Spatula-probe. The facetted shaft narrows above the bulb of the probe; the other end has an elaborate series of mouldings above a flexible spatula. Length 153mm. *[F769] MoL Acc No 18254*
XII.53. Lozenge-shaped sealbox with projections for string, catch, and hinge at the angles. The upper surface is decorated with small lozenges of green enamel, the lower has four holes; cf Allason-Jones and Miket

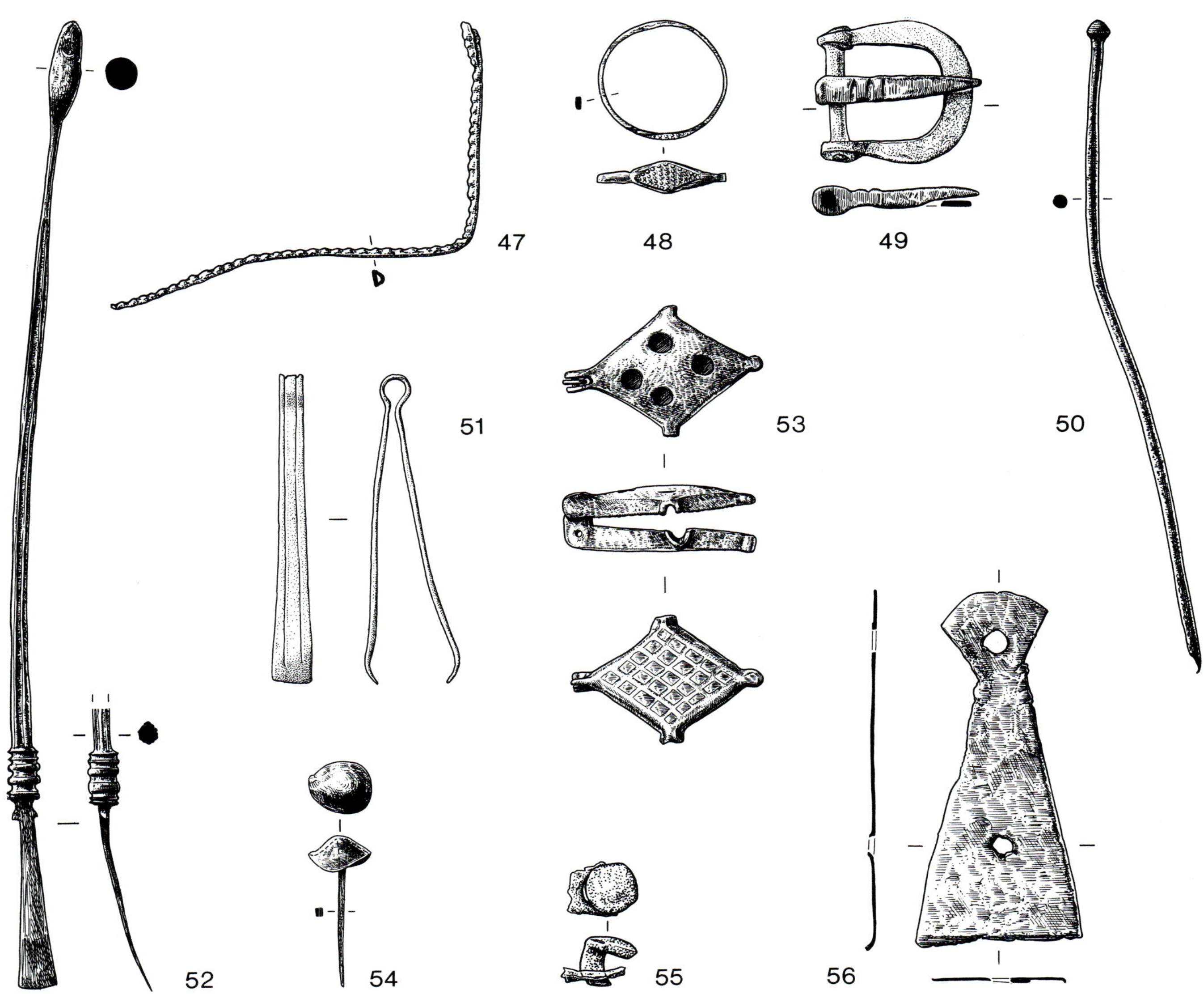

Fig 170 Period 1, Group XII copper alloy objects (scale 1:1)

1984, nos 3.376–7. Length 29mm. *[F763] MoL Acc No 18243*

XII.54. Stud with hollow domed head and long square pin; cf Goodburn 1984, fig 18, no 158. Length 25mm. *[F769] MoL Acc No 18256*

XII.55. Small stud or rivet, still attached through a fragment of sheet copper alloy. Length 8mm. *[F763] MoL Acc No 18245*

XII.56. Flat fitting with two punched holes; the metal from the holes is bent over at the back. Length 54mm. *[F771] MoL Acc No 18257*

Lead and lead alloy
Fig 171

XII.57. Candlestick, cut from one piece of sheet metal. The cylindrical sconce stands on a rectangular dish with four legs. Width 74mm; height 34mm. *[F762] MoL Acc No 18241*

XII.58. Squat, spool-shaped object; the constricted waist is worn smooth, as if by friction from a cord. Jones (1983, 59, no 28) suggests that this may be a fishing weight. Lead *[F765] MoL Acc No 18248*

Iron

XII.59. Finger-ring, worn on the inside. The intaglio is lost, but traces of adhesive remain in the setting. Cf LRT, fig 30, 16–18 Diameter 24.50 by 20mm. *[F763] MoL Acc No 18242*

XII.60. Stylus (Manning type 2); plain shaft, offset eraser and point. Length 112mm. *[BB351] MoL Acc No 18270 Not illustrated*

XII.61. Stylus (Manning type 4) with faceted shaft and offset eraser and point. Length 119mm *[BB354]*

XII.62. Knife blade, broken, shaped at the end to make a socket for the handle. A fragment of the wooden handle survives inside. Length 137mm. *[F768] MoL Acc No 18782*

XII.63. Knife blade, fragmentary and very corroded, surviving length 100mm. Narrow wedge-shaped section. Length 100mm *[BB347] MoL Acc No 18347 Not illustrated*

XII.64. Twisted handle, turned in to a ring at the end. Similar handles were used for many implements, including knives (Cunliffe 1971, fig 60, 43), ladles (ibid 1971, fig 60,55), rattles (LRT, pl xlviii, 2), and

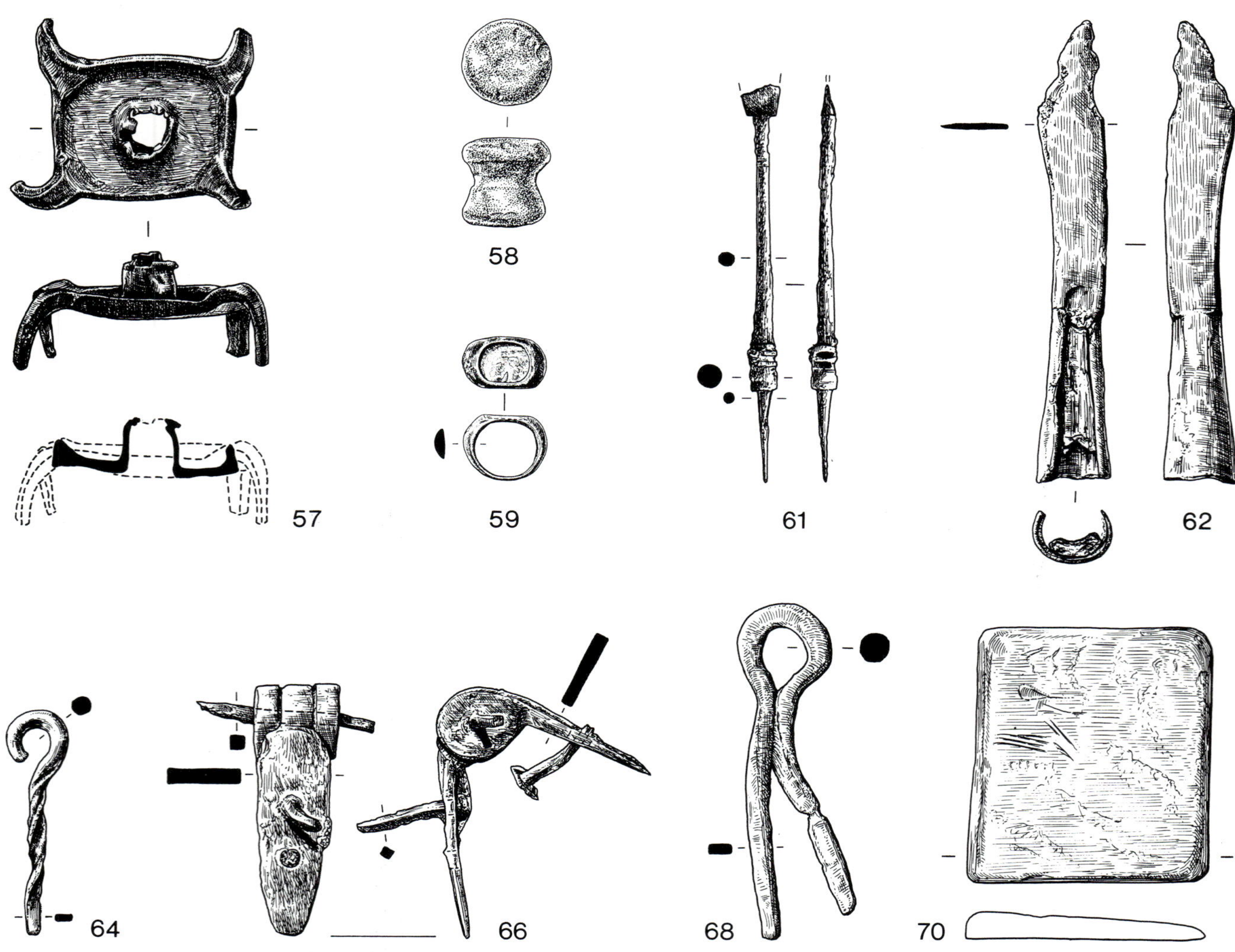

Fig 171 Period 1, Group XII small objects, excluding copper alloy (scale 1:2)

small fire-shovels (Manning 1972, fig 60, 6). Length 66mm *[F769] MoL Acc No 18255*
XII.65. Twisted iron bar, surviving 107mm long; probably a handle (cf nos 14 and 19 above). *[F768] Not illustrated*
XII.66. Heavy strap hinge, complete with pivot pin and attaching nails in place. Cf Cunliffe 1971, fig 56, 12–16. Length 74.5mm *[F759] MoL Acc No 18269*
XII.67. Joiner's dog or staple, 140mm long, with both arms broken. The rectangular shank (15 x 5mm) is considerably broader than the arms (7 by 5mm). *[BB354] MoL Acc No 18348 Not illustrated*
XII.68. Double-spiked loop, the arms slightly twisted. Cf Manning 1972, fig 68, 90–94. Length 99.5mm. *[F765] MoL Acc No 18249*
XII.69. Bolt composed of a flat-headed nail with a rivet attached; probably originally bolted through wood (cf Cunliffe 1971, fig 55, nos 6–7). Length 42mm overall; the head and rivet are corroded. *[F765] Not illustrated*

Stone

XII.70. Mixing palette, green slate. The upper surface is smooth and well finished, the underside scarred and irregular — the usual state in which such palettes are found (Crummy 1983, 57). The edges are rounded or bevelled. 75 by 67mm. *[F765] MoL Acc No 18247 XII*

Period 2 finds

Group VIII: second half of the third century

The finds catalogued and discussed below come from the following layers:

Cutting CA: 301, 302
Cutting CB: 116, 119, 260, 261, 262, 263, 264, 270, 281, 282, 319, 335, 350, 352, 352A, 355, 357, 358, 359
Cutting CD: 158, 159, 163, 165, 168, 169, 170, 172, 173, 174, 176
Cutting CE: 244 (internal), 259 (internal), 268 (exterior south side)

The original design of the Mithraeum was to have been a simple rectangular room with an apse at its western end (Fig 61). Two sleeper-walls each supported seven columns. During the laying of foundations, however, the wet soil conditions, which had dictated the nature of activity in all of the earlier phases, led to three supporting buttresses being built around the apse and relieving arches being included at the west end of the sleeper-walls. A dump of homogeneous soil was laid or had built up outside the Mithraeum up against its external wall; this was probably meant to enhance the cave-like qualities of the temple.

In its original form the nave floor was much lower than the west end of the temple where a solid dais supported cult sculptures. The entrance was at the opposite east end. Steps led from the latter into the nave and from the nave up to the dais. Group VIII contains the first four superimposed floors in the nave of the temple (Floors 1–4). This resulted in a surface level equal to that of the top of the sleeper-walls and higher than the aisle.

Pottery from these floors suggests a date from the mid-third century until the late third or early fourth century. Animal bone from these floors shows that chickens formed part of the ritual use of the temple.

Other objects from the Mithraeum floors are more prosaic, chiefly miscellaneous fittings (VIII.50), perhaps from the fabric of the building, but in addition there is an ornate iron stylus (VIII.47) inlaid with bands of copper alloy which could well be contemporary, as could an unusual open lamp (VIII.40). A pine cone (VIII.54) came from the surface of the first floor and can be interpreted as an item associated with the Mithraic liturgy.

The most striking small find was the jet handle from an ornamental sword or dagger with a distinctive military style, found above Floor 3 (Grimes 1968, 114) (VIII.55). This may well have formed part of the temple furnishings, perhaps part of a statue, a votive offering, or an item used in the Mithraic ritual. The dolphin handle mount (VIII.42), which may have been affixed to an elaborate vessel, was found outside the temple to the south, and although it is clearly an item of high quality its use in the temple cannot be proved. Contemporary levels west of the Mithraeum produced a drill bit and key (VIII.48 and VIII.49).

The vessels

Pottery
Tables 18 and 19

The Oxfordshire red colour-coated ware suggests a post-*c* AD 270 date but only a very small quantity is present (1%). Black-burnished 1 (20%) and Black-burnished style wares (11%) have particularly high ratios and Nene Valley colour-coated ware (7%) is also one of the main fabrics. Among the miscellaneous sand-tempered wares it is evident that the C306 is becoming more common, with four, possibly five vessels represented. The percentage of samian (37%) remains high. A late third-century date seems appropriate.

Catalogue of illustrated vessels
For code expansions see above, *Pottery codes and expansions*
Fig 172

VIII.1. Alice Holt/Farnham ware everted-rim jar (AHFA ERJ). Not illustrated
VIII.2. BB1 everted-rim jar (ERJ) with obtuse lattice decoration. *[CD173]*

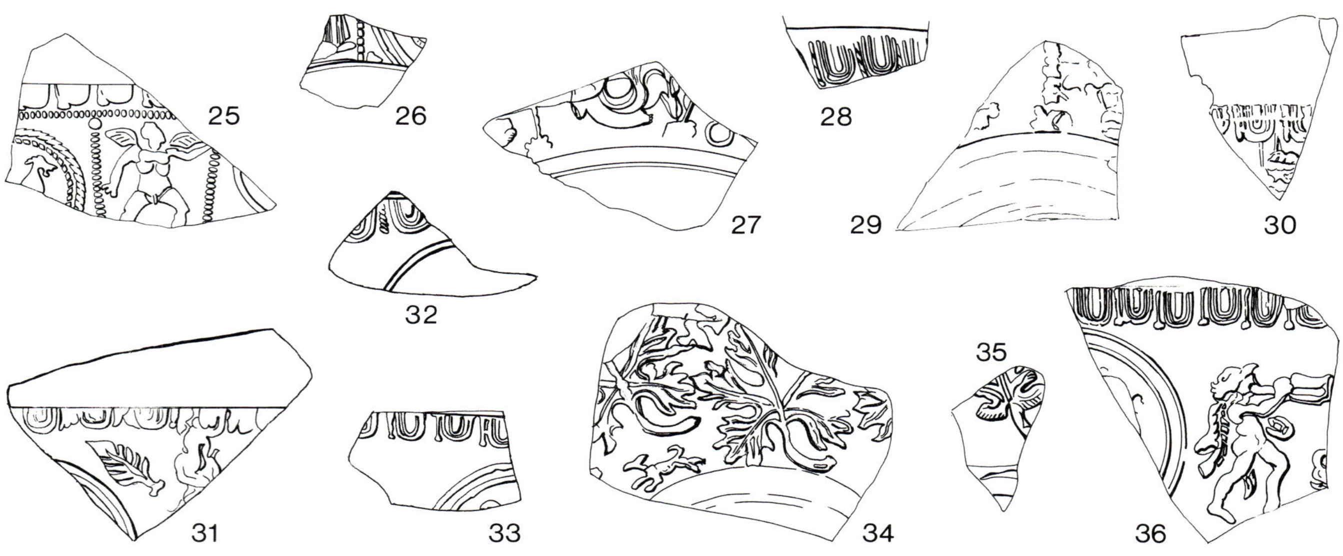

Fig 173 Period 2, Group VIII samian vessels (scale 1:2)

Selected samian
Fig 173

VIII.25. Dragendorff Form 37 in the style of Cinnamus of Lezoux. The ovolo is badly smeared, but may be Rogers 1974, B24, assigned to Cinnamus, who used similar beadrows and terminals (Stanfield and Simpson pl 158, no 22), the wreath (Rogers 1974, E16) and the cupid (Oswald 1936–7, 401). The cockerel is Oswald 1936–7, 2342. *c* AD 150–80. *[CB262] no 1*

VIII.26. Dragendorff Form 37, probably in the style of Doeccus of Lezoux. The figure is likely to be that on Stanfield and Simpson pl 150, no 51, with similar beads and medallion. Mid- to late Antonine. *[CB262] no 2*

VIII.27. Dragendorff Form 37, Central Gaul. The thin rectangular beads suggest the work of Laxtucissa or Paternus II (Stanfield and Simpson pls 99, no 21, 105, no 16). The rosette terminals and the circle motif were used by Censorinus, Laxtucissa and Paternus II (Stanfield and Simpson pls 97.7, 99.16, 101.10, 104.4 and 105.17). The dolphin is probably Oswald 1936–7, 2394. *c* AD 160–90. *[CB350] no 2*

VIII.28. Dragendorff Form 37, Rheinzabern. The ovolo, Ricken and Fischer 1963, E23, was used by a number of potters. Late second to first half of third century. *[CB260] no 1*

VIII.29. Dragendorff Form 37 in the style of Julius II–Julianus I of Rheinzabern. The cross is Ricken and Fischer 1963, O53, the beadrow Ricken and Fischer 1963, O256. Early to mid-third century. [CB261] no 1

VIII.30. Dragendorff Form 37, Rheinzabern. The ovolo, Ricken and Fischer 1963, E23, was used by several potters, but especially by Julius II–Julianus I and their associates. Very poorly finished. Early to mid-third century. *[CB264] no 9*

VIII.31. Dragendorff Form 37, Rheinzabern. The ovolo (Ricken and Fischer 1963, E40), boxer (Ricken and Fischer 1963, M196a), leaf (Ricken and Fischer 1963, P30) and medallion (Ricken and Fischer 1963, K17) were all used by Primitivus III (Ludowici and Ricken 1948, 1948, Taf 196, no 11, has all but the boxer); all but the medallion were also used by Attillus and Primitivus I. The bowl is 'waisted' at the top of the decoration, which is a late feature. Early to mid-third century. *[CB359] no 1*

VIII.32. Dragendorff Form 37, Rheinzabern. The ovolo, Ricken and Fischer 1963, E42, was used by Julius I and Lupus; the medallion is probably Ricken and Fischer 1963, K6, which they also used. End of the second to mid-third century. *[CB359] no 2*

VIII.33. Dragendorff Form 37, Rheinzabern. Ovolo Ricken and Fischer 1963, E17, medallion Ricken and Fischer 1963, K19: both shared by several potters. Late second to first half of the third century. *[CB359] no 3*

VIII.34. Dragendorff Form 37 in the style of Atto II of Rheinzabern. Ludowici and Ricken 1948, Taf 135, no 4, has the leaves (Ricken and Fischer 1963, P62) and dog (Ricken and Fischer 1963, T141c). Taf 135, no 5, has the bird (Ricken and Fischer 1963, T205a) and leaves. Later second to early third century. *[CD173] no 1*

VIII.35. Déchelette Form 72, Central Gaul. Applied leaf, smaller version of Déchelette's (1904) applied type 157; barbotine tendrils. Antonine. *[CB355] no 1*

VIII.36. The motifs (flautist Ricken and Fischer 1963, M165, ovolo Ricken and Fischer 1963, E17 and medallion Ricken and Fischer 1963, K19) were all used by Comitalis V: cf Ludowici and Ricken 1948, Taf 96, no 17, a bowl in similar style. Later second to first half of third century. *[CD174] no 1*

Samian ware stamps

VIII.37. Illixo, Lezoux (b), 3a, Dragendorff Form 33, *c* AD 150–180. *[CB359]*

VIII.38. Unidentified I[or]I, South Gaul, Dragendorff Form 18, *c* AD 50–100. *[BB357]*

Mica-dusted pedestal base
Fig 174

VIII.39. The fabric of this vessel is like Hoo ware but finished with mica dusting rather than a white slip. *[CB 359]*

Lamp

VIII.40. Open lamp. Very crudely made, with an unusually deep wall. Sandy whitish fabric with a black colour coat, probably manufactured in the London area. Length 140 mm; height of wall 35mm. *[CB 264] MoL Acc No 18733*

Graffiti

VIII.41. Colour-coated beaker. M[on the neck. *[CB 335]*

Lead or lead alloy

VIII.42. Handle in the shape of a dolphin, rather crudely modelled and partially hollowed underneath. There are signs of attachment at the mouth, and it was probably also fixed at the tail. Dolphin handles are common in copper alloys: cf Waugh and Goodburn 1972, fig 41, nos 133–5; no 135 is similarly hollowed and also enamelled, as are the dolphins supporting the upper part of an elaborate vessel from Ambleteuse (Henry 1933, fig 45, no 1). This humbler dolphin may have been attached in a similar position (Ralph Jackson kindly supplied a copy of the Ambleteuse illustration). Tin (MOL; Jones 1983, fig 7, no 17). Length 98mm; width of body 20mm. *[CE 268] MoL Acc No 18734 from poorly recorded deposits against the external face of the south wall of the Mithraeum*

Worked stone architectural fragment

Fig 175

VIII.43. Part of the base of one of the 14 original columns from Phase 1. Shelly, uneven-grained oolitic Jurassic limestone, probably from the Cotswold region. Traces of red paint in the angle of the cavetto moulding

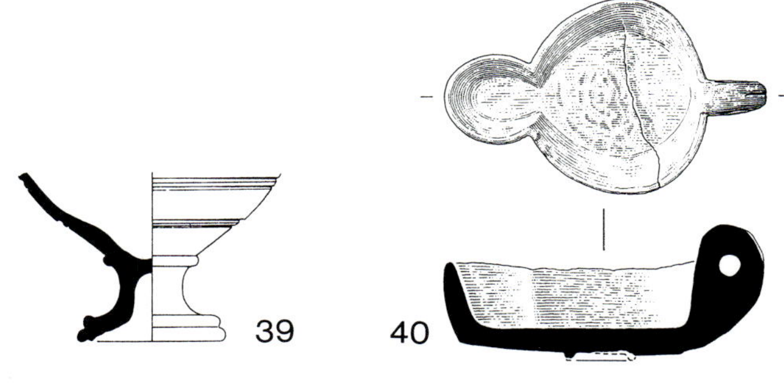

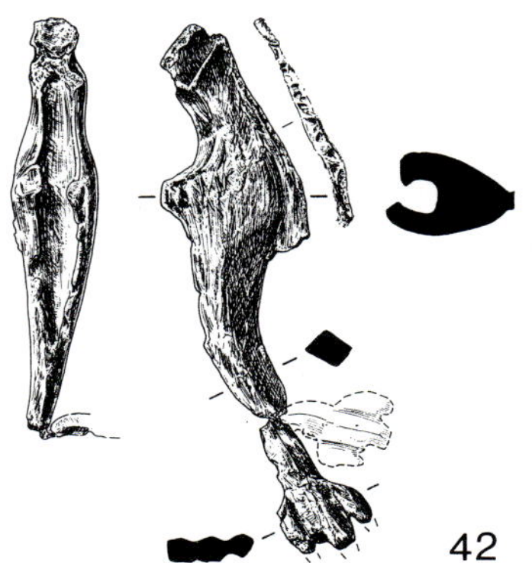

Fig 174 Period 2, Group VIII mica-dusted vessel, lamp and lead alloy vessels (nos 39, 40 scale 1:4; no 42 scale 1:2)

and the column shaft. A vertical rebate has been gouged into the side of the base, presumably to accommodate a wooden plank. *MoL Acc No 18500, partly displaced, from the packing over column pad N7 (Fig 82)*

The small objects

Fig 176

Copper alloy

VIII.44. Two links of S-shaped chain; the joining loops are more tightly closed than the ends. Length 37.5mm. *[CB 335] MoL Acc No 18834*
VIII.45. Corner of rectangular plate or mounting, surviving 54mm by 44mm, with a small square rivet-hole in the corner and another in the probable centre. *[CB 262] Not illustrated*
VIII.46. Two strips, 173mm long overall, welded together and overlapping for 50mm. The rectangular section is 18mm wide and 3mm thick. Three holes, 4mm in diameter, are pushed through from one side, 60mm apart; the ends are roughly cut. Perhaps a binding or reinforcement *[CB 357] MoL Acc No 18342. Not illustrated*

Iron

VIII.47. Stylus (Manning 1976 type IV) with plain offset eraser. Above the offset point are elaborate mouldings set with five narrow bands of copper alloy; the lowest

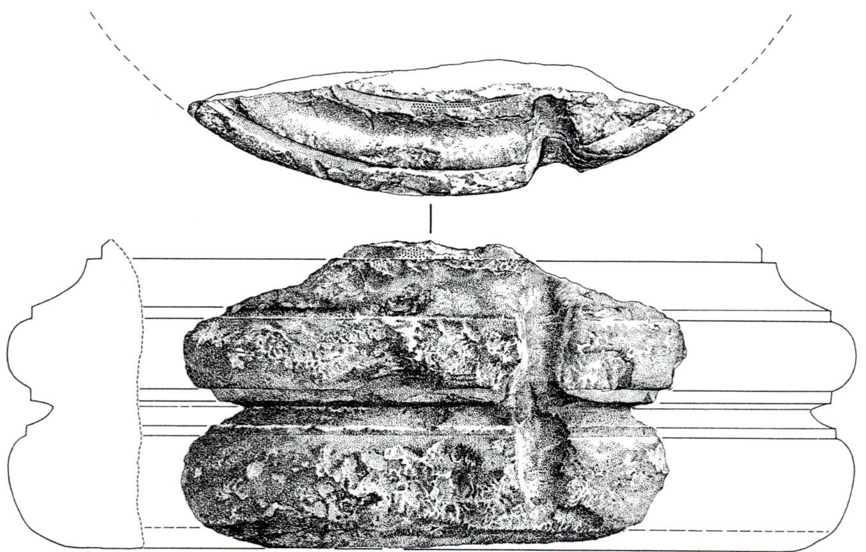

Fig 175 Period 2, Group VIII column base from over column pad N7 (scale 1:4)

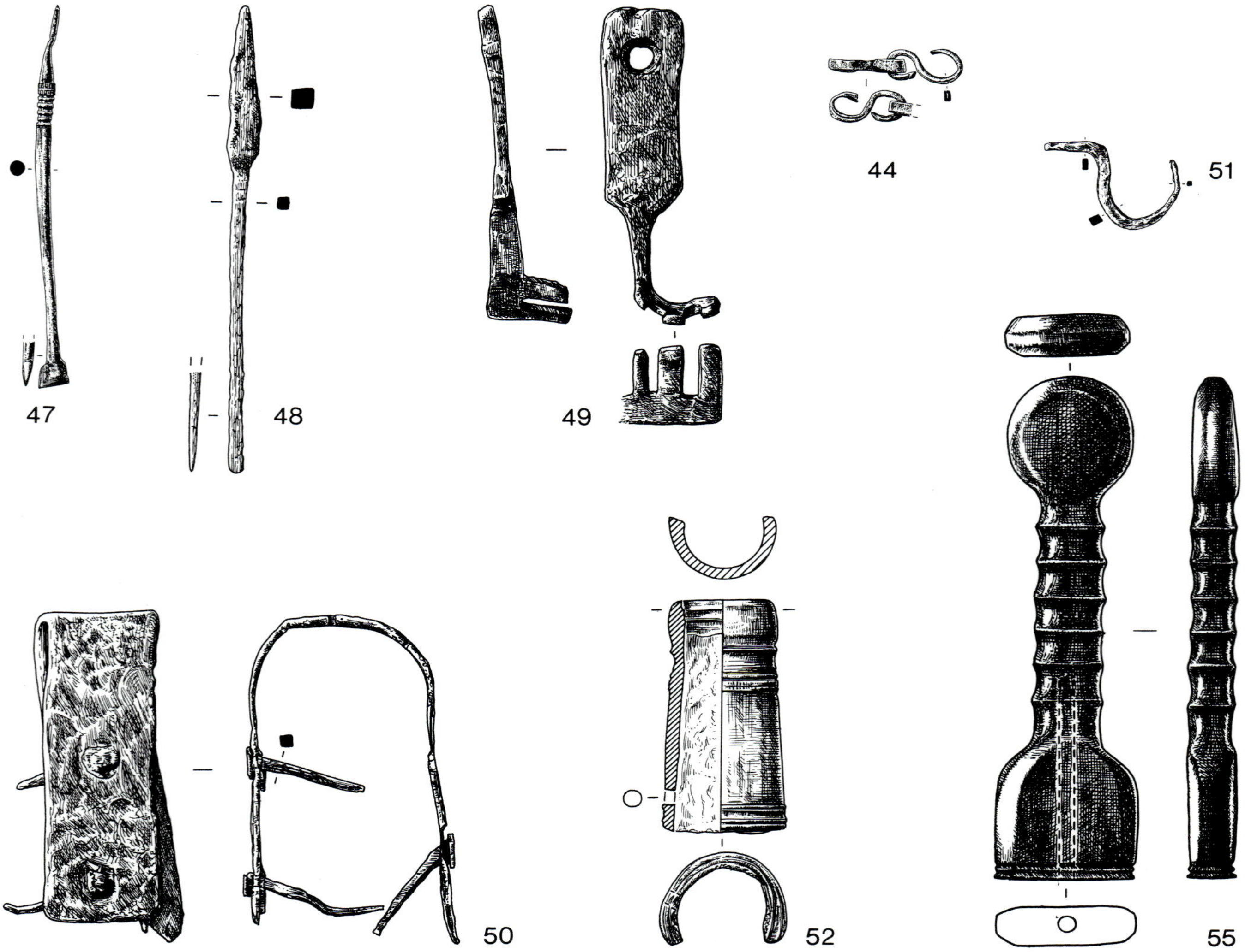

47 48 49 44 51 50 52 55

Fig 176 Period 2, Group VIII small objects (scale 1:2)

band has incised vertical lines. Cf LRT pl xxiv, 2, which has similar inlaid bands. Length 113.5mm. *[CB 355] MoL Acc No 18343*

VIII.48. Drill bit with long pyramidal head, square-sectioned shaft and flat blade, probably a diamond bit originally, as Manning (1985, 26, B23, pl 11 from Hod Hill and fig 5, 2). Length 140mm. *[CD 173] MoL Acc No 18186*

VIII.49. Tumbler-lock slide key with three heavy teeth on a curved bit. For discussion of the type see Manning 1972, 181; Manning 1985, 92 and fig 25,6. Length 95mm. *[CD 170] MoL Acc No 18187*

VIII.50. U-shaped band, probably a reinforcement for a wooden post or jamb. The attaching nails remain in position, cf Manning 1972, 188–9 and fig 70, 131–33. Length 92mm. *[CB 262] MoL Acc No 19836*

VIII.51. Hook with spike for attachment, cf Manning 1972, fig 68, nos 86–89. Length 55mm. *[CB 355] MoL Acc No 18345*

Bone and antler

VIII.52. Finely turned and polished long bone, perhaps a handle or an ornamental cover for an item such as the leg of a box. The wider end has mouldings, with a small hole on one side, presumably for securing the bone to a wooden core; the curved and moulded narrow end is roughly turned on the interior for 8mm. Length 70mm. *[CB 355] MoL Acc No 18344*

VIII.53. Shaft of plain hairpin, broken at each end. *[CB 270] MoL Acc No 18735. Not illustrated*

Pine cone

VIII.54. Cone of *Pinus pinea* (the Mediterranean stone pine), largely complete but partly burnt or scorched on one side. The pine cone was associated with Atys, who died beneath a pine tree, and was also used to tip the Bacchic thyrsus; it may have had a more general significance as a symbol of the afterlife (cf Henig 1984, 202–3), and would therefore not be inappropriate in a Mithraic context. Other British finds of pine cones are noted by Green (1976). Richmond (Richmond *et al* 1951, 6, n 2) notes that in Roman Egypt they were sold in tens or sixteens for burning as sacrifices or simply as gifts to friends: the Carrawburgh pine cones were also charred but they had not ignited. Tests showed that they had been intentionally carbonised by roasting for use as fuel. When a sample was burnt it gave off a pungent aroma of pine and burnt with a dark red glow. Other examples from the immediate vicinity of the London Mithraeum come from St Swithun's House (MoL Acc No 24195) and the National Safe Deposit Company, Bucklersbury (MoL Acc No 3831). *[CB 361] MoL Acc No 18501. Not illustrated*

Stone: jet

VIII.55. Handle, probably from an ornamental sword or dagger; highly polished. The circular head and faceted shaft resemble a legionary sword handle (cf the statue from Camomile Street bastion, Merrifield 1965, pl 95); the base is a shouldered rectangle, with a small circular hole for attaching a blade. Such an elaborate object may have served a ritual purpose or have been a votive offering; the Mithraic sculpture from Housesteads shows the god holding a dagger with a similar shouldered hilt and round terminal (Toynbee 1962, pl 74). Length 150mm. Found on Floor 3 (Grimes 1968, 114). *[CB 355] MoL Acc No 18263*

Window glass

VIII.56–7. Two fragments of cast matt/glossy, natural greenish blue window glass. [*CB 116] and [CD 158]. Not illustrated*

VIII.58. Small fragment of cylinder-blown window glass. Free-blown and flattened; natural blue-green. Third or fourth century. *[CB 261] Not illustrated*

Group IX: first half of the fourth century

The finds catalogued and discussed below come from the following layers:

Cutting CA: 134, 135, 242, 246, 247, 271, 272, 312, 321, 322, 323, 341
Cutting CB: 110, 115, 137, 138, 243, 245, 253, 310, 312, 314, 315, 320, 326, 330, 332, 340, 342, 344, 345, 346, 353
Cutting CE: 237 (internal)

Group IX consists of the make-up layers of Floors 5–7 and the floors themselves. This separation from Group VIII was intended to highlight the apparent change in interior layout, and possibly also function, during the early fourth century. The sleeper-walls had disappeared entirely from view and the columns had been removed. The interior was open in plan with only flimsy partitions. It is possible that severe structural problems, perhaps even a collapse, in the south-west corner and down the centres of both north and south walls prompted these alterations. The head of Minerva (IX.39) was found over one of the column pads and the head of Mithras (IX.38) came from a contemporary level in the north aisle nearby. Four sculptures (Serapis IX.40, Mercury group IX.41, the large marble hand of Mithras Tauroctonos IX.42, and the limestone hand of Mithras Tauroctonos IX.43) were buried in a pit cut into Floor 5 and the apse area was redesigned to take two new altars. It is argued above (Chapter 4, Modern disturbance in the temple) that three sculptures found in 1889 (IX.44, IX.45, IX.46) were also buried in this floor at the same time

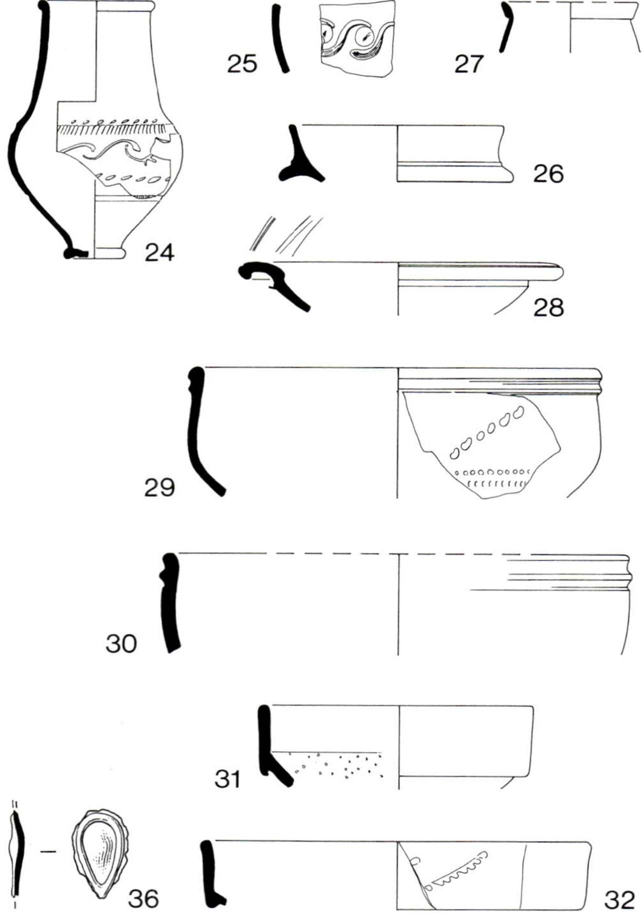

Fig 178 Period 2, Group IX pottery and glass vessels (nos 24-32 scale 1:4; no 36 scale 1:2)

IX.11. BB1 everted-rim jar (ERJ). *[CB115]*
IX.12. BB1 plain-rimmed dish with burnished decoration (IVJ BUD). *[CA135]*
IX.13. As above. *[CB243]*
IX.14. BB1 flanged bowl (FB). *[CA135]*
IX.15. BB1 flanged bowl with burnished decoration (FB BUD). *[CA321]*
IX.16. Black-burnished type ware, possibly BB1, flanged bowl with burnished decoration (BB1? FB BUD). *[CA 341]*
IX.17. Unidentified grey sandy ware Camulodunum type C306 bowl (SAND C306). *[CB 310]*
IX.18 As above. *[CB 310]*
IX.19. Late Roman Calcite-gritted ware necked jar (CALC NJ). [CA 272]
IX.20. Portchester 'D' ware necked jar (PORD NJ). *[CB 310]*
IX.21. Flagon, possibly Portchester 'D' ware (PORD? I). *[CB 310]*
IX.22. Oxfordshire parchment ware carinated bowl (OXPA CA). *[CA242]*
IX.23. Oxfordshire parchment ware necked bowl (OXPA NE). *[CA271]*
IX.24. Nene Valley colour-coated ware bead-rim beaker with white paint and rouletted decoration. (NVCC III BR WPD ROD). *[CA272], [CA273]and [CA289]*
IX.25. Nene Valley colour-coated ware beaker with white-painted decoration (NVCC III WPD). *[CA242]*
IX.26. Nene Valley colour-coated ware copy of a Dragendorff Form 38 (NVCC IV C Dragendorff Form 38). *[CA271], [CA272]*
IX.27. Colour-coated beaker with brown slip (CC III). *[CA323]*
IX.28. Oxfordshire red colour-coated ware copy of a Dragendorff Form 36 with white-painted decoration, Young type C48 (NVCC IV C Dragendorff Form 36 WPD C48). *[CB310]*
IX.29. Oxfordshire red colour-coated ware copy of a Dragendorff Form 37 with white-painted decoration (OXRC IV C Dragendorff Form 37 WPD). *[CA242]*
IX.30. As above but with only slight traces of white paint. *[CA242]*
IX.31. Oxfordshire red colour-coated ware mortarium, Young type C97 (OXRC MORT C97). *[CA246]*
IX.32. Oxfordshire red colour-coated ware mortarium with white-painted decoration, Young type C98. *[CB137]*
IX.33. Base of an Alice Holt/Farnham jar with very thick deposit, probably pitch, on the interior. *[CA272] MoL Acc. No. 19859. Not illustrated*

Graffiti

IX.34. Grog-tempered storage jar with two 'X's on the shoulder. *[CA 321]*

Glass

IX.35. Small fragment from the rim of an 'Airlie' style bowl. Late second or third century. *[CB110] Not illustrated.*
IX.36. Fragment of the body of a vessel with an applied oval prunt (cf Harden 1975, fig 198, 19 and 20). Applied to a free-blown form; colourless glass. Late third or fourth century. *[CB 110]*

Stone
Fig 179

IX.37. Laver or stoup. The body is set on a low footring with a roughly rectangular irregular depression in its centre; damage to one side. Even-grained oolitic limestone with crystalline matrix, Jurassic type, probably from the Gloucestershire area. Lavers have been found in other mithraic contexts, for example *in situ* at Rudchester (Gillam 1954, 211) and at

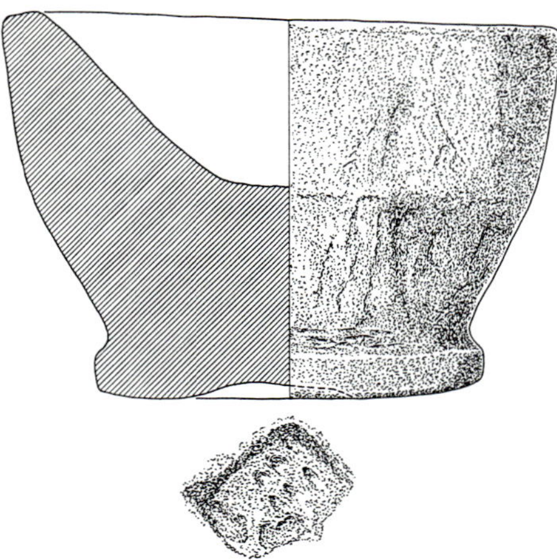

Fig 179 Period 2, Group IX stone laver, stoup or mixing bowl (scale 1:4)

Carrawburgh (Harris and Harris 1965, 20, 27, and note 9). Diameter 242mm; height 172mm. *From Pit A at the east end of the nave, found with the head of Serapis, the colossal hand and the Mercury group. MoL Acc No 18502*

Sculpture and worked stone sculptures found in 1954

IX.38. Head of Mithras, Figures 180–3: cf Toynbee (1986) 5–10; no 1; pl I; pls 1–3. Mithras is portrayed as a handsome beardless youth, with long curly hair and characteristic Phrygian cap. Originally the flesh parts were smooth and highly polished. When the head was found, most of the face and large portions of the hair were disfigured by dark smears of iron incrustation and staining (Fig 180). These have been cleaned off, leaving a light yellow colour and a slightly roughened surface. Since most of the head and neck is well preserved, the Mithras must have been carefully buried. It was found with a clean break between the head and neck just below the chin (Fig 183). The gash was made in antiquity, deliberately, before burial, and with a blunt instrument, perhaps an axe. Below the lower edge of the polished neck the bust terminates in a kind of tenon, triangular in shape and roughly worked with a point in the centre of the lower surface. The tenon, which was not meant to be visible, must have been let into a cavity between the shoulders of the body.

The carving of the head and neck of a statue in a block separate from the body was a common practice among sculptors of the Roman imperial period (Fig. 181). The draped parts of the figure may have been rendered in a coarser marble, stone or even stucco. In the base of the tenon there is an ancient hole, about 20mm square, into which a vertical metal bar could have been inserted to support the weight of the marble head.

The head of Mithras was clearly not intended to be viewed from the rear (Fig 182). It seems that the head was reshaped at the back to fit a group placed a short distance in front of a background. The head probably formed part of a bull-slaying scene. The eyes, wide open and far-seeing, are averted from the sight of his victim's anguish, perhaps a sign that Mithras takes no delight in the slaughter. The hairs of the eyebrows are not detailed nor the irises of the eyes incised, and these were probably painted. The pupils are deeply drilled in a crescent shape and glass paste or enamel may once have filled these hollows. The inside of the mouth has also been drilled out, with an upper row of teeth just visible between slightly parted lips. The hair is treated in an impressionistic manner, with drilled holes and grooves segmenting the individual locks.

Fig 180 Period 2, Group IX. The head of Mithras (IX.38)

For parallels to the head of Mithras found in mithraea, see Toynbee, but most noteworthy are those from Aquileia, now in Vienna (Vermaseren 1956, 262–3, no. 736, figs 203–4), two marble reliefs from the Palazzo dei Musei di Roma Mithraeum in Rome (Vermaseren 1956, 184–5, nos 435–7, figs 122–3) and a stucco head from the mithraeum under the Church of Santa Prisca in Rome (Vermaseren 1956, 196, no 479, fig 132). The general style and the technique used for working the hair indicate a date of *c* AD 180–200. Henig suggests a date of AD 180–220 (below, *Appendix 1*). Both the craftmanship and the material suggest it was carved in Italy.

The head is made from fine-grained saccharoidal marble, probably from Carrara, Italy. Dimensions; height 369mm; width at base of neck 168mm. Found in 1954, the head and neck were found lying close together. They had been deliberately buried in a shallow pit, overlying the dismantled stone colonnades of the temple and afterwards sealed by the later fourth-century floors of the temple, just east and slightly north of the site of the easternmost column of the northern colonnade. *MoL Acc No 20005*

Fig 181 Period 2, Group IX. Mithras (IX.38), front view

Fig 182 Period 2, Group IX. Mithras (IX.38), rear view

IX.39. Head of Minerva, Figures 184–5: cf Toynbee (1986) 10–13; no 2; pl II; pls 4, 5, 7. The head of Minerva is a finely carved, classicising and idealised representation. The surface of the face and neck have been highly polished. Under the lower edge of the polished neck there is a roughly surfaced tenon, rounded in shape. The supporting body into which the head was set was probably made of stone or coarser marble. Walker comments that it must have been intended as a part of a full-length figure (S Walker pers comm). The scale and pose of the head and the overall finish would have been wrong for a bust alone.

On the head a plain band runs over the brows and behind each ear over the thick, rope-like coil of hair on the nape of the neck. In addition the crown of the head is absent and the back of the head is roughly tooled and completely unfinished. It is pierced with two circular holes, each 13mm in diameter, set one behind the other.

Fig 183 Period 2, Group IX. Mithras (IX.38), detail of damage to neck

Fig 184 Period 2, Group IX. The head of Minerva (IX.39) in situ *east of column N1*

Fig 185 Period 2, Group IX. Minerva (IX.39), front view

These two features suggest that the goddess could have worn a metal helmet, probably crested. The two holes could have held metal bars which would have held the helmet firm. Walker has pointed out (pers comm) that although the goddess almost certainly wore a helmet, the band, as the base for the helmet, looks very like a *stephane* (diadem). In addition, some marble heads are known to have had crowns added in stucco or stone.

It seems that the head was meant to be turned very slightly towards the spectator's left, with the face tilted a little upwards. Two triangles of hair frame the face of Minerva in a series of round curls. Blagg remarks (pers comm) that the carving of the hair contrasts with the head of Mithras (IX.38) in the absence of drilled grooves and greater use of the chisel, an indication of an earlier date. The details of the eyebrows are not rendered and the eyes are plain. The pupils are not engraved and were presumably painted. The clear-cut brows, long straight nose, small neat mouth and oval cheeks combine to produce an idealised face, drawing on images created in classical Greece.

The head is perfectly preserved, apart from the loss of a small portion of the outer margin of the upper part of the right ear and some slight chipping along the edge of the neck above the tenon. Black staining, due to iron deposits, spreads over the side of the left cheek under the chin, over the left ear and the portion of the head directly behind. Other patches are visible on the right side of the chin.

There are no known instances of the worship of Minerva in other mithraea. The style and material indicate that the head was carved in Italy and was most probably produced between *c* AD 130–90.

The head is made from fine-grained saccharoidal marble, probably from Carrara, Italy. Dimensions: height 253mm; width at base of neck 152mm. Found in 1954, it was deliberately buried in a shallow pit cut into Floor 5 overlying the dismantled stone colonnades of the temple, just east of column N1. The head of Mithras (IX.38) came from the same area. *MoL Acc No 18491*

IX.40. Head of Serapis, Figures 186–7: cf Toynbee (1986) 13–18; no 3; pl III; pls 8, 9. The head of Serapis has liveliness and movement (Fig 186). Technically, it is a more accomplished carving than those of Mithras (IX.38) and of Minerva (IX.39), but it lacks the dynamism of the head of the former. The flesh surfaces are highly polished. The neck terminates in a roughly surfaced tenon, triangular in shape, like that of Mithras. Cut into its base, just to one side of the centre line, is an unevenly shaped deep slot, about 38mm square, into which there may have been some corresponding projection on the top of the body or bust that once supported the head.

Apart from a heavy abrasion on the nose, the head is intact. The chest is preserved to the waist on the right side but abdomen and legs are missing, as are the left arm and shoulder.

There are many parallels for the presence of water-deities in mithraic contexts. Most notably, Oceanus is depicted in the Dieburg mithraeum (Behn 1928, pl 2 and Vermaseren 1960, 104–6, no 1247, fig 324), from Virinum in Noricum (Vermaseren 1960, 159–161, no 1430, fig 366) and also at Heddernheim (Vermaseren 1960, 64–6, no 1083, fig 274). For large-scale representations of water-deities in Mithraea, it must be compared with the stucco figure in the Santa Prisca temple (Vermaseren 1956, 196, no 478, fig 131 and Vermaseren and van Essen 1965, pl 18, figs 1 and 19) and with a marble statue at Merida in Spain (Paris 1914, 8–9, no 8, fig 6 and Vermaseren 1956, 273, no 778, fig 212). It was likely to have been imported ready-sculptured from Italy. The treatment of the surfaces suggest that this figure was carved in the early to mid-second century AD. This would therefore make it earlier than either Mithras or Serapis, like the Minerva (IX.39), and it must be assumed that both had stood elsewhere before their dedication in the Walbrook temple. Since all the Italian marble pieces are probably imports, it is not necessarily the case that these earlier ones formerly stood elsewhere in London (Blagg pers comm). They could all have been imported from Italy at the same time, even though they are of different dates and workmanship.

The figure is made from fine-grained saccharoidal marble, probably from Carrara, Italy. Dimensions: height 343mm; width 266mm; thickness from back to front 140mm. It was found in 1889 during the building of offices, later destroyed in World War II. Said to have been found during 'sewerage works', near the middle of the Walbrook stream at a depth of 6.1–6.7m. As discussed above it seems most likely that this water-deity, the Genius (IX.45) and the Mithras Tauroctonos of Ulpius Silvanus (IX.46) were found when the concrete block foundation (Fig 55, L) was constructed. This was located next to the shallow pit containing Serapis (IX.40), Mercury (IX.41) and the hand (IX.42). *Mol Acc No A16931*

IX.45. Genius, Figures 194–5: cf Toynbee (1986) 27–9; no 9; pl XI; pl 15. The head of this statuette of a standing half-draped male is missing (Fig 194). The arms, torso and feet are bare. A thick cloak covers the back, hangs in folds over the left arm and diagonally across the hips and then drapes down to the ankles. The cloak must have been drawn as a veil over the now vanished head. Two necklace-like objects that encircle the neck appear to represent either metal torcs or flower garlands. In the left hand, the figure holds a cornucopia, brimming with vine leaves, grapes and other fruits. In his right hand, the figure holds a *patera* over a narrow rectangular altar. A snake rears up from behind the altar and twines itself around the figure's right wrist. To the right of the figure's left foot is the prow of a ship riding over waves.

The statuette was not meant to be viewed from behind, with little rendering of detail (Fig 195). The surfaces of both flesh and drapery are smooth but not polished. The figure depicted is that of a Genius and was perhaps a personification of London, with ship, waves, cornucopia and torcs or garlands alluding to the wealth and activities of a busy sea-port. The front shows a large number of black stains due to iron incrustation. As well as the missing head, the tips of two fingers on the left hand are lost, as is part of the stem of the cornucopia.

The mithraeum at Dieburg has produced two provincial stone reliefs of *Genius loci* (Behn 1928, 31–2, nos 6–7, figs 31–2 and Vermaseren 1960, 107–8, nos 1253 and 1255, figs 328 and 330). A Genius is also depicted on an altar dedicated to Mithras from Poetovio in Pannonia (Vermaseren 1960, 196, no.1591, fig 407). As with the Water-deity (IX.44), the treatment of the surfaces may indicate a mid-second-century date and the statuette must have stood elsewhere before it reached the Walbrook Mithraeum.

The statuette is made from fine-grained saccharoidal marble, probably from Carrara, Italy. Dimensions: height with base 585mm; height without base 528mm; width of base 255mm. It was found in 1889 at the same time and in the same place as the Water-deity (IX.44) and the Mithraic relief (IX.46). *Mol Acc No A16932*

IX.46. Relief of Mithras Tauroctonos, Figures 196–200: cf Toynbee (1986) 29–30; no 10; pl X. The central feature of the rectangular relief is a roundel or medallion in which the famous bull-slaying scene is carved in high relief (Fig 196). On the border of the roundel the 12 signs of the zodiac are worked in low relief, starting with the ram on the spectator's right and proceeding in an anticlockwise fashion. Outside the roundel in the upper left-hand corner is Sol driving his team of four horses to the right. Luna, in the corresponding corner on the right, sends her pair of bulls plunging headlong. In the lower corners are the busts of two wind-gods. The god on the left is old, fierce and bearded and may be Boreas, while the god on the right is young and smiling and may be Zephyrus.

In the roundel, Mithras wears his usual Phrygian cap, short-sleeved tunic, cloak and trousers. He turns his head away and upwards as he grasps the bull's nostrils with his left hand and plunges his knife into its shoulder. The god's cloak flies out behind him, although some of this garment has broken off. Cautes stands on the left of the scene, his left leg crossed over his right and a torch held erect in both hands. Cautes, the symbol of life, light and day, is balanced on the right by Cautopates, the symbol of death, darkness and night. He looks down, crossing his right leg over his left and holding a torch pointing downwards. A snake and dog rear up to drink the blood that gushes from the wound. These represent the life generated and nourished by the act of sacrifice as also does the scorpion which approaches the bull's genitals.

The modelling is crude and somewhat coarse. In the empty spaces an inscription in four separate parts has been squeezed, which may not be contemporary with the sculpture. To the left below Sol, it reads ULPI/US / SILVANUS (Fig 197); on the right below Luna, EMERI/TUS LEG(IONIS)/ II AUG(USTAE)/ VOTUM/ SOLVIT (Fig 198); to the right of Boreas, FAC/TUS (Fig 199), and to the left of Zephyrus, ARAU/SIONE (Fig 200). This is best translated as 'Ulpius Silvanus, veteran of the second Augustan legion, paid his vow: he was initiated at Orange'. The reading *(miles) factus,* 'enlisted', is supported by Alföldy (1966, 639). RIB cites its use by *vigiles* and legionary veterans of their original enrolment, and prefers that reading to 'initiated' (into a mithraic grade), partly because a mithraic grade would probably be specified, and also because *Arausio,* as colony of *legio* II *Augusta,* would have been a likely recruiting ground. However, Birley (1966, 228) points out that the colony was that of Caesar's *legio* II *Gallica,* and would not have had any special relationship with *legio* II *Augusta,* particularly in the third century, the date he attributes to the stone. Birley supports the reading 'initiated'; Harris and Harris (1956, 8) find this interpretation attractive, but knew of no parallel for its use with reference to a mithraic initiation. Vermaseren, however, notes the altar to the *dea* Semele in Cologne (CIL XIII 8244), on which Reginia Paterna describes herself as *mater nata et facta,* mother by birth and continuation (Vermaseren 1974, 30).

For parallels to this scene, compare the Mithras Tauroctonos altar in the Mithraeum under the Church of San Clemente in Rome (Vermaseren 1956,

Fig 194 Period 2, Group IX. Genius (IX.45), front view

Fig 195 Period 2, Group IX. Genius (IX.45), rear view

157, nos 339–40, fig 97), the Neuenheim 'altar-piece' (Cumont 1896, pl 5) and those from Heddernheim (Cumont 1896, pl 7) and Sarrebourg (Vermaseren 1956, 323–5, no 966, fig 236). The style and technique indicate the work is not Italian. It is likely that it was carved in the late second or early third century specifically for this Mithraeum. Henig comments that as the marble would seem to come from Carrara, it was presumably brought from a marble workshop in the Mediterranean region fully carved except, possibly, for the inscription *(Appendix 1)*.

The relief is made from fine-grained saccharoidal marble, probably from Carrara, Italy. Close inspection, during cleaning, revealed possible red paint in the bull's mouth, on the central figures and on some of the zodiac symbols. Dimensions: height 432mm; width 508mm; thickness at top 114mm. It was found in 1889 at the same time and in the same place as the Water-deity (IX.44) and Genius (IX.45). *Mol Acc No A16933*

Inscriptions
Figs 201–2

IX.47. Piece of moulded marble panelling, the back reused for the inscription [....]VGGGG/[.../...]INVIC-TO/[...]AD/[..]ENTEM. A pelta is carved on the right-hand side. Traces of red paint survive in some of the letters. Coarse-grained saccharoidal marble with sutured grains showing complex twinning, from Italy, Greece or Asia Minor.

RIB 4 restores this to *[Pro salute d(ominorum) n(ostrorum) Au]g(ustorum)/[et nob(ilissimi) Caes (aris)/deo Mithrae et Soli] Invicto/[ab] ad/[oriente occid]entem:* 'for the welfare of our August Emperors and most noble Caesar, to the god Mithras and the Invincible Sun from the east to the west'. The phrase *ab oriente, ad occidentem* should be read downwards, and was probably separated by a leaf-stop: a parallel for this comes from the Santa Prisca mithraeum in Rome (Vermaseren and van Essen 1965).

Fig 196 Period 2, Group IX. The Mithras Tauroctonos of Ulpius Silvanus (IX.46)

Fig 197 Period 2, Group IX. The Mithras Tauroctonos of Ulpius Silvanus (IX.46). Detail of inscription on left side

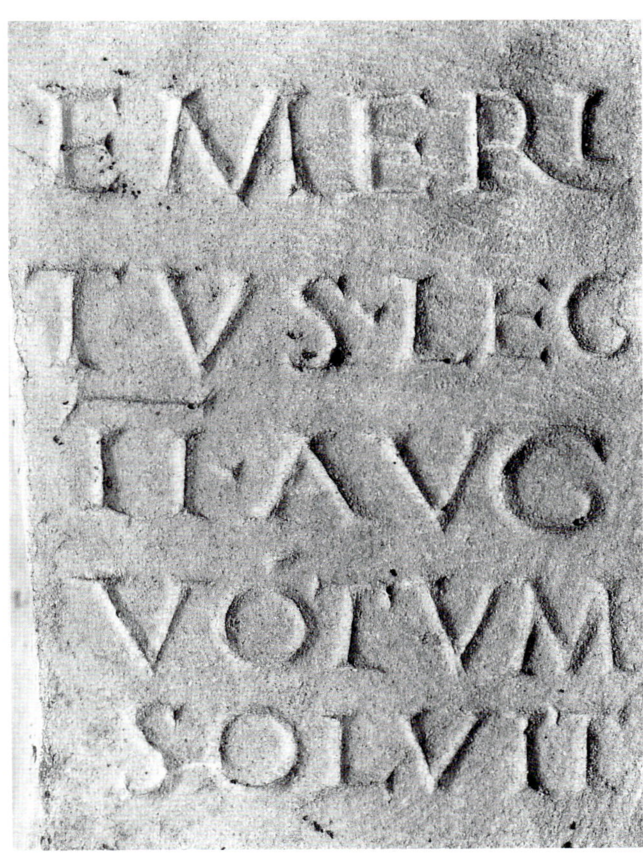

Fig 198 Period 2, Group IX. The Mithras Tauroctonos of Ulpius Silvanus (IX.46). Detail of inscription on right side

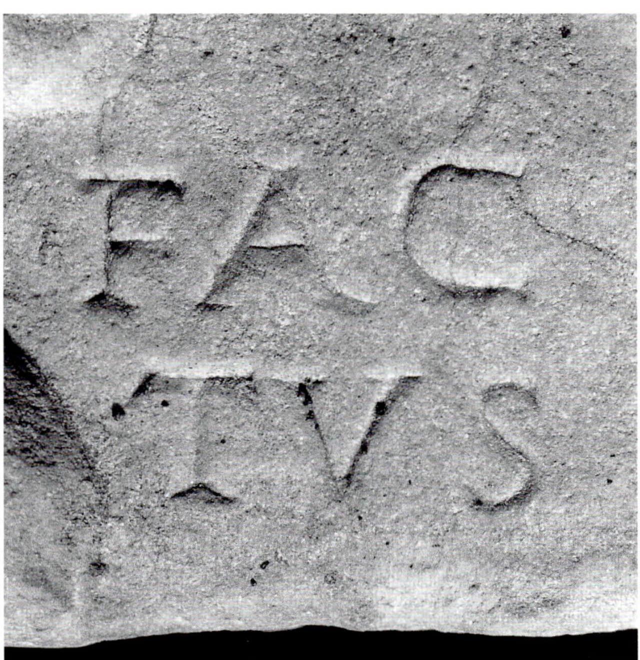

Fig 199 Period 2, Group IX. The Mithras Tauroctonos of Ulpius Silvanus (IX.46). Detail of inscription on lower left side

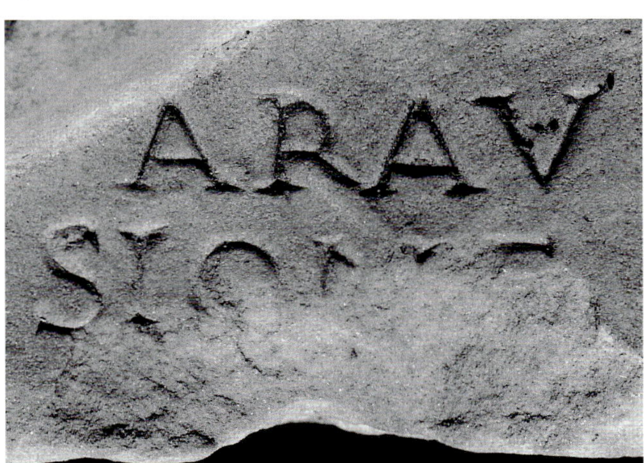

Fig 200 Period 2, Group IX. The Mithras Tauroctonos of Ulpius Silvanus (IX.46). Detail of inscription on lower right side

A drawn reconstruction of the stone (Fig 202) suggests that the RIB reading of line 1 should be slightly amended to *pro sal(ute)* rather than *pro salute* in full; assuming *dominorum* and *nostrorum* to be represented by four letters each to match *Augustorum,* the spacing would preclude having the word in full unless the whole inscription was much wider than the surviving letters indicate. The cramping of the final *o* of *Invicto* argues against a much wider spacing.

RIB dates the inscription between May 307 and May 308, when the four Augusti were Maximianus, Galerius, Constantine and Maxentius, with Maximinus II as Caesar. Found on Floor 6b at the east end of the temple. *MoL Acc No 18499*

Altars

IX.48, Figures 203–4. Limestone column base reused as an altar, original diameter 231mm, height 265mm. The cylindrical shaft has been reduced to a fairly regular quadrilateral section by dressing into four flat faces approximately at right-angles. The base has been correspondingly flattened but part of the original cavetto moulding survives. On the flat underside of the base is a square socket *c* 50 mm across. The area around it is hollowed, diameter *c* 120mm, suggesting a focus for the altar. *MoL Acc No 96.2. From Floor 7 (see Figs 101–2 for this altar* in situ)

IX.49, Figure 205, see also Figures 105–6. Altar with rectangular channel cut into the top. It stood on Floor 5 and was probably one of a pair, the other disappearing with the digging of the Group XI pit. This altar was removed from site in 1954 but it was not accessioned by the Guildhall Museum with other material from the site. It appears in photographs of the site taken on 18 and 19 September sitting on the side of the excavation at the south-west corner of the temple (Figs 180 and 14 respectively. In Figure 14 it can just be seen between the man and the woman on the left of the photograph. A shovel leans against it in Figure 83 — a print taken during the early part of September. It is missing in Figure 7, the overhead view taken at the end of the excavation in October).

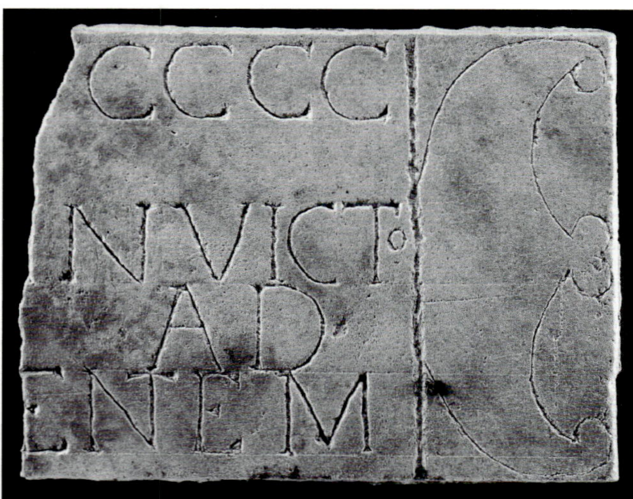

Fig 201 Period 2, Group IX. The Four Augusti inscription (IX.47)

The small objects
Fig 206

Iron

IX.50. Chisel, perhaps a morticing chisel, with plain round shaft and battered head; the shaft is cut back at the end to form a rather blunt chisel. The battering suggests that it was used with a heavy mallet to cut stone, cf Manning 1976, fig 16, no 69. Length 127mm *[CB 346]*

Bone and antler

IX.51. Antler terminal stiffener from a composite bow, as no II.125 where full references are given; broken at each end; Bishop *et al* forthcoming 4C02. Length 250mm. *[CA 242] MoL Acc No 20077. Not illustrated*

Stone: jet

IX.52. Fitting, probably a scabbard mount, and perhaps connected to VII/IX.8. The outer face is ribbed, with flat unpolished ends to fit a corresponding piece; the complete end has a small hole for a pin. 26mm by 38mm. From on the south sleeper-wall at the west end. *[CE 244] MoL Acc No 18267*

Window glass

IX.53. Fragment of cast matt/glossy, natural greenish blue window glass. *[CA 134]. Not illustrated*

Group VIII/IX: late third and fourth century

The finds catalogued and discussed below come from the following layers:

Cutting CA: 255
Cutting CE: 226 (external south-west corner), 236 (external south-west corner), 283 (external south side), 285 (external south side)
Cutting G: 5

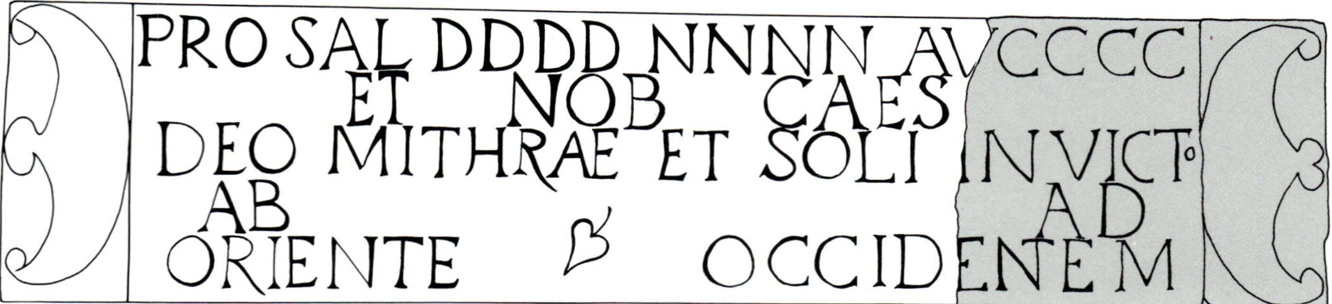

Fig 202 Period 2, Group IX. The Four Augusti inscription (IX.47). A suggested reading

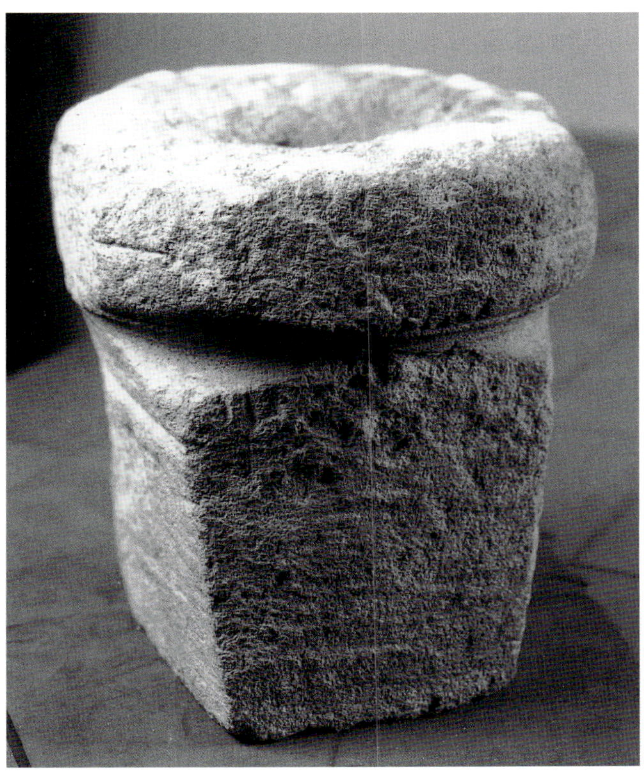

Fig 203 Period 2, Group IX. Column fragment (IX.48)

This group includes finds which come mainly from immediately outside the temple but which cannot, because of documentation ambiguities, be placed in either Group VIII or Group IX. The pottery from these layers layers is broadly late third- or fourth-century. None has been included here.

Three objects of interest came from these contexts immediately outside the temple, two ornamental jet mountings, probably from the same object (VIII/IX.9 and VIII/IX.10), and part of a pair of copper alloy tongs or shears (VIII/IX.3). Direct association with the Mithraeum is possible but not proven. The jet in particular is likely to be of a suitable date. A fragment of a pipeclay Venus figurine from a similar context is likely to be residual (VIII/IX.6). A catapult bolt apparently found within the temple (VIII/IX.3) is probably of earlier date and residual.

The small objects
Fig 207

Copper alloy

VIII/IX.1 Blade from a pair of tongs or shears. The wide tapering blade is set at right-angles to the handle which now has a double loop at its broken upper end,

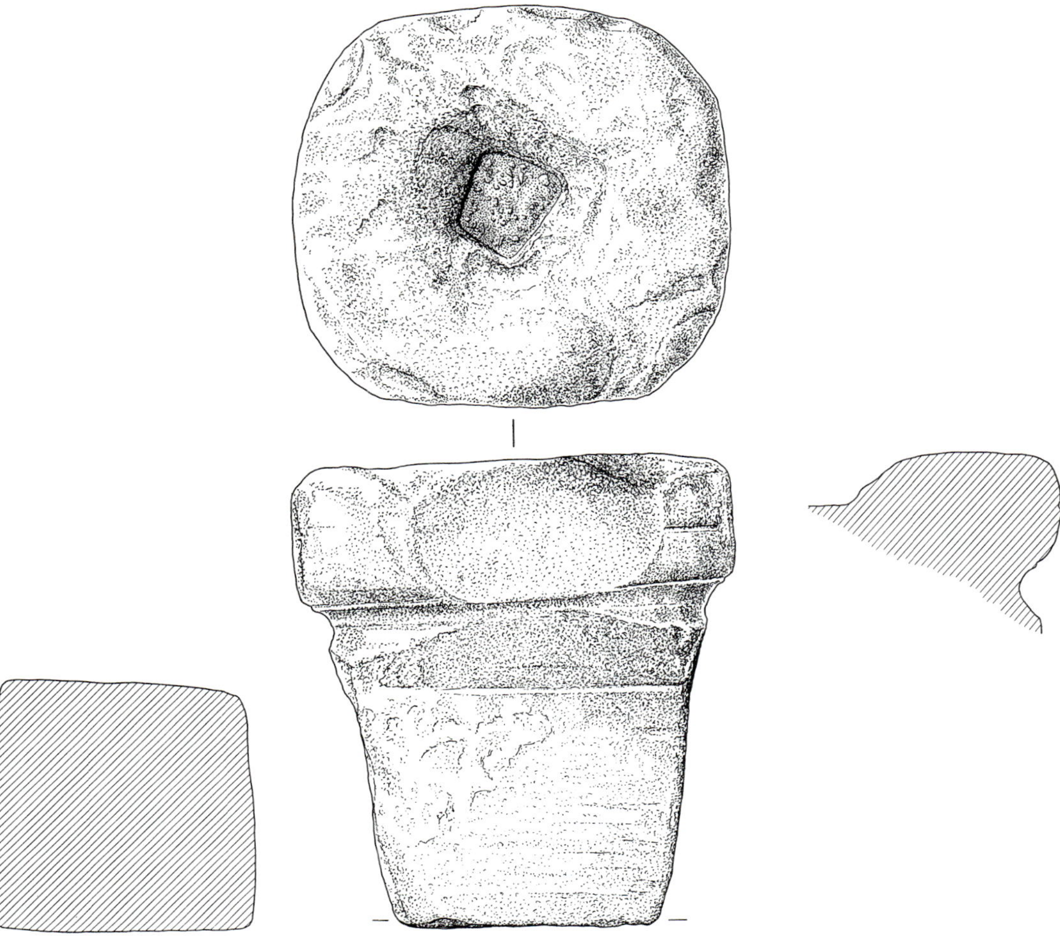

Fig 204 Period 2, Group IX. A drawing of the column fragment (IX.48) (scale 1:4)

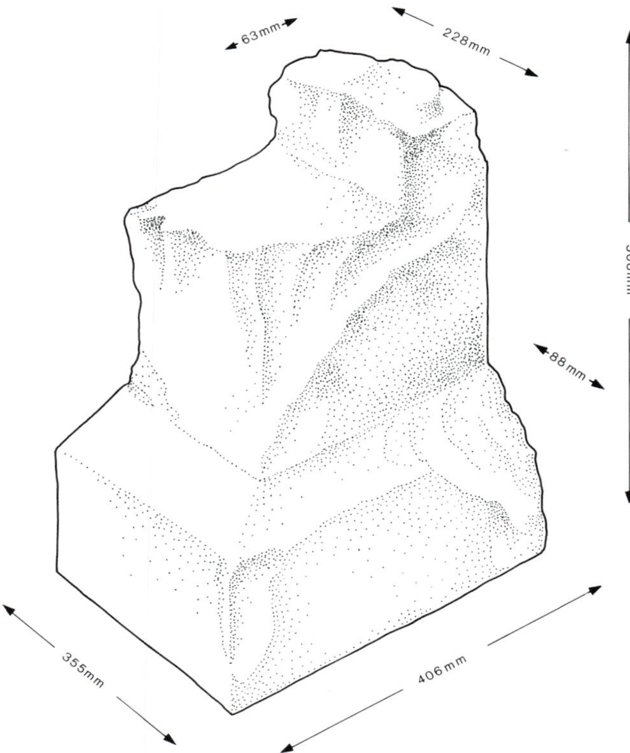

Fig 205 Period 2, Group IX. A drawing of the channelled altar

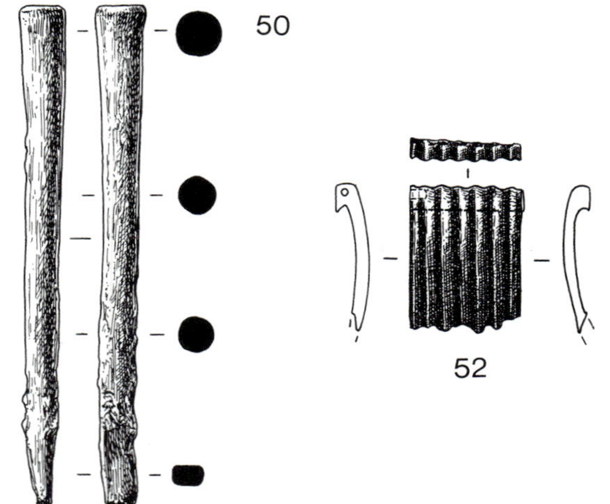

Fig 206 Period 2, Group IX small objects (scale 1:2)

presumably originally forming a spring. The upper edge of the blade is decoratively cut. Length 119mm. From poorly recorded deposits against the external face of the north wall of the Mithraeum. *MoL Acc No 19869*

VIII/IX.2. Candlestick formed from two small bowls with omphaloid bases, held by a rivet through the centre. The cylindrical sconce has a flange for attachment. Maximum diameter 57mm, height 44mm. From poorly recorded deposits against the external south face of the Mithraeum. *[CE 283] MoL Acc No 18261*

Iron

VIII/IX.3. Catapult bolt, square-sectioned and socketed. Similar bolts are common on military sites, eg Richmond 1968, fig 58, A1 a–c, and e; Curle 1911, pl xxxvii 11 and 20; other examples are illustrated in Bishop and Coulston 1993, 80, fig 44 3a-f; also Manning 1985, 170–1, Type 1, pls 62, 63. Length 101mm. *[CE 251] MoL Acc No 18266*

VIII/IX.4. Fragment of joiner's dog or staple, as no 37. Length 67mm. From poorly recorded deposits against the external south face of the Mithraeum. *[CE 283] Not illustrated*

VIII/IX.5 Ring, rounded in section. Diameter 28mm, thickness 5mm. *[CE 251] MoL Acc No 18264 Not illustrated*

Ceramic

VIII/IX.6. Fragment of mould-made pipeclay figurine, probably of Venus (cf LRT, pl xxi, 1–4), in fine micaceous cream fabric. These figurines were imported from the Allier region of Gaul from the first to the early third centuries AD (Jenkins 1974). Found in poorly recorded deposits over the external timber drain at the south-west corner of the Mithraeum. *[CE226] MoL Acc No 18237. Not illustrated*

Stone: jet

VIII/IX.7. Shouldered plaque, probably an ornamental mounting for an item such as a box or frame. The edges and front are highly polished, with a series of incised triangles containing incised vertical lines, along the bottom. The reverse is rough, with traces of adhesive, and is partly bevelled along the bottom. For similar plaques, cf Hagen 1937, Taf 41; Taf 42: Taf 22, B18 shows similar decoration on a jet bracelet. 46mm by 64mm. Found in poorly recorded deposits over the external timber drain at the south-west corner of the Mithraeum. *[CE 236] MoL Acc No 18238*

VIII/IX.8. Strip, possibly a mounting from the same object as IX.52. The front face has decorative notches along the bottom and halfway along the top; there are two grooves along half the upper edge, one along the lower edge, one halfway along the back, and one in the wider end which connects with a hole for an attachment pin. The surfaces are highly polished, with the exception of the back below and beyond the groove, and the upper edge beyond the groove, which has traces of adhesive. The two shaped ends are damaged. Length 202mm. Found in poorly recorded deposits over the external timber drain at the south-west corner of the Mithraeum. *[CE 236] MoL Acc No 18239*

VIII/IX.9. Fragment of a ring, perhaps a binding. The outer surface is curved, the inner flat with a slight offset; the narrower part is less well finished, suggesting that it was concealed. From within the Mithraeum but context no longer locatable. *[CE 319] MoL Acc No 18296*

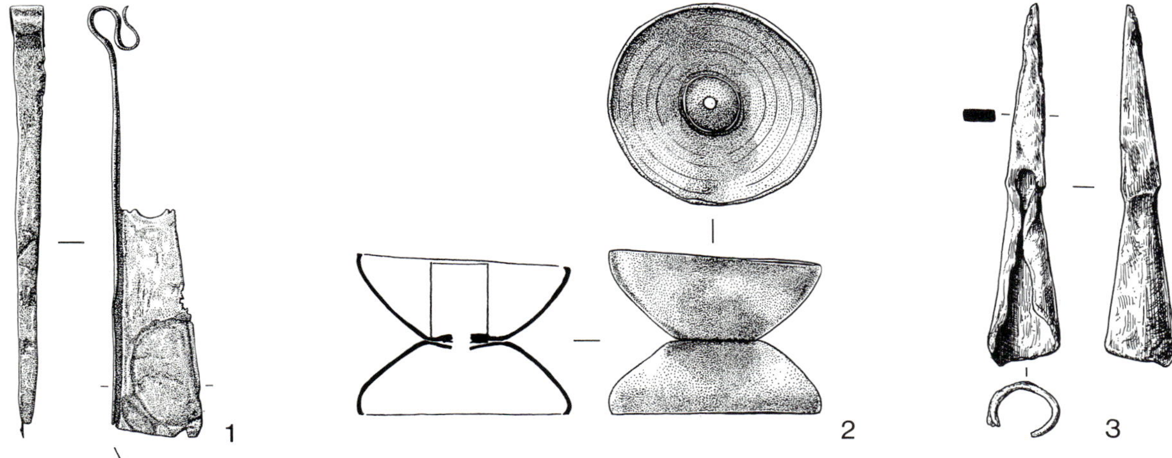

Glass

VIII/IX.10. Fragment of cast matt/glossy, natural greenish blue window glass. *[CE 285] Not illustrated*
VIII/IX.11. Fragment from the edge of a cylinder-blown double glossy window pane. Natural green glass. *[CE 266] Not illustrated*

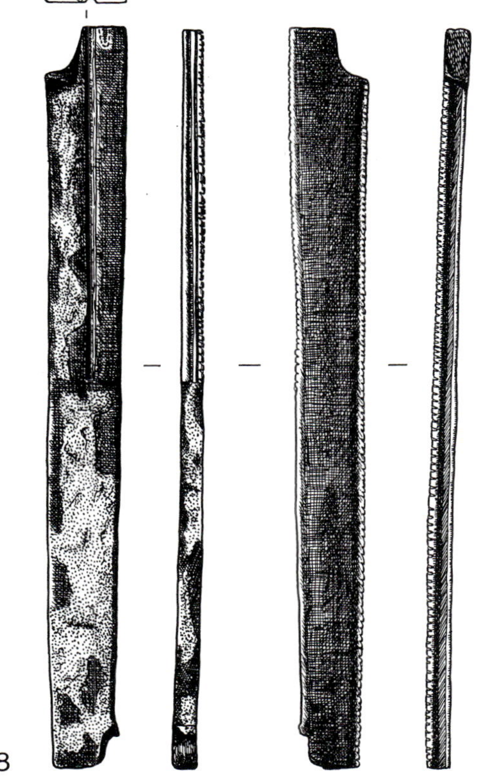

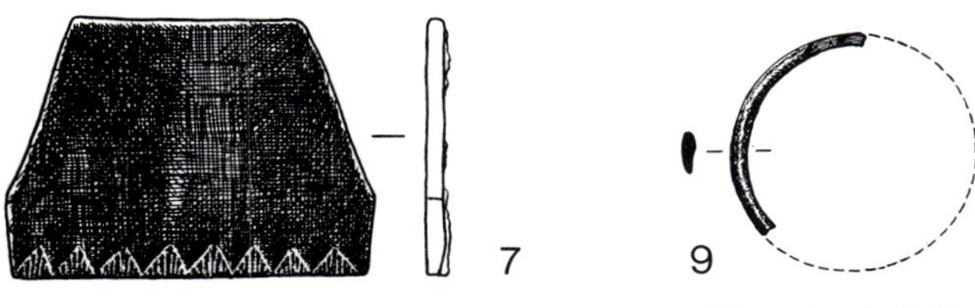

Fig 207 Period 2, Group VIII or IX small objects (scale 1:2)

Group VIII/IX/X: second half of third and fourth centuries

This group includes finds which come from layers directly associated with the temple but which cannot, because of documentation ambiguities, be placed in either Groups VIII, IX or Group X.

The vessels

Silver

VIII/IX/X.1. Figures 208–10. Casket and strainer. For full discussion see Toynbee (1986, 42–52), from which this brief description is taken. The hinged lid of the circular casket is covered with figure ornament, cast in relief and chased, with traces of gilding. The designs, of men and animals, with some landscape detail, fall into seven groups (ibid, 42). The side wall is similarly decorated with figures of men and animals set

Fig 208 Period 2, Group VIII, IX or X. The silver casket and strainer (VIII/IX/X.1)

Fig 209 Period 2, Group VIII/IX or X. The silver casket (VIII/IX/X.1) (scale 4:5)

in a landscape of trees and rocks, the frieze-like design arranged in four main scenes. The groups are all hunting scenes set in exotic landscapes, of animals hunted by men and animals hunting other beasts. The general style and workmanship indicate that the piece dates from the late third or early fourth century, perhaps made by a craftsman who worked in or came from the eastern Mediterranean (ibid, 51–2).

Technological examination of the base of the casket revealed evidence for repairs and the former existence of three feet. The base also has a scratched graffito, reading ISI VI, probably a personal name (ibid, 49).

Inside the casket was a strainer or filter, also made of silver, its base perforated with a series of small holes forming a decorative geometric pattern (Fig 210) with

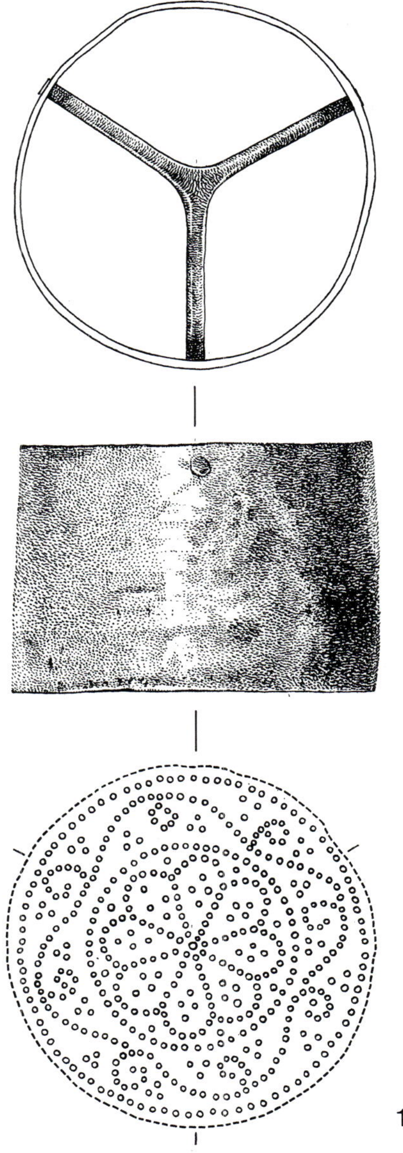

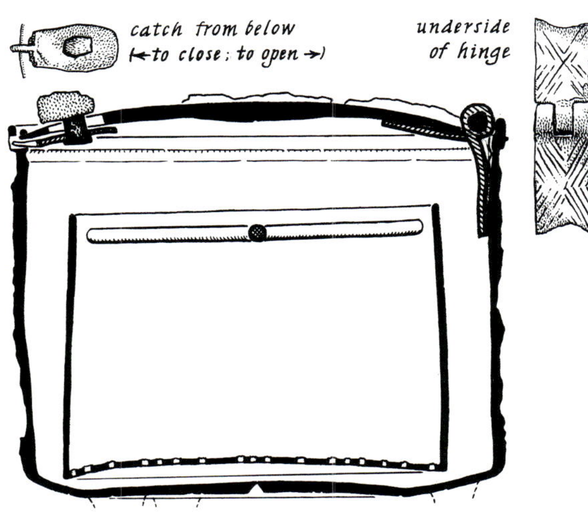

Fig 210 Period 2, Group VIII, IX or X. The silver strainer and a cross-section of the casket and strainer (VIII/IX/X.1) (scale 4:5)

an eight-petalled rosette at its centre. At the top of the strainer are three horizontal arms, secured by rivets, which presumably served as a handle.

The real significance of this object is the subject of debate. The late Ralph Merrifield believed it to be Mithraic, for the infusion of liquids used in the ceremonies, but Henig believes that a Bacchic association is equally possible. Their comments, including the last paper to be written by Dr Merrifield shortly before his death in 1995, are published below as *Appendixes 1 and 2.*

Dimensions: casket, height 63mm, diameter 79mm; lid diameter 77mm; strainer height 45mm, diameter 64–70mm, length of each arm 32mm. Unstratified, in the top of the north wall, and possibly originally hidden within the wall. *MoL Acc No 21579*

VIII/IX/X.2. Figure 211. Bowl. Fragments of a small hemispherical bowl in thin sheet silver, previously published by Bird (1986b, 52–4), where full discussion and references are given. The punched design which covered the exterior consists of a row of circles, outlined in dots and probably indented or faceted, alternating with foliage motifs, flanked by bands of geometric decoration. There are indications of a second row of circles below. Other examples, found in Britain and on the continent (ibid, 53) suggest that it was of Gaulish manufacture, and is of third-century date. Diameter of rim *c* 120mm. Found with the canister (VIII/IX/X.1). *MoL Acc No 21552*

Stone

VIII/IX/X.3. Figure 212. Large laver; half remaining, broken in antiquity. The underside is flat, the wall convex externally, with a moulded flat-topped rim, which is damaged. Inside, a flattened conical boss projects from the base, its sides carrying six concentric grooves. Its top has a central depression, probably a lathe-mark. Pisolithic limestone with Girvanella, Jurassic type, probably from the Gloucestershire region. Overall diameter of laver 596mm, height 152mm. *MoL Acc No 18503*

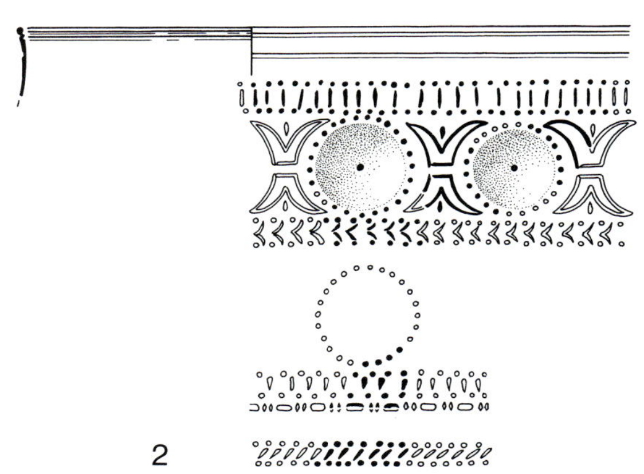

Fig 211 Period 2, Group VIII, IX or X. Silver bowl (VIII/IX/X.2) (scale 1:2)

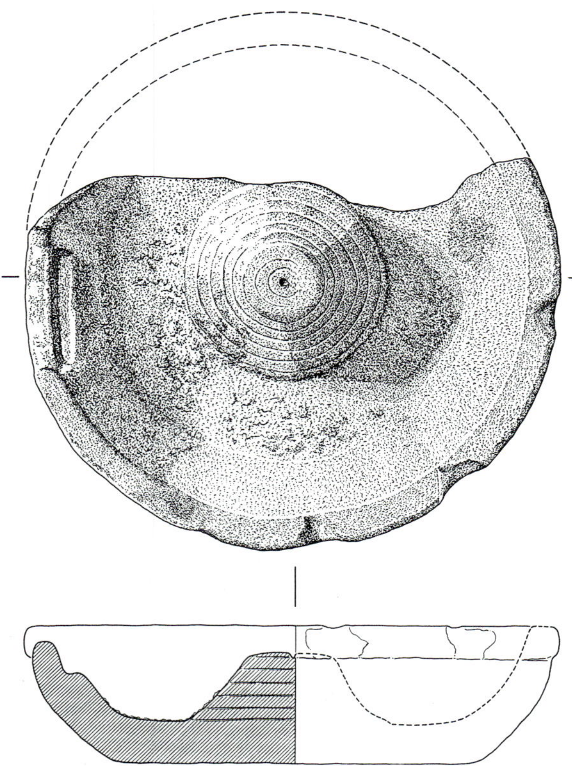

Fig 212 Period 2, Group VIII, IX or X. Large laver or stoup (VIII/IX/X.3) (scale 1:8)

Fig 213 Period 2, Group VIII, IX or X. Relief of Cautopates (VIII/IX/X.4)

Sculpture and worked stone

VIII/IX/X.4. Figure 213. Relief of Cautopates: cf Toynbee (1986) 32–4; no 12; pl 18. The relief shows the lower half, from just below the waist downwards, of the figure of Cautopates, carved in high relief in a deep curved niche hollowed out of the thickness of the stone. Below the floor of the niche is a low rectangular plinth. The monument was either hacked carelessly into two or it broke apart as a result of being hurled to the ground violently. Cautopates faces the spectator with his right leg crossed over his left leg. He holds a great lighted torch pointing downwards diagonally across his body. He wears a knee-length tunic, trousers, boots and a cloak. He would have worn a Phrygian cap and his head would have been bent downwards as he gazed at the ground. He represents the painful aspect of the sacrificial scene.

The piece is in a severely damaged state, since it is battered as well as broken. It might be expected that the temple once possessed the balancing figure of Cautes, also standing in his niche with an upward gaze and his torch held erect. Both figures would have been painted.

Similar figures have been found in the mithraeum at Carrawburgh on Hadrian's Wall (Richmond *et al* 1951, 14 and 32, figs 3–5 and 7) and in the Santa Prisca Mithraeum, Rome *(Commissione Archeologica Communale di Roma* 1940, 63 and 65–6, figs 3–5). It dates to the late second or early third century. As the stone is British, it is also most likely that the relief was sculptured in the workshop of a British or Gaulish carver. It was most probably carved specifically for the Walbrook Mithraeum.

The relief is made of pisolithic limestone of Jurassic type, probably from the Cotswold area. Dimensions: height 915mm; width across base 584mm; depth 265mm. It was found in 1954 just outside the south wall of the temple towards the eastern end (Cutting E). Found with the altar 2.68. *MoL Acc No 20006*

VIII/IX/X.5. Figure 214. Relief of a Dioscurus: cf Toynbee (1986) 34–6; no 13; pl 19. A fragmentary sculpture which shows one of the Dioscuri and his horse carved in relief. The figure stands on a heavy ledge in front of his horse. He is naked, save for a cloak which is fastened on his right shoulder. He wears the characteristic pointed cap *(pilleus)*, from under which appear the thick curls of hair that frame the face. In his right hand the Dioscurus grasps the shaft of his spear, the head of which is missing. His missing left hand must have held the bridle of his horse. The rump and hind-quarters are all that remain of the horse.

The back of the slab is roughly hewn and was not intended to be viewed. The upper portion of the slab is missing and with it the Dioscurus' right hand. On the right the background is broken away around his head

Fig 214 Period 2, Group VIII, IX or X. Relief of a Dioscurus (VIII/IX/X.5)

and left shoulder, losing the figure's left arm and leg and the head and fore-parts of the horse. It is also possible that this Dioscurus was accompanied by his brother in the missing portion.

The nearest parallel to the Walbrook Dioscurus is the relief found on the site of a Mithraeum at Vienne (Reinach 1912, 308, fig 2). The clumsy styling suggests a third-century date. The local stone indicates that the piece was carved in Britain by a native or north-west provincial craftsman.

Henig comments in Appendix 1 that there must have been other temples in the vicinity and that most mithraea seem to be sited in temple quarters. This being the case, it is possible that this sculpture came from a temple of the Castores. For comparison see Belot (1990) where a sculpture of two nude youths from Boulogne, although different from our example, presents this possibility.

The sculpture is made from oolitic limestone of Jurassic type, probably from the Cotswolds. Dimensions: height 555mm; greatest remaining width 355mm; overall thickness 114–29mm. It was found in May 1955, six months after the official investigations on site had ended, on the east bank of the Walbrook about 20m south of the temple and therefore not directly associated with the temple. It was found at a level over 3m above the primary deposits of the Walbrook stream. *MoL Acc No 20736*

Fig 215 Period 2, Group VIII, IX or X. Altar (VIII/IX/X.6) found with Cautopates relief

Altar

VIII/IX/X.6. Figure 215. Altar. Shelly, uneven-grained oolitic limestone, probably from Gloucestershire. Cutting E. Found with the Cautopates relief (VIII/IX/X.4). *MoL Acc No 18848*

Architectural fragment

VIII/IX/X.7. Column drum. Shelly, uneven-grained oolitic Jurassic limestone. Probably Cotswolds region. Height 0.86m. Diameter 0.28m. A 'tide-mark' of plaster and red paint, similar to that which can be seen on the column X.64, is modern, resulting from the display of the fragments in the Guildhall Museum

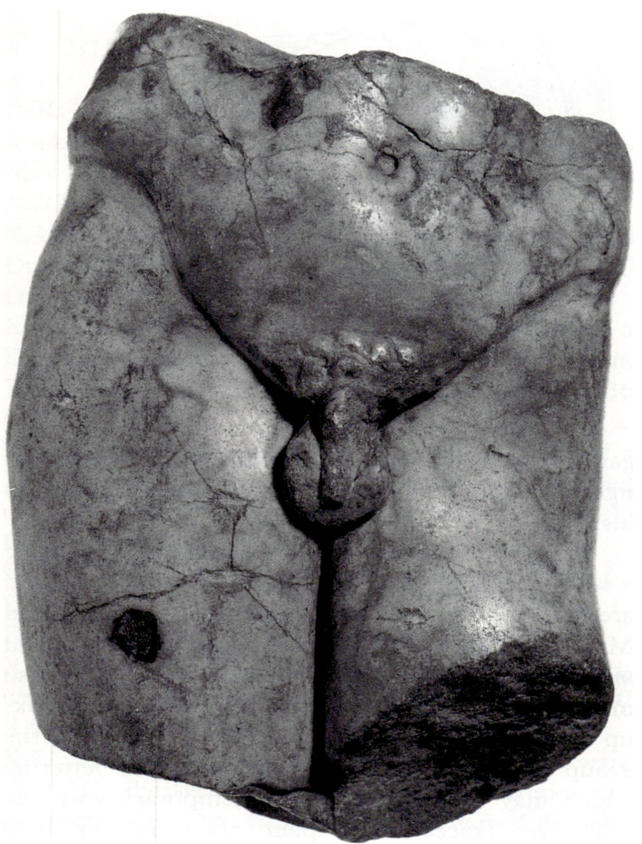

Fig 220 Period 2, Group X. Bacchus torso (X.58)

Fig 221 Period 2, Group X. Bacchic group (X.59) Front view

Fig 222 Period 2, Group X. Bacchic group (X.59) Rear view

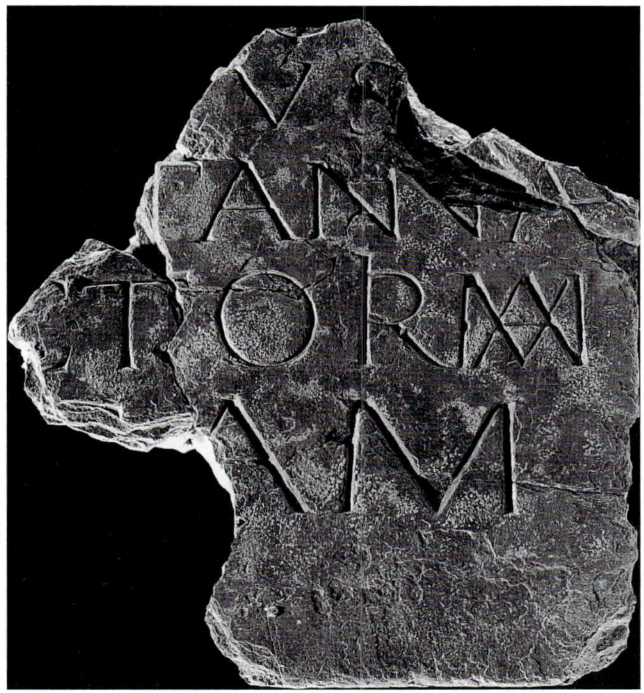

Fig 223 Period 2, Group X. Inscription X.60

Fig 224 Period 2, Group X. Inscription X.61

The sculpture is made from fine-grained saccharoidal marble, probably from Carrara, Italy. Dimensions: height 343mm; width at base 293mm; thickness at greatest extent 63mm. It was found in 1954 in the north aisle of the temple, close to the north wall just to the west of the wooden box-like structure and on the level of the latest floor. *MoL Acc No 18496*

Additional comment on the inscription of X.59
by M Hassall

It is noted in RIB 1 that the inscription may be a later addition to the sculpture, and certainly the lettering is much rougher than the workmanship of the rest. The substitution of B for V occurs on many inscriptions of the later centuries. Mann (1971, 221) cites this as his sole example of the substitution from Britain, and assumes that the inscription was added in Britain.

Inscriptions

X.60. Figure 223. Part of a slate panel inscribed ...]C[.../ ...]CVS[.../ ...]TANNAE/ [...]CTORIAM/ [...]CAM.

RIB 8 restores this to ... *le]g[atus Augusti iuridi]cvs [pro/vinciae Bri]tann[i]ae/ [ob vi]ctoriam/[Daci]cam*: 'imperial juridical legate of the province of Britain on account of the Dacian victory', a commemoration of Trajan's victory of AD 102 or 106.

Alföldy (1966, 639), considers that the ligatures, although they do occur earlier, imply a later, in this case Severan, date, with *Dacicam* replaced by *Parthicam* or *Germanicam.* He suggests that a more likely restoration would be on the lines of *.../c/.../.../cus/ leg(atus) /Aug(usti) pr(o) pr(aetore) Bri/tann/ia/ae//fecit ob vi/ctoriam//Parthi/cam,* or *Germani/cam.* Cagnat (1914, 206) includes *Arabicus, Adiabenicus* and *Britannicus* among Severus' titles, and these would be other alternatives for the last word. Wilkes (1981, 416) also considers that the lettering and ligatures make a Trajanic date doubtful. *[CE 217] MoL Acc No 18219. From the rubble overlying the south sleeper-wall*

X.61. Figure 224. Fragment of micaceous schistose marble slab. Identified as Cipollino from Carystos, Euboea. Inscribed ...]COS[.../ ...]OS ITEM[.../ ...]CVM[...

RIB 24 states that this is 'difficult to interpret as part of an official career' or as part of an inscription recording more than one imperial position, and suggests that it might be part of a list of accusatives, such as a temple inventory (cf CIL viii, 6981 and 6982, from Cirta, and CIL xiv, 2215 from Nemi).

Mark Hassall (pers comm), however, considers that the inscription might be part of a military career inscribed on a tombstone, as CIL xii, 2602, from Genève. There, the same formula, *co(n)sule item*, is used in a list of positions (ending as centurion of an urban cohort) held by M Carantius Macrinus. Found in the debris outside the south side of the temple. *MoL Acc No 19498*

X.62. Figure 225. Fragment from an altar of arenaceous glauconitic chert (silicified sandy limestone) of Lower Greensand type. Inscribed ...]BENT[... in rough lettering on the face. The block had apparently been cut down and reused as a base for a base for an altar or cult statue in the temple; RIB 34 gives

Fig 225 Period 2, Group X. Inscription X.62, taken from RIB 661

Fig 226 Period 2, Group X. Altar (X.63)

...li]bent[es..., '...freely...'. as an 'obvious but not exclusive' reading. The word *libentes* given in full is unusual, but it is not unknown in Britain: cf RIB 661, from York, and RIB 1594 from Housesteads. Found face down in the apse recess. *MoL Acc No 20009*

Altar

X.63. Figure 226. Altar. Shelly, uneven-grained oolitic limestone.From destruction debris over final floor. *M0L Acc No 18189*

Architectural fragment

X.64 Figure 227. Column and capital fragment. Pisolithic Jurassic limestone, probably from the Cotswold region. The tide-mark near the top of plaster and red paint, similar to that on the column drum VIII/IX/X.7, is modern, resulting from the display of the fragments in the Guildhall Museum display at the Royal Exchange between 1955–67. From the destruction debris over the final floor. Williams and Grimes believed that this column stood with another on the plinth on top of the dais on either side of the main Tauroctonos sculpture. However, its position among the building debris probably suggests that it comes from the final phase building. It is possible that it belongs to the canopy which may have been located in front of the apse, utilising the two pedestal altars and the plinth as bases. Height 0.76m. *MoL Acc No 20007*

The small objects
Fig 228

Iron

X.65. Handle, square in section, the end bent into a ring. Length 133mm *[CA 320] MoL Acc No 18349*
X.66. Hook (?); the tip and most of the suspension plate are lost. Length 56mm *[CD 152]*

Leather

X.67. Fragment of leather. The surface is gilded, apart from a band 6mm wide along the surviving edge. The decorated band, 8mm wide, is defined by pairs of incised lines and has double concentric circles stamped in an overlapping design. This is probably the piece which Waterer (1976, 192) suggested may have been part of a curtain. See also the fragment from a pre-temple layer (VII.52). *[CB 295] MoL Acc No 18448*

Group XI: late fourth century

The finds catalogued and discussed below come from the following layers:

Cutting CA: 232, 239, 241, 273, 274, 280, 289

A pit was cut during the late Roman period into the surface of Floor 9 in the vicinity of the apse. It is probable that a 'stirrup' altar, similar to that found standing on Floor 5 but covered up to the top by

Fig 227 Period 2, Group X. Column and capital fragment (X.64)

subsequent floors, was removed by this pit. It is not known if this pit cut or was sealed by any demolition or destruction debris.

The pottery is consistent with a late fourth-century date. Only an iron needle came from this feature (XI.7).

Group XI finds

The vessels

Pottery
Table 24

A very small group which on stratigraphic grounds must postdate *c* AD 350.

Catalogue of illustrated pottery vessels

For code expansions see above, *Pottery codes and expansions*
Fig 229

XI.1. Alice Holt/Farnham ware plain-rimmed dish (AHFA IVJ). *[CA232]*
XI.2. Alice Holt/Farnham ware flanged bowl (AHFA FB). *[CA239]*
XI.3. Alice Holt/Farnham ware uncertain form (AHFA ?form). *[CA232]*
XI.4. Black-burnished style ware flanged bowl (BBS FB). *[CA273]*

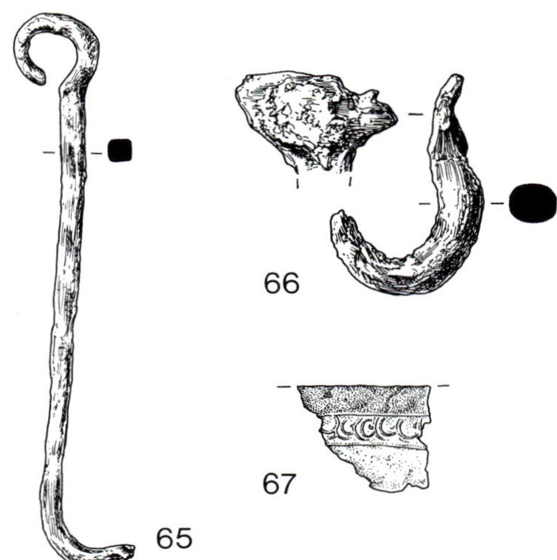

Fig 228 Period 2, Group X small objects

XI.5. Reduced sandy ware Camulodunum type 306 bowl (SAND C306). *[CA273]*
XI.6. Nene Valley colour-coated ware everted-rim beaker with white-painted decoration (NVCC III ER WPD), cf Howe *et al* 1981, type 54. *[CA273] and [CA325]*

Argonne ware

XI.7. Form Chenet 320; the roller stamp with eight decorative facets, is Chenet type 132. Chenet 1941, pl iii, 19 shows an identical bowl at the top of the kiln-stack. Hübener (1968) includes this stamp in a subsidiary section of his group 7, and dates it *c* AD ?390–?425. *[232] and [274]*

The small objects

Iron

XI.8. Needle. Plain round shaft, broken at each end, with a tapering groove below the eye. Surviving length 68mm. *[CA241]*

Table 24 Group XI pottery excluding samian

Fabric	*Forms*	*No of vessels (approx)*
AHFA	IVJ; FB; ?	3
BB1	IVJ(2)	2
BBS	FB	1
MOSL	III WPD motto; ?IV/VI	2
NVCC	IC; III BR WPD; III ER WPD	3
NVCC?	III WPD	1
SAND	C306	1
Total		13

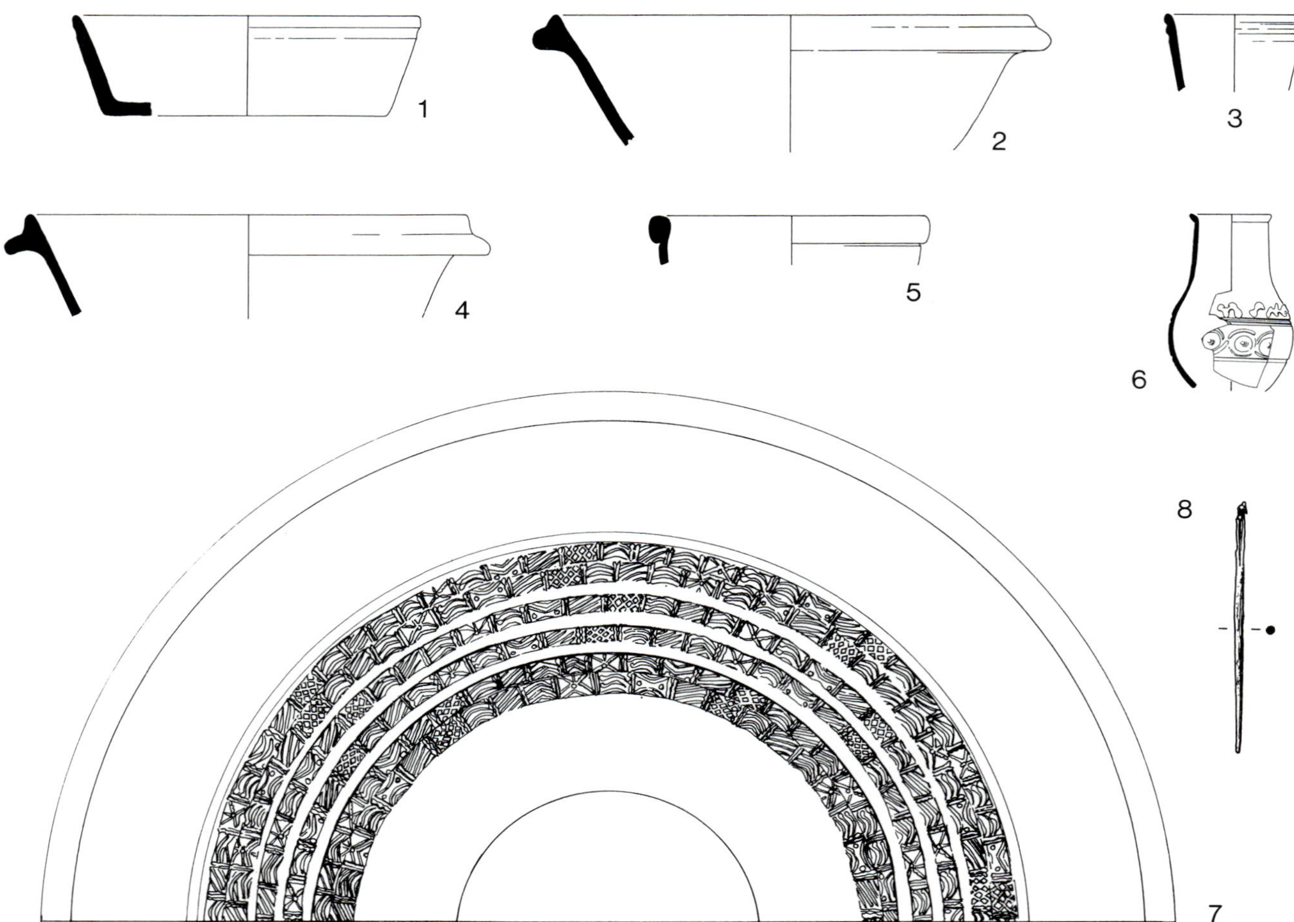

Fig 229 Period 2, Group XI pottery vessels and iron needle (nos 1-7 scale 1:4; no 8 scale 1:2)

Group XIII: mid- to late fourth century

The finds catalogued and discussed below come from the following layers:

Cutting AA: 500, 501, 516, 517
Cutting AB: 515
Cutting BB: 314, 325
Cutting F: 712, 713, 714, 715, 716, 718, 719, 721, 725, 736, 738, 746, 757, 758

The majority of the layers in this group come from the sequence of timber platforms in Cutting F associated with the unrevetted Walbrook stream bank. There were indications of small hut-like buildings set back from the stream edge.

The pottery belongs to the fourth century, especially the mid- to late fourth century.

The assemblage of small finds includes a bone hinge (XIII.22) together with residual window glass (XIII.26), a stylus (XIII.19) and a dagger blade (XIII.20). The last is of unusual type, and appears to be unsharpened. There has been some speculation that it may have formed part of a sculpture, perhaps held in the hand of Mithras, or that it served as a votive offering, but its findspot, at some distance from the Mithraeum and within another structure, would seem to preclude this.

The vessels

Pottery
Tables 25 and 26

Portchester 'D' ware places this small assemblage into the mid to late fourth century. The other fourth-century indicators are Late Roman calcite-gritted ware and Nene Valley colour-coated ware bowls. The quantity of samian (49%) and Verulamium region white ware (10%) shows there is a high degree of residuality.

Catalogue of illustrated pottery vessels

For code expansions see above, *Pottery codes and expansions*
Fig 230

XIII.1. Alice Holt/Farnham flanged bowl (AHFA FB). *[F716]*
XIII.2. BB1 everted-rim jar (ERJ). *[AB515] Not illustrated*
XIII.3. BB1 plain-rimmed dish with burnished decoration on interior and exterior (IVJ BUD). *[AB515]*
XIII.4. Late Roman calcite-gritted ware necked jar (CALC NJ). *[F736]*
XIII.5. Portchester 'D' ware bowl type P109 (PORD IV P109). *[F714]*

Table 25 Group XIII pottery excluding samian

Fabric	*Forms*	*No of vessels (approx)*
AHFA	IVJ; FB(3); SJ	5
AHSU	NJ	1
BB1	IIF(2); ERJ; IVJ; IVJ BUD(4); G226 BUD	9
BB2	IVH1(4); IVH	5
BB2?	IVH5?	1
BB2F	IVH5(5)	5
CALC	NJ	1
CC	III	1
OLC?		1
COMO	WAL	1
CGBL	FOB	1
HWC	IVF	1
KOLN	III; III BFD	2
MICA	IV	1
MOSL		1
NFSE	MORT HOF	1
OXID	I; III	2
OXID?	MORT BEF	1
OXID/SAND	II	1
OXMO	M17; M22	2
OXRC	IV CDR37; IV CDR38 C51(2); IV; MORT	5
NVCC	III CR; III BAD(2); III BFD; III ROD; III WPD; FOB SCD; FOB; IV; IV?	10
NVCC?	FOB	1
PORD	IV P109	1
SAND	C306	1
VRW	IB5; IIG(2); IVA; MORT HOF; MORT HOF?; TZ	7
VRW?	MORT HOF	1
Total		68

Table 26 Group XIII Samian

Source/ Fabric	*Forms*
SG	DR18(2); DR18R; DR27; DR29; DR37(2); RT12
MV	DR37
CG	CU21; DR27?; DR31(6); DR18/31; DR18/31 or 31(3); DR31 or 31R; DR33(12); DR36(2); CU11 or DR36; DR37(5); DR38; DR45; WA79
CG?	DR37
EG	DR18/31; DR31(2); DR33(3); DR37(5); DR38(6); LD; SMb
CG/EG	DR36
Total no of vessels (approx)	65

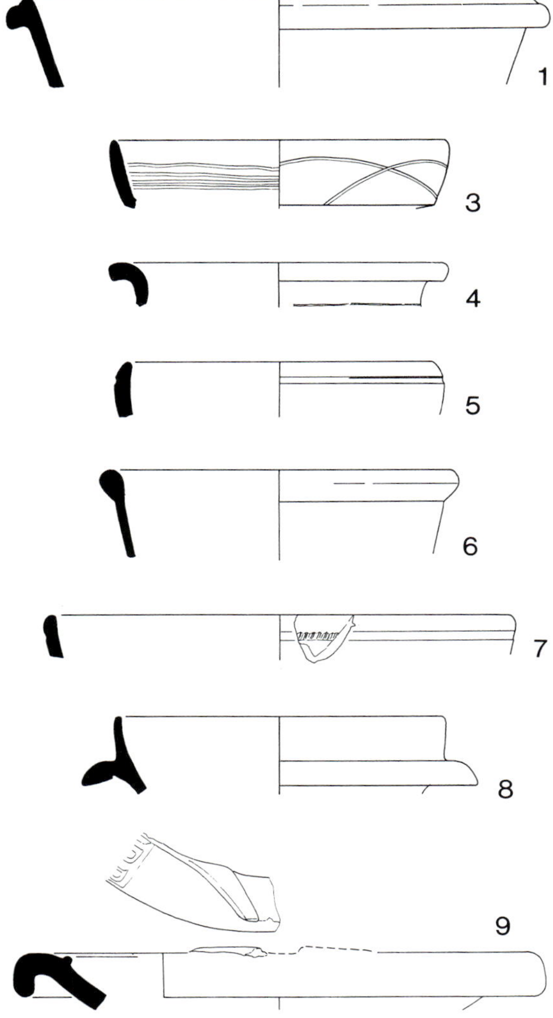

Fig 230 Period 2, Group XIII pottery vessels, excluding samian (scale 1:4)

XIII.6. Reduced sandy ware Camulodunum type 306 bowl (SAND C306). *[F736]*
XIII.7. Oxfordshire red colour-coated ware copy of a Dragendorff Form 37 (OXRC IV C Dragendorff Form 37). *[F718]*
XIII.8. Oxfordshire red colour-coated ware copy of a Dragendorff Form 38, Young type C51 (OXRC IV C Dragendorff Form 38 C51). *[F718]*

XIII.9. Verulamium region white ware hooked flange mortarium (KH)

The stamp, on the left of the spout, is an incomplete impression of Die A, reading P.PR.B( ) *in ansis;* there are three other examples noted, all from London.

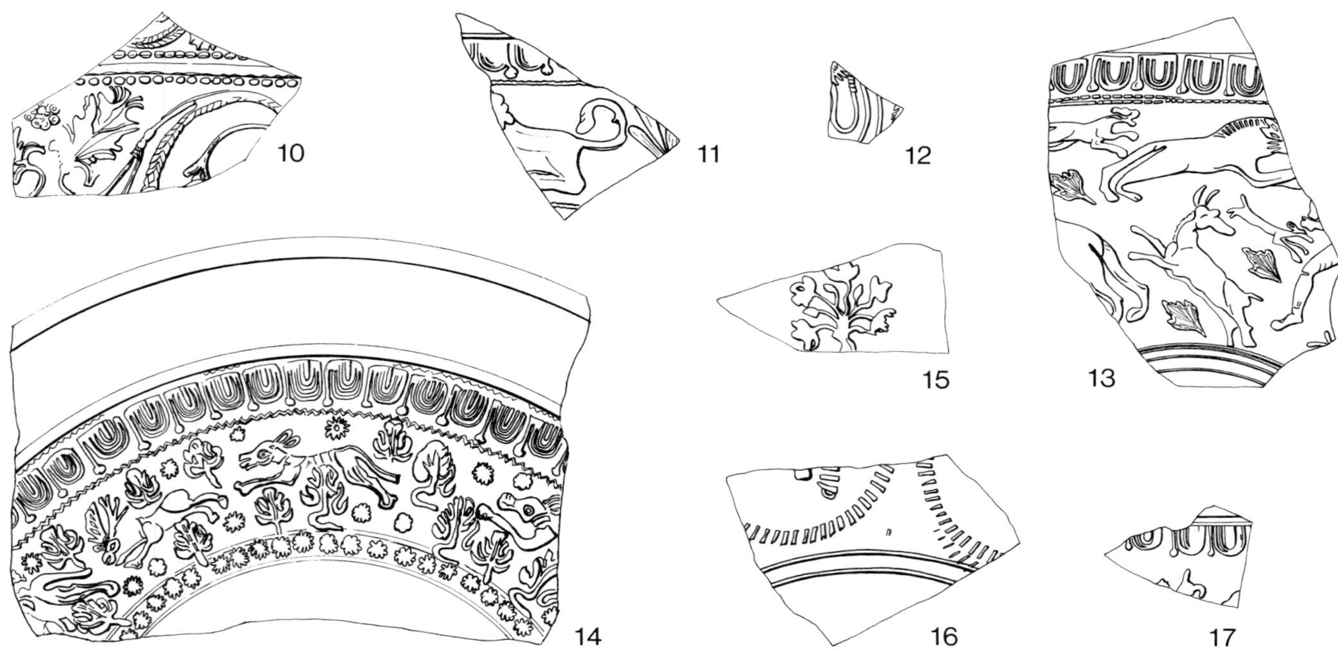

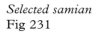

Fig 231 Period 2, Group XIII samian vessels (scale 1:2)

Die B, P.P.BR( ) is known from one mortarium, also in London, and is almost certainly the die used for the tile-stamp P.P.BR.LON (Merrifield 1965, 43–4). Die A has not been noted on a tile-stamp, but it is close in style to one reading P.PR.BR. The mortarium stamps, rather surprisingly, are from a larger die (Walters 1908, no M.2826). Examination of the tiles and mortaria proves fairly certainly that they were manufactured in the same workshop and that some dies could be used on either. There is no other instance in Britain of tiles and mortaria being manufactured together, but the practice was common in Italy.

As with the mortarium stamps, the tile stamps have only been found in London, with the exception of two fragments from a kiln at Brockley Hill (*JRS* 1956, 22). The reading PR*(ouinciae)* BRI*(tanniae)* LON*(dinensis)* is clear, and suggests that the tiles were manufactured with official sanction, and perhaps for use only in official buildings. The first P is more controversial, but probably signifies the procurator, who would be responsible for official building (see fuller discussion in Merrifield 1965, 43–4). The mortaria might have been produced for use in these official buildings, or may simply be a sideline of the brickworks; the small number of stamps and their restriction to London does not suggest large-scale production.

The evidence implies that tile and mortarium production was contracted out to potters with the use of an official stamp required as part of the terms. The mortaria date to *c* AD 80/90–130, with the proviso that all could be within the second century. In that period the Verulamium region potters were of outstanding importance and would have been the obvious choice for an official contract. *[F 714]*

Selected samian
Fig 231

XIII.10. Dragendorff Form 29, South Gaul. Corded scroll in both zones. The leaf and rosette have no apparent parallel. Corded scrolls are early: a date *c* AD 45–60 is likely. *[F758] no 1*

XIII.11. Dragendorff Form 37, South Gaul. Trident-tongued ovolo, too blurred to identify. The lion is probably Hermet 1934, pl 25, no 11, suggesting links with the Germanus group. *c* AD 85–110. *[F712] no 2*

XIII.12. Dragendorff Form 37, South Gaul. Scroll with beaded bindings. Flavian. *[F721] no 5*

XIII.13. Dragendorff Form 37 in the style of Butrio of Lezoux. The ovolo (Rogers 1974, B109) and boar to right (Oswald 1936–7, 1589) are on Stanfield and Simpson pl 58, no 656, stamped by Butrio; the ovolo, same boar, dog (Oswald 1936–7, 1926A) and panther (Oswald 1936–7, 1511) are on pl 57, no 653. Butrio regularly used the leaf, Rogers 1974, H151, shown with similar beads on pl 61, no 684. The second boar is close to Oswald 1936–7, 1621, the deer Oswald 1936–7, 1822J; the hunter is not identifiable. The overall style suggests that this bowl dates later in Butrio's range of *c* AD 120–40. *[F712] no 1*

XIII.14. Dragendorff Form 37 in the style of Gesatus of Lavoye. The motifs are all catalogued on Ricken 1934, Taf 13: the ovolo is B, the rosette probably 2, the leaves 10 and 11, the stag 27 and the hound 29. Both leaves, the stag, ovolo, rosette and border are on Muller 1968, Taf 17, no 449, assigned to Gesatus, while Oswald 1945, fig 7, nos 1, 2, both by Gesatus, have the ovolo, leaf and stag. Antonine. *[F736] no 1*

XIII.15. Dragendorff Form 37, Rheinzabern. The tree is a larger version of Ricken and Fischer 1963, P3.

Late second to first half of third century. *[F714] no 1*
XIII.16. Dragendorff Form 37 in the style of Afer of Trier. The festoon is Gard 1937, K68; the motif inside is probably the end of it used as an alternating arcade (cf Bird 1986, no 2.78). First half third century. *[F714] no 13*
XIII.17. Dragendorff Form 37, Rheinzabern. Ovolo Ricken and Fischer 1963, E17, used by several potters; the other motif is not identifiable. Late second to first half of third century. *[F718] no 1*

Graffiti

XIII.18. Nene Valley colour-coated ware cornice-rim beaker. Scored on top of rim. *[BB325]*

The small objects
Fig 232

Iron

XIII.19. Stylus (Manning 1976 type 4) with plain offset eraser and point; the round shaft has a band of inlaid copper alloy above the point, and a narrower strip further up. Length 99mm [F715] *MoL Acc No 18176*
XIII.20. Dagger blade, a flat ellipse in section, with a square tang to fit into a handle. The point is rounded, the edges have apparently never been keen, and the surfaces appear unfinished. There are no close military parallels for the type. Toynbee (1962, pl 74, 154, no 71) shows a dagger of similar proportions in the hand of Mithras, and it is possible that this dagger formed part of a sculpture or similar arrangement; alternatively, it may have served as a votive offering. Length of blade 279mm; of tang 132mm. *[F719] MoL Acc No18154*

Professor Grimes stated that a metal dagger blade was found with the jet dagger handle in the upper levels of the aisle floor on the north side (Grimes 1968, 114). This unsharpened iron dagger-blade, however, is the only one recorded in the finds archive, and it manifestly does not fit the delicate jet handle. The context in fact indicates that it came from the west bank of the Walbrook, not from within the Mithraeum. This provenance is supported by its uncorroded condition, quite different from that of the iron attached to the marble hand buried in the floor of the Mithraeum, but resembling iron finds from the stream bed or from the waterlogged silt deposited on the banks when the channel was recut. It should also be noted that the context number of the jet handle is located in the nave, not an aisle.
XIII.21. Hook with a tang at the back. Length 45.5mm *[F721] Not illustrated*

Bone and antler

XIII.22. Part of a hinge cut from a long bone; the complete end has two pairs of grooves, with a hole for an attachment peg cut through one side. The inside is roughly hollowed, and it would have been plugged with wood. For a full discussion of the working of these hinges see Waugh and Goodburn 1972, 149–50. Length 40mm *[F 718] MoL Acc No 18171*
XIII.23. Roughly worked peg, as no 10, 43mm long, with flat head and plain shaft tapering to a point. *[BB325] Not illustrated*

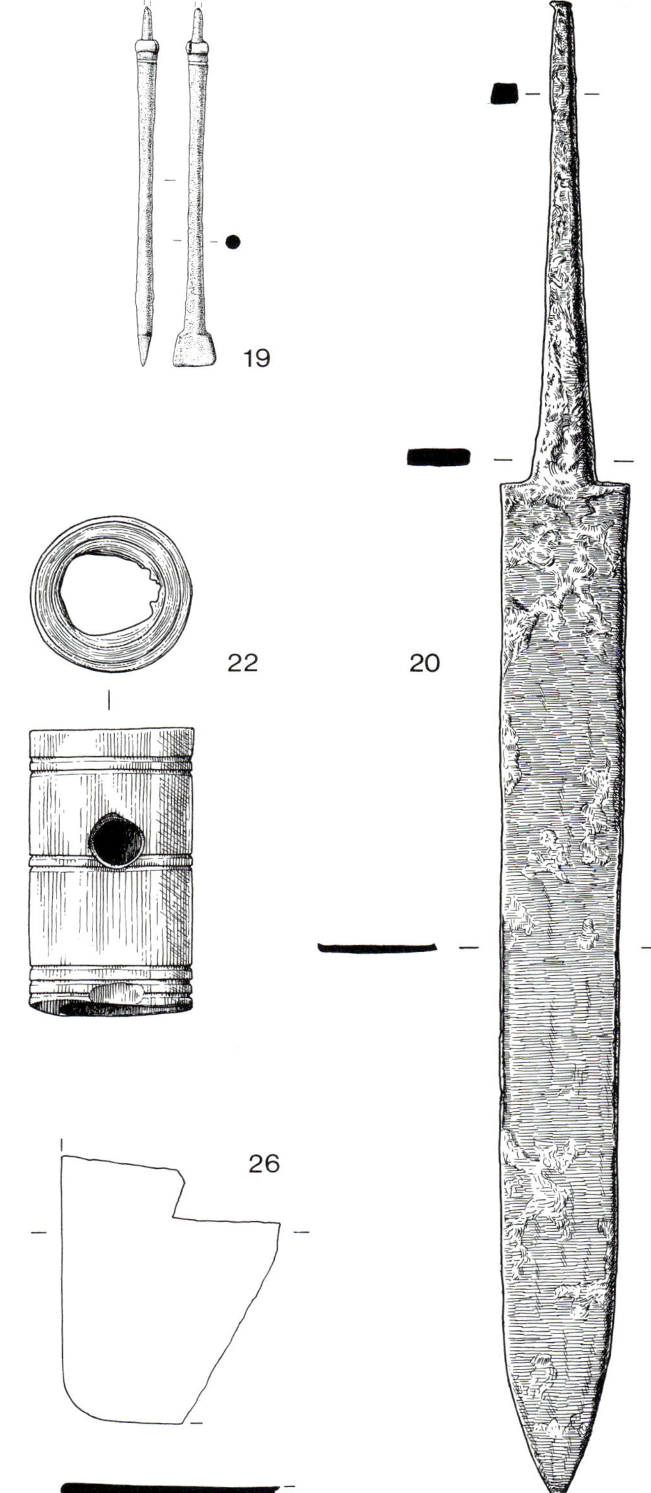

Fig 232 Period 2, Group XII small objects (nos 19, 20, 26 scale 1:2; no 22 scale 1:1)

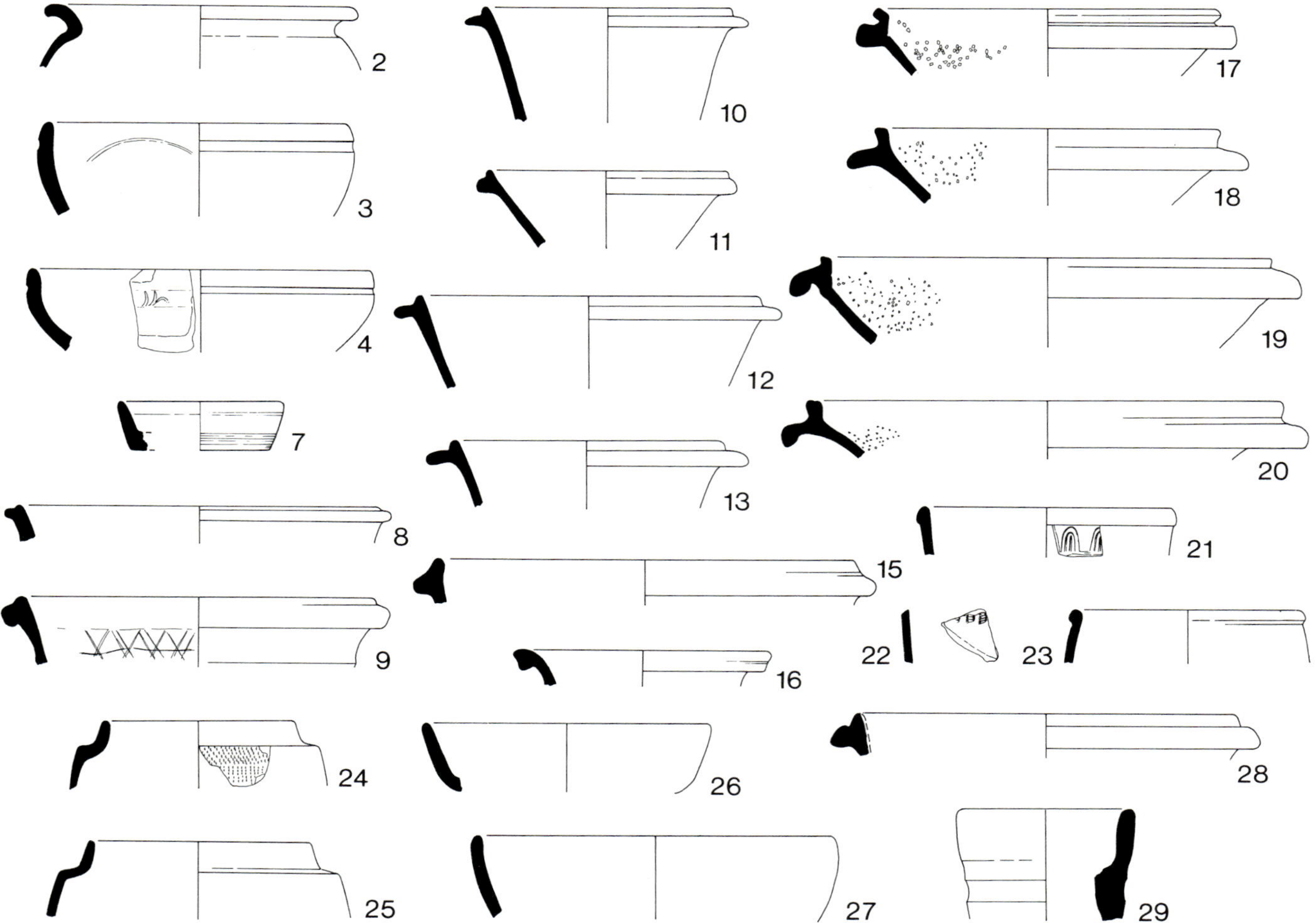

Fig 234 Period 2, Group XIV pottery vessels, excluding samian (scale 1:4)

XIV.15. Late Roman calcite-gritted ware flanged bowl (CALC FB). *[BB112]*

XIV.16. Porchester 'D' ware necked jar (PORD NJ). *[BB104]*

XIV.17. Oxfordshire mortarium, probably Young type M22 (OXMO M22?). *[BB114]*

XIV.18. Oxfordshire white-slipped red ware mortarium, Young type WC5 (OXWS MORT WC5). *[BB 43]*

XIV.19. Oxfordshire white-slipped red ware mortarium, Young type WC7 (OXWS MORT WC7). *[BB104]*

XIV.20. Oxfordshire white-slipped red ware mortarium (OXWS MORT). *[BB104]*

XIV.21. Oxfordshire red colour-coated ware copy of a Dragendorff Form 37 with stamped decoration (OXRC IV C Dragendorff Form 37 STD). *[BB74]*

XIV.22. As above but body sherd only (OXRC IV C Dragendorff Form 37 STD). *[BB112]*

XIV.23. Oxfordshire red colour-coated ware? bowl possibly a copy of a Dragendorff Form 37 (OXRC? IV C Dragendorff Form 37?). *[BB32]*

XIV.24. Nene Valley colour-coated ware box with rouletted decoration (NVCC BX ROD). *[BB106]*

XIV.25. As above but undecorated (NVCC BX). *[BB44]*

XIV.26. Nene Valley colour-coated ware plain-rimmed dish (NVCC IVJ). *[BB75]*

XIV.27. As above (NVCC IVJ). *[BB95]*

XIV.28. Nene Valley colour-coated ware flanged bowl (NVCC FB). *[BB32]*

XIV.29. Amphora (AMPH), possibly North African cf Peacock and Williams (1986) type LV.A, p162. *[BB110]*

Selected samian
Fig 235

XIV.30. Dragendorff Form 29, South Gaul, with scroll in upper zone. *c* AD 70–85. *[BB311] no 2. Not illustrated*

XIV.31. Dragendorff Form 37, South Gaul. Characteristic Flavian arrangement of triple medallion above foliage motifs. The bud is close to one on a Dragendorff Form 30 in the style of the M Crestio group (Knorr 1919, Taf 99, B). The figure may be a maenad, a smaller version of Oswald 1936–7, 370. Mid- to later Flavian. *[BB94] no 1*

XIV.32. Dragendorff Form 37, South Gaul. Trident-tongued ovolo, probably one used by Sabinus iv and Sulpicius. Below is a common Flavian wreath. *[BB94] no 2*

XIV.33. Dragendorff Form 37, South Gaul. Incomplete trident-tongued ovolo above panels, including a bud tendril, with coarse borders. *c* AD 85–110.*[BB311]no 6*
XIV.34. Dragendorff Form 37 in the style of Sacer of Lezoux. The ovolo is on Stanfield and Simpson pl 82, no 1, with the lion whose tail is present here; the panther is on pl 82, no 4. The third animal is probably a deer. For the leaf, cf pl 82, no 3, and pl 83, no 10. Burnt. *c* AD 125–50. *[BB45] no 1*
XIV.35. Dragendorff Form 37 in the style of Cobnertus III of Rheinzabern. Ludowici and Ricken 1948, Taf 27, no 14, has the ovolo (Ricken and Fischer 1963, E40), beads (Ricken and Fischer 1963, O264), leaf (Ricken and Fischer 1963, P88) and medallion; the figure is not identifiable. Mid- to late Antonine. *[BB42] no 1*

Samian stamp

XIV.36. Donnaucus Les-Martres-de-Veyre (a) 2a. Dragendorff Form 42 *c* AD 100–25. *[BB94]*

Parting vessel

XIV.37. A sherd of a BB1 bowl (IVJ BUD) which has been used as a parting vessel, for the separation of gold and silver. This process, and the archaeological evidence for it, are discussed in detail by Bayley (1991).

The core and surfaces of the vessel are white (except where they are masked by residues) due to oxidisation which has occurred during use. A dark-coloured deposit covers the interior of the vessel to just below the rim. This deposit has a pinkish colouration and specular haematite, which are characteristic of parting vessels. The same deposit is present on the upper part of the vessel exterior but it is patchy. On the interior the deposit, in addition to coating the surface, is also raised above it, giving it the appearance of rough-casting. There is also a concreted whitish deposit on the basal exterior which could be the remains of clay luting. *[BB75]*

Lamp chimney

XIV.38. Fragment of lamp chimney in coarse sandy buff fabric. *[BB45] Not illustrated*

Glass

XIV.39. Rim of a jar or a small dish (eg Isings form 67 or 42 respectively). Free-blown; natural green-blue glass. Rim folded inwards to form a hollow tubular lip and folded out and down. Late first or second century. *[BB308]*
XIV.40. Fragment from the rim and side of a beaker (Isings form 12). Free-blown; natural green glass. Cracked off rim ground smooth with a wheel-ground band around the lip. The rim curves slightly inwards. Mid- to late first century. *[BB 311]*

XIV.41. Fragment from the rim and part of the side of an indented beaker (eg Isings form 34). Free-blown; colourless glass. Rim slightly outsplayed, cracked off and ground smooth. Body decorated with deep circular indentations. Second century. *[BB 91–92]*

Sculpture

XIV.42. Figure 236. Fragment of a statuette of (?)Bacchus: cf Toynbee 1986, 24–25; no 7; pl VII; pl 14. A fragment of a mutilated nude male statuette, possibly Bacchus. The torso is the same scale as the one above (X.58), although it varies in its rendering. Unlike the other, it has no traces of support and no tooling marks to the rear indicating it could have been more visible. The upper cut is similar but is flat across the top. The lower cut truncates the left thigh at a higher level.

The surface is pitted and no longer polished. There is a large circular chip out of the left buttock and a large abrasion on the side of the right thigh. There is a grey stain down the left thigh. It is clearly of the same date, technique and style as X.58 and must come from the same workshop. See Henig's comments for X.58 above.

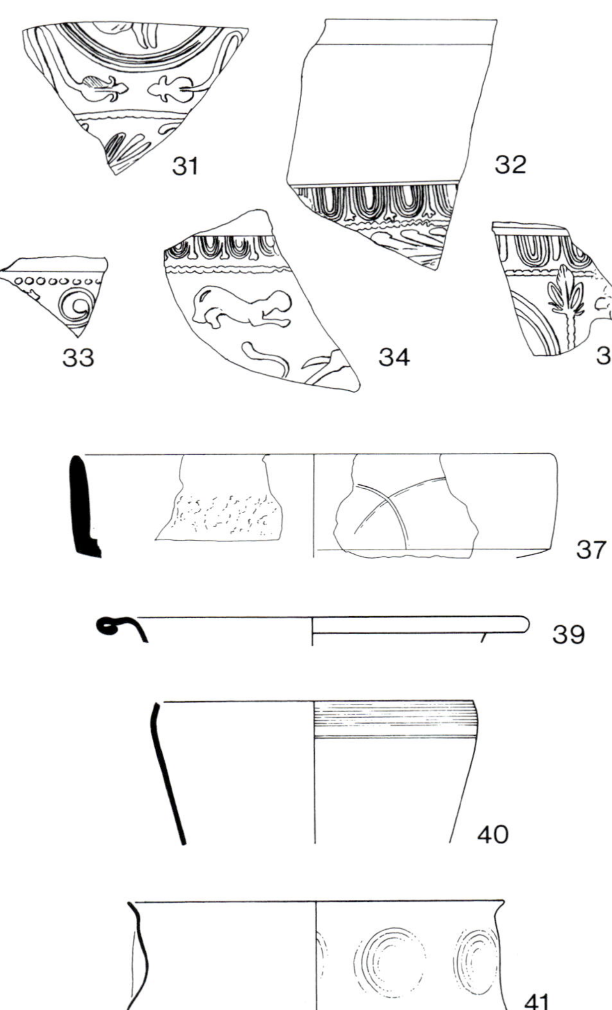

Fig 235 Period 2, Group XIV samian vessels, parting bowl and glass vessels (no 37 scale 1:4; rest scale 1:2)

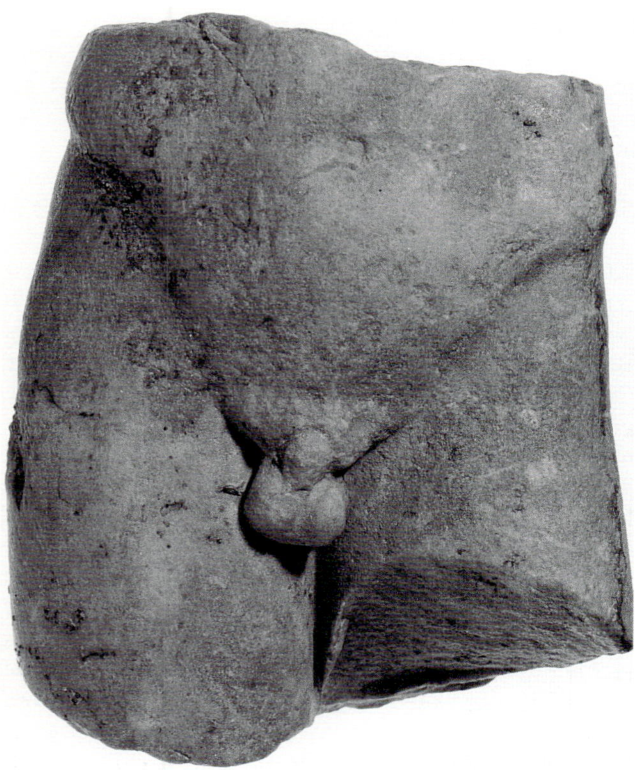

Fig 236 Period 2, Group XIV. Bacchus torso (XIV.42)

The statuette is made from fine-grained saccharoidal marble, probably from Carrara, Italy. Dimensions: height 185mm; width across 153mm; thickness 96mm. Found in 1952, reused in a late Roman foundation block of masonry, west of the Walbrook stream and about 183m from the temple. *MoL Acc No 18015*

The small objects
Fig 237

Copper alloy

XIV.43. Fragment of spiral, perhaps a binding, made from folded sheet copper alloy. Length 15mm. *[F710] MoL Acc No 18215*

Iron

XIV.44. T-shaped staple, as 1.64, with long rectangular shank and short arms. Length 147mm *[BB104] MoL Acc No 18124*

Group XV: late fourth century

The finds catalogued and discussed below come from the following layers:

Cutting BB: 14, 15, 18, 33, 39, 40, 41
Cutting F: 100, 700, 702, 703, 704, 705, 706, 707, 711, 717

Group XV deposits sealed both Cuttings BB and F. The ungrouped layers at the top of Cuttings AA and AB most probably belong here also. The layers were virtually featureless and consisted primarily of dark, almost black, soil.

The pottery was very mixed but included late fourth-century forms and fabrics. A few intrusive medieval sherds were also noted, but not included in this report. The only find of note was a bone peg (XV.25) and some residual window glass.

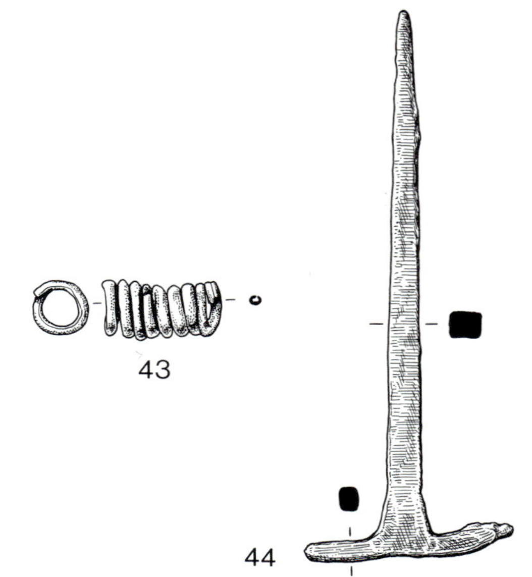

Fig 237 Period 2, Group XIV small objects (no 43 scale 1:1; no 44 scale 1:2)

The vessels

Pottery
Tables 29 and 30

The Oxfordshire industries are the most prominent (20%), followed by those from the Nene Valley (15%) and Alice Holt/Farnham (15%). The stamped Oxfordshire red colour-coated sherd (IV Dragendorff Form 37) shows that the group post dates *c* AD 345 and is likely to be later than *c* AD 350 because of the dating of Group XIV. There is one possible medieval sherd [BB 41], which, if it is post-Roman, is presumably intrusive. Even in this late group samian accounts for 34% of the assemblage.

Table 29 Group XV pottery excluding samian

Fabric	*Forms*	*No of vessels (approx)*
AHFA	II, ERJ(5), IVJ(2), FB(2)	10
AHFA?	IIF?; ERJ; FB	3
BB1	IVJ BUD; FB; FB BUD(4); G226 BUD(2)	8
BB1?	FB BUD	1
BB2	IVH; IVH; IVJ BUD	3
BB2F	IVH5(3)	3
BBS	IIF; ERJ(2); IVJ	4
EIFL	IV	1
HWC	IVF	1
KOLN	III BAD; III RC	2
LOMI?	IF/G	1
LRRA		1
MOSL	III motto	1
NVCC	III BAD; III BR WPD; III BR; III CR(4); III; III ER; FB; IV?	11
NVCC?	II ROD; ?(handle)	2
OXID		1
OXMO	M17(4); MORT(2)	6
OXMO?	M22?	1
OXPA	CA	1
OXRC	IV CDR37(3); IV CDR37 STD; IV CDR38 WPD; IV CDR38; NE?	7
OXWS	MORT ?WC4	1
SAND	NJ; IVJ; IV	3
VCWS	MORT BEF	1
VRW	MORT HOF	1
Total		75

Catalogue of illustrated vessels
For code expansions see above, *Pottery codes and expansions*
Fig 238

XV.1. Alice Holt/Farnham ware lidded jar (AHFA II LJ). *[BB14]*
XV.2. Alice Holt/Farnham ware flanged bowl (AHFA FB). *[BB14]*
XV.3. BB1 plain-rimmed dish with burnished decoration (IVJ BUD). *[F705]*
XV.4. BB1 flanged bowl with burnished decoration (BB1 FB BUD). *[F700]*
XV.5. As above (BB1 FB BUD). *[F706]*
XV.6. Reduced sandy ware plain-rimmed dish (SAND IVJ). *[F700]*
XV.7. Eifelkeramik bowl (EIFL IV). *[BB18]*
XV.8. Oxfordshire parchment ware carinated bowl (OXPA CA). *[F706]*
XV.9. Oxfordshire mortarium, Young type 22 (OXMO M22). *[F703]*
XV.10. Oxfordshire white-slipped red ware bead and flange mortarium (OXWS MORT BEF). *[BB 41]*
XV.11. Oxfordshire red colour-coated ware copy of a Dragendorff Form 37 with rouletted decoration (OXRC IV C Dragendorff Form 37 ROD). *[BB14]*
XV.12. As above but with stamped decoration (OXRC IV C Dragendorff Form 37 STD). *[F711]*
XV.13. Oxfordshire red colour-coated ware copy of a Dragendorff Form 38 with white-painted decoration, Young type C52 (OXRC IV C Dragendorff Form 38 WPD C52). *[F700]*
XV.14. Oxfordshire red colour-coated ware possibly a necked bowl (OXRC NE?) see Young type C75. *[F700]*
XV.15. Nene Valley colour-coated ware everted-rim beaker (NVCC III ER). *[F705]*
XV.16. Nene Valley colour-coated ware bead-rim beaker with white-painted decoration and rouletting (NVCC III BR WPD ROD). *[F700]*
XV.17. Nene Valley colour-coated ware flanged bowl (NVCC FB). *[F707]*
XV.18. Nene Valley colour-coated ware? jar with rouletted decoration (NVCC? II ROD), cf Howe et al 1981, type 74. *[F706]*

Table 30 Group XV samian

Source/ Fabric	*Forms*	
SG	CU11; DR18; DR30; DR37(2)	
CG	CU11; DR27; DR31(3); DR18/31; DR33(2); DR37(3);DR38(2; DR45	
EG	CU21; DR31(5); DR33(2); DR37(2); DR37R(2); DR38(2); DR45(2); MORT(2); I/II/III?	
Total no of vessels (approx)		38

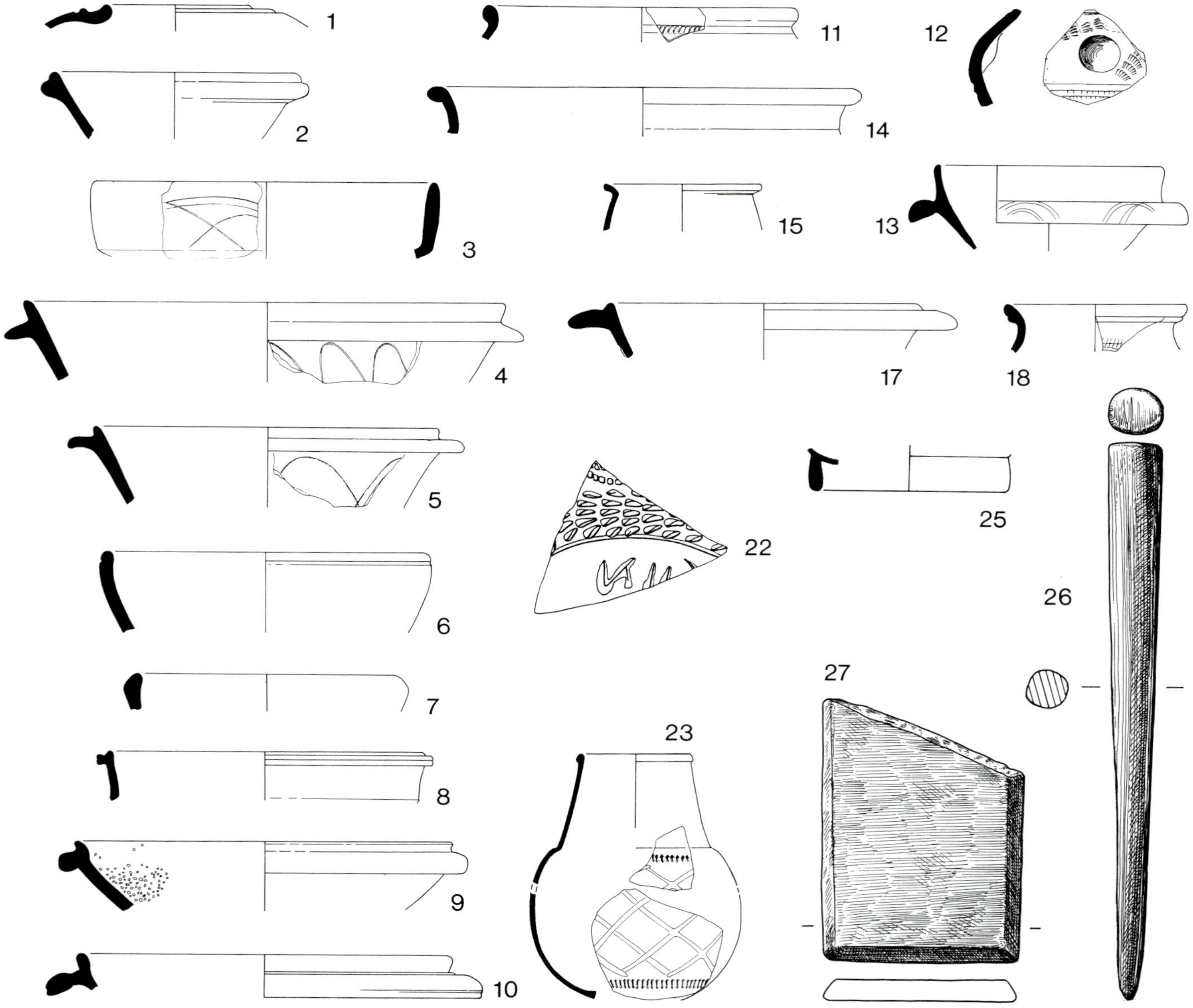

Fig 238 Period 2, Group XV pottery vessels and small objects (nos 1-18, 23 scale 1:4; nos 22, 25 scale 1:2; nos 26-27 scale 1:1)

Mortarium stamp

XV.19. Verulamium region white ware hooked flange mortarium. Only the edge of the stamp survives but the border indicates that it may belong to Driccius of Radlett. Eleven of his stamps are known from Radlett and four from Brockley Hill, which may represent a branchworks. *c* AD 85–130. *[F705]*

Mortarium graffiti 'stamp'

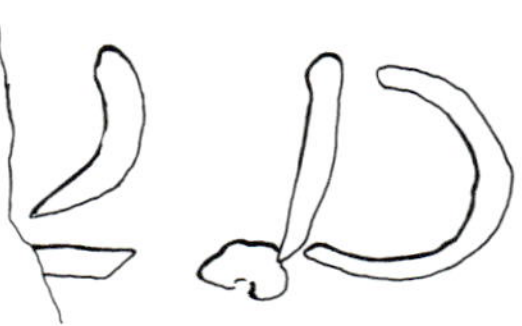

XV.20. Verulamium coarse white-slipped bead and flange mortarium. A pre-firing graffito potter's stamp cut on the right of the spout with the vessel inverted reads ( )Q.D. The circle of the Q is cut in two strokes, with the horizontal tail cut more deeply; the D is cut in a one curved stroke one vertical. The intevening stop has been placed on the lower line. Dated by vessel form to *c* AD 140–200. *[F700] [F706]*

Lamp chimney

XV.21. Fragment of lamp chimney in coarse sandy buff fabric *[BB14] Not illustrated*

Selected samian

XV.22 Dragendorff Form 37, South Gaul, with part of mould signature below the decoration of Censor i of La Graufesenque, where his signatures are recorded. Above is a basal wreath of palmettes and cogged festoon or medallion. *c* AD 70–90. *[AA/AB 529]*
XV.23. Dragendorff Form 37 in the style of Criciro of Trier. The ovolo is on Bird 1986, no 2.71, and the motif in the upper row of festoons is probably the cockerel on that bowl. The beaded festoon occurs regularly on stamped bowls of Censor, with whom Criciro was associated, and the acanthus ornament in the lower row of festoons is also on Censor-group bowls (Fölzer 1913, Taf 16, nos 12, 37). The bowl is heavy and thick, the relief rather shallow: a early to mid-third-century date is likely. Partly burnt. *[F702]*

Samian ware stamps

XV.24. Unidentified,]-F, CG, Dragendorff Form 38, Antonine? *[F705]*

Glass

XV.25. Fragment from the base of a small bowl or beaker. Free-blown; natural green glass. Applied high true-base ring. Late third or fourth century. *[F707]*

The small objects

Bone and antler

XV.26. Peg with flat head and plain shaft, tapering to a blunt point; cf Crummy 1983, fig 199. Length 88mm. *[F704] MoL Acc No 18172*

Stone

XV.27. Mixing palette. Rectangular with neatly bevelled edges. *[F702]*

Window glass

XV.28. A fragment of cylinder-blown double glossy window glass. *[BB 33]. Not illustrated*

Unstratified finds of interest

Included here are those objects of interest from layers which can no longer be located on the site.

The vessels
Fig 239

Pottery

Lamps

0.1. *Firmalampe,* burnt; part of the shoulder and base. Stamped EV( ) in relief on base. Probably Eucarpus, who worked in Gaul or North Italy. Late Neronian–Trajanic (information from D Bailey, BM) Central Gaulish fabric. *[F727, layer not located] no 17*

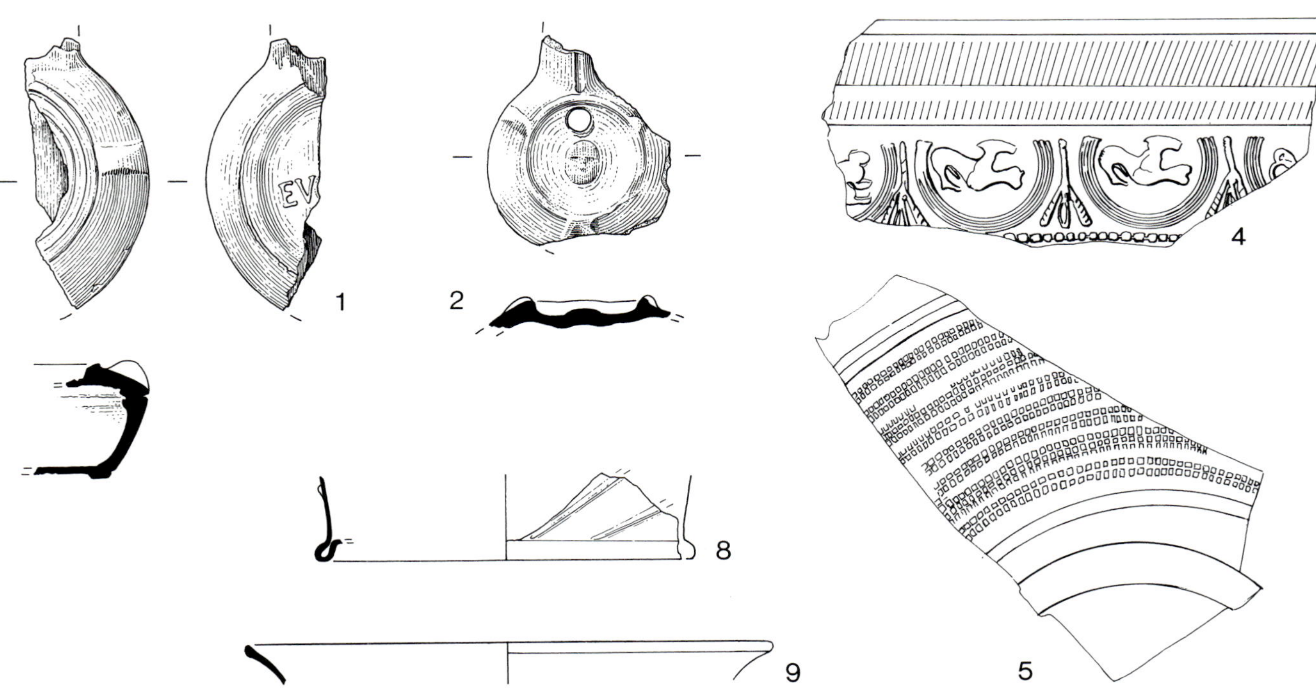

Fig 239 Period 2, Group 0 unstratified pottery vessels of interest (scale 1:2)

0.2. *Firmalampe* with moulded dramatic mask on the discus (cf Bailey 1963, pl 10 e–g). Loeschke Type IX. Provincial manufacture in Local mica-dusted ware. Later first to second century. *[B331, layer not located] no 16*

Lamp chimney

0.3. Fragment of lamp chimney in coarse sandy buff fabric. *[B12, layer not located] Not illustrated*

Selected samian

0.4. Dragendorff Form 29, South Gaul. Upper zone has triple festoons with trifid tassels. Similar festoon frieze with the same dog (as Oswald 1936–7, 1963 but smaller) on a lower zone at Verulamium (Hartley 1972, fig 89, no 69), a bowl whose upper zone has links with the work of Crucuro. No apparent parallels in South Gaul for other animals, probably squirrel and ibis-like bird. *c* AD 70–85. *[F732, layer not located]*

Argonne ware

0.5. Form Chenet 320. Decorated with a roller-stamp of three small squares; no exact parallel in Chenet (1941), but cf types 303 and 304. Hübener 1968 puts these stamps in group 2, dated *c* AD 330–?67. *[D810, layer not located]*

Graffiti

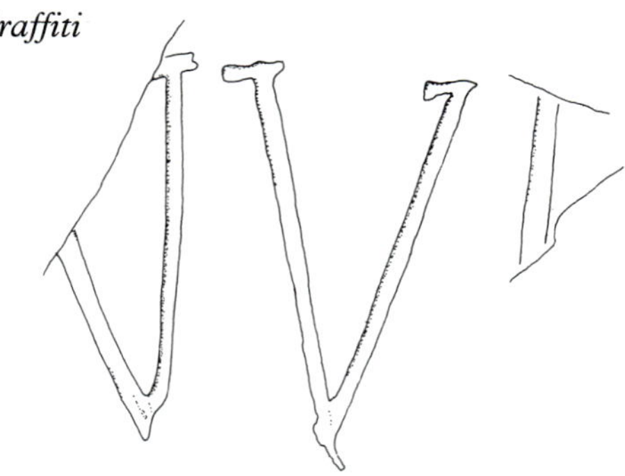

0.6 Colour-coated ware,]NVI[on exterior. *[CE266, layer not located]*

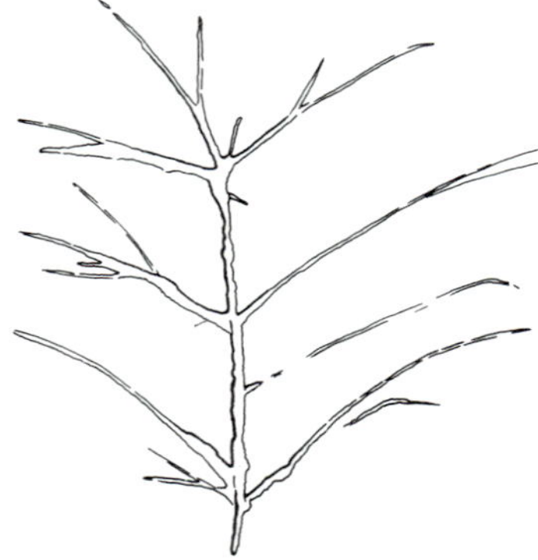

0.7. Samian, Dragendorff Form 33 (South Gaulish). A 'tree'. *[F713, layer not located]*

Glass

0.8. Fragment from base and lower part of straight-sided tankard or bowl (see Isings form 37 for straight-sided one-handled tankard, form 41 for bowl). Optic-blown; colourless glass with a green tint. Base pushed in to form wide hollow tubular base-ring. Body decorated with high relief optic-blown diagonal ribs. Mid- to late first century. *[WFG44/45 unstrat]*

0.9. Fragment from the rim of beaker. Free-blown, ground and polished; colourless glass with yellowish tint. Rim thickened and ground round. Very abraded. Late first century. *[F100, 1952 layer not located but probably at top of Group XV layers. See Fig 36]*

Stone

0.10. Mortar. Fragment of rim; basalt. *[E807, layer not located]*

The small objects
Fig 240

Copper alloy

0.11. Bent rod with acorn finial; other end is cut straight. Possibly a long handle, cut down. Length 134mm *[BB unstrat] MoL Acc No 18120*

0.12. Stud, shaped into a hollow boss with a groove round the edge; pin short and square. Diameter of head 19.5mm. *[CA unstrat] MoL Acc No 18404*

Iron

0.13. Knife. Flat leaf-shaped blade and a centrally placed twisted handle with a ring terminal. Length 134mm. *[WFG44/45 unstrat]*

Bone

0.14. Upper part of hairpin, with plain shaft and rounded conical head, cut flat on one face (cf Crummy 1983, fig 19, Type 3) Length 63mm. *[CE237: layer not located] MoL Acc No 18273.*

Wood

0.15. Rounded bung or stopper, chamfered. Diameter 64mm, thickness 30mm. *[F unstrat] MoL Acc No 18195*

0.16. Turned knob or finial; one end has a shallow socket, the other a tenon. Probably a furniture fitting; cf the couch legs shown in a number of tombstones (Liversidge 1955, especially pls 2, 6–12). Wood type uncertain. Length 105mm. *[C complex 220] MoL Acc No 18262*

0.17. Carved fragment, probably from a piece of furniture (as 1.105 above). *Quercus* (oak). Length 50mm. *[CD unstrat] MoL Acc No 18265*

0.18. Fragment of writing tablet. *Abies* (silver fir). *[F unstrat] M+L Acc No22243. Not illustrated*

0.19. Fragment of writing tablet. *?Quercus* (oak). *[F unstrat] MoL Acc No 22244 Not illustrated*

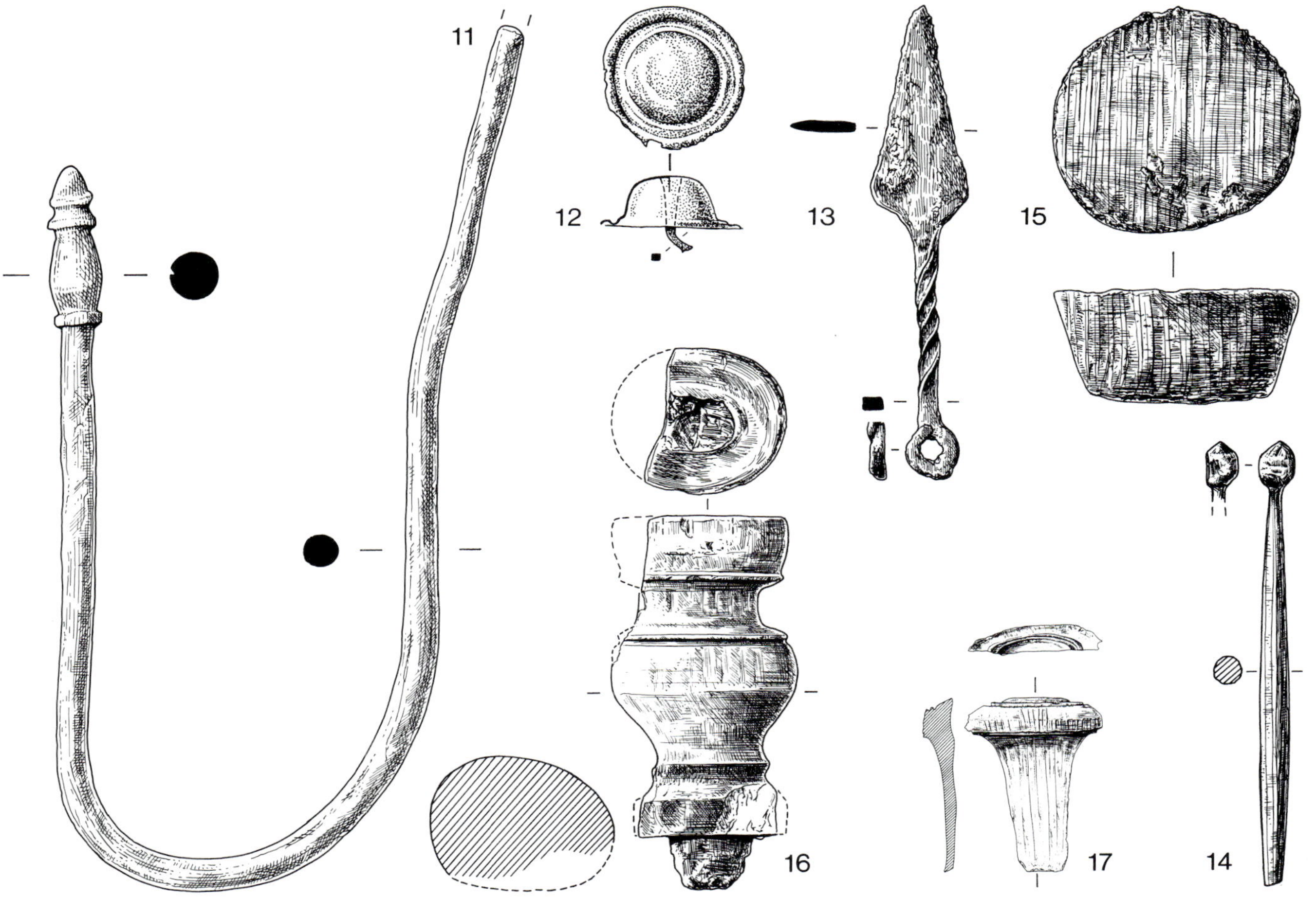

Fig 240 Period 2, Group 0 unstratified small objects of interest (nos 11,12,14 scale 1:1; rest scale 1:2)

6 The environmental evidence

The animal bones

by S Macready and J Sidell (written by the second author from notes and original work by the first author)

Introduction

For such a large site, the bone assemblage from the Mithraeum and surrounding areas is relatively small. A number of factors are likely to have contributed to the nature and type of bones recovered. There may have been a degree of selection, during both antiquity and the excavation, affecting bones from within the temple and its surrounding area. The assemblage is also likely to have been biased because no sieving programme was used during the excavations and because of the different digging conditions in the different areas. This will have favoured the recovery of large bone fragments, easily visible in the field, at the expense of small pieces. Normally this is compounded by natural decomposition, which also favours the survival of more robust and larger bones. However, the exceptional conditions of preservation on the site, thanks to a high degree of waterlogging which hinders microbial activity and therefore the process of organic degradation, mean that this factor is unlikely to have had much effect. It also needs to be noted that in any case, regardless of the effect of all these factors, the size of the assemblage is too small to sustain statistical analysis.

There are a number of ways in which the bones are likely to have been deposited on the site. One possibility which must be borne in mind for the smaller assemblages (for example where only a few small fragments of bone were found with no obvious significance) is that of 'background noise'. This occurs where previously deposited bone is reworked into new deposits, or occasional bone fragments are thrown and discarded in a random manner. In this specific case, bones may have entered the temple if make-up was needed to level the surface before laying a new floor. A further possibility is that the bones are by-products of practices associated with the cult. The likelihood is that such bones would generally have been cleared out of the temple area, and that the bones recovered are from a much larger original assemblage. However, in some cases within the temple, groups of bones of one species or a group of charred bones may indicate the remains of one individual incident which was incorporated into the fabric of the temple.

The bone fragments which were examined and identified numbered 445. Measurements were taken after von den Driesch (1976) and tooth wear was recorded after Grant (1975). The majority of bones (390) came from the temple area, Cutting C, with most of these coming from within the temple itself. The remainder of the bones came from Cuttings A, B and F.

Tables 31 and 32 show the breakdown of bone and bone fragments by species.

Each floor filling in the temple was treated as one layer, although some bones, in particular chicken, seem to have been deliberately deposited in groups within the floor surfaces or make-up for (and between) these surfaces. Where this occurs, the contents of the specific assemblages are listed in detail below (seeTables 33–42).

Bones related to temple use

As mentioned above, a number of groups of bones were isolated as probably having originated from cult practices. These are listed in Tables 33-42 and collated in Table 43. Table 33 lists the material from CA149, a dump layer immediately pre-dating the construction of the temple. Tables 34, 35 and 36 show selected deposits from Floors 2 and 3, the period when it is suggested the

Table 31 Breakdown of bones/bone fragments of cattle, pig and sheep. It was not possible to distinguish rib fragments of sheep from those of pig

Bone		***Species***	
	Cattle	*Pig*	*Sheep*
Horn core	29		1
Skull	3	2	1
Maxilla	3	1	
Mandible	14	11	12
Scapula	1	3	
Humerus	1	9	2
Radius		2	2
Ulna		5	1
Metacarpus	6	2	4
Ribs	8		
Innominate	1	2	
Femur	5		1
Tibia	2	1	1
Metatasus	1		1
Tarsals			1
1st phalanx	1		
2nd phalanx	3		
3rd phalanx			
Atlas	1		
Axis	1		
Cervical vertebrae	10		
Thoracic vertebrae	4		
Lumbar vertebrae			
Sacrum			
Caudal vertebrae			
Loose (pre) molars	4	3	1
Loose canines		13	
Loose incisors		4	

building was in use as a mithraeum, and Tables 37–42 show a selection from Floors 6–9, the phase postdating the burial of the Mithraic sculptures. A further group resting on Floor 5, to be included with the latter, was CB269, a collection of charred bones found within a pot set beside an altar. These bones were set aside for detailed examination, and unfortunately were subsequently lost. The only notes made at the time of their discovery were to the effect that the material included chicken bones.

The bones from the selected groups may be the traces of cult practices, such as feasting or possibly sacrifices.

Table 32 Breakdown of bones/bone fragments of chicken and other birds

Bone	***Species***					
	Chicken	*Domestic duck*	*Duck Sp.*	*Goose*	*Wood-cock*	*Raven*
Skull	1					
Maxilla	2					
Mandible	1					
Furculum	6					
Coracoid	13					
Scapula	4					
Humerus	20	3		1		
Radius	18		1			
Ulna	24				1	
Carpometa-carpus	7					1
Ribs	9					
Innominate	5					
Femur	17					
Tibiotarsus	40	1	1			
Fibula	2					
Tarsometa-tarsus	13					
Phalanges	2					
Vertebrae	1					
Synsacrum	7					

Table 33 Bone concentration from CA149, construction layer of the temple

Bone	***Species***	
	Chicken	*Pig*
Humerus	5	
Coracoid	2	
Femur	3	
Tibiotarsus	4	
Ulna	5	
Radius	3	
Scapula	1	
Sternum	1	
Synsacrum	1	
Innominate		1

Table 34 Bone concentration found in CB354, a small hole in Floor surface 2, in the north-west angle of the south sleeper-wall

Bone	***Species***			
	Chicken	*Cattle*	*Pig*	*Sheep*
Humerus	3			
Coracoid	7			
Femur	7			1
Tibiotarsus	8			
Ulna	6		2	
Radius	4			
Tarsometatarsus	1			
Scapula	1		1	
Carpometacarpus	5			
Sternum	3			
Synsacrum	3			
Innominate	2			
Skull	1			
Maxilla	2		1	
Mandible	1			
Ribs	4	1		
Furculum	2			
Metacarpal		1		
Metapodial			1	

Table 35 Bone concentration in CB358, beneath floor 3

Bone	***Species***				
	Chicken	*Pig*	*Sheep*	*?Sheep*	*Cattle*
Humerus	2	1	1		
Coracoid	1				
Femur	1				1
Tibiotarsus	3				
Ulna	1				
Radius	1				
Innominate		1			
Metatarsal			1		
Long bone Fragment				1	

Table 36 Concentration of bone from CB347, in gully related to Floor 3, next to north sleeper-wall

Bone	***Species***						
	Chicken	*?Chicken*	*Pig*	*Sheep*	*Sheep-sized*	*Cattle*	*Duck*
Ulna	1						
Radius	1		1	1			
Humerus	2		1				2
Tibio-tarsus	3						
Femur	1						
Rib		1			1	1	
Skull			1				

Butchery

With the exception of the skull with the horns sawn off, the horn cores were generally found with a fragment of the frontal part attached, many showing clear signs of having been deliberately cut or smashed some way below the base of the horn. None of the cores came from the temple itself: 2 came from beneath the temple, 1 from above it, 10 from Cutting CD outside the temple, 15 from Cutting F, 2 from Cutting A and 2 from Cutting B. It seems likely that the majority of these are waste from horn-working activities, as seen at Angel Court, Walbrook (Clutton-Brock and Armitage 1974), and No 1 Poultry (Pipe, pers comm). A large number of horn cores were found here, although relatively more post-cranial material was also present. It is possible that the material from the Mithraeum area may relate to these activities, but in more secondary deposits. Most of the cores from Cutting F and the two skulls with horn cores and traces came from the filling of the stream bed, and may have been tossed in deliberately to clear them out of the way. (No details are available on the preservation, or it might have been possible to see whether they were rolled and had been carried within the Walbrook.) In addition to the horn cores, several other elements showed signs of butchery. One femur and a metacarpal both had cut marks on the shaft close to the proximal epiphysis. These were possibly knife marks caused during secondary butchery, during food production rather than primary jointing. One first phalange had a cut mark on the midshaft, which may well have been from primary butchery when the feet were removed from the carcass. A femur head had been chopped from its shaft, and this again probably falls into the primary butchery class, the creation of the basic joints of meat.

Pathology

Three of the cattle bones showed signs of severe osteoarthritis: a seventh cervical vertebra in which the articular surfaces of the centrum were very highly eburnated, a fused and compacted seventh cervical and a first thoracic vertebra. In these the vertebral bodies had not yet reached maturity, indicating an animal under five years old. The third pillar of the third molar was missing in one mandible, and the second molar was absent from three further mandibles.

Domestic pig *(Sus scrofa)*

The majority of the pig bones come from Cutting C and most of these from within the temple itself. They are represented mainly by mandibles, teeth and forelimb bones. The bias towards mandibles and teeth in particular may suggest a degree of differential preservation, teeth being the most robust elements of a carcass. They may also be from primary butchery waste, when the head is removed before jointing. However, the presence of limb bones would seem to indicate that this is not the case.

Table 44 Juvenile pig bones

CE303	metacarpal 3	unfused	distal	right	under 2 years
CB107	metacarpal 4	unfused	distal	right	under 2 years
CB336	humerus	unfused	shaft	left	under 1 year
CB336	radius	unfused	shaft	left	under 1 year
CE347	humerus	unfused	shaft	left	under 1 year
CE347	humerus	unfused	proximal	right	under 4 years
CE347	radius	unfused	shaft	right	under 1 year
CB354	scapula	unfused	proximal	left	under 1 year
CB354	metapodial	unfused	distal		subadult
CB354	ulna	unfused	shaft	left	under 3 years
CE288	metapodial	unfused	distal		under 1 year
CE288	ulna	unfused	proximal	right	under 3 years
CE292	radius	unfused	shaft	right	under 1 year
CE292	humerus	unfused	shaft	left	under 1 year
CA320	vertebra	unfused	body		subadult

Table 45 Juvenile pig/sheep bones

CE292	vertebra	unfused	body	subadult
CB336	vertebra	unfused	body	subadult
CB354	vertebra	unfused	body	subadult

The preponderance of forelimb bones to hindlimb bones is difficult to explain. It could be coincidence and a factor of the small sample size, but 17 (one of these a scapula) of the 21 bones in question are from the temple itself. One possibility is that joints of the forelimb were preferred in cult meals. Most of the pig bones consist of isolated finds with no evidence of joints or partial skeletons, with the exceptions of some groups listed in Tables 33–42, and the left radius and humerus of a neonatal animal from CB336.

Age

Unfused epiphyses indicated that a proportion of the material came from immature animals It was not possible to differentiate in a few cases between sheep and pig (Table 45).

Two skull fragments of neonatal individuals were also found in CA292 and CB347. Some of the mandibles were in a fairly fragmentary condition, but in at least 60% of those with cheek teeth present, the teeth were generally unworn and/or the third molar unerupted. Most of the loose canines were well developed.

Butchery

Butchery marks were not common, and consisted of cut marks on two half mandibles on the inner surface close to the mandibular symphysis. As suggested above, the mandibles may be products of butchery, and these cuts result from meat being taken off the bone. Also a right humerus had a cut mark on the shaft just above the distal end. This may be a knife mark incurred during food preparation, in the secondary butchery phase.

Domestic sheep/goat *(Ovis aries/Capra hircus)*

It was possible in CB329 to identify the fronto-parietal suture of a skull fragment as sheep. Otherwise all fragments have been classed as sheep/goat, henceforth referred to as sheep for convenience. Many of the bones came from within the temple itself. Most of the finds are mandibles, which may be owing either to purposeful selection or differential preservation. Of the remaining bones, both fore- and hindlimbs are represented, although forelimb bones are more common.

There is no evidence for joints or any articulated material, with the exception of some of the material listed in Tables 33–42.

Age

A small number of unfused bones was recovered (Table 46). A left metatarsal, proximal end, obviously belongs to a young animal although it is fused. In six out of the ten mandibles, the third molar had erupted and was in wear. Eruption is thought to be at 36–48 months in hill sheep (after Silver 1969), but approximately 18–24 months in improved breeds. In goats they erupt at the same age in improved breeds, and at approximately 30 months in rough breeds. Teeth generally come into wear about 5 months after eruption. In the remaining four mandibles the fourth deciduous premolar was present and the third permanent molars unerupted, in one case just visible in the jaw. Unfortunately it is not possible with such a small sample to form any interpretations concerning the age structure of this group.

Butchery

There was no clear evidence of butchery or working marks on any of the bones.

Pathology

One of the mandibles was affected by a disease resulting in the thickening of the ramus close to the mandibular symphysis.

Table 46 Juvenile sheep/goat bones

CA206	radius	unfused	shaft	right	under 10 months
BA319	femur	unfused	distal	left	under 3.5 years
CB358	humerus	unfused	distal	right	under 10 months
C345	meta-carpal	unfused	distal	left	under 20 months
CB329	ulna	unfused	proxi-mal	left	under 2.5 years
CE292	humerus	unfused	distal	right	under 10 months
CB107	meta-tarsal	unfused	distal	left	under 28 months
CB326	tibia	unfused	distal	left	under 2 years

Domestic dog *(Canis familiaris)*

Seven bones were identified as domestic dog. These were a right humerus, two right halves of mandibles, a right radius, a skull and mandible and a slightly pathological metapodial.

Domestic cat *(Felis cattus)*

Two complete cat skulls came from BB320. One had small cut marks at the top of the skull, which may indicate skinning (P Armitage pers comm).

Red deer *(Cervus elaphus)*

One antler base came from CE217, overlying the temple. It had been worked, sawn beneath the beam and brow tine.

Hare *(Lepus sp)*

A right femur was found in CB131 below the north aisle, approximately 220mm above the underlying geology.

The birds

Domestic fowl *(Gallus gallus)*

Chicken bones were the commonest bones recovered, almost all of which came from Cutting C. Of these 32 came from the temple itself. The high proportion of these bones recovered from within the temple may be a result of several factors; more careful excavation of the temple area, differential preservation, or the frequent use of chickens in Mithraic practices (see above). The number of chicken bones in the temple compared to the number of other bones may be a factor of their size. Smaller material will be more easily incorporated into the floor matrix, whereas bones of larger species would be more obstructive and more likely to have been cleared efficiently.

All parts of the body was represented, but the most commonly found bones were the tibiotarsus, ulna, humerus, radius, femur, tarsometatarsus and coracoid. Large groups of bones representing 1–3 (MNI) birds occurred frequently throughout the temple floors (see Tables 33–42).

Age

The majority were fully adult. Only four were immature, and these were of adult size.

Sex

In 2 of the 13 tarsometatarsi it was not possible to determine sex, as only the extreme proximal or distal ends had survived. All the remaining 11 carried spurs or, on one bone from CB345, a spur scar. The majority of tarsometatarsi (nine, including the two whose sex could not be determined) came from within the temple. The percentage of male birds as seen from the tarsometatarsi is therefore between 84–100%. This figure bears no resemblance to those of a normal breeding population in the Roman period, where a cock to hen ratio of between 1:3 and 1:5 was more usual (White 1970). This seems to point strongly to the use of cocks in preference to hens, although it must be borne in mind that this is a small sample. Again this is paralleled at Carrawburgh where the male of the species predominated (Richmond *et al* 1951). The cock seems to have been preferred, although whether this was stipulated by ritual is uncertain. It may that larger birds were needed, for instance in the use of chicken gut for tying the hands of initiates.

Butchery

No cut marks were observed on any of the bones.

Pathology

One right humerus from CB347 showed fairly severe periostitis, with a spongy-looking outgrowth approximately 25mm long covering the lateral surface at the midshaft.

Domestic duck *(Anas platyrhynchus)*

Four bones of this species were found: a right humerus, a left humerus (from a different bird, both from CB347), a proximal right tibiotarsus and a left humerus, both from the fill of Floor 6 (CA344 and CA323). All came from groups thought to be by-products of cult practices (see Tables 33-42).

Duck *(Anas* sp)

Two duck bones were recovered which could not be identified to species. These were a left humerus (CA323) and a right tibiotarsus (CB336).

Raven *(Corvus corax)*

One bone was recovered of this species. It was a left carpometacarpus from CB353, Floor 3 of the nave. Ravens are known to have been tamed by the Romans. The raven played a large part in Mithraic belief, being the bird that carried the message to Mithras to slay the bull, and also ministered food in the feast with Helios. The raven was also one of the seven grades of Mithraism. The findspot may indicate a tamed bird, or one deliberately introduced into temple, but on the evidence of one bone this is no more than a possibility and must be treated with caution.

Domestic/greylag goose *(Anser anser)*

One bone was recovered of this species, a left humerus from CA320, beneath the fill of Floor 8. This may be a remnant from a cult meal, but its isolation may point more towards it being part of make-up for the floors.

Woodcock *(Scolopax rusticola)*

One bone was recovered of this species, a left ulna from CE303, in the fill beneath Floor 5. Again it may have been part of a feast or part of the make–up for floor levels but cannot be interpreted any further.

Summary

The animals and birds identified from the Walbrook Mithraeum produced no rarities for this period in London, and the number of bones involved was also quite small. The majority of species were of domestic creatures, with the exceptions being red deer, hare, woodcock and possibly wild duck. Domestic cattle, fowl, pig and sheep/goat were all common finds, although the cattle were generally outside the temple, and were rarer within the walls. Most of the material recovered is presumed to have been eaten.

Outside the temple itself, most bone groups were made up of only one of two bones per species. Another factor which contributed to the high numbers of cattle was the presence of large amounts of horn cores, presumed to be the product of hornworking activities in the area. Within the temple there were various concentrations of bones, representing larger proportions of the skeleton per species or individual than was the case elsewhere (particularly domestic fowl). These concentrations were almost certainly the by-products of cult activities such as feasting or sacrifice. Around the apse these concentrations consisted of burnt bone, but elsewhere there was no sign of burning. From the bone evidence, domestic fowl was the most common faunal species included in the rituals, followed by sheep (or goat) and pigs (both adult and domestic), domestic duck, and possibly goose and cattle. However, the bones that were recovered may not be an accurate reflection of the activities which produced them. A number of factors must be considered, such as the probability that large bones would have been cleared out after feasts or other celebratory events. Unfortunately, only a limited level of interpretation may therefore be based on this bone assemblage.

It would seem that the specific groups isolated in Tables 33–42 are from cult meals, and generally consist of chicken, pig, and sheep (or goat), with occasional fragments of cattle, while some of the other bones are probably part of the make-up of the structure of the temple. This selection of species is common as food generally, but is paralleled at the Carrawburgh Mithraeum (Richmond *et al* 1951). A comparison may be drawn with offerings identified from the Roman Eastern Cemetery, London (see Sidell and Rielly (in press) and Rielly in Barber and Bowsher (forthcoming). It also seems possible that the chickens were also sacrificed as part of the ritual before being consumed or left as offerings. It has therefore been possible to isolate a number of activities from the faunal material excavated in the area of the Walbrook Mithraeum, providing good information on the use of birds and animals in the Mithraic practices.

Report on soil sample associated with waterlogged piles and stakes

by I W Cornwall

The material was a grey sandy loam, with occasional bright orange ferruginous patches, these mostly in contact with wood and clearly secondary. There were, besides, occasional larger fragments of white lime mortar and plaster and of red brick or tile, and a single potsherd. The sample was full of amorphous organic matter and of fragments of wood and charcoal, some of macroscopic size, but largely very finely comminuted. Plant remains other than wood were not found.

Preliminary chemical results: pH 5.9 (distinctly acid), loss on ignition 20% of dry weight (mostly wood and charcoal). Phosphate present in large quantity, under reducing conditions. Alkali-soluble humus 25 mgs/gm (amorphous organic matter). A quantity of the sample was first heated with dilute 'Calgon' solution to disperse clay and, after washing on a 0.2mm sieve, further treated with hydrogen peroxide to destroy the humified organic matter and to clean individual grains for visual inspection. Neither treatment would remove ferruginous concretions from sand grains.

The washed and dried residue of medium-sand grade and upwards, was further subdivided by sieves into four size-fractions, 5.0, 2.0, 0.6, 0.2mm, and these were individually examined under the binocular microscope.

Particles of uncarbonised wood and charcoal formed an important component. The loss in weight on ignition includes these with the amorphous humus. Only a very few larger fragments of bone and molluscan shell were found, which had survived acid solution. These might be one source of the massive phosphate concentration which, today, clearly resides mainly in the amorphous organic matter.

The mineral part, 80% in total, consisted of a few small irregularly shaped flints and occasional pieces of sandstone, most being quartz sand including a few rounded grains of green glauconite, probably from the Greensand of the Weald. Artificial mineral materials, including red brick or tile, white mortar or plaster, were prominent because of their colours but probably contributed no more than 5% of the weight. Half a dozen tiny flint spalls were obviously the products of flintworking. There was one small wheel-made potsherd.

The mortar and plaster were present only in the coarser grades — smaller particles presumably having dissolved away completely in the acid conditions. One fragment showed a plane face which was well finished with a finer coat than the body and was evidently wall- or ceiling-plaster. Some of the mortar and plaster contained glauconite grains and was perhaps the source of those noted above with the other sand grains.

The coarser sand-grade quartzes, both in the sediment as a whole and in the plaster, were clean, well rounded and in some cases water-polluted, suggesting beach rather than river sand as their immediate source. Perhaps beach sand was imported from down the estuary rather than obtained locally, for Roman building operations. Local sand would have been sharper and almost certainly ferruginous, and it would have been hard to find sand which did not have to be quarried and washed before use. As a whole, the material might be characterised as a sandy flood or tidal loam, laid down in no more than a gentle current. It was heavily contaminated with organic detritus, mainly it would seem from the associated piles but probably also with contributions from sewage (phosphate), ashes (carbonised wood), building rubbish (brick and mortar) and occasional food debris (bone and shell). It was evidently formed under rather acid reducing conditions, being almost permanently waterlogged and only occasionally and locally oxidised by surface water percolating along channels through and beside the timbers, which laid down the secondary iron.

Examination of peat samples

by Elizabeth M Knox

Extract from a letter to Professor Grimes dated 5 August 1954:

> The peat proved interesting in that it contains vast quantities of pollen, but of very few varieties. Here are the results of a rough count:-

Betula (Birch)	44%
Alnus (Alder)	43%
Grass	8%
Quercus (Oak)	6%
Sedge	2%

> There were in addition a few odd grains representative of Caryophyllaceae, Compositae, *Potentilla* and Chenopodiaceae.
>
> I was most surprised at the lack of variety. The pollen grains of Alder and Birch were not always easy to distinguish from one another, as they seemed to be distorted in a curious manner. It would appear that at the time of the early Roman settlement the Walbrook area must have been a pretty dense 'forest' of Alder and Birch — with not very much in the way of undergrowth.

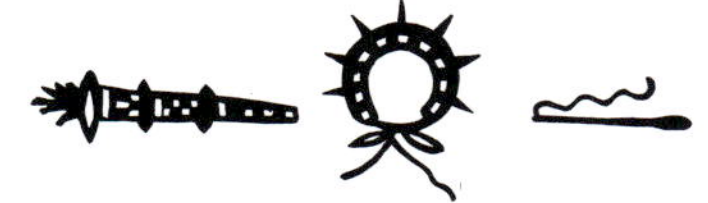

7 Conclusions: the Walbrook and the temple in context

Introduction

The RMLEC excavations at Bucklersbury House between 1952–4 were the first to examine the Walbrook stream and its valley in any detail. The discovery of the temple was, as Grimes put it, 'a fluke' and distracted the attention of the archaeological world and the public away from the original objectives of the excavation. Grimes, however, continued with the pursuit of the details of the stream and its valley both at the time of excavation and, as his archive shows, during the post-excavation work on the site. The following chapter, therefore, takes into account the entire Roman sequence at Bucklersbury House.

It begins with a summary of the pre-urban aspects of the site, in particular the shape and nature of the stream and valley. Unfortunately, detailed environmental evidence was not collected at the time. Roman occupation in this part of the valley is briefly examined with reference to recent statements made by Merrifield and Wilmott about the nature of the deposition of the large small finds assemblage from this area of the Walbrook. The discussion of the temple as a mithraeum examines the form of the building, a brief statement about the nature of the cult itself, and comparisons between features of the London building and other mithraea. Dr Martin Henig's proposal that the building was converted for use by followers of another pagan cult, probably that of Bacchus, is also presented here (see *Appendix 1,* by Henig, for a more detailed paper on this subject).

The natural Walbrook valley

Before the RMLEC programme of 1952–4 at Bucklersbury House it was generally agreed that the dark, waterlogged deposits which were found in many places along the entire course of the Walbrook stream were the fills of the actual stream channel. For example, they were recorded at St Swithin's House in 1951, just on the east side of the modern street called Walbrook and directly opposite the location of the Cutting C complex described above. Their presence there was not regarded as exceptional by the excavator, Ivor Nöel Hume, who duly interpreted them as '...the eastern edge of the Walbrook stream...' (St Swithin's House, 1949–50, archive notes). This interpretation was well in keeping with the established belief that before the arrival of the Romans to London and during the early Roman period, at least, the Walbrook flowed southwards to the Thames as a broad stream or river with proportions similar to the River Fleet to the west.

It was in this broad form that the Walbrook was reproduced on the map published with the RCHM inventory of Roman London (RCHM 1928). Wheeler, the author of the introduction to that volume, believed that the information which had accumulated even by the time he was writing in the late 1920s was '...enough to make it unlikely that any subsequent evidence will throw much fresh light on the subject...' (RCHM 1928, 15). However, he was sceptical about the size and character of the stream as suggested by some of his predecessors. Though ambiguous on the nature of the pre-Roman stream, he believed that, for the Roman period itself, the stream united from a number of small tributaries in the northern part of the city and flowed at the bottom of a gradually broadening depression. He believed that it was only towards the end of the Roman period that the stream was confined to a quite narrow channel, even near its mouth at Cannon Street. In general, he saw the valley itself as being 'rubbish filled' (ibid, 44) and not conducive to use of any other kind.

It has been noted on a number of occasions in the preceding chapters that the prime objective of the RMLEC excavations at Bucklersbury House was to examine in greater detail the nature of the valley of the Walbrook stream. The 1952 cuttings were accordingly located in positions which would obtain an almost complete profile of the Walbrook (Cuttings A, C and F) as well as a longitudinal section of the deposits contained within it (Cutting B). The results of these excavations showed that Wheeler's scepticism was justified — the main watercourse, seen in the eastern end of Cutting F at a point *c* 365m (400yds) to the north of the present riverfront, flowed, as Wheeler had suggested, in the bottom of a broad, shallow depression. The RMLEC excavations revealed this to be *c* 91.5m (300ft) in width, with its west edge coinciding approximately with the pre-development line of Sise Lane and its east edge with the Walbrook street. However, in the early Roman period (late first century, see *Chapter 3, Cutting F*) the stream itself was contained in a narrow, shallow channel at least 3m wide. It was slightly narrower during the late Roman period (see *Chapter 4, Cutting F: Group XV)* but this was more the result of neglect rather than the canalisation implied by Wheeler (RCHM 1928, 44).

Unfortunately, the true nature of the pre-Roman stream and the environment on its banks could not be determined from the RMLEC excavations. The natural surface of the stream valley was not examined in detail due to the wet conditions of the excavations but the recorded sections do not show any pre-Roman land surfaces. This could mean that, as seen elsewhere in the city, the earliest Roman activity represented the clearing and deturfing of the site or, perhaps due to clearance of vegetation, the natural surface had become eroded with surface run-off of rainwater (T Barham and J Hill pers comm). It is now impossible to know. To compound this problem, detailed environmental

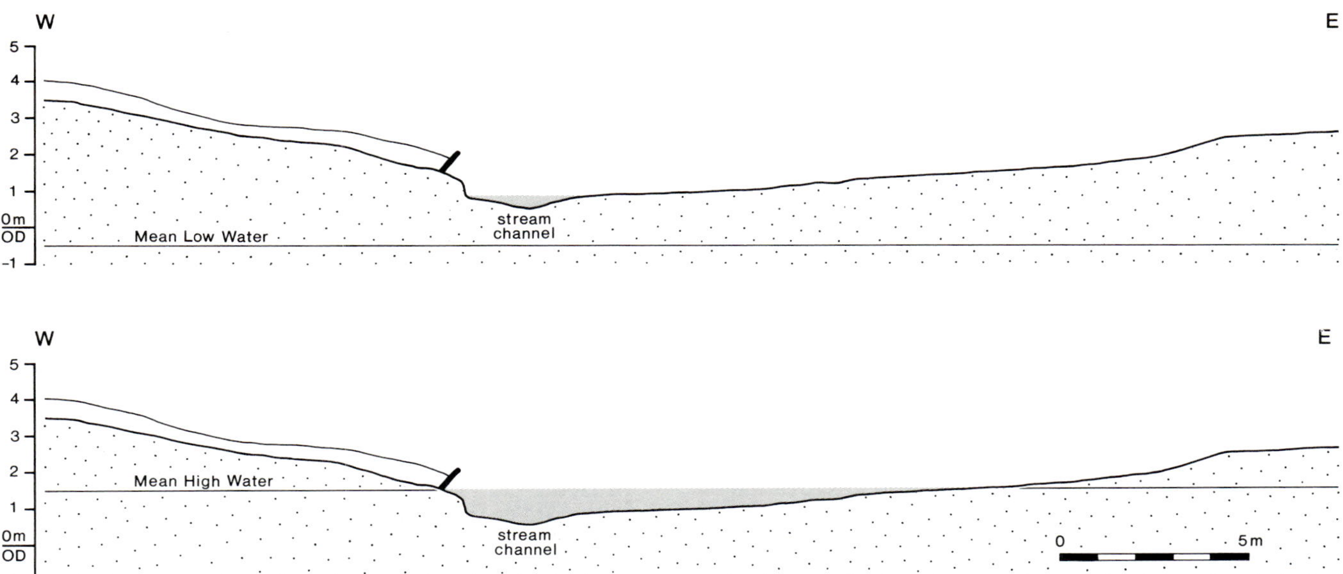

Fig 241 The tidal range of the Thames projected against the section through the Walbrook valley. For the late first century at least, the Walbrook channel was between the lowest and highest tides

sampling was not carried out. The one sample which was taken came from the peat deposits at the base of Cuttings CA and CD (Group I or II: late first or early second century). A formal report for these no longer survives in the archive, but a letter from Knox to Grimes (*Chapter 6, Examination of peat samples*) gives an indication of the content of these samples. This led Grimes to suggest that 'remnants of birch and alder thickets ...would no doubt have been its natural vegetation...' (Grimes 1968, 97).

Although the environmental picture of the valley is not clear, Grimes's detailed recording of the sections across the deepest part of the valley (Cuttings CA, CD and F) contains some items of information which may have an important bearing upon the nature of the watercourse itself during the pre-Roman and early Roman periods. Recent work conducted by the Department of Urban Archaeology, Museum of London, on the Thames waterfront has focused attention upon the tidal range of the Thames during the Roman and medieval periods. In part this has shown that a number of the building programmes on the Thames waterfront were initiated in response to long-term fluctuations in the tidal range of the river (see Brigham 1990 for a discussion of the late Roman waterfront with references to earlier structures). During the late first century the range has been estimated at *c* –0.5 m to 0m OD Mean Low Water level to *c* 1.5m OD Mean High Water Spring level. This gives an amplitude of 1.5 to 2m. But between the late first century and the middle of the third century there was a substantial fall of about 1.5m (Milne 1985, 79–86 and Brigham 1990, 143–5).

The lowest point in Cutting F, the base of the stream channel at the eastern end of the cutting, was recorded by Grimes at *c* 0.47m OD (Figs 35 and 36). This is the lowest level of the *c* 3m wide rectangular cut which was probably formed by the initial manual clearing of the channel (*Chapter 3, Cutting F: natural deposits*). If the slopes of the banks of the Walbrook are projected over this cut they meet at a point only *c* 0.25m above. The probable level of the bottom of the natural stream channel before the first cleaning in the early Roman period was therefore *c* 0.75m OD. Both these figures, ie the surface of the projected profile of the natural valley (*c* 0.75m OD) and the recorded level of the man-made cut (*c* 0.47m OD), fall within the tidal range of the Thames during the first and second centuries as recorded by the recent work on the waterfront referred to above. It is possible to suggest, therefore, that during the pre-Roman and early Roman periods the level of water in the Walbrook valley as far north, at least, as the position of Cutting F was influenced by the range of the tides (Fig 241). With water flowing towards the Thames from the tributaries higher up in the northern part of the city and beyond, and the level of the Thames itself varying with the tides, the area which falls within the tidal range would be better described as a tidal creek rather than simply a stream. This would have had a major effect upon the initial layout and planning of the Roman town, in particular the siting of the main east–west road running parallel with the Thames. This subject is unfortunately beyond the scope of the present study but an opportunity to examine this further should arise with the interpretation of the earliest sequence at No 1 Poultry to the north of Bucklersbury House. At the time of writing this site is under analysis by the Museum of London Archaeology Service.

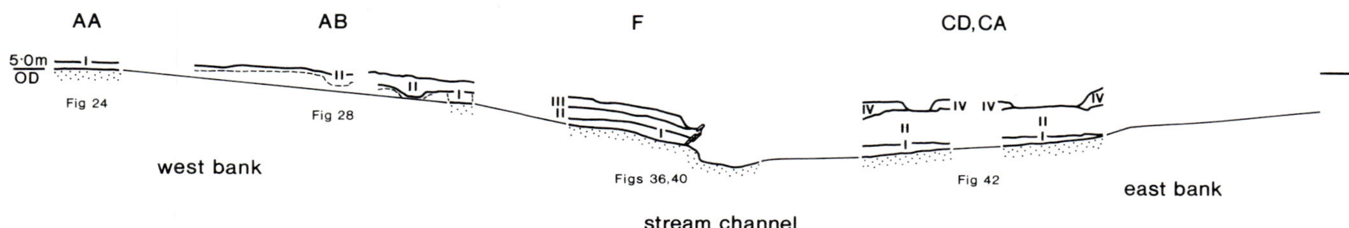

Fig 242 First- and second-century groups

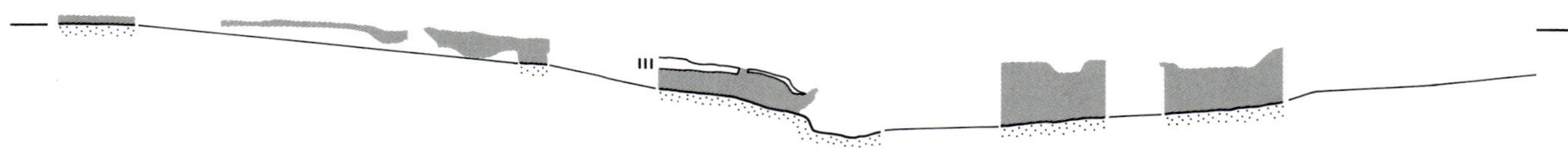

Fig 243 Second-century clay and gravel dumps

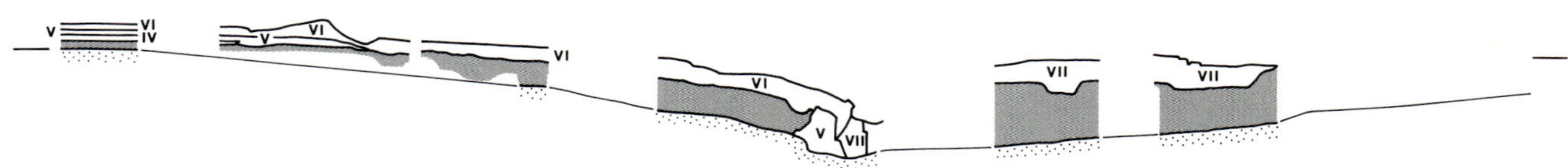

Fig 244 The early third-century valley

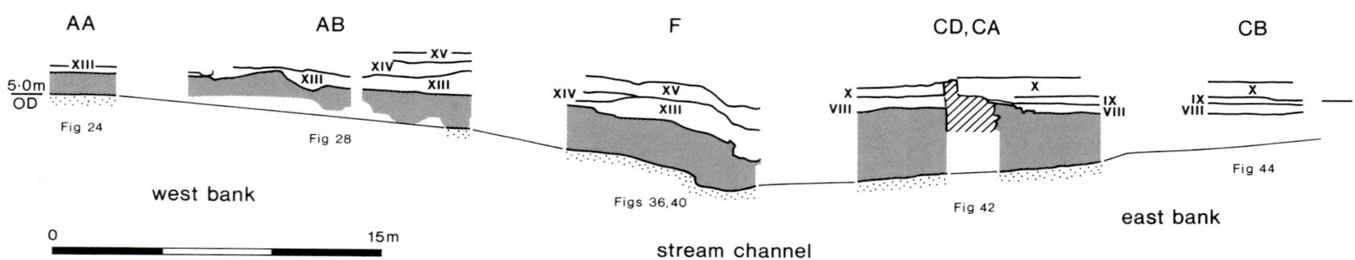

Fig 245 The temple and contemporary groups

The siting and construction of the temple

When the temple was built, it would appear that the west bank was occupied by timber structures with their platforms extending as far as the stream bank. This was still revetted but the revetment had probably already started to slump into the stream. On the east bank, the nature of occupation immediately alongside the stream was very different. As indicated above there were no timber platforms on the scale of those on the west bank. Instead there were a number of individual features, many cut into the surface of the east bank, and the single chalk and flint foundation.

Further to the east of the RMLEC excavations, observations made by Ivor Nöel Hume in 1949 for the Guildhall Museum at the St Swithin's House site noted evidence of masonry buildings of the late second century onwards which may have been contemporary for a time with the temple (Wilmott 1991, 41). Unfortunately, their true relationship with the temple is not known. The difficult conditions with which Nöel Hume had to contend on this site meant that his site records were not as complete as would normally have been the case (Nöel Hume 1978, 14). It would be unwise, therefore, to attempt to link together these two sites using only the records which currently exist. In any case, the modern street called the Walbrook divides the two sites. No doubt many answers to the positioning of the temple in this particular area will be found beneath that street but, for the record here, it is interesting to note that Grimes and Sorrell, in their reconstruction drawings of the temple seen from the west (Fig 246), show a Roman street in the same

Fig 246 Reconstruction by Alan Sorrell of the temple, seen from the west

position and alignment as the modern street. The result of postulating a road in that position was the very shallow narthex of the temple. Furthermore, the temple appeared in these reconstruction drawings as a free-standing building apparently isolated on the east bank of the stream. But if there was no road the rooms at the east end of the temple, which Grimes called the narthex, may have extended eastwards to join with the St Swithin's House buildings. The temple could therefore have been part of a larger complex of rooms (Fig 247).

It is therefore not certain whether the temple was constructed in a pre-existing religious zone or precinct, whether it was built in an undeveloped area with no religious affinities whatsoever, or whether it was added to a private building which extended further to the east. As a mithraeum, the building would no doubt have attracted soldiers and merchants among its congregation. It should be emphasised, however, that during the third century, in particular the second half of the third century when the Mithraeum was in use, it is unlikely that the Cripplegate fort was still in use (Shepherd forthcoming). This would not exclude the presence of troops who could be garrisoned elsewhere in the town, but would remove the need to associate the location of the Mithraeum with a defined military presence. Furthermore, the temple was also set at a distance from the riverside and the forum and basilica. It is probable, therefore, that its location in the Walbrook valley was simply through convenience. It is safe to assume that London was so frequented by soldiers and merchants that proximity to one area of the town was not an advantage.

The sequence of events during the construction of the temple is described in detail above *(Chapter 4, The construction of the temple)*. It is important to note that the builders were hampered in their efforts by the wet and unstable nature of the accumulation of deposits on the east bank. It is unlikely that such poor conditions would have been improved or even stabilised by the mere presence of the new building. Indeed, Grimes's observation that the adverse effects of the high level of ground water in this area caused the raising of the floor levels on at least eight subsequent occasions following the initial construction is still valid. It is also probable that these conditions also caused the slumping and collapse of part of the building which may have necessitated or provoked the radical alterations made to the interior plan of the building. This is discussed below in the section on the end of Mithraism at Walbrook.

The date of the construction of the Mithraeum was placed by Grimes initially in his 1968 report as occurring at some time during the end of the second century. This was based upon a single coin (no 3) and a cursory examination of the pottery from the levels which immediately pre-dated the temple (Group VII). However, following the detailed study of all the pottery from the site by Joanna Bird during the early 1970s, and reproduced in edited form by Jo Groves and Joanna Bird above, he revised this date to *c* AD240–50.

The latest datable samian in Group VII dates to the early to mid-third century (eg VII.40: see *Chapter 5, The samian: general summary and discussion*) and the other pottery can be broadly dated from the mid-third century to *c* AD 300 *(Chapter 5, Group VII: pottery)*. Since the evidence from the early floors of the temple suggests that they were in use during the second half of the third century, the early part of this broad date range for the pottery is more likely as a deposition date.

The foundations of the temple were trench-built of mortared ragstone rubble with no piles to support them. The walls of the building were constructed in coursed ragstone blocks interspersed with tile coursing. The latter was not regular. At the west end, the arrangement of ragstone courses and tiles was regular but this was not the case for the two main walls of the building. It is likely, however, that these walls had undergone substantial rebuilding and patching during the life of the building and so the elevations as recorded (Figs 65–6) show the final state of these walls and not their original appearance.

Access to the building was from the east. The excavation of the rooms attached to the east wall of the temple, the so-called narthex, was hampered by the cramped conditions (see Fig 136) and the precise relationship of the sequence of walls there with the main building is not certain. It would appear that the two main east–west aligned walls of the temple were originally planned to extend further eastwards. A clay slab which covers these two extensions suggests that they were never completed. The broad narthex (Narthex 2) was added to the east end, but at what date is not clear. It is certain that it was in existence during the final years of the temple.

The floor levels in the narthex appear to have remained constant throughout the life of this part of the structure and never overlapped the stone sill of the entrance-way into the temple. This sill had fittings for two narrow doors which would have swung into the temple. At a later date, a timber sill was installed, probably to consolidate the eastern end of the later floors which had encroached upon and over the original stone threshold. It is not clear, however, if the same double-door arrangement was retained. Throughout the life of the temple, this doorway remained the only access into it.

Initially, as suggested by the sequence of events during its construction, the builders intended the temple to be of rectangular plan with an apse at the west end. The apse contained a raised, solid foundation, or dais, which was to be the focal point of the building. The addition of the buttresses was, as described above, a feature caused by necessity rather than design: the unstable conditions had already begun to affect the building. The rectangular body of the temple was divided into three by two low sleeper-walls on which were placed seven pairs of columns. These, no doubt, supported the roof timbers but, contrary to the reconstructions produced by Grimes and Sorrell in 1954 and 1957, even though the ground-plan appeared 'basilican' in style it is perhaps not necessary to reconstruct the elevation as basilican with a clerestory supported above these columns (see Brigham, *Appendix 3*).

The level of the floors of the two side aisles was higher than that of the central nave of the building. They matched the level of the door-sill, whereas the nave surface was *c* 0.9m below this level. Two steps gave access from the door-sill into the nave and, at the opposite end, two steps led up to the floor of the dais. This tripartite form with raised aisles conforms well with the general range of known mithraea but the excavators did not make this association until the discovery of the Head of Mithras (IX.38) on the last day of excavation. When the building was first discovered in 1952 the presence of the large block set into the face of the dais and an altar positioned on Floor 5, which covered the entire floor area of the building, led them to interpret the building as a temple, but to an unknown cult (see Figs 8–9

Just as the design of Roman forts follows certain basic principles, and yet no two forts are exactly the same, so too with mithraea. Certain elements in the ground-plan appear to have been necessary at the outset, eg the sunken nave, the focal point, the aisles for the location of benches or podia for the congregation, but there is no standard style or size, as the numerous mithraea from Ostia demonstrate. It is evident that these predetermined elements were related to the liturgy of the cult of Mithras itself. However, this is not the place to enter into a detailed discussion of the complex and, frequently, contentious debate concerning the nature of this secret religion. It is hoped that this publication will permit others more qualified in the intricate study of Roman Mithraism to apply the results of more recent research to the London building. Until then, however, and so that the function of this building can be put into its proper context, a very brief and cursory digression to examine Roman Mithraism is necessary.

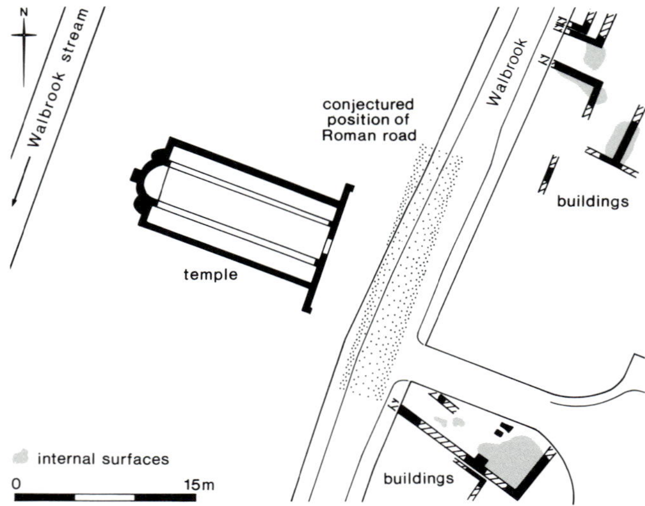

Fig 247 The temple with contemporary walls of a building to the east

Roman Mithraism

At the time when Grimes completed the excavation of the London Mithraeum in 1954 the accepted interpretation of the nature of Roman Mithraism was that proposed by Franz Cumont, the excavator of the mithraeum at Dura Europos, in what can still be regarded as the only comprehensive monograph on Mithraism (Cumont 1896–99). His main conclusion was that the Roman cult had its origins in Persian religion and that it spread westwards as a result of the patronage of the Roman military.

In the Roman world, Mithras was first mentioned by Plutarch in his life of Pompey the Great during the first century BC. While discussing the Cilician pirates he recorded that they followed certain mysteries, including Mithraism (*Pompey,* 24). The cult, however, did not become established in the empire until during the late first century AD, and thereafter it spread via the Roman military throughout the Balkans and the western Empire. As the Unconquered he appealed to the army, especially the officer ranks, and to merchants and traders. The cult spread quickly and by the third century was well established in parts of Britain (see below, *The temple as a mithraeum*).

According to the Cumont theory, his legend could be reconstructed from the iconography of the cult. He is said to have been born from a rock, naked except for his Phrygian cap, holding a dagger and torch. The principal feature of his life was the pursuit and capture of the primeval bull, which personified power, energy, vitality and life. After a struggle, Mithras dragged the bull to a cave, said to represent the celestial canopy, and killed the beast.

The ubiquitous bull-slaying scene *(Tauroctonos),* an icon central to the Roman cult, depicts the moment when the dagger was thrust into the bull. A dog and snake lapped up the blood and a scorpion attacked the genitals of the bull. Corn grew from the bull's tail. In attendance were two torchbearers, Cautes with a raised torch, and Cautopates with a lowered torch, signifying light and dark and symbolising the contrasts of the seasons and of night and day. In other, rarer scenes, Mithras is seen feasting with the Sun, who had sent him a raven to deliver the message to kill the bull. This feast was to have an important role in the liturgy of the Roman cult. Indeed, as his popularity spread, Mithras and the Sun became entwined and the address DEO INVICTO SOLI MITHRAE, 'To the Unconquered Sun, Mithras', appears on many dedicatory altars and reliefs, including one from the London Mithraeum (*Chapter 5, The finds catalogue, Period 2 finds, IX.47* and Fig 202).

The cult declined during the fourth century but it is debatable whether this was a result of the rise in Christianity or the preference for other pagan religions. This subject, too, is beyond the scope of this report (but see Sauer 1996), but it should be noted that the revised evidence presented below (see below, *The end of Mithraism at Walbrook* and *Appendix 1*) favours a non-iconoclastic end to the Mithraic occupation of the London temple.

During the last 25 years, however, the symbolism of the various elements of the Mithraic iconography have undergone vigorous reinterpretation, focusing upon astronomical and cosmological origins for these scenes. Prime among these has been the correlation of the Tauroctonos with the arrangement of constellations and their visibility at certain times of the year. The Tauroctonos, it is suggested, should be interpreted as a cosmic map portrayed as a narrative with Mithras, the Unconquered Sun, at its centre. Unfortunately this is not the place to examine the details of this exciting reinterpretation, but Beck (1984) provides an extremely useful summary of research into Roman Mithraism during the 1970s and early 80s, when this subject was being re-examined. For the uninitiated, who may require some balance to this study, Swerdlow (1990) is recommended for his less than enthusiastic interpretation of the cult.

Mithraea and Mithraic liturgy

For the purposes of this study on the London Mithraeum, what is known of the function of mithraea and the liturgical aspects of the cult practised within them should be briefly described. The form of the Roman mithraeum was a coalescence of a number of themes central to the cult, in particular the cave in which Mithras killed the bull and where he feasted with Sol, the banquet itself and the cult's grade system. Many mithraea are built below ground or, as in the case of the London building with its lowered floor, to create the impression of being in a confined subterranean space.

No doubt various ceremonies were performed in the mithraea and these must have included initiations of cult members. It is known, for example, that the followers of the cult were divided into seven ascending grades and that transfer from one grade to the next was by means of initiation. The names of these grades are given by St Jerome (*Ep* CVII.2 *ad Laetam*) and wall paintings in the mithraeum beneath the church of Santa Prisca in Rome (Vermaseren and van Essen 1965) and the nave mosaic on the floor of the mithraeum of Felicissimus at Ostia (Fig 248) supply us with details of their dress and the symbols of the grades. These can be summarised as follows. The first three grades, the lower orders of the cult, were:

(Corax) Raven. This was the first of the grades under the protection of Mercury, represented by a *caduceus.* A cup was its symbol although the meaning of this is not clear. St Augustine tells us that at the ritual feast in the mithraeum he wore a raven headdress and wings (Ambrosiaster, *Quaestiones veteris et novi testamenti* 113, 11). The grade is depicted in the Santa Prisca wall paintings by a man wearing a dark red tunic.

Nymphos (Male bride). To translate the name of this grade as 'bride' may be too simplistic. Women were excluded from the cult and so all the cult names were masculine. It is probable that this word conjures up a paradoxical entity in keeping with the multivalence which permeates the cult. The protective deity was, fittingly, Venus and the lamp, representing the light brought to the ceremonies by the grade. A painted inscription at Santa Prisca, with a *Nymphos* wearing a yellow veil and carrying a lamp, can be translated as 'Behold *Nymphos,* Hail *Nymphos,* Hail New Light'. A wall painting at Ostia shows a *Nymphos* wearing a short yellow tunic with red bands and carrying a red cloth in his hands.

Miles (Soldier). Under the protection of Mars, the symbols of this grade were the spear and helmet. It is possible to reconstruct the initiation ceremony into this grade from Tertullian (*De corona,* 15) and wall paintings in a mithraeum at Santa Maria di Capua Vetere near Naples (Vermaseren 1971, 36–42). The kneeling initiate, naked and blindfolded, was offered a crown on the point of a sword. Once crowned he was expected to order immediately that the crown be removed and placed on his shoulder, insisting that Mithras was his 'divine crown'. In both the Santa Prisca and Capua wall paintings, the *Miles* wears a white tunic with red stripes at the wrist and, in another Santa Prisca scene, he appears in a brown tunic.

The remaining four were the senior grades. They were:

Leo (Lion). Under the protection of Jupiter, indicated by a thunderbolt on the Felicissimus mosaic, the symbols for this grade were the fire shovel and the sistrum. St Augustine tells of initiates growling like lions and a figure wearing a lion headdress appears on a relief from Konjic, former Yugoslavia. Porphyry (*De antro nympharum,* 15) records that the Lion had his hands washed and his tongue anointed with honey and that, now in the grade representing the element of fire, he was not to touch water during the ceremonies. The Santa Prisca depictions show Lions, wearing red tunics with their sleeves striped with purple and also white tunics with red stripes on their sleeves, bringing in the food and paraphernalia for the ritual feast.

Perses (Persian). Honey was also used as a purifying agent during the initiation of this grade. The Santa Prisca paintings show him in a white tunic with yellow stripes at the wrist and, at Ostia, he appears in a red tunic with red bands. The grade came under the protection of the moon and its symbols were ears of corn and the sickle.

Heliodromus (Courier of the Sun). This grade came under the protection of the Sun. Its symbols were the attributes of the Sun God — the radiate crown, torch and whip. Its dress was a red tunic, yellow belt and a red cloak.

Pater (Father). The seventh and highest grade came under the protection of Saturn and was the most senior member of the Mithraic community, responsible for the organisation, teaching and discipline of that community. The Phrygian cap and the staff of authority were its symbols. At Santa Prisca he is shown dressed in a red tunic with long sleeves with yellow stripes, and a yellow belt.

The initiation of the *Miles* is described briefly above but other details also survive in literature. In connection with this grade, Ambrosiaster (*Quaestiones veteris et novi testamenti* 113, 11) tells that the initiate's hands were bound with chicken-gut, and that he was blindfolded and forced to leap across a trench of water. He was then freed of his bindings by a single stroke of a sword. In a passage not specific to any particular grade, Tertullian tells of 'the forgiveness of sins through baptism' and

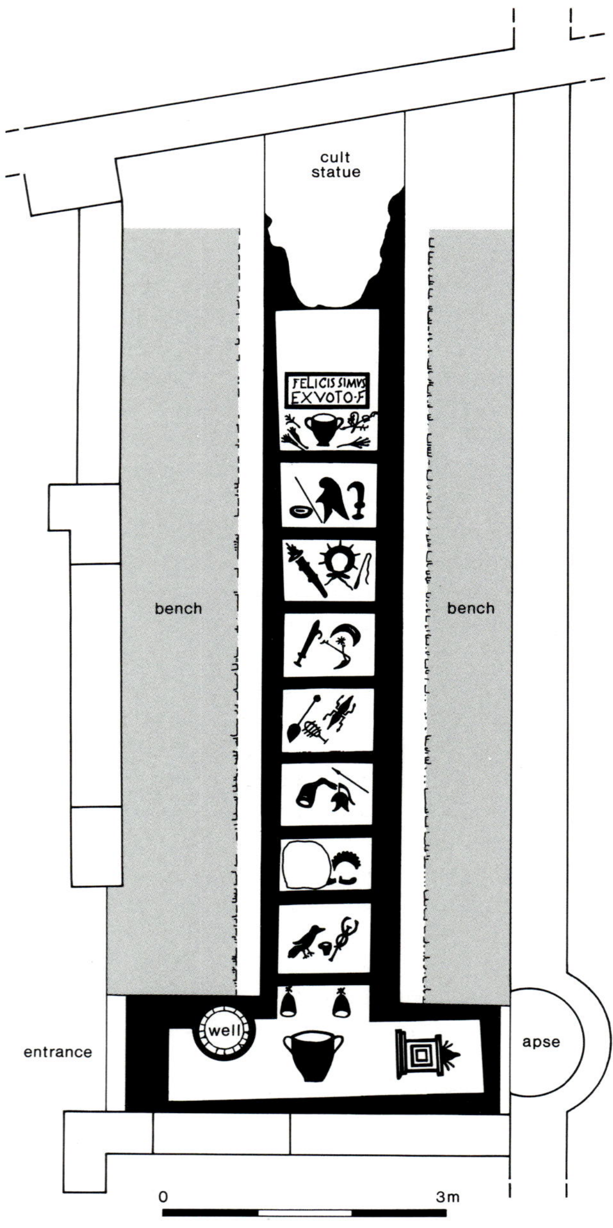

Fig 248 The mithraeum of Felicissimus, Ostia (after Becatti 1954)

recalls that the followers were marked on their foreheads with the 'sign of Mithras', that there was a mock resurrection and an offering of bread (*De praescriptione haereticorum,* 40). Justin also tells of bread and water being taken during initiations (*Apol* I, 66). Bread appears in the hands of the Lions bearing food on the Santa Prisca murals and the Konjic ritual feast relief also shows a quartered loaf of bread. Furthermore, Gregory Nazianzen mentions tortures, brandings and orgies in mithraea (*Orationes* IV *Adv Julianum,* Chapter LXXX; *Orationes* XXXIX *In sancta lumina,* Chapter V and *Ad Nemesium,* VII, 265 respectively).

The temple as a mithraeum

To return to the London building, it has been noted above that the Head of Mithras came from a small pit dug into the floor of Floor 5. As will be seen, the laying of this floor appears to have marked the end of the use of the building as a mithraeum and the introduction of a new pagan cult, perhaps Bacchus. Before examining this further it is necessary to describe the sequence and the dates of the alterations which took place within the building when it was in use as a mithraeum, any distinctive similarities with other mithraea other than the general arrangement, and any objects which might have had a liturgical function and their parallels with other mithraea.

The building was initially designed with a sunken nave and, on either side of this, a raised aisle or podium. The focal point of the temple was the dais at the far end of the nave immediately opposite the entrance. No doubt the dais would have supported the main cult statue of Mithras slaying the bull. A well was located at the west end of the south aisle. This general arrangement, with the inclusion of a water source or receptacle, conforms well with the design of the great majority of mithraea throughout the western empire. As we have already noted, however, no two mithraea are exactly the same and the London Mithraeum similarly does not have a direct parallel. However, there are certain features of the London building which are not common to the majority and which have few parallels. In particular, these are the apsidal end containing the solid dais and the sleeper-walls. The significance of these parallels is not certain and in the absence of a detailed study of Roman mithraea, another subject requiring a volume of its own, there is little further to do than to record here the details of these similarities.

It has been mentioned above that the original intention of the builders of the London Mithraeum was to give the building simply a round, apsidal end. However, buttresses had to be incorporated into the external design of the building, giving what must have been a bastion-like impression of the building when seen from the west. On the interior, however, the apse appeared to be recessed into the west end of the building and contained the solid dais for the cult image. This stood on a low plinth on the edge of the dais. Below this, in the face of the dais and just above the top step leading up from the floor of the nave, a square-shaped hole probably contained a smaller relief or dedicatory slab. It is probable that this was the Tauroctonos of Ulpius Silvanus (see below, *The end of Mithraism at Walbrook*).

Surprisingly, the inclusion of apses in the designs of mithraea is not a common feature. In general, the cult statue stood on a raised dais or plinth which projected from a straight wall into the nave or, in many cases, simply stood on the floor of the central nave. Mithraea with external projecting square or rectangular niches are known and it may be significant that they are found mainly in the north-west provinces, eg at Carrawburgh (third century: Richmond *et al* 1951), Rudchester (third century: Gillam 1954), Nida-Heddernheim (Nida I, second/third century; Nida II, early third century; Nida III, second century; Nida IV, second/third century: Huld-Zetsche 1986, 17–41: Fig 249) and Lillebonne (not dated: Gauthier 1982). The mithraeum at Lillebonne also had low sleeper-walls separating the nave from the aisles and on which columns once stood, another uncommon feature. However, the number of columns is not known.

Only one other mithraeum with a projecting apsidal end is known to the author and this is at Lambaesis, Algeria (Vermaseren 1956, no 138a: Fig 250). Built in the late second century, it was situated at the end of the 'Avenue Sacrée', east of the Asclepeium and its baths. The main rectangular component of this mithraeum measures 16.4m by 8.4m, the internal measurements of the apse are 2m in width, 1.8m deep with the top of the dais at 1m above the level of the nave floor. At London, the Mithraeum measures 18.3m by 7.6m. The apse is 3.1m across, 1.7m deep and 0.80m above the level of the nave floor. The Lambaesis building also had low sleeper-walls which supported four pairs of columns. Considering that there were seven grades in the cult, it is possible that the seven pairs of columns in the London Mithraeum held some significance. The mithraeum of Felicissimus at Ostia (Fig 248), with its mosaic covering the nave floor divided into eight sections (seven grades and one dedicatory panel), might suggest that the design of the London building also included some graphic representations of the grades associated with the pairs of columns. The floors of the London building were not elaborate, so any indication of the grades must have been painted on the columns or have been portable, such as painted panels fixed against the columns.

The floors of the nave of the London Mithraeum were raised on at least three occasions. The first (Floor 2) raised the nave to the level of the lower steps at both the west and east end. A small wooden box was sunk in the centre of the nave. The function of this is not clear. Floor 3 raised the level of the nave up to the top of the remaining steps, thus diminishing the sunken aspect of the building. A timber-lined channel was built into this floor against the face of the north

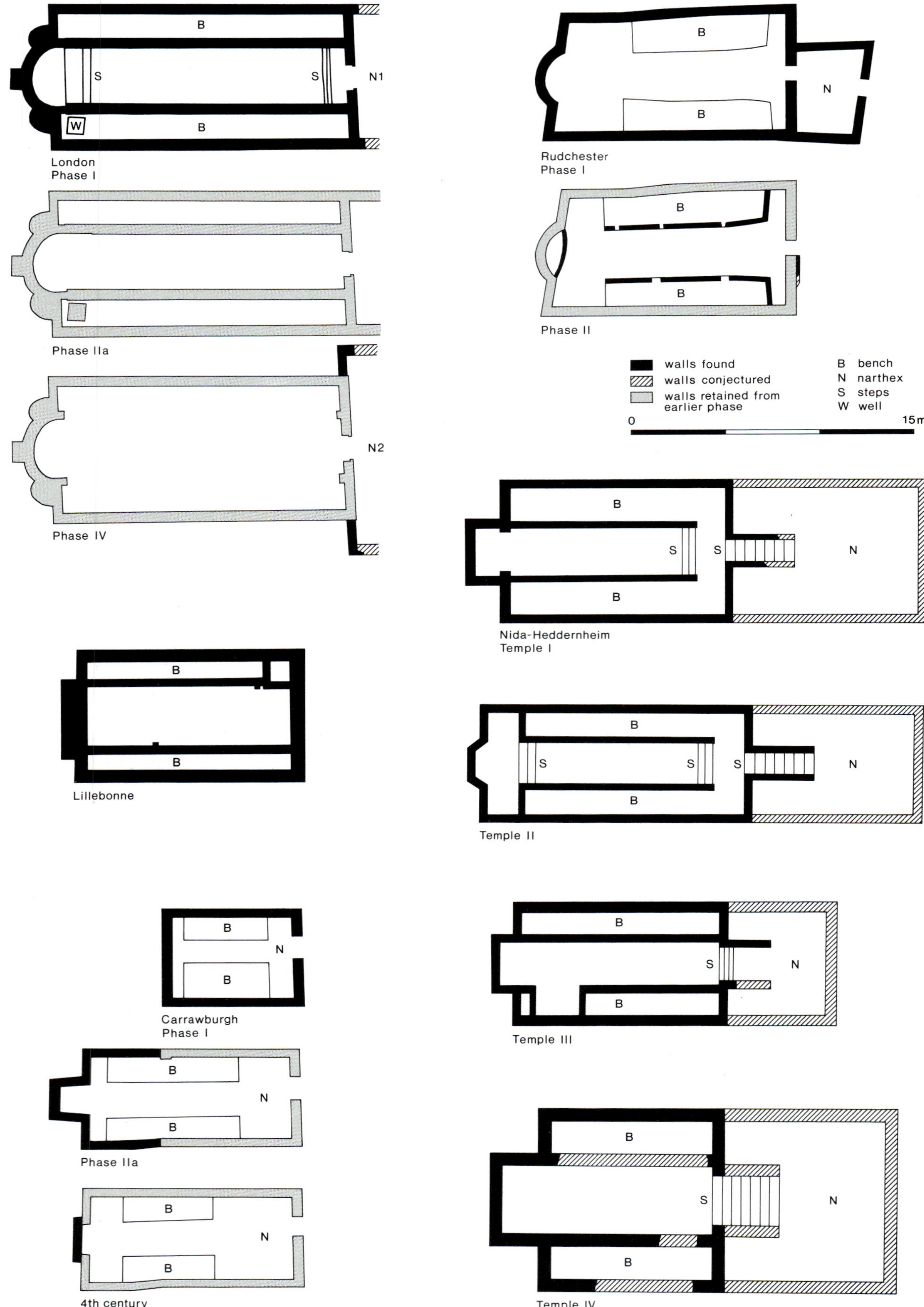

Fig 249 Comparative plans of mithraea in the north-west provinces

sleeper-wall. Presumably this was intended to contain water, but once again this is not certain. A coin of the obscure usurper Marius (AD 268) from the surface of Floor 3 provides *a terminus post* quem for later activity.

The laying of Floor 4 brought the level of the nave above that of the sleeper-walls. Evidently, it was felt necessary to retain the levels of the aisles, which had only partially been raised since the construction of the building. In order to retain Floor 4, squat walls were constructed between the columns, enclosing their bases. The single remaining fragment of one of these columns shows signs of a chiselled vertical groove which was aligned with the axis of the sleeper-wall. This would suggest that, before the squat walls were inserted, vertically set planks existed between the columns. These were probably the fronts of the benches arranged in the aisles, or the bases of rails or fences.

During the use of Floors 3 and 4, a large timber frame was constructed in the centre of the south aisle. The function of this is not clear but it looks as if it was intended to bear a considerable weight. It is possible that this was to support another cult image. It is interesting to note that Oikonomides, inspired by the relief from Bologna, Italy, has imaginatively suggested that the London temple would have housed a larger than life-sized Tauroctonos. This would have included the hand (IX.42) as the only surviving part of Mithras, the Head of Mithras (IX.38) reinterpreted as the head of Cautopates standing on the viewer's right looking up at Mithras, with the heads of Serapis (IX.40), reinterpreted by Oikonomides as Saturn, and Minerva (IX.39), as Luna, placed in a zone above the bull-slaying scene and the Water–deity (IX.44) below (Oikonomides 1975, 11-22).

Of the small finds from the Mithraeum which might have had a ceremonial significance, reference should be made to the stone lavers (IX.37 found with the hoard of sculptures and VII/IX/X.3), suitable receptacles for the water and honey used for purifying the initiates. The well in the south aisle, the small wooden box in Floor 3 and the channel in Floor 3 may all have played a similar role. Another item which may have been used in the initiations is the jet dagger handle (VIII.55). No doubt the silver canister (VIII/IX/X.1), if it was Mithraic (see Merrifield, *Appendix 2,* but also Henig, *Appendix 1,* who believes that it could belong to the later phase of the temple) would have played a very significant part in the ceremonies.

Perhaps the most telling indication that ritual meals of some sort were carried out in this building, other than the benches for reclining, is the presence in this and other mithraea of the detritus from these meals. At London a large number of chicken bones, especially cock birds, were scattered throughout the floor levels of the Mithraeum and also, though to a lesser extent, the post-Mithraeum floors. Chicken bones were also found in quantity at Carrawburgh (Richmond 1951, 16).

The end of Mithraism at Walbrook

The end of the worship of Mithras in this temple appears to have happened long before the building was finally abandoned. Whether this end also equates with the end of Mithraism in London, however, is not certain. It should be noted that, on the basis of current knowledge, the only evidence for the worship of Mithras in Londinium at any date appears in this temple. It might be argued that insufficient evidence has come from Londinium to inform us of its shrines and temples and that more might still await discovery, but it is a fact of the archaeological record at the time of writing that this building contains the only Mithraic assemblage from Roman London.

During the first quarter of the fourth century, three definable events took place in the Mithraeum:

1 part of the building suffered a collapse
2 the colonnades were removed, resulting in a more open plan with one floor (Floor 5) covering the entire building other than the dais
3 a number of cult icons were buried in this floor and a new arrangement was installed at the west end of the building

First, the building finally succumbed to the unstable ground conditions. The south wall leant outwards and, in what must have been a single devastating moment, the south-west corner of the building separated from the rest causing a deep fissure. This crack was so wide that it must have caused the partial collapse of the roof in that part of the building. This in turn may have precipitated a domino-like collapse of the columns on the south side. For how long the building showed signs of collapse before this moment is not certain. The exterior and interior faces of both long walls of the building show many signs of repair and patching, leading to the uneven disposition of the tile coursing, but it is possible that much of this work was carried out when the south-west corner was repaired. It is evident that, from the position of the major repairs midway along the lengths of both walls and the discrepancies in levels between the east and west ends of the building, the west end had subsided into the soft underlying ground whereas the east end, on more stable ground, had remained almost level. The building, therefore, may also have broken its back as well as suffering the major collapse in the south-west corner.

Apart from the patching and repair of the long walls, the rebuilding involved filling the hole in the south-west corner at ground level with a single column drum. This must have necessitated the removal of masonry from the exterior face so that the column could underpin the wall. It has often been suggested that this column drum came from the interior of the building. However, it is too narrow to be part of the colonnade of the Mithraeum. Its source is unknown.

The second major change occurred in the interior of the building. The columns were dismantled and the resulting holes between the squat walls were packed with rubble. Only one small fragment of the original colonnade survives (VIII.43). It can only be assumed that these columns were removed for reuse elsewhere. A search of the Museum of London archaeological archive for similar architectural fragments has produced none of similar dimensions.

The removal of the columns led to the laying of Floor 5, which produced, for the first time, an open hall-like structure. Some temporary roof supports may have been included at this stage, as indicated by the groups of post-holes along the line of the old sleeper-walls, but these would not have been as substantial as the colonnades. Indeed, since the colonnades had served a structural function this would also suggest that a new roof structure was installed. Brigham's new reconstruction of the late building shows the roof supported on joists which run from one wall to the other. Grimes was not certain how such a space could be covered over, but recent discoveries on the riverfront of structural timbers even longer than those required to span the width of the temple at Walbrook show that the roofing of this structure would not have caused any problems.

Finally, once the new Floor 5 had been laid two new altars, of which only one was found, were installed at the west end of the building. It may be significant that the tops of these matched the top of the cult plinth on the dais and that their position in front of the dais formed a square with this plinth. It is possible, therefore, that rather than being altars these stones and the plinth served as the base for a platform or canopy *(baldachino)*, a regular way of housing a god in a pagan shrine (see Henig, *Appendix 1*). This would imply that the original cult images at this end of the Mithraeum had been removed. It is probably no coincidence, therefore, to discover that a number of sculptures, the heads of Mithras, Serapis and Minerva, the large hand, the forearm from a Tauroctonos and the Mercury group, in addition to a stone laver, had been buried in pits cut into the surface of Floor 5. Furthermore, to this list should probably be added the three sculptures found in 1889, the Genius, the Water-deity and the Ulpius Silvanus Tauroctonos. It is argued above (*Chapter 4, Modern disturbance in the temple*) that these were discovered during the excavation in 1889 of the foundation stanchion which penetrated the floors of the temple immediately to the west of the 1954 discoveries. If it is accepted that this was the original findspot of these sculptures the similarity in the dimensions of the Ulpius Silvanus relief with the square hole in the face of the dais might not be simple coincidence. Ulpius Silvanus is generally accepted to have been a *Pater* of a Mithraic community (see Vermaseren 1974, 31), in which case, if his relief was originally in such a prominent position in the building under the main cult sculpture and at the

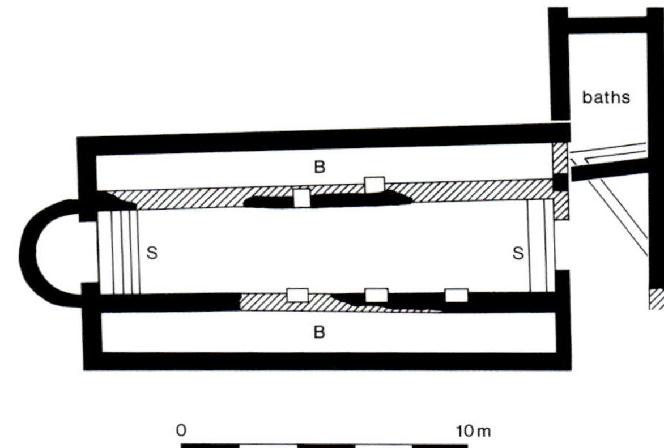

Fig 250 The mithraeum at Lambaesis

top of the steps leading up to the dais, his role might have been more than just one of the leaders of the community. One possibility is that he was responsible for the building of the Mithraeum.

The reasons for the burial of these sculptures has often been blamed upon the Christian community, or at least an anti-pagan policy of the government. This argument is based on two strands of evidence. First, the date of the burial during the first quarter of the fourth century might give a context for an anti-pagan policy, and secondly, the presence of what appears to be an axe-cut on the side of the head of Mithras, separating it from its shoulders, might suggest iconoclasm. However, if the sequence of events described above is taken into account, there may be a much simpler explanation for the deposition of these sculptures. They may simply have been buried with reverence and respect by Mithraists or other followers of a pagan cult when the building was converted into a hall-like structure.

The alterations to the Mithraeum during the second half of the third century show that the building was being maintained by a Mithraic community. How large or enthusiastic this community was during the period when the building underwent its collapse and restoration cannot, however, be quantified. The archaeological record shows that, following the restoration of the building, it continued to be used by a pagan community throughout the fourth century (see Henig, *Appendix 1*). Logic would suggest that those who laid Floor 5 and installed the new arrangements at the west end of the temple may also have been responsible for clearing out the icons of the old cult and burying them in their new shrine.There is no need to suppose a Christian presence, which according to the archaeological record was even rarer in Londinium than Mithraism, and no need even to consider the presence of any threat causing a panic burial of the cult icons. Such panic burials, no doubt, did take place, as has been suggested by the excavators of the hoard of 24 pieces of marble statuary buried in a shrine at Tomis (Constantza, Romania). It has been suggested that their burial took place sometime around AD 250 to

260 at a time of massive Gothic incursions into the Empire (Canarache 1963, 139). Nothing similar can be claimed as the cause of the burial for the London sculptures.

Finally, if the sculptures were buried by people who were not concerned with the Mysteries of Mithras but who had sufficient sensibility, awe and fear to respect the power of the god and those deities worshipped with him in the old temple, it would not be necessary to explain why they were never recovered. Their burial in the floor of the new temple was intended to be their final resting place.

The temple in the fourth century

The use of the building in the fourth century and the probability that it was the cult of Bacchus which was introduced into this building is discussed below by Henig *(Appendix 1)*.

The interior plan of the building described above, with Floor 5 extending across its entire width, was maintained throughout the fourth century until the final abandonment of the building. At least four new floors were laid during this period, resulting in the channelled stone altars in front of the dais being covered almost to their maximum height. The final floors (Floors 8 and 9) reached up to the floor level of the dais. This was raised at some time during this period by a layer of *opus signinum.*

The presence of timbers running down the length of the building, approximately over the original lines of the hidden sleeper-walls, might suggest some form of internal partitioning either by screens or rails. It may be that their coincidence of position with the earlier sleeper walls resulted from them being aligned with the square pilasters on either side of the dais and the entrance-way.

At the east end, the raising of the floors partially covered the site of the burial of the sculptures and brought the floor levels above that of the stone sill of the entrance-way. A new timber sill was installed and a rough step-like arrangement was constructed to lead up from the entrance into the building — a complete reversal of the original plan of the building.

Unfortunately, the dates for these specific alterations cannot be determined. The ceramic assemblages include fourth-century material and, in the case of the final floors, some fabrics belong to industries which might have continued into the early fifth century (see above *Chapter 5, The finds catalogue, Period 2 finds Group X: pottery,* especially X.52). This distinctive, though unidentifiable, pedestalled cup from the latest phase of the temple is unlike any other vessel yet found in London and no parallels can be found for it elsewhere. It has been tentatively suggested that it belongs to a non-Roman tradition.

The last years of the temple

It is possible to summarise the final years of this building in just a few words. There is no evidence for a violent end to its life. Although interior fittings, including perhaps any large cult statues, may have been removed the building was simply left to decay. The digging of the Group XI pit may indicate that the abandoned building had been briefly occupied, but it does not appear to have been occupation of any significance.

The final floor of the building was covered with decayed plaster and building rubble. The walls and foundations remained intact with no evidence of robbing. It is likely, therefore, to have survived as a free-standing ruin into the post-Roman period, making it eligible to be added to the growing list of Roman structures which would have remained visible amid the undergrowth in the walled city during the Saxon period.

Appendix 1 The temple as a *bacchium* or *sacrarium* in the fourth century

by Martin Henig

The form of the late 'temple' was conditioned by the survival of the outer walls of the Mithraeum, but the space within would appear to have been used somewhat differently (see *Appendix 3, New reconstructions of the third-century mithraeum and the fourth-century* bacchium *or* sacrarium, by Trevor Brigham). Worship was centred to the front of the apse where there appears to have been a low platform, presumably for the cult image, surmounted by a *baldachino.* This was a regular way of housing a god in a pagan shrine, as many works of art attest (see Henig 1990). The double rows of columns down the nave were not replaced in the rebuild; however, the tripartite arrangement seems to have been maintained as attested by two parallel beams, perhaps for low screens. This, together with the use of C306 bowls before and after the break in occupation, could be adduced as evidence for the continuity of Mithraism here, though as we shall see the ceremonies of worshippers of Bacchus, who will be proposed as the new tenants of the site, also consisted largely of sacred feasts. Collins-Clinton (1977, 23) even suggests that the arrangement of couches in the mithraeum at Cosa may have been the inspiration for the couch in the nearby shrine of Liber (Bacchus).

Evidence for a fairly radical change in the nature of the cult is supported first by the treatment of the Mithraic sculptures and then by new cult material from the upper levels of the temple. The Mithraic sculptures were buried towards the entrance of the temple but, as noted above, they were not abused. This suggests that the new owners of the site were not Mithraists, but equally they did not hate idols: they were not Christians. Their behaviour, relegating unwanted religious items to a sacred repository or *favissa,* was normal throughout pagan antiquity. There may, however, have been an additional nuance in this particular case, as we shall see.

Not one of the later sculptures is Mithraic. Most exotic is the roundel depicting the Danubian riders with a female figure (goddess) between them before a table on which lies a fish. In the lower register, imagery includes a hound and a cantharus. Clearly we are dealing with a Mystery Cult with chthonic (underworldly) associations, but the imagery does not seem to me any more Mithraic than, say, Bacchic, and Marjorie Mackintosh rightly compares such rites of this cult known from art with those shown on the Mysteries Mosaic in Trier (Mackintosh 1995, 58–64). The plaque could have been imported to the 'temple' by a votary from the Lower Danube in either phase or have been associated with a nearby independent shrine of the Castores, as a relief of a Dioscurus was found nearby.

Much more unequivocal evidence for a new dedication is the marble statuette of Bacchus with his retinue inscribed with the acclamation *Hominibus Bagis Bitam*, 'You give life to wandering men!'. This was presumably a votive gift. The dating of the group has been disputed but it should be pointed out that marble statuettes of Bacchus have been found in fourth-century contexts in Britain, at the temple on Maiden Castle (Henig 1983) and in the grave of one of the owners of the Spoonley Wood villa (Henig 1993, 3–4, no. 1), and at the Chiragan villa in southern Gaul (Hannestad 1994, 134, 136, fig. 89). Elaine Gazda, in discussing other Late Antique marble groups, mentions the London Mithraeum group and places it with them (Gazda 1981, 167, n. 58). She also cites the diatribe against idols by Theodoret, Bishop of Cyrrhus between 423 and *c* 466, who singles out figures of Dionysus (Bacchus) 'that limb-loosener and effeminate creature' *(Ellenikon therapeutike pathematon* 3, 79–84).

There are two broken torsos of Bacchus, one from inside the 'temple' and the other outside. It is thought that they were of earlier date, perhaps late second or third century. They are so similar that it is tempting to think that breakage in this manner, preserving the generative parts of the image, was no coincidence. Perhaps the answer lies not in iconoclasm but in Bacchic myth and ritual. The cult was in essence connected with the annual vegetative cycle and with the natural forces of generation. There were dark and disturbing elements in the cult. For example, dismemberment played a part, as readers of Euripides' *Bacchae* will know; the followers of the god (his *thiasos*) dismembered living creatures, which in some sense were regarded as substitutes for the god himself (see Thomson 1979). Less well known is that in an Orphic story Bacchus had himself been dismembered by the Titans and was later resurrected as Dionysus Zagraeus (see Roscher 1937, cols 532–8), a myth which seems to be recalled on the Littlecote mosaic (Walters 1984). Should we see here such a ritual of death and rebirth being re-enacted with old, discarded figures of the god? Incidentally, as far as the users of the building were concerned, there may have been thoughts of the other buried statuary being in some way resurrected too.

Like Mithraism, the cult of Bacchus demanded a building, either in a house (see Parrish 1995) or purpose-built, where dining and revelry could take place. It was called a *bacchium, sacrarium,* or *stibadium* (Collins-Clinton 1977, 16–23). The last takes its name from the semi-circular couch *(stibas)* on which revellers reclined in some such meeting place. In the

Walbrook example the couches were likely to have been straight, following earlier Mithraic examples (see Collins-Clinton 1977 19–20, n 27). For the Walbrook building, the term *bacchium* or *sacrarium* might be less ambiguous.

It is very tempting to attribute the actual use of the silver bowl and the casket and infusor to the late, post-Mithraic period of the Bacchic *stibadium.* Although the silver objects date to the later third century, the casket shows considerable wear and signs of repair. My late friend Ralph Merrifield, with whom I was engaged in fruitful correspondence just before his death, agreed that the infusor was filled with 'a dry herbal preparation which would produce a drug of known strength and efficiency' but preferred to leave it in the context of the Mysteries of Mithras (see *Appendix 2*). However, the iconography of the casket with its wild and exotic beasts, felines and elephants still seems to me to fit what we know of the Bacchic cult better than that of Mithras, for these are the creatures especially connected with Dionysus and associated with his Indian Triumph, so often shown on sarcophagi like the famous example in the Walters Art gallery, Baltimore (Richmond 1950, 30–1, pl iii). It may be regarded as a miniature *cista mystica,* a little box containing sacred things used especially in the Dionysiac mysteries — according to one story the heart of Zagraeus, collected by Athena, but in actuality a phallus or a snake (Lenormant 1887); here the infusor, surely used for lacing wine with a measured quantity of narcotics, offers another symbol of life very much at home in the Bacchic worship. As Professor George Thomson has shown, the 'life' offered on the inscription was probably not so far removed from the mind-blowing, drug-induced 'mystical' experiences of the 1960s. He and Dr Bernard Barnett have suggested that the physical manifestations of Bacchic ecstasy, as shown in literature and art, agree with the symptoms of strychnine poisoning: 'if the wine was laced without the novice's knowledge, he would believe the added potency to be inherent in the wine itself, and the effect would be, according to the dosage, either euphoric or traumatic' (Thomson 1979, 442–3). However, the plants that the Greeks called *strychnos* were not the tropical vines from which strychnine is derived but covered several species, including perhaps black nightshade and the highly poisonous thorn-apple, and it may be fruitless to speculate about the exact chemical composition of the ecstasy-inducing 'herbs' (see Sherratt 1995, 29–32 for the infusing of drugs and Goodman *et al* 1995 for the use of drugs in antiquity). The bowl reminds us of the much earlier vessel being offered to a votary (young satyr) by Silenus on the famous fresco of the mid-first century BC at the Villa of the Mysteries, just outside Pompeii (Lehmann 1962, 66–7, pl xii). However, I suspect the recipient of the bowl is not merely looking at his reflection but is about to drink the — drugged — wine.

Whether the wine was regularly drunk from the silver bowl is another matter. In many instances it will have been decanted. Among the vessels, C306 bowls have been found in the Mithraic phase as stated above but are especially common later. They are not well made and suggest drinking ceremonies in which the pots were often broken, either accidentally or deliberately. The ceramic evidence, which includes Alice Holt Farnham and Oxfordshire wares, shows that such rituals perhaps continued as late as the fifth century.

As a later fourth-century Mithraeum, the building by the Walbrook would have been anomalous in Britain, though Mithras certainly continued to be worshipped in continental Europe during the century (Merkelbach 1984, 245–50; Walters 1974, 3–30; Sauer 1996). The form of the structure is paralleled by the so-called church at Silchester (Fig 251), sited near the basilica,

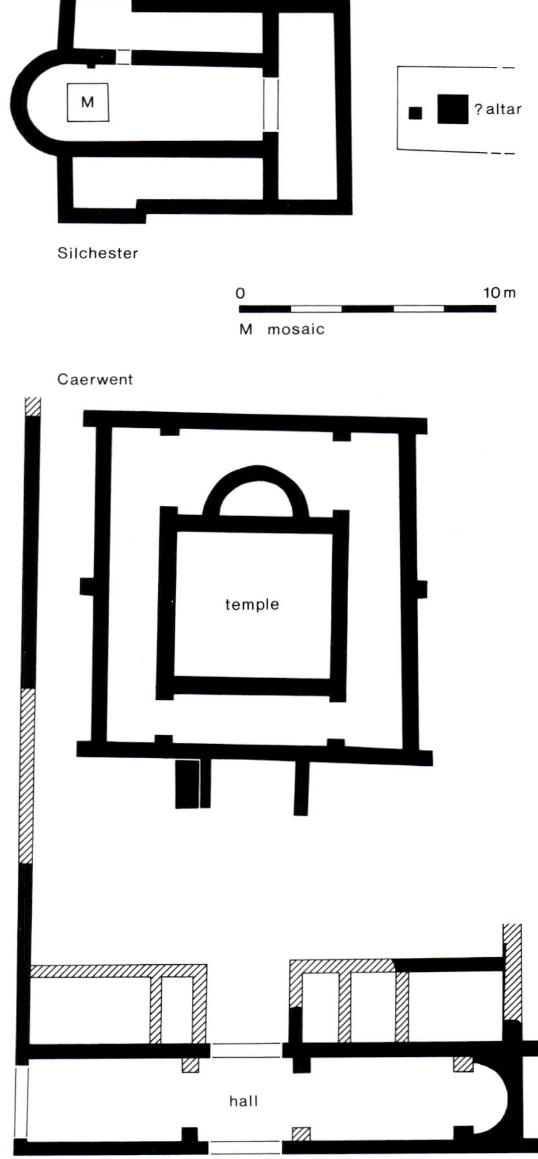

Fig 251 Late Roman buildings at Silchester and Caerwent

where I follow Anthony King (1983) in doubting any Christian connection. It had an apsidal west end before which was a square of mosaic corresponding to the platform in the Walbrook building. Perhaps an image was placed there. In front of the Silchester building was a tiled base which I am tempted to see as the seating for an altar. No cult material of any sort is recorded here, and it is possible to see the building used for civic ceremony, rather like the hall with an eastern apse placed across the entrance to the fourth-century temple at Caerwent (*Britannia* xvi, 1985, 260–1, fig 8). With regard to function the best parallel may be a third building with a triconch west end; this is the famous hall with Orpheus mosaic dated to *c* AD 360 at Littlecote, Wiltshire (Walters 1984), associated with a villa and surely a Bacchic *stibadium.* Here the complex imagery is related to Bacchus and Apollo as well as to Orpheus, who reconciles these two powers. Bacchus was venerated in his Orphic aspect as Zagraeus, and a bronze appliqué found nearby shows a bust of the young god emerging from a calyx of leaves (Walters and Henig 1988). It is apposite here to mention the Thetford Treasure (Johns and Potter 1983); the building where the relevant *collegium* of Faunus met has not been preserved, but clearly we have here spoons and other objects which provide clear evidence for a Bacchic-type cult engaged in eating and drinking in late fourth-century East Anglia. It is assumed to have used a temple, presumably of Romano-Celtic type, unfortunately destroyed when a factory was built.

Outside Britain, a *triclinium* of a villa at Las Coperos, Spain, was decorated with a mosaic showing rather staid votaries of Bacchus (Blazquez *et al* 1989, 26–7, pl 12) but the best parallel is the fourth-century shrine of *Liber Pater* (Bacchus) set in a reused building in the forum at Cosa (Fig 252) (Collins-Clinton 1977). Here the cult image of a youthful Bacchus set upon a pedestal survived. It was set against the back wall but spur walls show it was given an architectural setting. The space within the shrine was divided by partition walls, roughly dividing the area into three sections as in London (Collins-Clinton 1977, 10). Collins-Clinton (1977, 21–3) cites other Bacchic meeting places at Athens, Pegamum and Magnesia on the Meander. David Parrish has suggested that certain works of art from domestic contexts show continuity of Dionysiac/Bacchic cult (Parrish 1995).

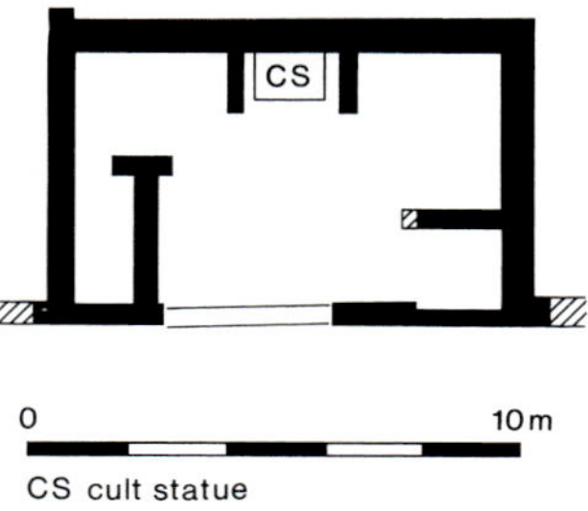

Fig 252 The temple of Liber Pater *at Cosa*

Especially notable are the mosaics depicting the birth and triumph of the god in a house at Nea Paphos, Cyprus (Parrish 1995, 323-6), while as late as the sixth century a mosaic floor showing scenes of the cult from Sarrin, Syria, may indicate that the Dionysiac religion was 'still vital and active' in the provincial eastern zone at a late date (Parrish 1995, 308-13). An interesting feature at Cosa was the presence of ceramic vessels with appliqués of the sort generally associated with Sabazios. These are also recorded near the Walbrook Mithraeum but in a pre-Mithraic context (Toynbee 1964, 395, pl lxxxviiid).

I suspect that a cult connected with Bacchus and Sabazios existed through the third century in the vicinity of the Mithraeum, alongside other shrines which may have included one devoted to the Dioscuri, Castor and Pollux. Mithraea were often situated in the near vicinity of other shrines, the Altbachtal of Trier being a well known example, and friendly relations probably existed between the polytheistic devotees of various gods even where there was not a degree of assimilation (Walters 1974, 42–9). Bacchus was popular and widely venerated in Roman Britain (Hutchinson 1986) and attested in third-century London by openwork appliqué (Hall 1982) and the Leadenhall Street mosaic (Smith 1977, 109 no 8, pl 6.xxi b), among other examples. When the Mithraeum was abandoned such neighbouring cults would without doubt have cast covetous eyes on a vacant site which had a reparable building. So the new occupants need not have been total newcomers to the Walbrook valley, nor lacking in sympathy with what had gone before. In a world of syncretism Mithras was not so much ousted as replaced by another manifestation of the divine.

Appendix 2 A Mithraic interpretation for the silver casket and strainer

by Ralph Merrifield

I have never been convinced by Professor Toynbee's interpretation either of the way in which the strainer was used or of the significance of the figures in relief on the casket that contained it (Figs 208–10). In lectures and (briefly) on museum labels I have always favoured an alternative hypothesis, though I have not hitherto set out the case for this on paper. I did, however, put at least the first part of my argument, relating to the use of the strainer, to Professor Toynbee herself, and it is only fair to say that she rejected it (Toynbee 1986, 49–50), though the reasons she gave for doing so were partly based on a misunderstanding. I have since developed further the alternative interpretation of the iconography of the container, which gives some support to my suggestion of the purpose of the strainer. I am convinced that this is the most important single find from the Mithraeum, and the one most likely to contribute to our further understanding of Mithraism. I make no such claim for my own hypothesis, but I believe its full publication might stimulate debate among scholars better qualified to discuss this difficult subject, if only in irritation at my presumption.

First, then, let us consider the use of the strainer, which I have always preferred to call an infusor. I do not think it would be possible at normal temperatures to strain honey through the tiny holes in the base, thereby separating it from fragments of honeycomb and other impurities. It is also unlikely to have been thinned by dissolving in water, since the purpose of using honey for purification of the Lion Grade was as a substitute for water, which was considered incompatible with the Lions, who were associated with the element of fire (Vermaseren 1963, 146–7). I suggest that the true use of the strainer is indicated by the triple bar at the top, which is identical with those of Roman measures of volume for dry, loose material such as grain. This had the practical purpose of ensuring that the same quantity filled the measure each time without compression, as would happen if the measure were loosely filled, with any surplus brushed off at the level of the bars. The strainer was therefore a precise measure, I suggest, for a dry herbal preparation which would produce a drug of known strength and efficacy if the strainer were suspended in the correct volume of water. I did not suggest, as Jocelyn Toynbee supposed, that the infusion was made in the container, which is hardly bigger than the strainer itself. There was, however, a silver bowl that was apparently concealed in the north wall of the Mithraeum with the strainer and its container, evidently inverted over the latter (Fig 211). The strainer in its container escaped destruction by a hairsbreadth when the temple wall was lowered to accommodate the nineteenth-century foundation that overlay it; the bowl, however, was less fortunate, and only portions of the side and rim remained. The most important part of this infusion kit was clearly the measure, which would have been difficult to replace, and therefore had its special container. It is believed that the primary initiation into the Mithraic society involved the apparent death and resurrection of the initiate, who first had to endure ordeals by heat and cold. Sometimes, it appears, he was temporarily buried below ground level, and a pit in the Mithraeum at Carrawburgh may have been used for this purpose. It is clear that initiation was a painful and dangerous business, and oblivion by means of a powerful drug would not only produce the appearance of death, but also perhaps give the candidate a better chance of survival.

The dramatic emergence of the revived initiate appears on both the lid and side of the silver container, where he is depicted being helped out of a wheeled box — a symbol of his rebirth that may actually illustrate how this rite was performed (Fig 209). The initiate is shown more clearly on the side of the container, where his head seems to be covered by a cloth that descends to the base of his neck, presumably the veil of the *Nymphus* which he has lifted from his face on regaining consciousness. He is being helped out by a man wearing a pointed hat, who with his right hand clasps that of the emerging initiate, while something that might be a purse is passing from one hand to the other. It is possible that three separate events have here been merged together: the emergence of the initiate, the oath he takes while clasping the hand of his mentor, and the payment of his entrance fee. The man receiving him has a sword or dagger, and could be a senior member of the grade of Soldiers that the initiate is about to join, but is more probably of a superior grade such as Persian or even the *Pater* himself, who was responsible for dispensing initiation to the various grades and for accepting new members (Vermaseren 1959, 153). According to Vermaseren a sword was required at several stages in the initiation, so the *Pater* as mystagogue might well wear one (ibid, 132–3, 145). A special emblem both of this grade and of the Persian, however, was the sickle, shown in paintings of Santa Prisca with a sword-like hilt (ibid, 149, fig 59; 152, fig 62). Fine detail on the silver container has been lost by corrosion, and it is just possible that there was originally a crescentic extension downward near the point of the weapon worn by the figure receiving the initiate, indicating that it represents a sickle, emblem of the harvest of new recruits that is being reaped.

The very similar scene on the lid adds little more information. In this case a third figure, naked and nondescript, assists by raising part of the wheeled

Sun, and it is possible that his round headdress or wig is intended to represent the nimbus worn by the Mithraist dressed for this part. For this is no divine manifestation, but a very human runner. Nowhere in fact on the casket is there any attempt to depict the divine or even the supernatural, and only in the representation of Lions and Griffins as real animals rather than men in costume, and in the weird landscape with other animals, is there any departure from a sober depiction of ritual as it might actually have been performed in the place where the casket was made, considered by Toynbee to be somewhere in the eastern Mediterranean. A Lion represented as the animal is shown using a pestle with his forepaws in a mixing-vessel at Sarmizagetusa (Vermaseren 1963, 147, fig 58)

At worst we can identify five of the seven Mithraic grades in the characters represented — *Cryphii* or *Gryphi* (replacing Ravens), *Nymphi,* Soldiers, Lions and the *Pater* on his throne. Persis (the Persian) can probably be recognised in the second (standing) mystagogue seen receiving a *Nymphus* emerging from his box, while the curved object behind him might represent the crescent moon and the weapon at his side a sickle, both of which are emblems of that grade (Vermaseren 1963, 149, fig 59). Acceptance of the figure with globe and (?)torch as *Heliodromus* would complete the seven.

The other animals and the strange trees with unrecognisable flowers seem to have sprung from a rich tradition of animal legends that might be African rather than European or Asiatic. Their sole purpose here may be to stress the conflict that is an essential part of nature. One scene twice repeated, and centrally placed on the lid, may, however, display symbolism that is commonly associated with a Mithraic deity. The group consists of the forepart only of an elephant subduing another animal with its trunk and tusks, while a large snake is coiled round its right foreleg and body, looping over its head. Both extremities of the snake are concealed on the far side of the elephant's body. If, as it appears, this was a three-sided contest, it is the only one represented; all other conflicts convey the dualism that is the dominant principle of Mithraic philosophy. It is possible, therefore, that the snake is not attacking the elephant, but is the symbol of eternity commonly shown encircling Aion (Persian, *Zervan),* the Time God, also identified with Chronos or Saturn. This primeval deity was often represented in Mithraea with a ferocious lion's head, but there seems to be no parallel for the substitution of an elephant. Nevertheless, the association of a symbol of eternity with an image centrally placed on the lid, might suggest that here some important legend of a primeval contest is depicted.

Two parts of the interpretation suggested here require special scrutiny by those with a wider knowledge of Mithraism, for if correct they appear to throw a new and perhaps unexpected light on the roles of two Mithraic grades in the process of primary initiation and subsequent promotion. First, the *Cryfii,* whatever the derivation of their name, seem sometimes by the late third or fourth century because of its similarity to *Gryphi* to have been regarded as Griffins and disguised accordingly, replacing the Raven costume. Their concern with the primary initiation was limited to its first phase, culminating in the ritual 'death' of the initiate, in which they acted as porters and general attendants under the instruction of the mystagogue. Those permitted to take part in the second phase of 'rebirth', revealed themselves by discarding their costume of death, and were presumably thereby promoted to *Nymphus,* the grade eligible for initiation. That is what appears to be happening in sequence on the lid of the silver box.

Secondly, the Lions in their animal form appear to be in conflict with Soldiers in two separate scenes on the wall of the box, though unfortunately in one of these the Lion is almost obliterated by corrosion holes. As there is unlikely to have been real antagonism between two grades of the same society, it must be assumed that this was a ritual struggle in which the courage of the Soldiers was being tested by their seniors, presumably with a view to promotion. Whether this was a real fight as depicted or some more subtle test administered by the Lions can only be surmised, although the former cannot be ruled out. Presumably the Soldiers were equipped with blunt weapons, like the unsharpened dagger found in the west bank of the Walbrook outside the London Mithraeum (XIII.20), and the outcome was probably predetermined in favour of the Lions. In each scene a Soldier has been overthrown and seems about to succumb to a Lion's attack. He may, however, be destined for promotion because he did not give ground. Whatever the nature of the test, it seems likely to have been a necessary preliminary to becoming a Lion, and it is interesting that the Lions themselves apparently administered it.

Two assumptions have been made: firstly, that the figures represented on the counter are meaningful, though the meaning may not be obvious, and secondly that they should be interpreted in Mithraic terms. As we have seen, this is quite possible, though in one or two doubtful cases requires some exercise of the imagination. It can hardly be doubted, however, that the main subject of the silver container is Mithraic initiation, and from this the identification of several Mithraic grades performing their generally accepted roles logically follows. The idea that the pre-initiation grade of 'Hidden Ones' is represented by griffins will be reluctantly approved, since it depends on a bad pun and on the development of a new significance for these creatures, from guardians of treasure and tombs to symbols of the death that must precede rebirth as an initiate. An alternative explanation of their presence, however, is hard to find.

Appendix 3 New reconstructions of the third-century Mithraeum and fourth-century *bacchium* or *sacrarium*

by Trevor Brigham

The new reconstructions of the Mithraeum show the structure at two stages in its evolution: the primary stage, and the final rebuilding. The eastern narthex, whose complete plan is not known, and whose certain interpretation remains unclear, is shown as a foundation only in the later reconstruction; similarly, two foundations below the narthex which project from the east wall in the initial phase are shown but no attempt is made to interpret them. The intention of the reconstructions was simply to show the main structure.

The reconstructions differ from previous attempts in one important respect: there is no clerestory. The two main purposes of a clerestory are to introduce light and height into an aisled building. In the case of a mithraeum, it is generally assumed that light was largely excluded. Extra headroom was also gained in this instance by ground reduction, so that the central aisle was reached by two steps leading down from the main entrance. The only grounds for introducing a clerestory would therefore be for decorative purposes. However, the lack of internal supports within the structure following the removal of the aisle colonnades demonstrates that the building in its later stages is unlikely to have had a clerestory roof for structural reasons. There is therefore no need to postulate such a feature in the early period either.

The principal elements of the two reconstructions will now be discussed.

Primary phase

The interior was dominated by twin colonnades set on masonry stylobates. The diameter of the column bases suggests that they supported dwarf columns, probably

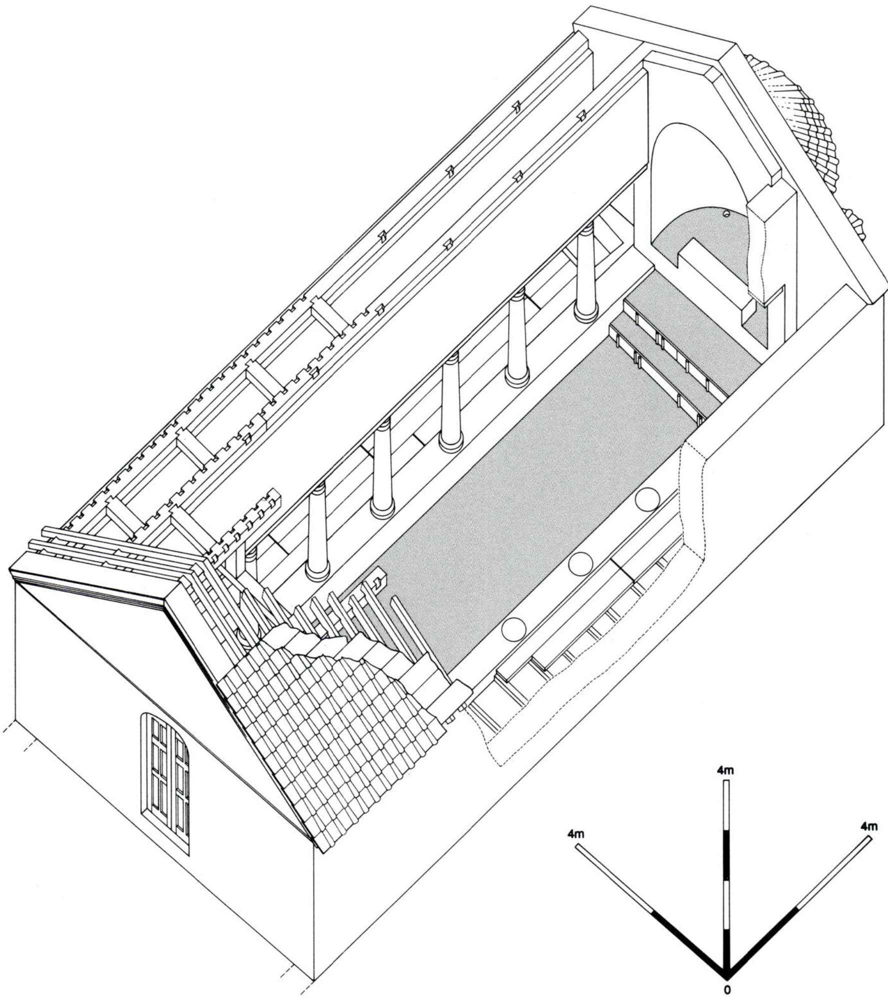

Fig 253 Reconstruction of the temple: Phase I Mithraeum

around 2.0m high and in the Tuscan order common in Britain. A column base and capital in this style, both of similar dimensions, have been found at Regis House (*c* 1930: KWS94) and Suffolk House (1994). These were of Cotswold-type limestone.

The colonnade is shown supporting a continuous entablature, which engages projecting buttresses in the east and west walls. The architrave may have consisted simply of stone lintels, although there may have been some carved decoration. There is no evidence that the entablature held a decorated frieze, and it was probably plain, possibly of plastered brickwork. There may have been a cornice, probably of stucco, but again, there is no evidence to support this.

The line of the colonnade is exactly half the distance between the centre of the outer walls and the apex of the end gables. The entablature is shown supporting wall plates which act as purlins to support the centre of the roof rafters; the outer ends of the gables are similarly supported by wall plates, with a central ridge beam connecting the gables. The wall plates, purlins and ridge beams are shown notched at intervals to locate the rafters, which would be similarly notched on the soffit and nailed in place. Two sections of a probable wall plate with similar notches have recently been found at Regis House. The angle of the notches reflects the angle of the roof pitch, which in the Regis House examples was around 3:1. A similar pitch has been used in the Mithraeum reconstructions.

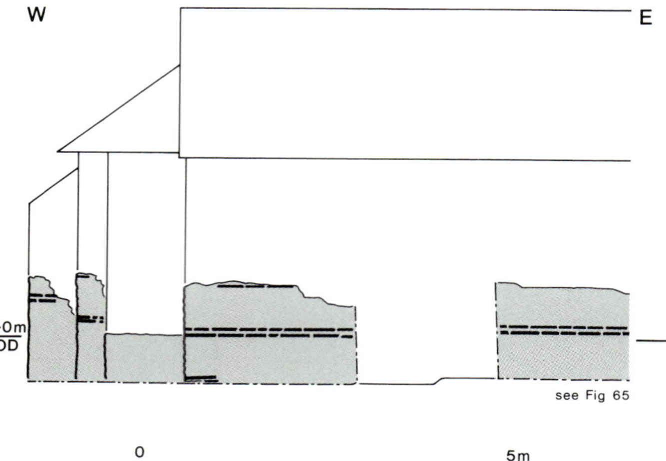

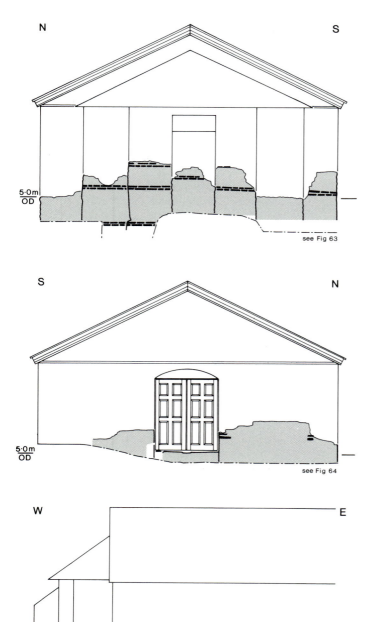

Fig 254 Exterior views of the temple

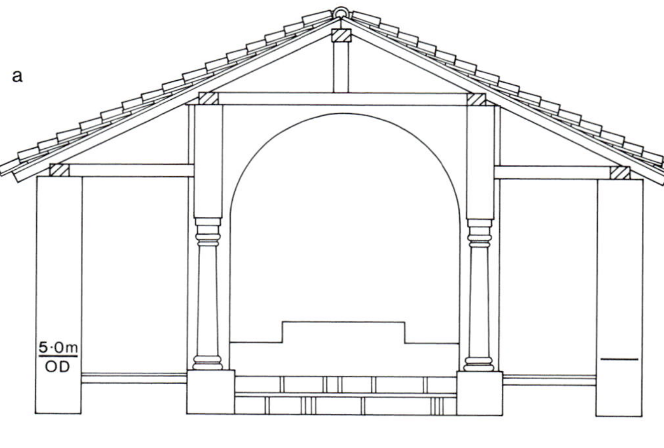

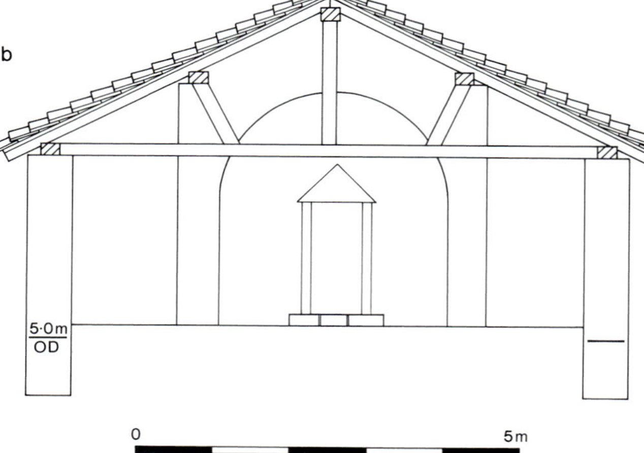

Fig 255 Cross-sections through the temple: a) Phase I Mithraeum, b) Phase IV temple (bacchium *or* sacrarium)

Tie beams are shown crossing the aisles at the same intervals as the columns. Socketed into the entablatures, and jointed to the wall plates, these counter the outward thrust of the roof which act against the walls. Similarly, collar beams tie the purlins together, preventing movement of the underlying colonnades. These support short king posts, which support the ridge beam.

The joints shown were those most commonly used in Roman carpentry. Tie beams and collar beams are joined to horizontal plates by dovetails. Lengths of plates are attached together using edge-halfed scarfs. The king posts are attached to the collar beams and ridge pieces by means of a mortise and tenon joint.

The rafters are shown here covered by a plank base for the tiled roof. Alternatively, laths could have been used, in which case planking may have been attached to the soffits of the rafters to create a ceiling which was draughtproof, waterproof and lightproof.

Final phase

(Figs 255b and 256)

Following the removal of the colonnades, the roof appears to have been supported temporarily by groups of posts driven at intervals into the contemporary floor along one side of the central aisle. The intervals matched those of the robbed columns. Each group of posts formed two small clusters on either side of the column position, suggesting that they had supported a horizontal tie, which in turn supported elements of the roof. The posts were only traced at the south side of the aisle, and were covered by the final floors. They can therefore be identified as temporary, possibly even part of a scaffold propping up the remains of the roof following the collapse on the south side, especially the south-west corner, and assisting the removal of the old roof. This would obviously have

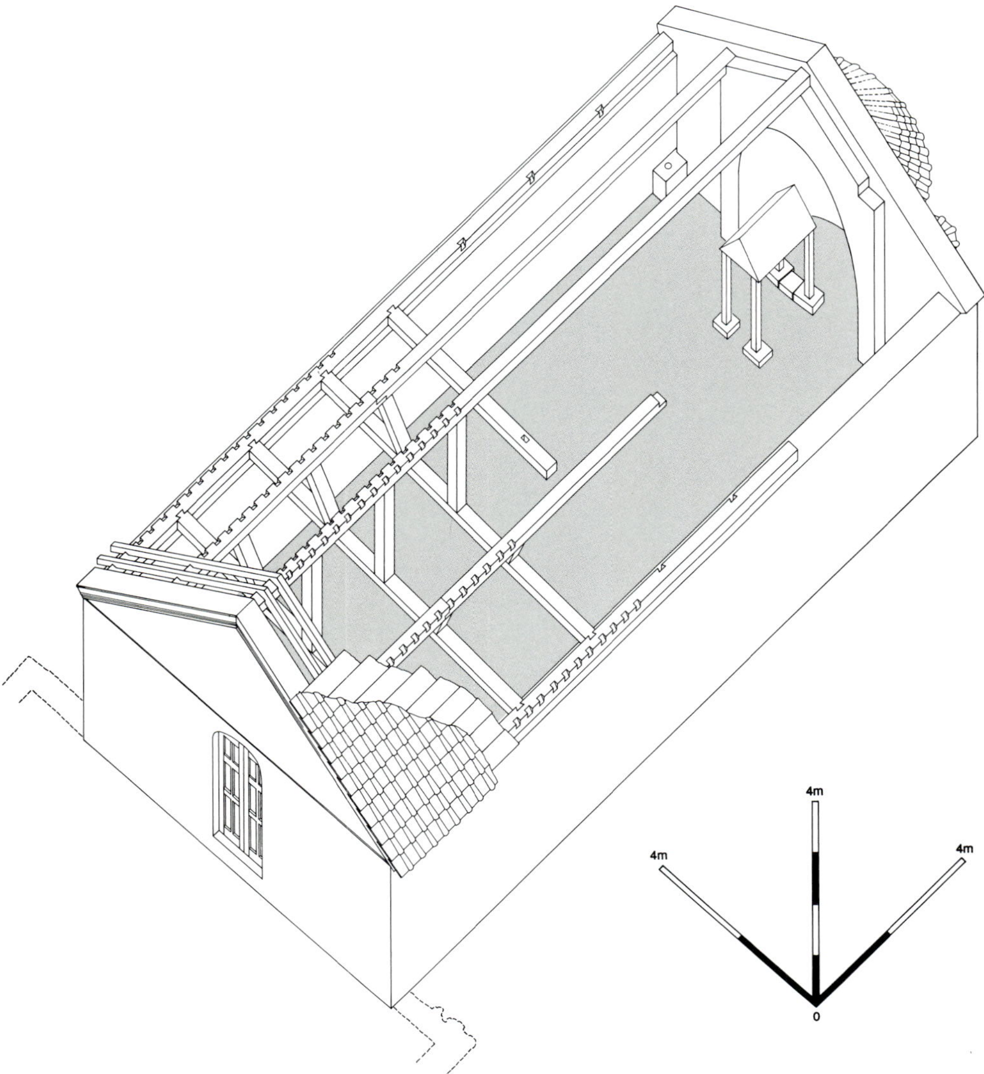

Fig 256 Reconstruction of the temple: Phase IV bacchium *or* sacrarium

been necessary once the columns had gone since the entablature would also have been demolished.

The tripartite division of the original structure was largely swept away, with a single floor level throughout. Horizontal beams lying on the floor might indicate the positions of timber partitions or rails. The roof which replaced the early arrangement appears to have survived without support. This is perfectly feasible given the small size of the building, and a suggested structure is shown in the second reconstruction. Here, the interrupted tie beam/collar beam arrangement has been replaced by ties crossing the full width of the building. These support king posts or struts, which have the dual function of supporting the ridge beam and preventing the tie beams from sagging or hogging. Angled struts support the purlins, which are in the same position as formerly, set half-way along the rafters. The roof construction is as previously.

Appendix 4 Context locations and descriptions

Cutting AA

(Figs 24–6)

No	*Group*	*Description*
19	XIII/XIV	-
29	XIII/XIV	-
31	XIII/XIV	-
500	XIII	-
501	XIII	Red brown gravelly soil over [514]
503	VI	Gravelly deposit below [501]
510	I	-
514	VI	Black soil below burnt brick rubble (Group XIII layers)
516	XIII	Burnt brick and debris over [517]
517	VI	Dense black soil with tile
518	VI	Dirty black clay, same as [520] & [522]
519	VI	Dirty black clay below [522]
520	VI	Dirty black clay
521	VI	Stony black soil below [520]
522	VI	Dirty black clay, same as [520]
523	VI	Timber in dirty black clay ie [520] & [522]
524	V	From among Group V timbers
532	V	From wicker floor at east end of cutting
533	V	From among Group V timbers
534	IV	-
535	V	From the surface of a wooden floor, at the same level as the wicker floor [532]
536	IV	Buff gravelly layer below timber layer
537	IV	From under wicker floor [532]
538	I	Stony black soil at base of cutting Same as [538a]
538a	I	Stony black soil at base of cutting Same as [538]

Cutting AB

(Figs 27-9)

No	*Group*	*Description*
510	I	-
515	XIII	Dirty clay speckled with brick rubble
530	V	Black soil from drain at the west end of the cutting
531	V	Black soil over east end of cutting
540	VI	Dirty clay over whole area of cutting
541	II	Dirty clay in gully *
542	I	-
543	VI	Black soil
544	VI	Mixed sticky black clay and gravel soil over the whole of cutting
546	VI	Black soil
547	VI	-
548a	II	-
549	II	Black gravelly filling in gully *
553	II	Black soil in gully *
554	II	Buff grey brickearth under [553]
555	II	Buff grey brickearth under a Group II timber floor

Cutting BB

(Figs 30–4)

No	*Group*	*Description*
3	XIII/XIV	-
12	0	-
14	XV	Loam deposit
15	XV	-
18	XV	Loam deposit
24	XIV	Loam deposit
32	XIV	Loam deposit
33	XV	Loam deposit
37	XIV	Loam deposit
39	XV	Dense soft black soil overlying [90]–[94] inclusive
40	XV	Loam deposit
41	XV	Loam deposit
42	XIV	Loam deposit
43	XIV	Loam deposit
44	XIV	Loam deposit
45	XIV	Loam deposit
74	XIV	Loam deposit
75	XIV	Loam deposit
91	XIV	Red brown burnt soil
93	XIV	Red brown burnt soil above [95], [115], and [308]
94	XIV	Red brown burnt soil above [95], [115], and [308]
95	XIV	From layer above [300]
104	XIV	Loam deposit
106	XIV	Loam deposit
107	XIV	Loam deposit
108	XIV	Loam deposit
110	XIV	Loam deposit
111	XIV	Loam deposit
112	XIV	Loam deposit
114	XIV	Loam deposit
115	XII	From layer above [300], below [308]
300	V	Mixed loam layer
301	V	Mixed loam layer
303	V	Mixed loam layer

No	Group	Description
308	XIV	From layer above [115]
310	VI	from black loamy clay to west of timbers, above [343]–[340] inclusive
311	XIV	From base of thick loam deposit
313	XII	From same stony clay as [316] but higher level
314	XIII	Loam clay over [316]
315	VI	From same stony clay as [344] but higher level
316	VI	Same as [315]
320	V	From same stony clay as [344] at east end of cutting
321	V	Same as [320]
322	II	From east end of cutting below timbers, same as [337]
323a	VI	Same as [310]
323b	XII	Among timbers, at higher level than [326]
324	XII	From immediately above timbers
325	XIII	Black mixed loam at top of channel
326	XII	As for [352]
326a	XII	-
327	XII	From east end of cutting at bottom of timbers
329	V	From a sticky grey clay among the timbers
331	0	-
333	IV	From wood layer, and just above it. Above [356]
334	V	From gravel and loam layer overlying deposits containing [333] and [335]
335	IV	Same as [333]
337	II	From east end of cutting at bottom of timbers. Same as [322]
338	II	-
339	XII	As for [352]
340	V	From a stiff, peaty clay to the west of timbers Above [341]
341	V	As for [340] but below [340]
342	V	As for [340] but below [341]
343	II	Stiff peaty clay
344	VI	Stony clay soil, close to timbers, above [349]
345	VI	As for [344]
347	XII	As for [352]
348	II	-
349	II	From bottom of cutting, near timbers
350	II	From timber floor, above [356]
351	XII	As for [352]
352	XII	From above timbers, above [353] and [354]
353	XII	From deposits among timbers at base of cutting
354	XII	As for [353]
356	II	From mixed dirty loam overlying timber floor sealing deposit containing [350]
357	II	From mixed dirty loam layer under [350] and [356]

Cutting CA

(Figs 41–2 and 91–6)

No	*Group*	*Description*
134	IX	Dirty grey clay from the make-up of Floor 6 in the south-east corner of Cutting CA, immediately east of modern foundation G
135	IX	As for [134]
139	X	Soil around wooden plank on Floor 8 at west end against the pilaster on the north side of the apse
143	VII	Very mixed clay loam layer resting on timber planks and backfilling the pre-Mithraeum cut feature
144	VII	Very mixed clay loam, the same as [143]
149	VII	Mixed dark brown clay loam layer backfilling the pre-Mithraeum cut feature beneath Floor 1, slightly to the east of the apse
150	VII	Mixed brown clay loam layer, 'vaguely horizontal', underlying the very mixed clay loam containing [143], [144] and [149]. It backfilled the pre-Mithraeum cut feature
153	VII	Part of the make-up of second step of first phase Temple at the western end
156	VII	Very mixed clay and tile layer backfilling the subsidence into the pre-Mithraeum cut feature and sealed by the make-up for the steps at the west end of the first phase Temple
161	IV	Dark brown mixed clay
162	II	'Peaty soil'
164	VII	Layer of very mixed clay with some stones, sloping down from beneath Floor 1 near the centre of the Temple to underlie the mixed clay loam containing [143], [144] and [149]
189	II	A dirty brown soil, a mixture of clay and wood fibre, directly beneath the mixed clay layer containing [202], [203] & [204] (Group IV) and the mixed organic (?) loam layer containing [196] (Group VII)
190	II	Greyish coarse loam layer underlying layer containing [197]
193	VII	Layer, not described, backfilling

		pre-Mithraeum cut feature
196	IV	A mixed dark unstratified (organic?) loam underlying a grey clay layer below the step area Above this lies the mixed loam containing [150]
197	II	Black peaty soil underlying [189]. This overlay [190]
202	IV	Organic loam layer beneath 'step' area under [150]
203	IV	As for [202]
204	IV	As for [202]
205	II	A black peaty layer underlying [190] and [197]
206	II	Dirty coarse gravelly soil, containing much peat, below [205]
211	II	A buff clay layer, containing much peat, below [206]
212	II	Very dirty grey clay below [211]
215	I	Clean brown clay overlaying natural soil in west end of Cutting CA under [212]
232	XI	Black soil in fill of latest pit. Same as [239], [273] and [241]
239	XI	Black soil in fill of latest pit. Same as [232], [273] and [241]
240	X	Make-up of Floor 7
241	XI	Black soil in fill of latest pit. Same as [232], [239] and [273]
242	IX	Very black clayey soil, covering whole of area, serving as a make-up layer for Floor 8
246	IX	From crushed tile make-up layer for Floor 7 in nave
247	IX	Make-up of Floor 7, described as 'black soil'
252	VII	From construction layer of Floor 1 below the steps at the west end
258	VII	From construction layer of Floor 1 below the steps at the west end
271	IX	Make-up of Floor 7
272	IX	Make-up of Floor 7
273	XI	Black soil from fill of latest pit. Same as [232], [239] and [241]
274	X	Black soil in make-up of Floor 8
280	XI	From mixed soil beneath wooden panel in west end of nave. Beneath Floor 6
288	X	Black soil between timbers below the final altar slab in the face of podium
289	XI	From mixed soil beneath wooden panel in west end of nave. Beneath Floor 6
292	X	Black soil between timbers below the final altar slab in the face of podium
296	IX	Make-up of Floor 5, under wooden panel
297	IX	As for [296]
301	VIII	Make-up of Floor 4 above [302]
302	VIII	Make-up of Floor 4 below [301]
312	IX	Mixed soil overlying hole in apse, make-up of Floor 5 at level of Floor 4
320	X	Make-up of Floor 8 containing much oyster shell
321	IX	Mortar/fragmentary tile layer (Floor 7)
322	IX	Make-up of Floor 7 below [321]
323	IX	Black soil make-up of Floor 6 below [322]
341	IX	Details unclear but associated with Floors 6 and 7

Cutting CB

(Figs 43–4 and 91–6))

No	*Group*	*Description*
107	X	Pink mortar debris against the top face of the north wall
112	X	Black soil and stones beneath mortar debris [107]
113	X	The same as [112]
115	IX	Grey clay above [116]
116	VIII	Grey clay from above Floor 1 of north aisle
119	IX	Black soil over north aisle and above top level of north sleeper wall
120	IV	Yellow sticky clay containing some wall plaster fragments. Same as [123]
121	IV	Very fine layer of black gravel with in [120] and [123]
123	IV	Yellow sticky clay containing some wall plaster fragments. Same as [120]
124	II	Peat and wood layer below clay layer [120/123]. With some horizontal grey clay banding
126	II	Same as [124] but lower down in section
127	II	Same as [124] and [126] but lower down in section
128	II	Dark brown clay loam below [127]
129	II	The fill, not specified, of a shallow gully seen in plan but not recorded in section. Above [128], below [127]
130	II	A thin layer of very black coarse gravel Below [128]
131	II	Thick peat layer below [128] and [130]
132	I	Dirty clay under peat layer [131] in east end of Cutting CB
133	I	Black gravel, under [132], overlying clean clay in east end of

		stoneless, clay layer overlying thick horizontal timber
729	II	From dense clay layer over [739], [740], [744], and [745]
730	II	As for [729]
731	II	As for [729]
732	0	-
734	II	As for [729]
735	II	As for [729]
736	XIII	From stream bed above [738]
737	III	From dirty buff clay layer over [739], [740], [744], and [745]
738	XIII	From stream bed above [757]
739	I	Brown timber deposit in west end of Cutting F
740	II	As for [739] but from a slightly higher level
742	I	Brown soil, under [740], on natural
743	III	Black loam layer over [733]
744	II	Deposits of mixed loamy clay, alternating with floors, over natural
745	II	As for [739] but from a slightly higher level
746	XIII	As for [746]
747	V	Among small timber revetment (Revetment 1)
748	V	Mixed deposits of shingle, loam and clay in and against Revetment 1
749	V	As for [748]
751	V	As for [748]
752	II	As for [729]
753	V	As for [748]
756	V	As for [748]
757	XIII	From stream bed above [759]
758	XIII	Same as [757]
759	XII	From stream bed above [762]
760	V	Clay and shingle layer against Revetment 1, cut by Revetment 2
762	XII	From stream bed above [763]
763	XII	From stream bed above [765]
764	VI	Dense black loam below timber floor against Revetment 2. Over [747]
765	XII	From stream bed above [767]
766	III	As for [728]
767	XII	From stream bed above [769]
768	XII	From stream bed below quernstone
769	XII	As for [771] but from a slightly higher level
771	XII	From stream bed, at bottom
772	XII	Same as [771]

Appendix 5 Animal bone data

1 Minimum numbers of individuals

Species	*MNI*
Sheep	21
Chicken	39
Cattle	56
Pig	31
Dog	6
Cat	2
Red Deer	1

I - Total MNI for all stratified bone from all cuttings, treating each bag separately

Species	*MNI*
Sheep	20
Chicken	34 *
Cattle	51**
Pig	29***
Dog	6
Cat	2
Red Deer	1

II - Total MNI, treating bags from floor fills together
** - 36 if bones in Floor 3 treated separately from fill*
*** - 52 if ditto*
**** - 30 if ditto*

Species	*MNI -1*	*MNI -2*
Sheep	8	7
Chicken	27	22*
Cattle	15	10**
Pig	17	15***
Dog	3	3

III - MNI from nave and aisles of temple, 1 treating each bag separately, 2 treating bags from floor fills together
** 24 if Floor 3 is separate*
*** 11 if ditto *** 16 if ditto*

Species	*CA/CE/CB*	*CD*	*AA/AB*	*F*	*BB*
Sheep	15 (8)	2	1	1	2
Chicken	35 (27)	1			3
Cattle	24 (15)	9	2	13	8
Pig	23 (17)		2	2	4
Dog	3 (3)	2		1	
Cat					2
Red Deer	1				
Total	101	14	5	17	19

IV - MNI by cutting, treating bags separately Numbers in brackets are those from the temple

Species	*Phase I*	*Phase II*	*Phase III*
Sheep	8	5	8
Chicken	4	8	27
Cattle	12	27	17
Pig	8	6	17
Dog		4	2
Cat	2		
Red Deer			1
Total	34	50	72

V - MNI by phase, treating bags separately
NB The phases are unequal in terms of length. Phase I = c 90 years, Phase II = c 120 years,
Phase III = c 160 years. The MNI of the animals found in each phase conform approximately to these differences, but the sample size is so small that this may be coincidence rather than a valid factor and should be treated with caution.

2 Measurements

Bone	*Number*	*1*	*2*	*3*	*4*	*5*	*6*	*7*
Tarsometatarsus	320	76.4	12.8	6.5	14.7			
Tarsometatarsus	333	84.2	14.5	7.6	13.3			
Tarsometatarsus	180	80.0	12.6	6.5	12.7			
Tarsometatarsus	202	80.0	14.2	6.9	14.7			
Tarsometatarsus	116	75.9	12.8	5.7				
Tarsometatarsus	353	84.5	13.0	6.9	13.4			
Tarsometatarsus	353	97.0	16.7	8.8	16.3			
Tarsometatarsus	345	82.8	12.4	5.9	12.7			
Coracoid	344	53.4	51.1		11.3			
Coracoid	292	54.4	51.7	13.7	11.3			
Coracoid	358	55.8	53.4		12.1			
Coracoid	354	56.1	52.6	15.3	13.4			
Coracoid	354	59.5	56.9	15.4	12.2			
Coracoid	354	56.4	54.3		11.5			
Coracoid	354	53.4	51.1	16.5	13.5			
Coracoid	354	53.6	50.8		10.9			
Coracoid	354	55.1	52.6	15.6	13.5			
Carpometacarpus	333	43		12.5	8.1			

Carpometacarpus	344	40.3		11.3	7.2			
Carpometacarpus	354	39.7		11.3	7.2			
Carpometacarpus	354	40.8		12.0	8.2			
Carpometacarpus	354	40.7		11.9	7.6			
Radius	107	65.3	3.3	7.3				
Radius	343	66.2	3.2	7.0				
Radius	343	68.3	3.0	7.4				
Radius	347	67.6	3.3	7.5				
Radius	358	63.5	6.7	3.2?				
Ulna	301	69.5	13.2	8.4	4.4	9.6		
Ulna	302	63.3	11.8	7.7	4.3	8.7		
Ulna	323	77.0	14.6	9.1	4.3	10.8		
Ulna	336	74.2	13.5	9	4.3	10.4		
Ulna	336	6.8	14	8.9	4.6	10.5		
Ulna	336	74.7	13.5	8.9	4.7	10.4		
Ulna	341	75.1	14.1	9.0	4.6	10.6		
Ulna	341	74.8	13.6	8.5	4.6	9.9		
Ulna	343	72.9	13.2	8.5	4.7	10.2		
Ulna	343	69.8	12.9	8.1	4.1	9.4		
Ulna	344	75.9	14.0	8.8	4.7	10.4		
Ulna	354	70.4	13.5	9.0	4.7	10.2		
Ulna	312	73.7	14.3	8.7	4.2	10.4		
Humerus	143	72.6	19.1	6.8	15.1			
Humerus	204	75.0	19.5	5.9	15.4			
Humerus	336	73.3	19.7	7.1	16.1			
Humerus	341	72.9	20.0	6.9	15.9			
Humerus	341	77.4	21.4	7.4	16.4			
Humerus	347	69.2	19.9	7.2	15.7			
Humerus	345	73.6	19.8	7.2	15.9			
Humerus	345	74.7	19.5	7.0	15.9			
Humerus	360	73.7	19.8	6.9	15.6			
Humerus	358	76.1	19.9	7.3	15.2			
Humerus	358	73.5	19.0	6.8	15.5			
Humerus	354	70.1	19.5	7.2	15.6			
Humerus	354	74.9	19.9	7.3	16.0			
Humerus	286	73.9	20.1	7.2	16.1			
Tibiotarsus	144	118.5	114.0	21.1	6.1	12.0	11.6	
Tibiotarsus	153	122	118.4		5.9	11.7	12.1	
Tibiotarsus	124	102.9	99.4	18.2	4.9	10.0	10.6	
Tibiotarsus	127	118.6	114.5	22.0	6.9	12.0	12.5	
Tibiotarsus	323	113.1	109.2	19.7	6.2	11.7	11.1	
Tibiotarsus	323	123	119.1		6.3	12.2.	12.3	
Tibiotarsus	336	122	118	22.5				
Tibiotarsus	345	125.0	121.4	22.0	6.5	11.9	12.5	
Tibiotarsus	347	108.7	104.8	20	5.7	10.9	11.3	
Tibiotarsus	354	123.3	118.7	21.6	6.2	11.5	11.2	
Tibiotarsus	354	111.9	107.5		6.1			
Tibiotarsus	354	115.8	112.6	19.8	6.0	10.8	12	
Tibiotarsus	354	115.5	109.9	20.7	6.2	11.3	11.9	
Tibiotarsus	312	114.7	110.8	21.0	5.8	11.2	11.6	
Tibiotarsus	312	129.3	125.5	22.0	6.9			
Femur	341	80.2	75.8	16.7	10.4	6.7	15.6	13.1
Femur	358	79.4	74.1	15.9	10.9	7.2	15.6	13.2
Femur	300	80.2	75.4	15.6	10.5	6.4	15.6	13.8
Femur	312	70.2	64.0	13.9	10.7	6.7	14.3	12.2

I - Measurements of chicken bones

Number	44	45	46	47
108	128	36.5	42	145
112	136	38.5	48	158
131	185	43.5	66.5	
175	225	59.5	77.5	
178	127	34.5	45	138
179	208	52.5	75.5	235*
179	171	44	60.5	250*
192	120	31	43	125
192	179	51.5	61.5	220*
208	135	33	54	121
340	132	34	47	160
340	154	42	53	174
515	223	58.9	80	200*
515	117	28	43.5	155*
746	139	38.5	47	140
746	123	33	45	155
746	135	37	45.5	165*
748	128	28.5	50.5	105**
748	128	29	49.5	100**
748	132	34.5	47.1	131
748	146	39	47.9	116
748	160	43.4	54.5	
748	132	34.5	45	138
749	103	26	36.5	93
749	157	42	55	
749	116	31	41.5	90
753	120	33	44	
768	140	35	54	155*
768	105	27	38.5	106*

II - Measurements of cattle horn cores.
** = estimated*
***= paired*

3 Tooth wear stages

Number	P2	P3	P4	DPM4	M1	M2	M3	Value	Side
C7						K			L
11			L		L	K	H	44E	R
11			F		l	K	J	45	L
CB116	L	P	G		L				L
CB131	L	P	C		H	G	F"	36	R
CB131	V	E		J	J	G	.5	30	L
CB131	C	E		J	H	G	.5	29	R
165						J			L
CD177	L	V		K	H	F	0.5	28	R
CD192	L	P		B	E			3	L
CA206		L	F		l	K	G	43	L
CE300	P	P			D			46E	L
CE302					D				
310	P	P	J		l	K	L	46E	L
317						K			L
317							G		R
324	L	P	G		L				R
BB338	A	P	F		l	G		40E	R
341							K		R
BB345	L	L	H		l	K	K	46	L
360	E	V		K	J	F	E	28	L
360	P	P		K	K	F		30E	R
551	A	L	H		o	l	K	50	R
F704					K				L
F748	A	P	C		K	G		38E	L
F748						J			L
F768	P	P	F		K	K	G*	42	L

I - cattle tooth wear stages
**Third pillar very worn down*
"Third pillar absent
A = congenitally absent P = present L - lost

Number	P2	P3	P4	DPM4	M1	M2	M3	Value	Side
3	L	L	F		K	H	G		R
10								B	
127	L	P	F*		G	G	B	31	L
CB131	L	P	F*		G	F	C	31	L
CB132	A	P	F		H	G	G	37	R
CA140	L	P	L		H	G	E		L
152?	L(D)		P(D)			C	L		R
CA153						F			R
CD179	L	L	H		K	G	G	49	L
CA205	P	P		H	G	D	V	23	R
CA206	L	P	G		G	F	C	31	L
BB326	L	L	L		L	G	E	35E	L
CB329	L	L	H		H	G		37E	L
AB541	L	P		J	F	D	-	22E	L
F753	L	P		L	G	E	C	23	L

II - Sheep tooth wear stages(D)
= deciduous
** possible caries*
- indeterminable

Number	P1	P2	P3	P4	DPM4	M1	M2	M3	Value	Side
15?	L	L	L	A		F	B	L	20E	R
15?		L	L	D		J			R	
CB131	P	P	P	F		l			L	
CB132							A	C	16E	R
CA204	L	L(D)		L(D)			A	V	UE	UE
2	L									
292								A		
BB300		L	P	D		M	H	B	37	L
CE318	L	L	L	B		H	D		27E	R
324							F		R	
341					A	C			1	L
354					A					
AB541		P	P	B		C	B	.5	19	L
AB541			P	B		K	D	-	29E	R
F751	P	P	P		G	B			L	

III - Pig tooth wear stages
UE - unerupted with no crypt visible

Bibliography

Abbreviations

CIL	*Corpus Inscriptionum Latinarum 1863—*
Isings	Isings, C, 1957 *Roman glass from dated finds*, Groningen/Djakarta
JRS	Journal of Roman Studies
MOL	Museum of London
MoLAS	Museum of London Archaeological Service
LRT	London Museum, 1930 *Catalogue No 3: London in Roman times*, London
RIB	Collingwood, R G, and Wright, R P, 1965 and 1990 *Roman inscriptions in Britain* 1 and 2
Stanfield and Simpson	Stanfield, J A and Simpson, G, 1958 *Central Gaulish potters*, London
Young	Young, C J, 1977 *Oxfordshire Roman pottery*, Brit Archaeol Rep Brit Ser, 43, Oxford

Alföldy, G, 1966 Review of Collingwood and Wright 1965, *Bonner Jahrbücher*, **166**, 639

Allason-Jones, L, and Miket, R, 1984 *The catalogue of small finds from South Shields Roman fort*, Soc Antiq Newcastle upon Tyne Monograph Ser, **2**, Newcastle

Anderson, A C, and Anderson, A S, (eds) *Roman Pottery Research in Britain and North-west Europe. Papers Presented to Graham Webster* Brit Archaeol Rep Int Ser **13**, Oxford

Arthur, P and Marsh, G (eds) 1978 *Early fine wares in Roman Britain*, Brit Archaeol Rep, **57**, 119–224, Oxford

Atkinson, D, 1914 A hoard of samian ware from Pompeii, *J Roman Stud*, **4**, 27–64

Bailey, D M, 1963 *Greek and Roman pottery lamps*, London

Barber, B and Bowsher, D, forthcoming *The eastern cemetery of Roman London: excavations 1983-90* MoLAS Monograph Series. Museum of London Archaeology Service

Bayley, J, 1991 Archaeological evidence for parting, in *Archaeometry '90: proceedings of the 27th international symposium on archaeometry, Heidelberg*, (eds E Pernicka and G A Wagner), Basel, 19–28

Becatti, G, 1954 *Scavi di Ostia II: I Mitrei*, Rome

Beck, R, 1984 Mithraism since Franz Cumont *Aufstieg und Niedergang der Romischen Welt* (eds H Temporini and W Haase), **II**, 17, 4, 2002–2115, Barlin/New York

Behn, F, 1928, *Das Mithrasheiligtum zu Dieburg*, Römisch-Germanische Forschungen **I**, Berlin/Leipzig

Belot, E, 1990 Dioscures ou dadophores? A propos des sculptures "mithriaques" et du "Mithraeum" de Boulogne-sur-Mer. Présence des cultes orientaux à Boulogne et en Morinie, *Revue du Nord*, **72 no 286**, 1 35-62

Bird, J, and Marsh, G, 1978 Decorated samian, in *Southwark excavations 1972–74* (eds J Bird, A H Graham, H Sheldon and P Townend), London Middlesex Archaeol Soc and Surrey Archaeol Soc Joint Pub, **1**, London

Bird, J, 1986a Samian wares, in L Miller, J Schofield and M Rhodes, *The Roman quay at St Magnus House, London* (ed T Dyson), London Middlesex Archaeol Soc Special Paper, **8**, 139–185

Bird, J, 1986b The silver bowl, in Toynbee 1986, 52–54

Bird, J, 1993 *Walbrook: the samian catalogue*, MOL Grimes Archive

Bird, J, no date, *The Mithraeum: summary of the dating evidence*, MOL Grimes Archive

Bird, J, 1996 Frogs from the Walbrook: a cult pot and its attributions, in *Interpreting Roman London: papers in memory of Hugh Chapman* (eds J Bird, M Hassal and H Sheldon), 119–128

Birley, E, 1966 Review of Collingwood and Wright 1965, *J Roman Stud*, **56**, 226–31

Bishop, M, Coulston, J C N, Greep, S, and Griffiths, N, forthcoming *Museum of London military corpus*

Bishop, M C, and Coulston, J C N, 1993 *Roman military equipment*, London

Bittner, F K, 1986 Zur Forsetzung der Diskussion um die Chronologie der Rheinzaberner Reliefttöpfer, *Bayerische Vorgeschichtsblätter*, **51**, 233-59

Blazquez, J M, Lopez Monteagudo, G, Neira Jimenez, M L, and san Nicolas Pedraz, M P, 1989, Mosaicos Romanos del Museom Arqueologico Nacional *Corpus de Mosaicos de Espana*, Madrid

Brigham, T, 1990, The Late Roman waterfront in London, *Britannia* **21**, 99–183

Brown, D, 1976 Bronze and pewter, in Strong and Brown 1976, 25–41

Bushe-Fox, J P, 1949 *Excavations of the Roman Fort at Richborough IV*, Rep Res Comm Soc Antiq London, **16**, London

Cagnat, R, 1914 *Cours d'Epigraphie Latine*, Paris

Callender, M H, 1965 *Roman amphorae*, Oxford

Canarache, V, Radulescu, A, Aricescu, A, and Barbu, V, 1963 Le dépôt des monuments sculpturaux récemment découverts à Constanta *Acta Antiqua Philippopolitana: studia archaeologica*, Sofia

Chaplin, R E, 1971 *The study of animal bones from archaeological sites*, London

Charlesworth, D, 1972 The glass, in Frere 1972

Chenet, G, 1941 *La ceramique gallo-romaine d'Argonne du IVe siècle et la terre sigillée decorée à la molette*, Maçon

Clutton-Brock, J, and Armitage, P, 1977 Excavations at Angel Court, Walbrook 1974, *Trans London and Middlesex Archaeol Soc* **26**, 14–100

Coleman, M, and Walker, S, 1979 Stable isotope identification of Greek and Turkish marbles, *Archaeometry*, **21**, 107–112

Collingwood, R G, and Wright, R P, 1965 *The Roman inscriptions of Britain*, 1, London

Collingwood, R G, and Wright, R P, 1990 *The Roman inscriptions of Britain*, 2, Stroud

Collingwood, R G, and Wright, R P, 1993 *The Roman inscriptions of Britain*, **Vol II, fasc 5**, (eds S S Frere and R S O Tomlin), Oxford

Collins-Clinton, J, 1977 *A Late Antique shrine of Liber Pater at Cosa*, Etudes préliminaire aux religions orientales dans l'Empire Romain, Leiden

Commissione Archeologica Communale di Roma, 1940 *Bullettino*, **68**

Craig, H, 1957 Isotopic standards for carbon and oxygen and correction factors for mass-spectrometric analysis of carbon dioxide, *Geochim Cosmochim Acta*, **12**, 133–149

Craig, H, and Craig, V, 1972 Greek marbles: determination of provenance by isotopic analysis, *Science*, **176**, 401–403

Crummy, N, 1983 *The Roman small finds from excavations in Colchester 1971–9*, Colchester Archaeol Rep 2, Colchester

Cumont, F, 1896–99 *Textes et monuments figures relatifs aux mysteres de Mithra*, **Vols i and ii**, Brussels

Cunliffe, B W, 1971 *Excavations at Fishbourne 1961–69, Vol 2: the finds*, Rep Res Comm Soc Antiq London, **27**, Leeds

Cunliffe, B W, 1975 *Excavations at Portchester Castle Vol I, Roman*, Rep Res Comm Soc Antiq London, **32**, London

Curle, J, 1911 *A Roman frontier post and its people: the fort of Newstead in the parish of Melrose*, Glasgow

Daicoviciu, H, 1969 [Catalogue entries] in *Römer in Rumänien. Ausstellung des Römisch-Germanischen Museums Köln und des Historischen Museums Cluj*, Köln

Dannell, G B, 1971 The samian pottery, in Cunliffe 1971, 260–316

Dechelette, J, 1904 *Les vases céramiques ornés de la Gaule Romaine*, Paris

Dragendorff, H, 1895–6 Terra Sigillata, *Bonner Jahrbücher* **96**, 18–155 and **97**, 54-163

Drexel, F, 1910 Das Kastell Stockstadt, *Der Obergerm.-Raet. Limes des Romerreiches*

Dunning, G C 1945 Two fires of Roman London, *Antiq J* **25**, 48–77

English Heritage, 1991 *The management of archaeological projects*, London [commonly known as MAP2]

Fölzer, E, 1913 *Die Bilderschussein der ostgallischen sigillata-Manufakturen*, Romische Keramik, Trier, **1**, Bonn

Frere, S S, 1972 *Verulamium excavations Vol 1*, Rep Res Comm Soc Antiq London, **28**, London

Fulford, M, 1975 The pottery, in Cunliffe 1975, 271–367

Gard, L, 1937 *Reliefsigillata des 3. und 4. Jahrhunderts aus den Werkstätten von Trier* (Unpublished dissertation, University of Tübingen)

Gazda, E K, 1981 A marble group of Ganymede and the Eagle from the Age of Augustine, in Humphrey, J H, *Excavations at Carthage VI*, 125–7, Ann Arbor

Gauthier N, 1982, Un Mithrée a Lillebonne? *Centres de Reccherches Archéologiques en Haute-Normandie*, Bulletin no. **3**

Gillam, J P, 1954 The Temple of Mithras at Rudchester, *Archaeologia Aeliana*, 4th ser. **32**, 176-219

Gillam, J P, 1970 *Types of Roman coarse pottery vessels in northern Britain* (third edition), Newcastle upon Tyne

Goodburn, R, 1984 Non-ferrous metal objects in S Frere, *Verulamium excavations Vol 3*, Oxford Univ Comm Archaeol Monograph, **1**, 18–68, Oxford

Goodman, J, Lovejoy, P E, Sherratt, A, 1995 *Consuming habits: drugs in history and anthropology*, London and New York

Gose, E, 1950 Gefässtypen der römischen Keramik im Rheinland, *Beihefte Bonner Jahrbücher*, **1**, Bonn; reprint Köln 1975

Grant, A, 1975, Appendix B: The use of tooth wear as a guide to the age of domestic animals — a brief explanation, in Cunliffe 1975, 437–50

Green, M J, 1976 *The religions of civilian Roman Britain*, Brit Archaeol Rep Brit Ser, **24**, Oxford

Grimes, W F, 1968 *The excavation of Roman and medieval London*, London

Guildhall Catalogue, 1908 *Catalogue of the London antiquities in the Guildhall Museum*, London

Hagen, W, 1937 Kaiserzeitliche Gagarbeiten aus dem rheinische Germanien, *Bonner Jahrbücher*, **142**, 77-144

Hall, J, 1982 A Roman silver mount from London, *Antiq J*, **62** 363–5

Hannestad, N, 1994 *Tradition in Late Antique sculpture. Conservation, modernization, production*, Aarhus

Harden, D B, 1975 The glass, in Cunliffe 1975, 368–74

Harris, E, and Harris, J R, 1965 *The oriental cults in Roman Britain*, Études Préliminaires aux Religions Orientales dans l'Empire Romain, 6, Leiden

Hartley, B R, 1972 The samian ware, in Frere 1972, 216–262

Hawkes, C F C, and Hull, M R, 1947 *Camulodunum: first report on the excavations at Colchester, 1930-39* Rep Res Comm Soc Antiq London, **14**, London

Henig, M, 1983 The Maiden Castle 'Diana': a case of mistaken identity, *Proc Dorset Nat Hist and Arch Soc*, **105**, 160–2

Henig, M, 1984 *Religion in Roman Britain*, London

Henig, M, 1990 A house for Minerva: temples, aedicula shrines, and signet-rings, in Henig, M, *Architecture and architectural sculpture in the Roman Empire*, Oxford University Comm Archaeol Monograph, **29**, 152–62

Henig, M, 1993 *Roman sculpture in the Cotswold region*, Corpus Signorum Imperii Romani Great Britain, I **fasc** 7, Oxford

Henry, F, 1933 Émailleurs d'occident, *Préhistoire*, **2**, 65-146

Hermet, F, 1934 *La Graufesenque (Condatomago)*, Paris

Herz, N, 1987 Carbon and oxygen isotope ratios: a data base for classical Greek and Roman marble, *Archaeometry* **29** 35–43

Hinnels, J, 1975 *Mithraic studies*, Manchester

Holden, C H, and Holden, W G, 1951 *The City of London: a record of destruction and survival*, London

Howe, M D, Perrin, J R, and Mackreth, D F, 1981 *Roman pottery from the Nene Valley: a guide*, Peterborough Cit Mus Occas Pap, **2**, Peterborough

Hübener W, 1968 Eine Studie zur spätrömischen Rädchensigillata (Argonnen-sigillata), *Bonner Jahrbücher*, **168**, 241–98

Huld-Zetsche I, 1986, *Mithras in Nida-Heddernheim. Gesamtkatalog* Museum für Vor- und Frühgeschichte Frankfurt am Main, Archäoogische Reihe **6**, Frankfurt am Main

Hull, M R, 1958 *Roman Colchester*, Res Rep Comm Soc Antiq London **20**, London

Hutchinson, V J, 1986 *Bacchus in Roman Britain, the evidence for his cult*, Brit Archaeol Rep Brit Ser, **151**, Oxford

Isings, C, 1957 *Roman glass from dated finds*, Groningen/Djakarta

Jenkins, F, 1974 Review of Rouvier-Jeanlin, 1972, Les figurines Gallo-Romaines en terre cuite au Museé des Antiquités Nationales, *Gallia* Supplement 24, *Britannia*, **5**, 485–6

Johns, C, and Potter, T, 1983 *The Thetford Treasure. Roman jewellery and silver*, London

Jones, C E E, 1983 A review of Roman lead-alloy material recovered from the Walbrook valley in the City of London, *Trans London Middlesex Archaeol Soc*, **34**, 49–59

King, A, 1983 The Roman church at Silchester reconsidered *Oxford J Archaeol*, **2**, 225–37

Knorr, R, 1919 *Topfer und Fabriken verzierter Terrasigillata des ersten Jahrhunderts*, Stuttgart

Knorr, R, 1952 *Terra-sigillata-gefasse des ersten Jahrhunderts mit Topfernamen*, Stuttgart

Knorr, R and Sprater, F, 1927 *Die Westpfälzischen Sigillata-Töpfereien von Blickweiler und Eschweiler Hof*, Speyer

Lauffer, S, 1971 *Diokletians Preisedikt*, Berlin

Leese, M N, 1988, Statistical treatment of stable isotope data, in *Classical marble: geochemistry, technology, trade* (eds N Herz and M Waelkens), 347–354, Kluwer, Dordrecht

Lehmann, K, 1962 Ignorance and search in the Villa of the Mysteries, *J Roman Stud*, **52**, 62–8

Lenormant, F, 1887 Cista Mystica in Daremberg, C, and Saglio, E, *Dictionnaire des Antiquites Grecques et Romains*, **Vol 1**, Paris

Liversidge, J, 1955 *Furniture in Roman Britain*, London

Loeschcke, S, 1909 Antike Lanternen und Lichthäuschen, *Bonner Jahrbücher*, **118**, 370-430 and Taf 28-36

London Museum, 1930 *Catalogue No 3: London in Roman times*, London

Ludowici, H, and Ricken, H, 1948 *Die Bilderschüsseln der Römischen Töpfer von Rheinzabern: Tafelband*, Speyer

Lyne, M A B, and Jefferies, R S, 1979 *The Alice Holt/Farnham Roman pottery industry*, Counc Brit Archaeol Res Rep, **30**, London

MacGregor, A, 1985 *Bone, antler, ivory and horn*, London

Mackintosh, M, 1995 *The Divine Rider in the art of the Western Roman Empire*, Brit Archaeol Rep Int Ser, **607**, Oxford

Macready, S, no date, *Walbrook coarse pottery*, MOL Grimes Archive

Macready, S, no date *Pottery from the Walbrook 1954*, MOL Grimes Archive

Mann, J C, 1971 Spoken Latin in Britain as evidenced in the inscriptions, *Britannia*, **2**, 218–24

Manning, W H, 1972 The iron objects, in Frere 1972, 163–95

Manning, W H, 1976 *Catalogue of Romano-British ironwork in the Museum of Antiquities, Newcastle upon Tyne*, Newcastle upon Tyne

Manning, W H, 1985 *Catalogue of the Romano-British iron tools, fittings and weapons in the British Museum*, London

Marney, P T, 1989 *Roman and Belgic pottery from excavations in Milton Keynes 1972–82*, Buckinghamshire Archaeol Soc Mon Ser, **2**, Aylesbury

Marsden, E, 1969 *Greek and Roman artillery: historical development*, London

Marsh, G, 1978 Early second century fine wares in the London area, in Arthur and Marsh 1978, 119–24

Marsh, G, 1981 London's samian supply and its relationship to the development of the Gallic samian industry, in Anderson and Anderson 1981, 173-238

Matthews, K J, 1988, Variability in stable isotope analysis: implications for joining fragments, in *Classical marble: geochemistry, technology, trade* (eds N Herz and M Waelkens), 339–346, Kluwer, Dordrecht

McCrea, J M, 1950, The isotopic chemistry of carbonates and a palaeotemperature scale, *J Chem Phys*, **18**, 849–857

Merkelbach, R, 1984 *Mithras*, Hain

Merrifield, R, 1962 Coins from the bed of the Walbrook and their significance, *Antiq J*, **42**, 38–52

Merrifield, R, 1965 *The Roman City of London*, London

Merrifield, R, 1995 Roman metalwork from the Walbrook — rubbish, ritual or redundancy, *Trans London Middlesex Archaeol Soc* **46**, 27–44

Milne, G, 1985 *The port of Roman London*, London

Milne, G, 1985 *St Bride's Church London: archaeological research 1952–60 and 1992–5* English Heritage Archaeol Rep **11**, London

Milne, G, forthcoming *The RMWC excavations in Cripplegate, London: post-Roman developments*

Monaghan, J, 1987 *Upchurch and Thameside Roman pottery*, Brit Archaeol Rep, **173**, Oxford

Muller, G, 1968 *Das Lagerdorf des Kastells Butzbach. Die reliefverzierte Terra Sigillata*, Limesforschungen, **5**, Berlin

Noël Hume, I, 1978 Into the jaws of death walked one, in *Collectanea Londiniensia; papers presented to Ralph Merrifield* (eds J Bird, H Chapman and J Clark), London Middlesex Archaeol Soc Special paper **2**, 7–23, London

Oikonomides, A N, 1975 *Mithraic art — a search for unpublished and unidentified monuments*, Chicago

Oswald, F, 1936–7 Index of figure-types on terra sigillata (samian ware), *Annals Archaeol Anthropol*, **23**, 1–4

Oswald, F, 1945 Decorated ware from Lavoye, *J Roman Stud*, **35**, 49–57

Paris, P, 1914 Restes du culte de Mithra en Espagne, *Revue Archéologique* ser. 4, **24**

Parrish, D, 1995 A mythological theme in the decoration of Late Roman dining rooms: Dionysos and his circle, *Revue Archéologique*, 307-32

Peacock, D P S, and Williams, D F, 1986 *Amphorae and the Roman economy: an introductory guide*, London

Pritchard, F, 1986 Ornamental stonework in Roman London *Britannia*, **17**, 169–89

Reinach, S, 1912 *Repertoire de reliefs grecs et romains,* **ii**, Paris

Richardson, B, 1986, Pottery, 96-138, in *The Roman quay at St Magnus House, London: excavations at New Fresh Wharf, Lower Thames Street, London 1974–78* by L Miller, J Schofield and M Rhodes (ed T Dyson) London Middlesex Archaeol Soc Special Paper **8**, London

Richmond, I A, 1950 *Archaeology and the after-life in pagan and Christian imagery*, Oxford.

Richmond, I A, 1968 *Hod Hill II: excavations carried out between 1951 and 1958 for the Trustees of the British Museum*, London

Richmond, I A, Gillam, J P, and Birley, E, 1951 The Temple of Mithras at Carrawburgh, *Archaeologia Aeliana*, **29**, 1–92 and Pls 1–XV

Ricken, H, and Fischer, C (ed), 1963 *Die Bilderschussein der romischen Topfer von Rheinzabern. Textband mit typenbildern, Materialen romisch-germanischen Keramik*, **7**, Bonn

Ricken, H, 1934 Die Bilderschussein der Kastelle Saalburg und Zugmantel, *Saalburg Jahrbuch*, **8**, 130–182

Ristow, G, 1974 *Mithras im römischen Köln*, Études Préliminaires aux Religions Orientales dans l'Empire Romain, **42**, Leiden

Ritterling, E, 1913 *Das frühromische Lager bei Hofheim im Taunus*, Annalen des Vereins für Nassauische Altertumskunde und Geschichtforschung *40*, Wiesbaden

Rogers, G B, 1974 *Potteries sigillées de la Gaule Centrale, 1: les motifs non figures, Gallia* Supplement, **28**, Paris

Roscher, W H, 1937 *Ausfürliches Lexicon der Griechischen und Römischen Mithologie*, **VI**, Leipzig and Berlin

Ross, L A, 1972 *Romano-British shoes from London* Unpublished MA dissertation, Institute of Archaeology, University of London

Rossi, L, 1971 *Trajan's column and the Dacian Wars*, London

Rostovtzeff, M C, Brown, F E, and Welles, C B, (eds) 1939 *The excavations at Dura-Europos: preliminary report of the seventh and eighth seasons of work, 1933–4 and 1934–5*, New Haven

RCHM (Royal Commission on Ancient and Historical Monuments of England), 1928 *London: 3, Roman London*, London

Sauer, E 1996 *The end of paganism in the north-western provinces of the Roman empire: the examples of the Mithras cult*, Brit Archaeol Rep Int Ser, **634**, Oxford

Saxl, F, 1930 *Mithras: Typengeschichtliche Untersuchungen*, Berlin

Sheldon, H L, 1971 Excavations at Lefevre Road, Old Ford, E3, *Trans London Middlesex Archaeol Soc*, **23**, 1

Shepherd J D, and Heyworth M, 1991 Le travail du verre dans Londres romain (Londinium): un état de la question, 13-22, in *Ateliers de Verriers de l'Antiquité à la Periode Pré-industrielle* (eds D Foy and G Sennequier), Association Française pour l'Archéologie du Verre. Actes des 4ème Rencontres — Rouen 24–5 Nov 1989, Rouen

Shepherd, J, forthcoming *The Roman fort at Cripplegate, London: post-war excavations by W F Grimes and A Williams*

Sherratt A, 1995 Alcohol and its alternatives: symbol and substance in pre-industrial cultures, 11-46, in Goodman *et al* 1995

Sidell, J, and Rielly, K, *Recent evidence for the ritual use of animals in Roman London.* Journal of Roman Archaeology Monograph Series

Simpson, G, 1968 The decorated samian pottery, in Cunliffe 1968, 148–162

Silver, I A, 1968 The ageing of domestic animals, in Brothwell and Higgs, *Science in archaeology*, 283-302, London

Smith, D J, 1977 Mythological figures and scenes in Romano-British mosaics, in Munby, J, and Henig, M, *Roman life and art in Britain*, Brit Archaeol Rep Brit Ser, **41**, 105–93, Oxford

Stanfield J A, 1930 Further examples of Claudian Terra Sigillata from London, *Antiq J*, **10**, 114–25

Stanfield, J A and Simpson, G, 1958 *Central Gaulish potters*, London

Strong, D, and Brown, D (eds), 1976 *Roman crafts*, London

Swerdlow, N M, 1990 On the cosmical mysteries of Mithras, *Classical Philol*, **85**, 48–63

Symonds, R P, and Tomber, R S, 1991 Late Roman London: an assessment of the ceramic evidence from the City of London, *Trans London Middlesex Archaeol Soc*, 42, 59-99

Symonds, R P, and Wade, S M, forthcoming *The Roman pottery from excavations at Colchester 1971–85*, Colchester Archaeol Rep

Thomson, G, 1979 The problem of the Bacchae *Epistemonike Epeteris tes Philosophikes Scholes tou Aristoteleiou Panepistemiou Thessalonikes*, **18**, 424–46

Toynbee, J M C, 1962 *Art in Roman Britain*, London

Toynbee, J M C, 1964 *Art in Britain under the Romans*, Oxford

Toynbee J M C, 1986 *The Roman art treasures from the Temple of Mithras*, London Middlesex Archaeol Soc Special Pap, 7, London

Tyers, I, 1988 *MoLAS Environmental Archaeology Section, Wood Identification Report ID02/92*, MOL Early Department: Roman and Prehistoric Objects

Ulbert, T, 1963 Römische Gefässe mit Schlangen- und Eidechsenauflagen aus Bayern, *Bayerische Vorgeschichtsblätter*, **28**, 57–66

Ulbert, G, 1969 *Die Römischen Donau-kastelle Aislingen und Burghöfe*, Limesforschungen **1**, Berlin

Vermaseren, M J, 1956 *Corpus inscriptionum et monumentorum religionis Mithriacae*, The Hague

Vermaseren, M J, 1959 *Mithras de Geheimzinnige God*, Amsterdam

Vermaseren, M J, 1960 *Mithras, ce dieu mystérieux*, Paris/Brussels

Vermaseren, M J, 1963 *Mithras the secret god*, London

Vermaseren, M J, and van Essen, C C, 1965 *The excavation in the Mithraeum of the Church of Santa Prisca in Rome*, Leiden

Von den Driesch, A, 1976 *A guide to the measurement of animal bones from archaeological sites*, Peabody Mus Bull **1**, Cambridge, Mass

Walker, S, and Matthews, K, 1988 Recent work in stable isotope analysis of white marble at the British Museum, in *Ancient marble quarrying and trade* (ed J C Fant), Brit Archaeol Rep Int Ser, **453**, 117–126, Oxford

Walters, B, 1984 The 'Orpheus' mosaic in Littlecote Park, England, in Campanati, R F, *III Colloquio Internazionale sul Mosaico Antico Ravenna*, 433–42, Ravenna

Walters, B, and Henig, M, 1988 Two busts from Littlecote, *Britannia*, **19**, 407–10

Walters, H B, 1908 *Catalogue of the Roman pottery in the British Museum*, London

Walters, H B, 1921 *Catalogue of the silver plate in the British Museum: Greek, Etruscan, and Roman*, London

Walters, V, 1974 *The cult of Mithras in the Roman provinces of Gaul*, Leiden

Waterer, J W, 1976 Leatherwork, in Strong and Brown 1976, 179–193

Waugh, H, and Goodburn, R, 1972 The non-ferrous objects, in Frere 1972, 115–62

Wheeler, R E M, 1923 Segontium and the Roman occupation of Wales (*Y Cymmrodor*, **33**), London

White K D, 1970 *Roman farming*, London

Wilkes, J, 1981 Review of *Roman London* by P Marsden, *Britannia* **12**, 412–16

Wilmott, T, 1991 *Excavations in the Middle Walbrook Valley, City of London, 1927–1960*, London and Middlesex Archaeol Soc Special Paper **13**, London

Young, C J, 1977 *Oxfordshire Roman pottery*, Brit Archaeol Rep Brit Ser, **43**, Oxford

Index

by Susan Vaughan

Illustrations are indicated by page numbers in *italics* or by *(illus)* where figures are scattered throughout the text. Places are in London unless otherwise indicated.